# Twin Star Exorcists

ONMYOJI

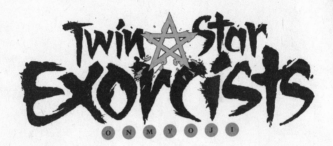

# Twin ☆ Star Exorcists

O N M Y O J I

## 11

STORY & ART
**YOSHIAKI SUKENO**

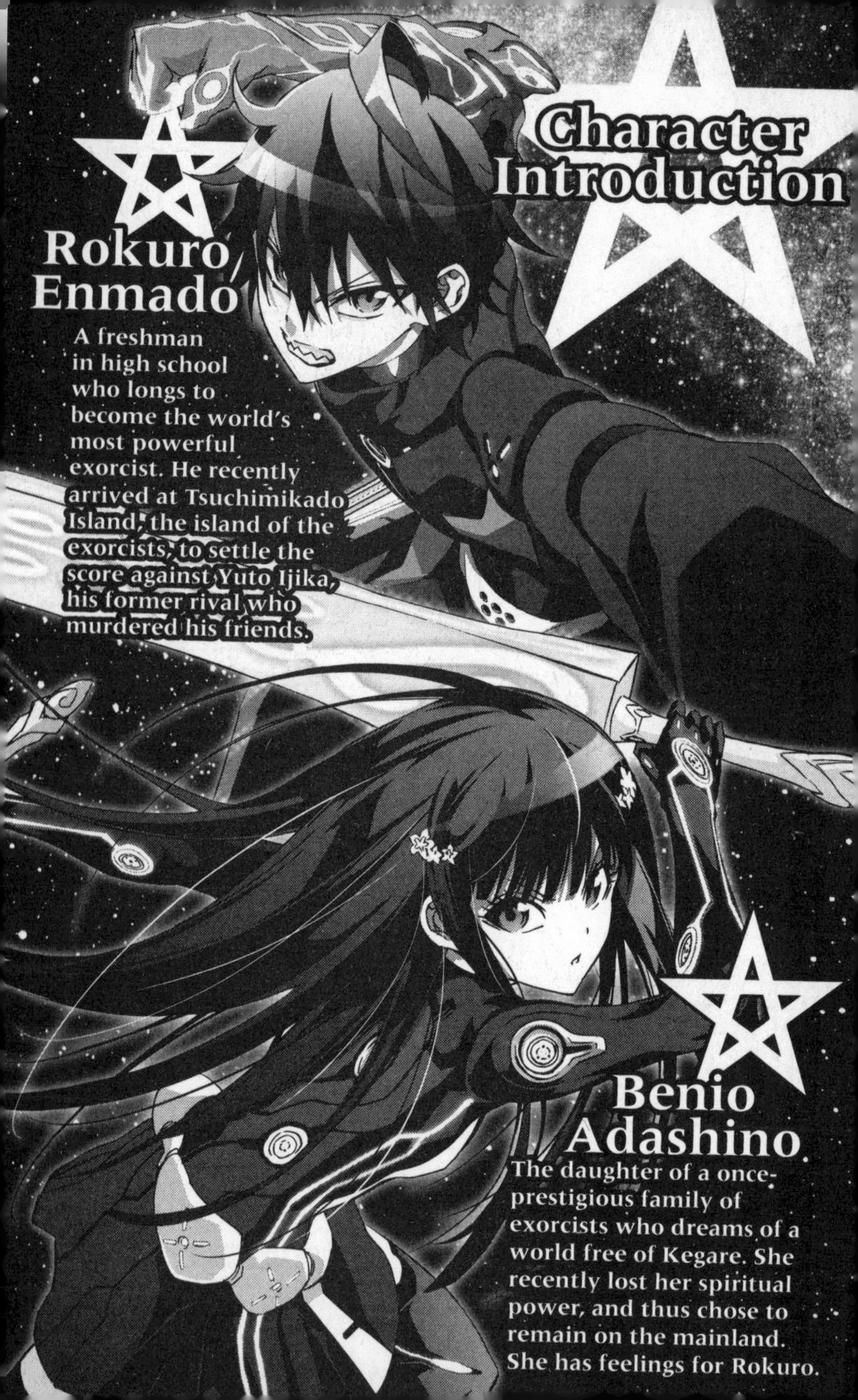
Character Introduction
Rokuro Enmado
A freshman in high school who longs to become the world's most powerful exorcist. He recently arrived at Tsuchimikado Island, the island of the exorcists, to settle the score against Yuto Ijika, his former rival who murdered his friends.
Benio Adashino
The daughter of a once-prestigious family of exorcists who dreams of a world free of Kegare. She recently lost her spiritual power, and thus chose to remain on the mainland. She has feelings for Rokuro.

## Kinako

A shikigami created by Benio who serves the Adashino family and remains on their estate awaiting her return.

## Mayura Otomi

Rokuro's childhood friend. During a fierce battle in Magano, her commitment to protecting others earned her the spiritual protector White Tiger.

## Kamui

A high-ranking Kegare called a Basara who has the ability to communicate in the human tongue. Kamui killed Benio's parents.

## Yuto Ijika

Benio's twin brother. He was the mastermind behind the Hinatsuki Tragedy and is eagerly awaiting Rokuro's arrival in the Magano underworld beneath Tsuchimikado Island.

## Arima Tsuchimikado

The Chief Exorcist of the Association of Unified Exorcists, an organization that presides over all exorcists. To fulfill a prophecy, he is determined to get Rokuro and Benio together.

## Shizuru Ioroi

A daughter of the Ioroi Family. She has contempt for Rokuro, but he rescued her when her life was in danger.

### Story Thus Far...

Kegare are creatures from Magano, the underworld, and it is the duty of an exorcist to hunt, exorcise and purify them. Rokuro and Benio are the Twin Star Exorcists, fated to bear the Prophesied Child who will defeat the Kegare. Their goal is to go to Tsuchimikado Island to get revenge on Yuto.

After two years of training, Rokuro qualifies to go to the island, but an attack by a Basara robs Benio of her spiritual power, so instead, Rokuro goes with his childhood friend and newbie exorcist Mayura. Intimidated by the Twelve Guardian families on the island, Rokuro decides to establish his own Enmado family with the aid of shikigami Kinako, in hopes of building a team to compete in a tournament and thus qualifying to join a mission to take out Yuto.

Meanwhile, stuck on the mainland, Benio is reunited with the Basara Kamui inside Magano...

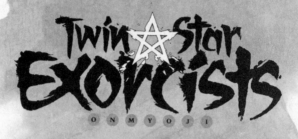

# Twin Star Exorcists

O N M Y O J I

## EXORCISMS



11

**ONMYOJI** have worked for the Imperial Court since the Heian era. In addition to exorcising evil spirits, as civil servants they performed a variety of roles, including advising nobles by foretelling the future, creating the calendar, observing the movements of the stars, measuring time...

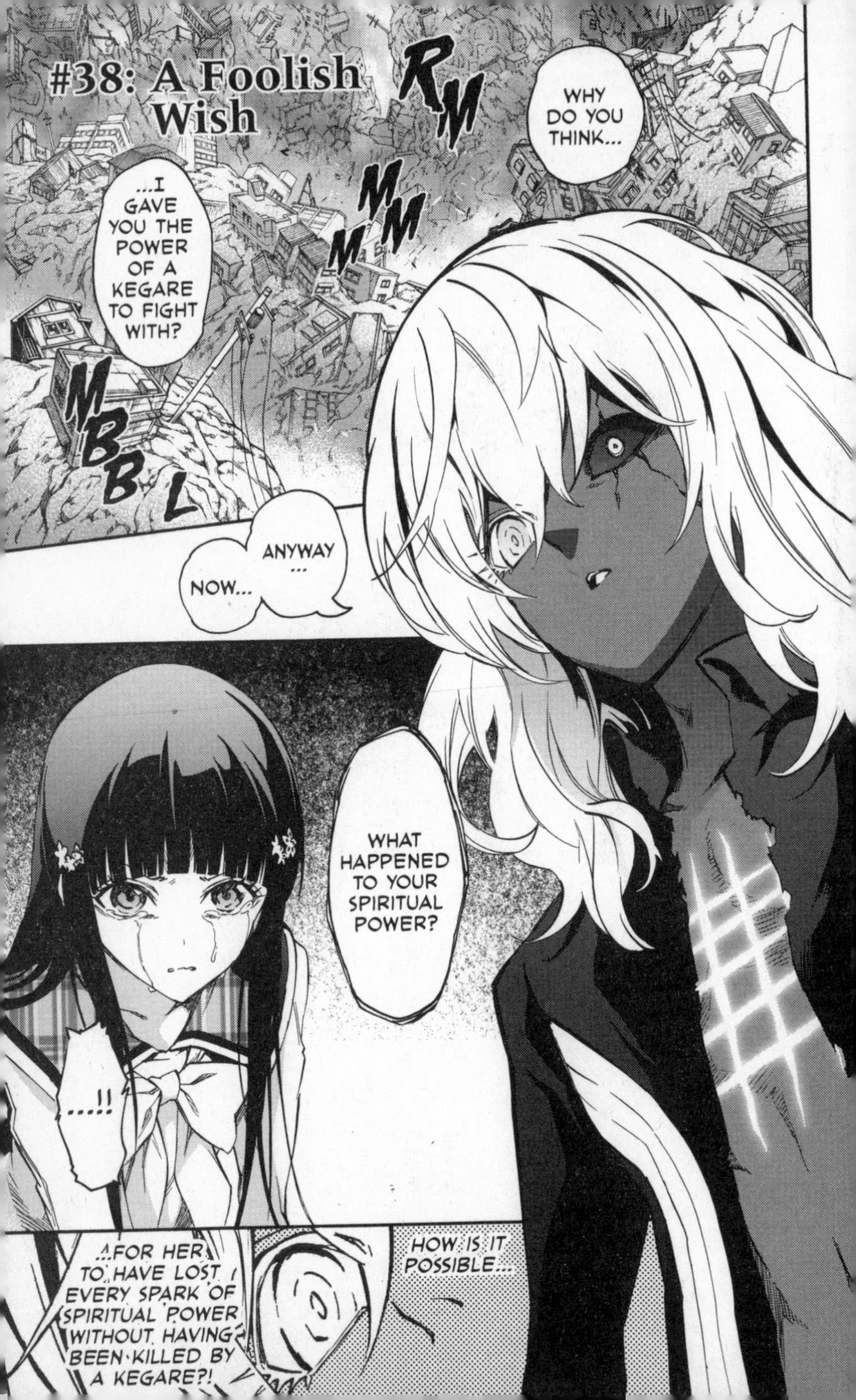
#38: A Foolish Wish
WHY DO YOU THINK...
RMMMM
...I GAVE YOU THE POWER OF A KEGARE TO FIGHT WITH?
MBBL
ANYWAY... NOW...
WHAT HAPPENED TO YOUR SPIRITUAL POWER?
...!!
HOW IS IT POSSIBLE...
...FOR HER TO HAVE LOST EVERY SPARK OF SPIRITUAL POWER WITHOUT HAVING BEEN KILLED BY A KEGARE?!

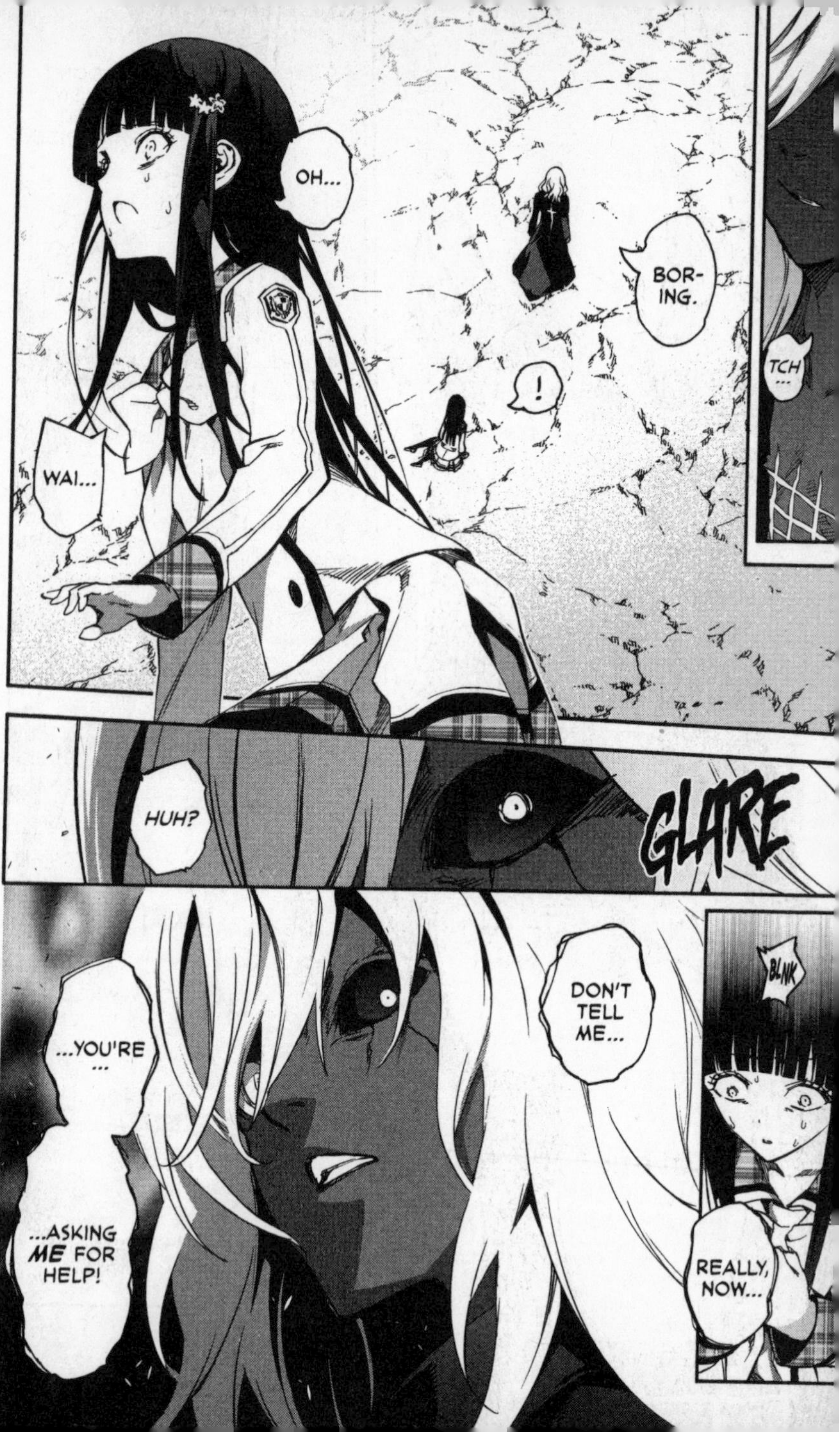
TCH...
BOR-ING.
!
OH...
WAI...
GLARE
HUH?
BLNK
DON'T TELL ME...
...YOU'RE...
...ASKING *ME* FOR HELP!
REALLY, NOW...

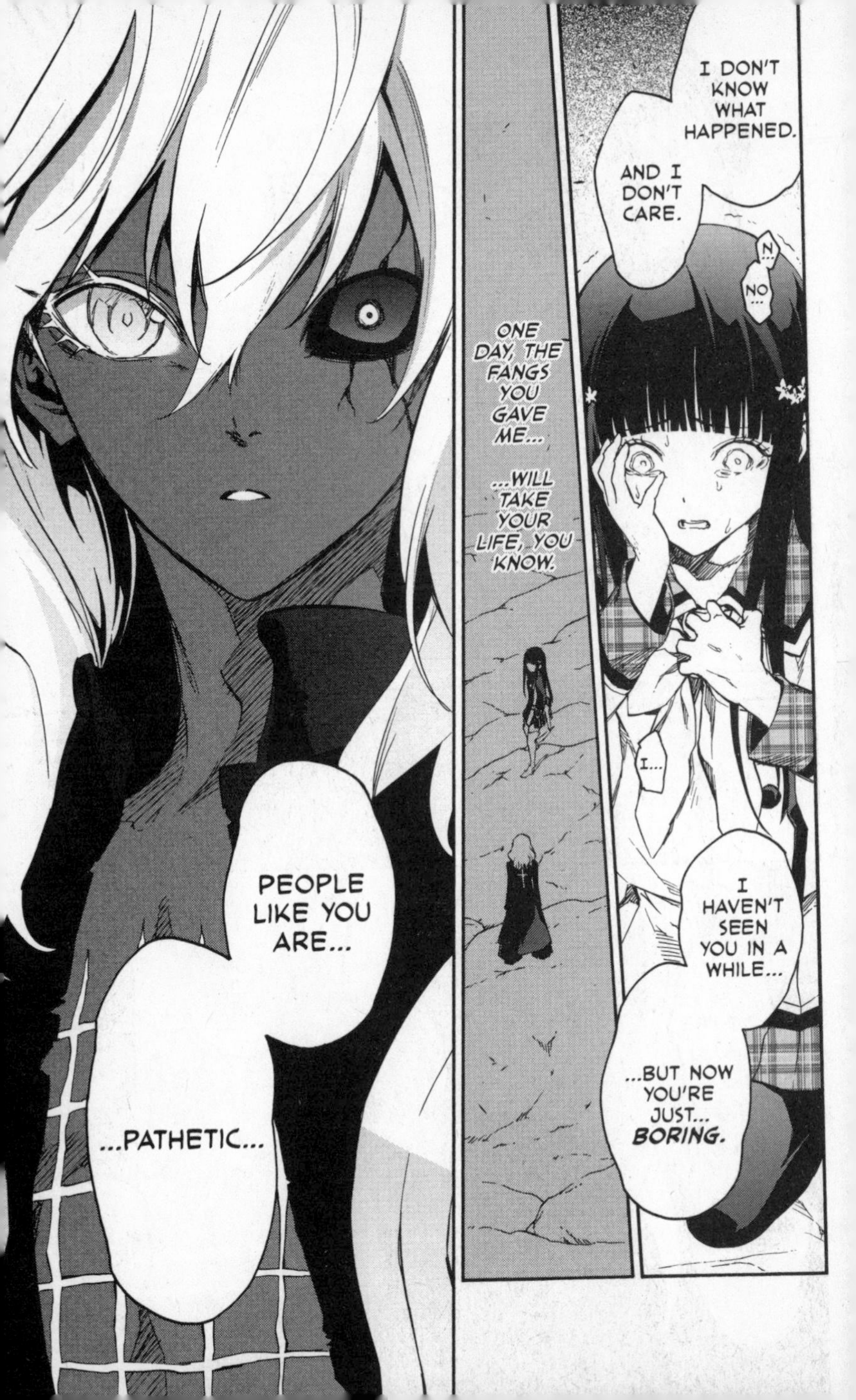
I DON'T KNOW WHAT HAPPENED.
AND I DON'T CARE.
N...
NO...
I...
I HAVEN'T SEEN YOU IN A WHILE...
...BUT NOW YOU'RE JUST... ***BORING.***
ONE DAY, THE FANGS YOU GAVE ME...
...WILL TAKE YOUR LIFE, YOU KNOW.
PEOPLE LIKE YOU ARE...
...PATHETIC...

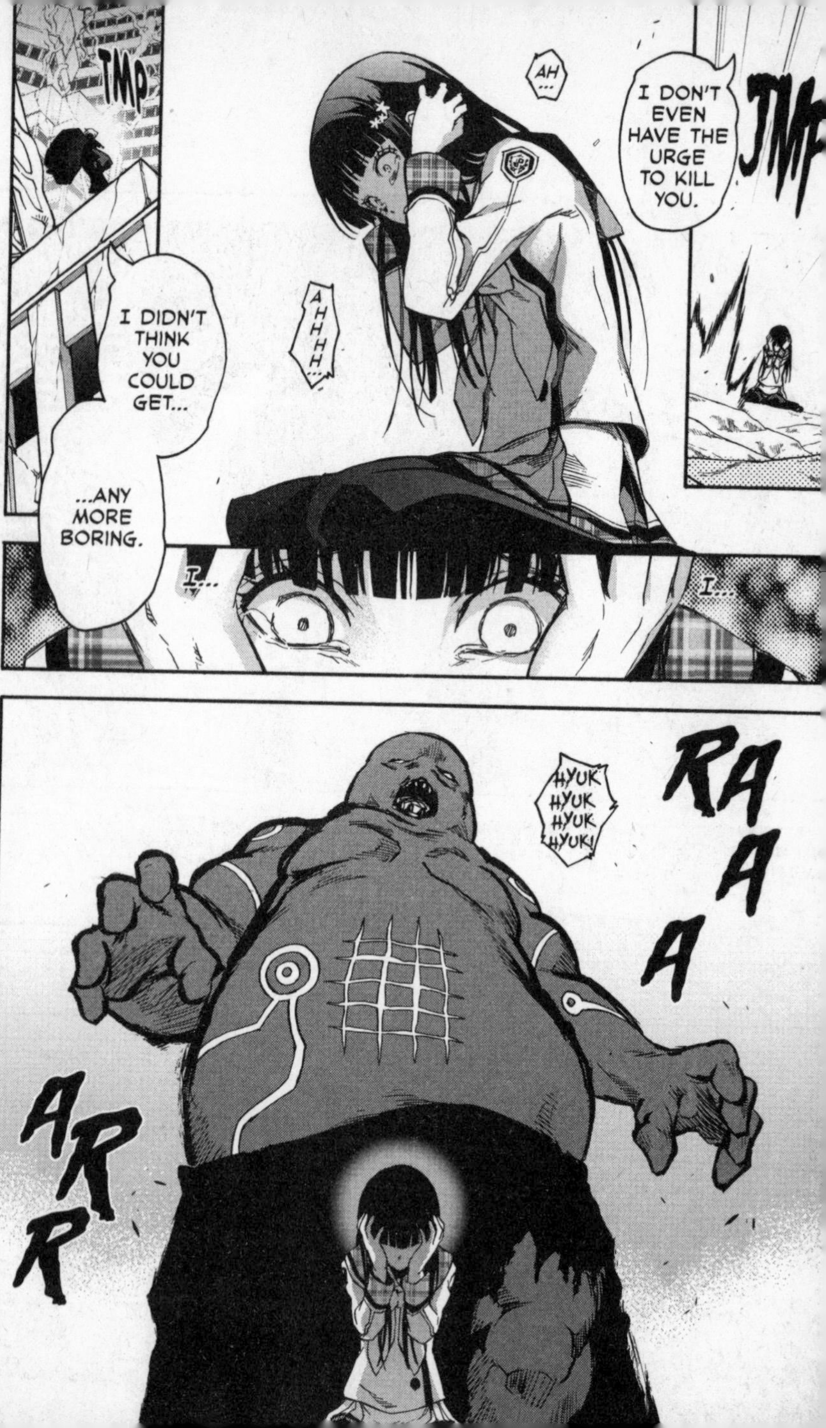
JMP
I DON'T EVEN HAVE THE URGE TO KILL YOU.
AH...
AHHHH...
I DIDN'T THINK YOU COULD GET...
...ANY MORE BORING.
TMP
I...
I...
RAAA
HYUK HYUK HYUK HYUK!
ARR

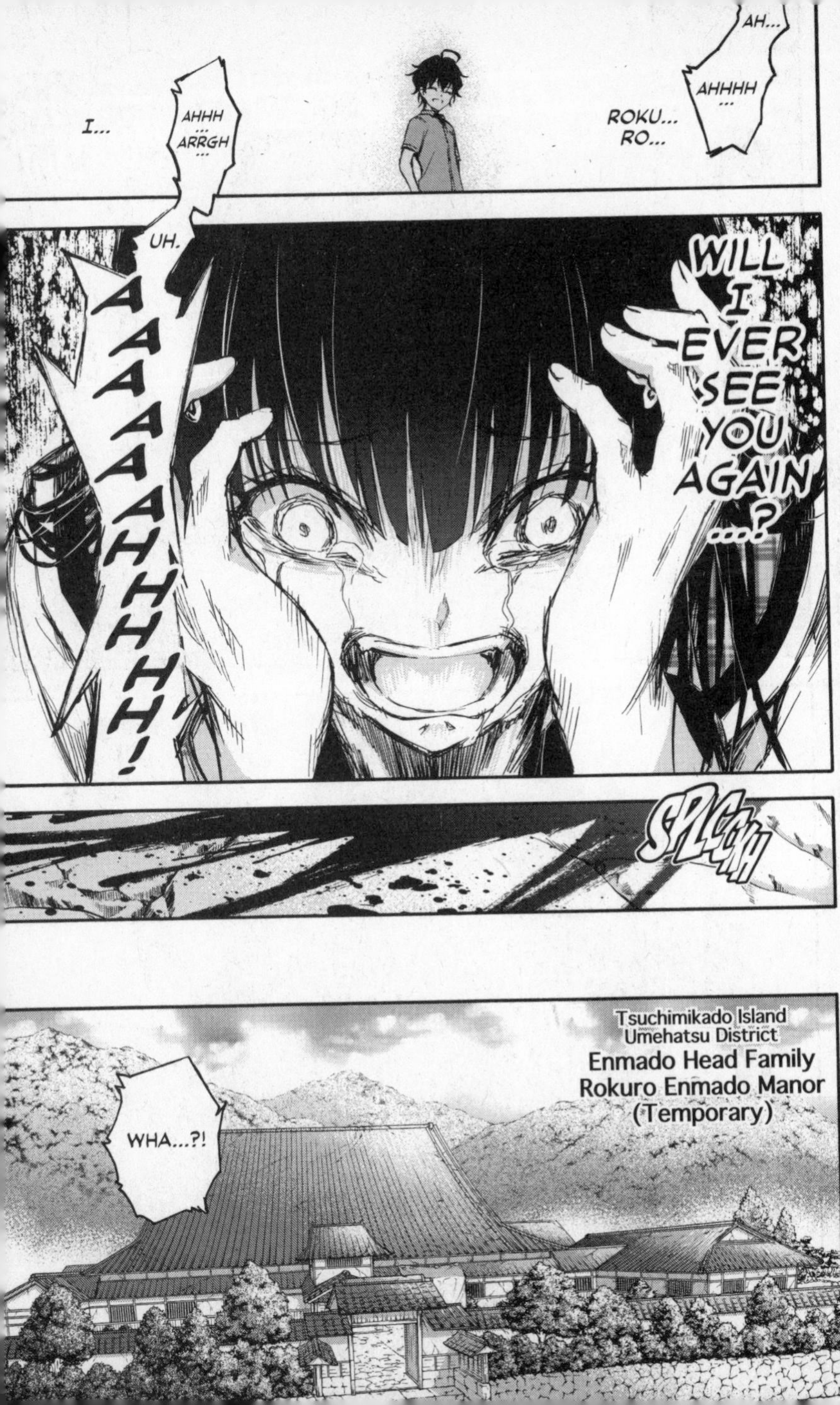
AH... AHHHH...
ROKU... RO...
AHHH... ARRGH...
I...
WILL I EVER SEE YOU AGAIN...?
UH.
AAAAAAHHHHHH!
SPLCCKH
Tsuchimikado Island
Umehatsu District
Enmado Head Family
Rokuro Enmado Manor
(Temporary)
WHA...?!

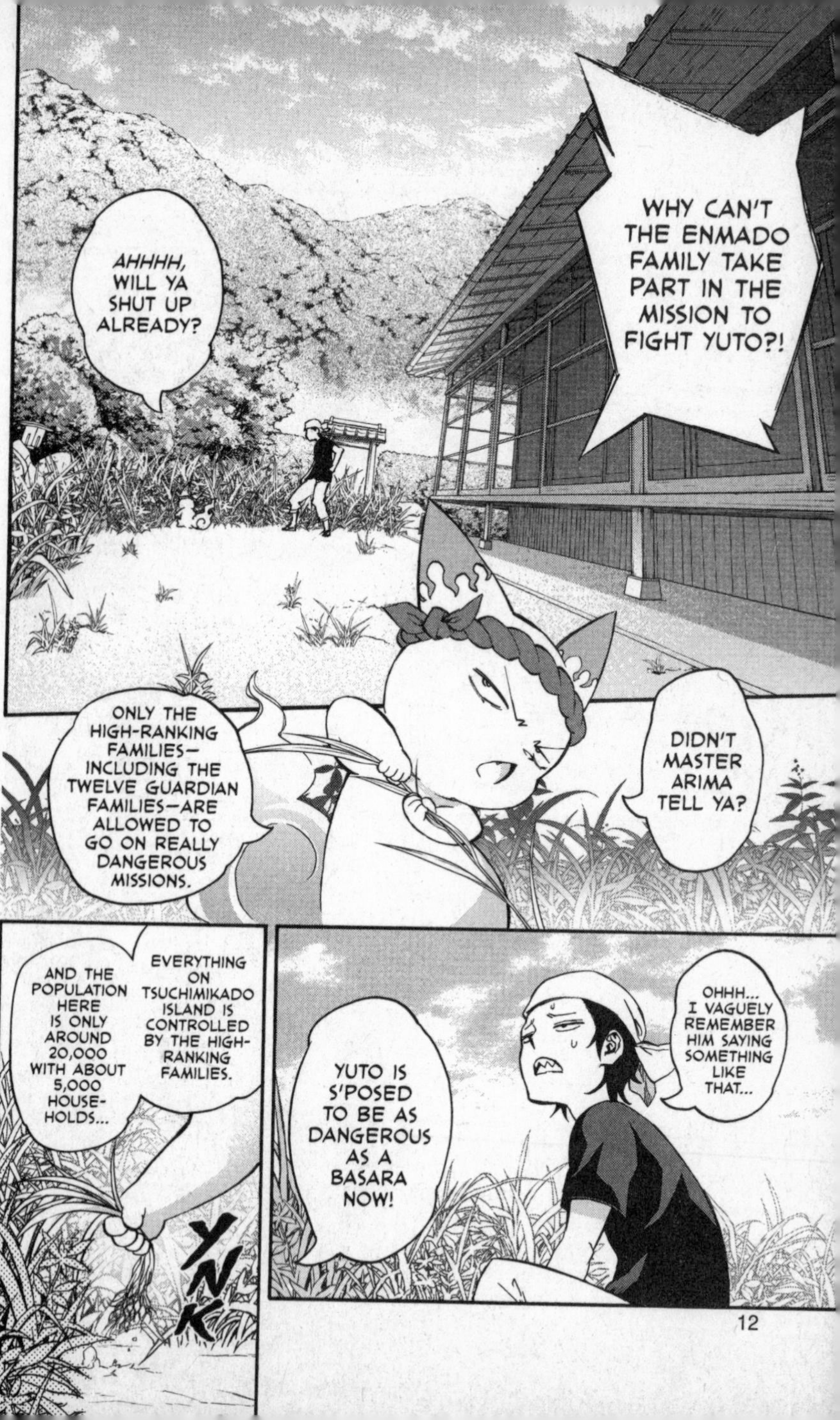
WHY CAN'T THE ENMADO FAMILY TAKE PART IN THE MISSION TO FIGHT YUTO?!
*AHHHH,* WILL YA SHUT UP ALREADY?
DIDN'T MASTER ARIMA TELL YA?
ONLY THE HIGH-RANKING FAMILIES—INCLUDING THE TWELVE GUARDIAN FAMILIES—ARE ALLOWED TO GO ON REALLY DANGEROUS MISSIONS.
OHHH... I VAGUELY REMEMBER HIM SAYING SOMETHING LIKE THAT...
YUTO IS S'POSED TO BE AS DANGEROUS AS A BASARA NOW!
EVERYTHING ON TSUCHIMIKADO ISLAND IS CONTROLLED BY THE HIGH-RANKING FAMILIES.
AND THE POPULATION HERE IS ONLY AROUND 20,000 WITH ABOUT 5,000 HOUSE-HOLDS...
YNK

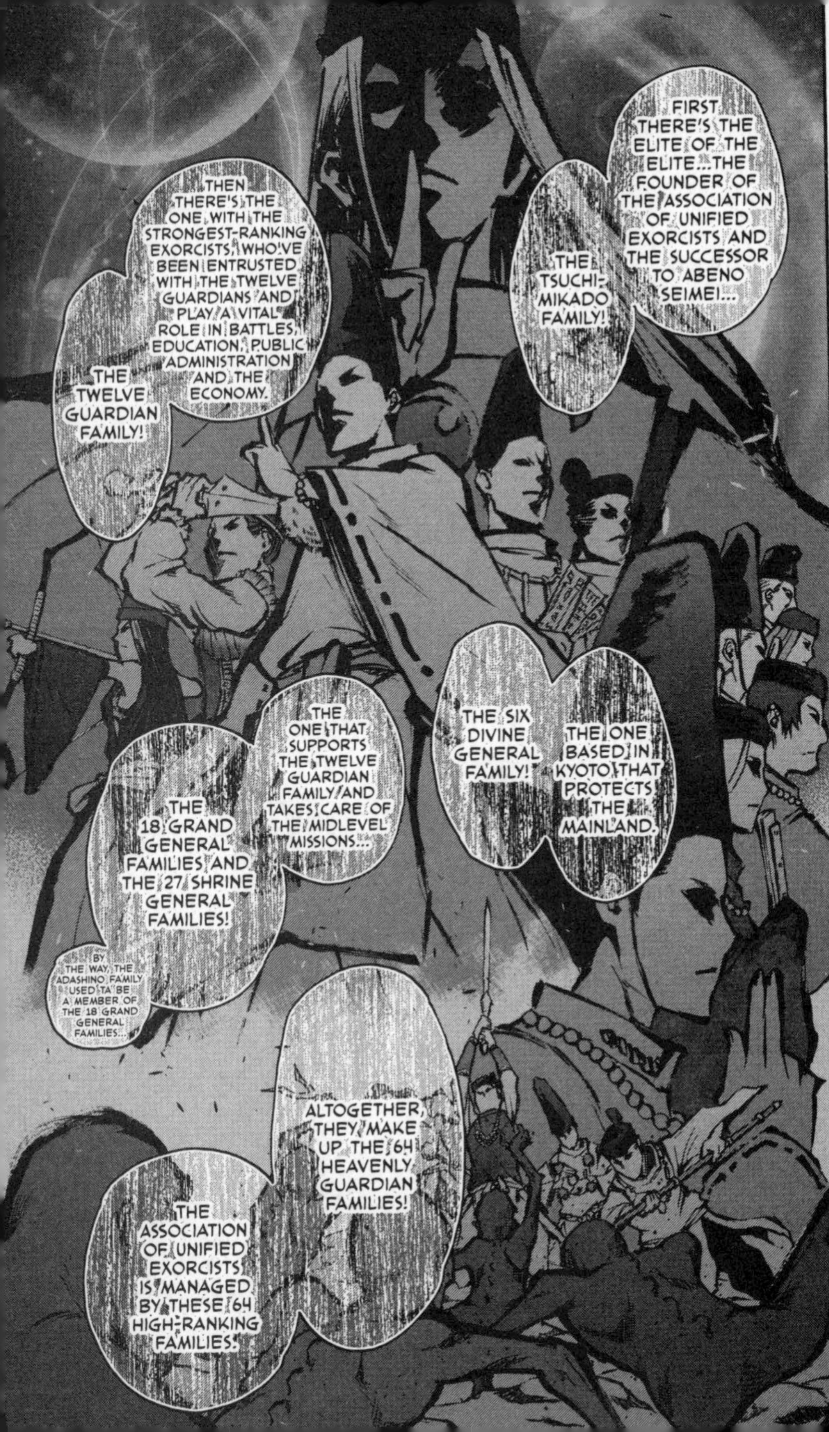
FIRST THERE'S THE ELITE OF THE ELITE...THE FOUNDER OF THE ASSOCIATION OF UNIFIED EXORCISTS AND THE SUCCESSOR TO ABENO SEIMEI...
THE TSUCHIMIKADO FAMILY!
THEN THERE'S THE ONE WITH THE STRONGEST-RANKING EXORCISTS, WHO'VE BEEN ENTRUSTED WITH THE TWELVE GUARDIANS AND PLAY A VITAL ROLE IN BATTLES, EDUCATION, PUBLIC ADMINISTRATION AND THE ECONOMY.
THE TWELVE GUARDIAN FAMILY!
THE ONE BASED IN KYOTO THAT PROTECTS THE MAINLAND.
THE SIX DIVINE GENERAL FAMILY!
THE ONE THAT SUPPORTS THE TWELVE GUARDIAN FAMILY AND TAKES CARE OF THE MIDLEVEL MISSIONS...
THE 18 GRAND GENERAL FAMILIES AND THE 27 SHRINE GENERAL FAMILIES!
BY THE WAY, THE ADASHINO FAMILY USED TA BE A MEMBER OF THE 18 GRAND GENERAL FAMILIES...
ALTOGETHER, THEY MAKE UP THE 64 HEAVENLY GUARDIAN FAMILIES!
THE ASSOCIATION OF UNIFIED EXORCISTS IS MANAGED BY THESE 64 HIGH-RANKING FAMILIES.

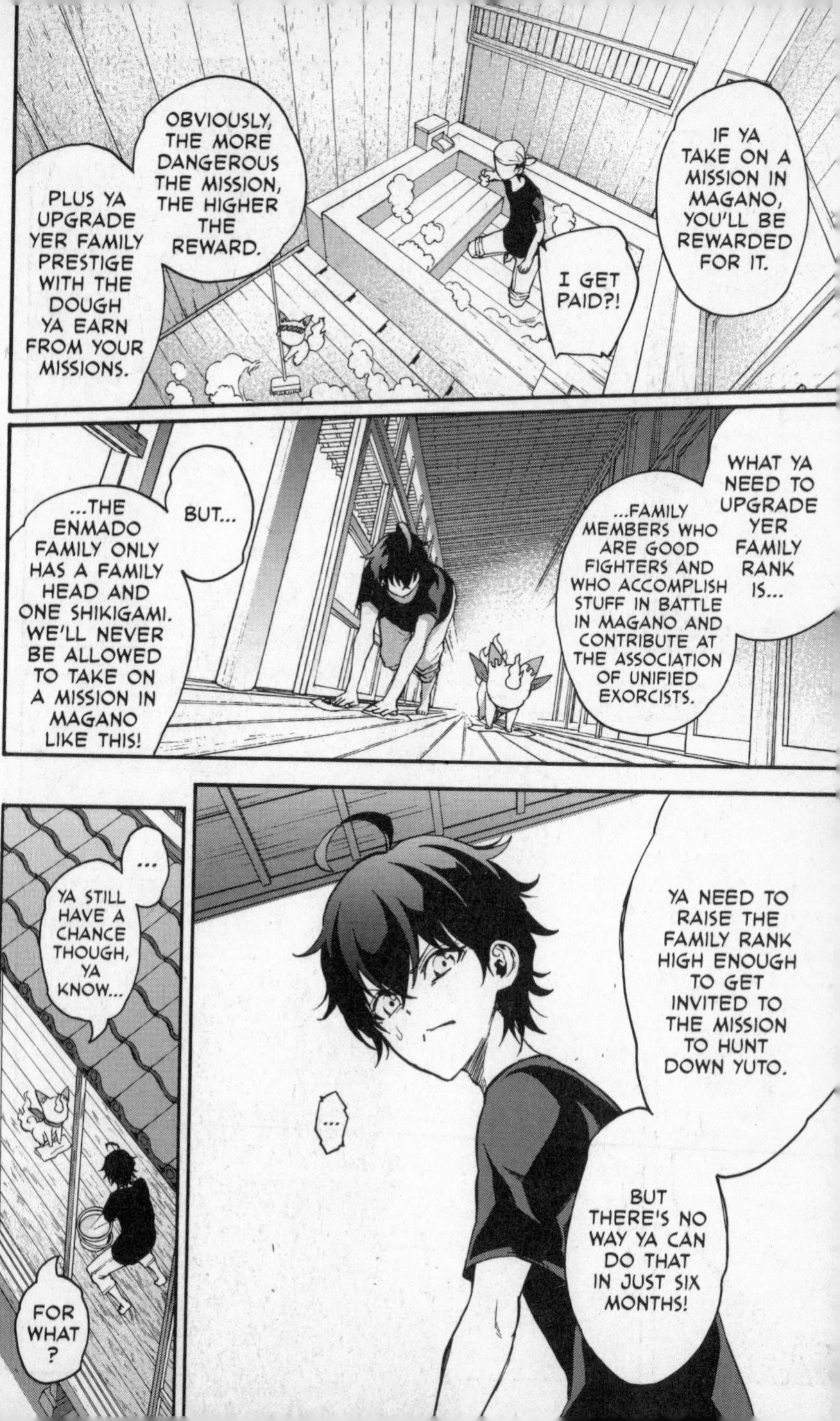
IF YA TAKE ON A MISSION IN MAGANO, YOU'LL BE REWARDED FOR IT.
I GET PAID?!
OBVIOUSLY, THE MORE DANGEROUS THE MISSION, THE HIGHER THE REWARD.
PLUS YA UPGRADE YER FAMILY PRESTIGE WITH THE DOUGH YA EARN FROM YOUR MISSIONS.
WHAT YA NEED TO UPGRADE YER FAMILY RANK IS...
...FAMILY MEMBERS WHO ARE GOOD FIGHTERS AND WHO ACCOMPLISH STUFF IN BATTLE IN MAGANO AND CONTRIBUTE AT THE ASSOCIATION OF UNIFIED EXORCISTS.
BUT...
...THE ENMADO FAMILY ONLY HAS A FAMILY HEAD AND ONE SHIKIGAMI. WE'LL NEVER BE ALLOWED TO TAKE ON A MISSION IN MAGANO LIKE THIS!
YA NEED TO RAISE THE FAMILY RANK HIGH ENOUGH TO GET INVITED TO THE MISSION TO HUNT DOWN YUTO.
...
BUT THERE'S NO WAY YA CAN DO THAT IN JUST SIX MONTHS!
...
YA STILL HAVE A CHANCE THOUGH, YA KNOW...
FOR WHAT?

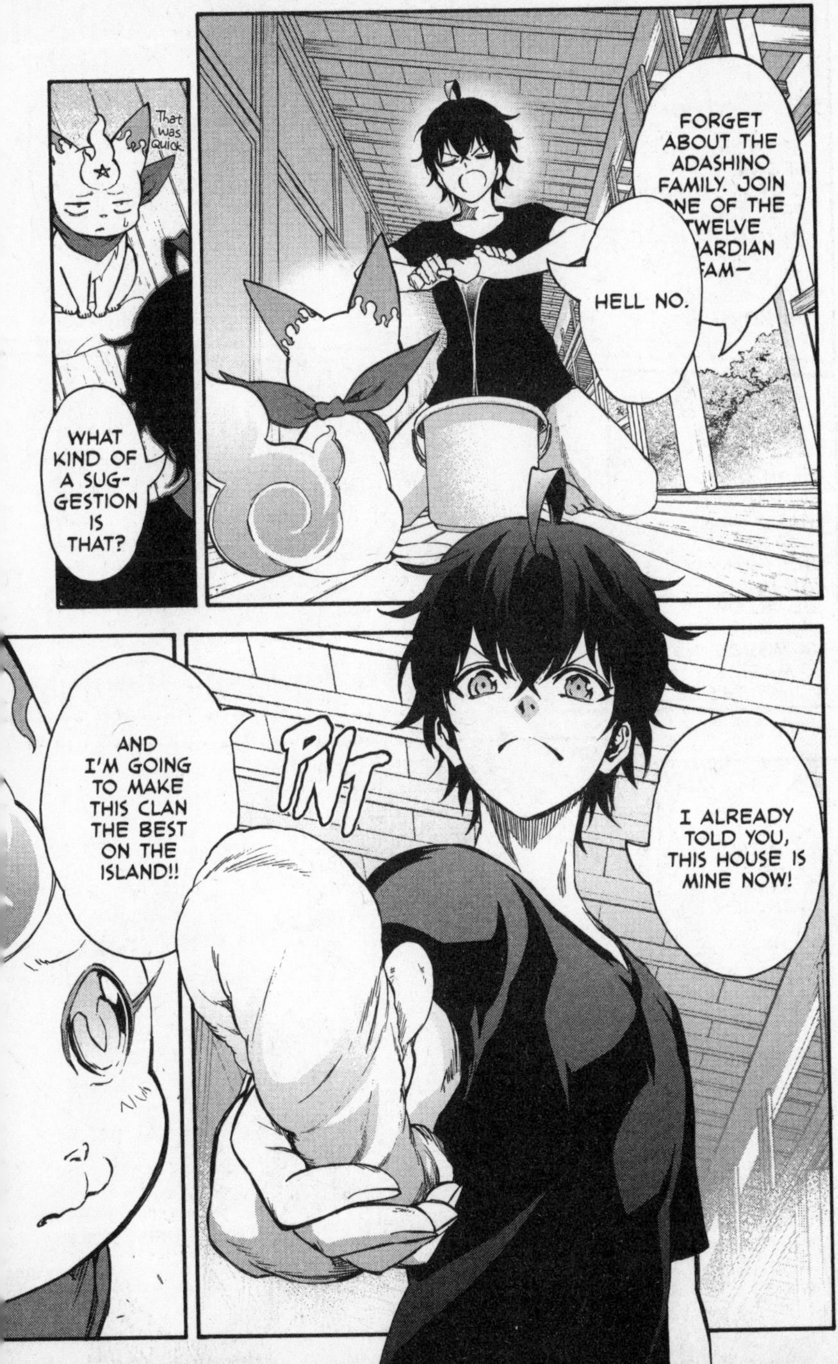
FORGET ABOUT THE ADASHINO FAMILY. JOIN ONE OF THE TWELVE GUARDIAN FAM—
HELL NO.
That was Quick
WHAT KIND OF A SUG-GESTION IS THAT?
PNT
I ALREADY TOLD YOU, THIS HOUSE IS MINE NOW!
AND I'M GOING TO MAKE THIS CLAN THE BEST ON THE ISLAND!!

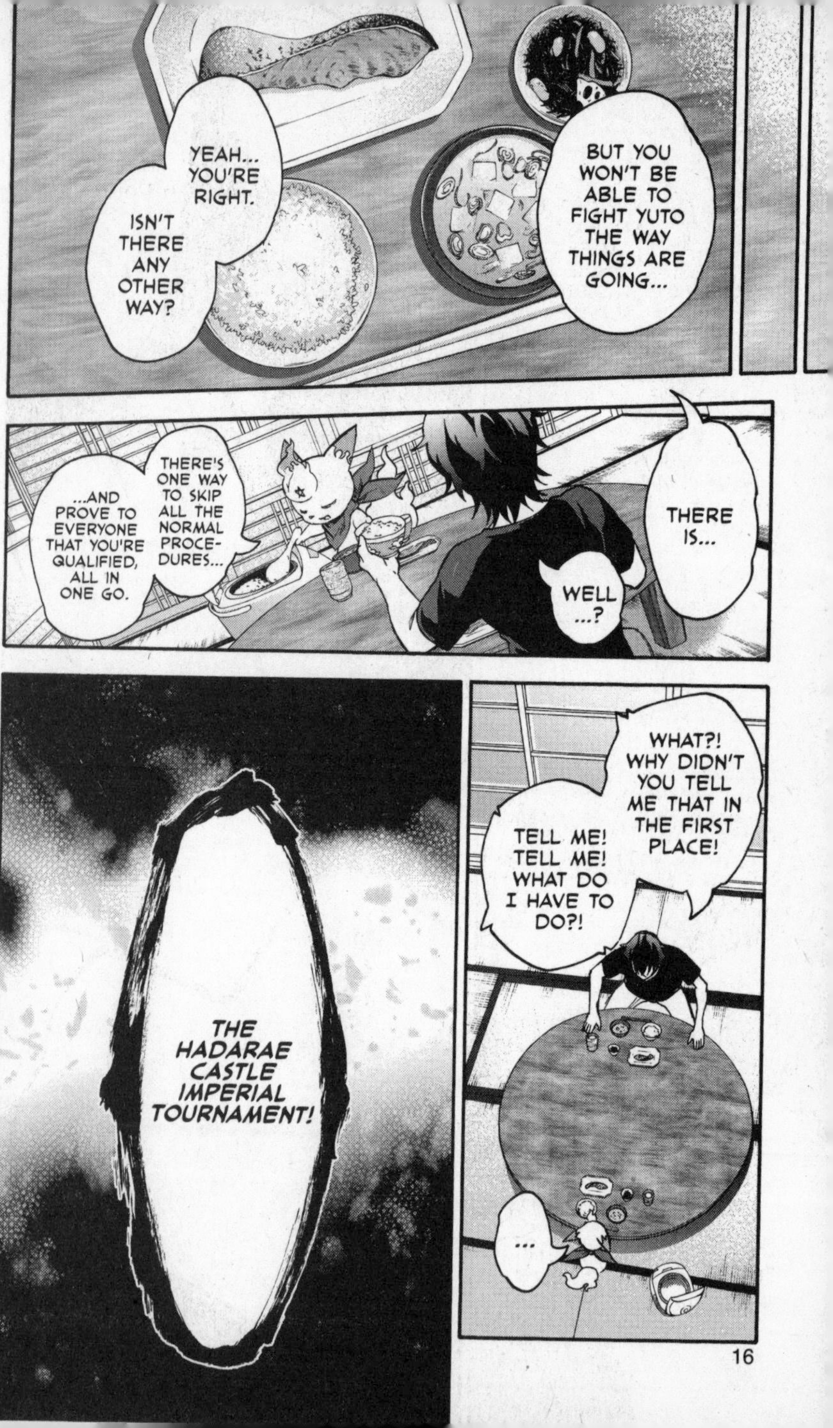
BUT YOU WON'T BE ABLE TO FIGHT YUTO THE WAY THINGS ARE GOING...
YEAH... YOU'RE RIGHT.
ISN'T THERE ANY OTHER WAY?
THERE IS...
WELL ...?
THERE'S ONE WAY TO SKIP ALL THE NORMAL PROCE- DURES...
...AND PROVE TO EVERYONE THAT YOU'RE QUALIFIED, ALL IN ONE GO.
WHAT?! WHY DIDN'T YOU TELL ME THAT IN THE FIRST PLACE!
TELL ME! TELL ME! WHAT DO I HAVE TO DO?!
...
THE HADARAE CASTLE IMPERIAL TOURNAMENT!

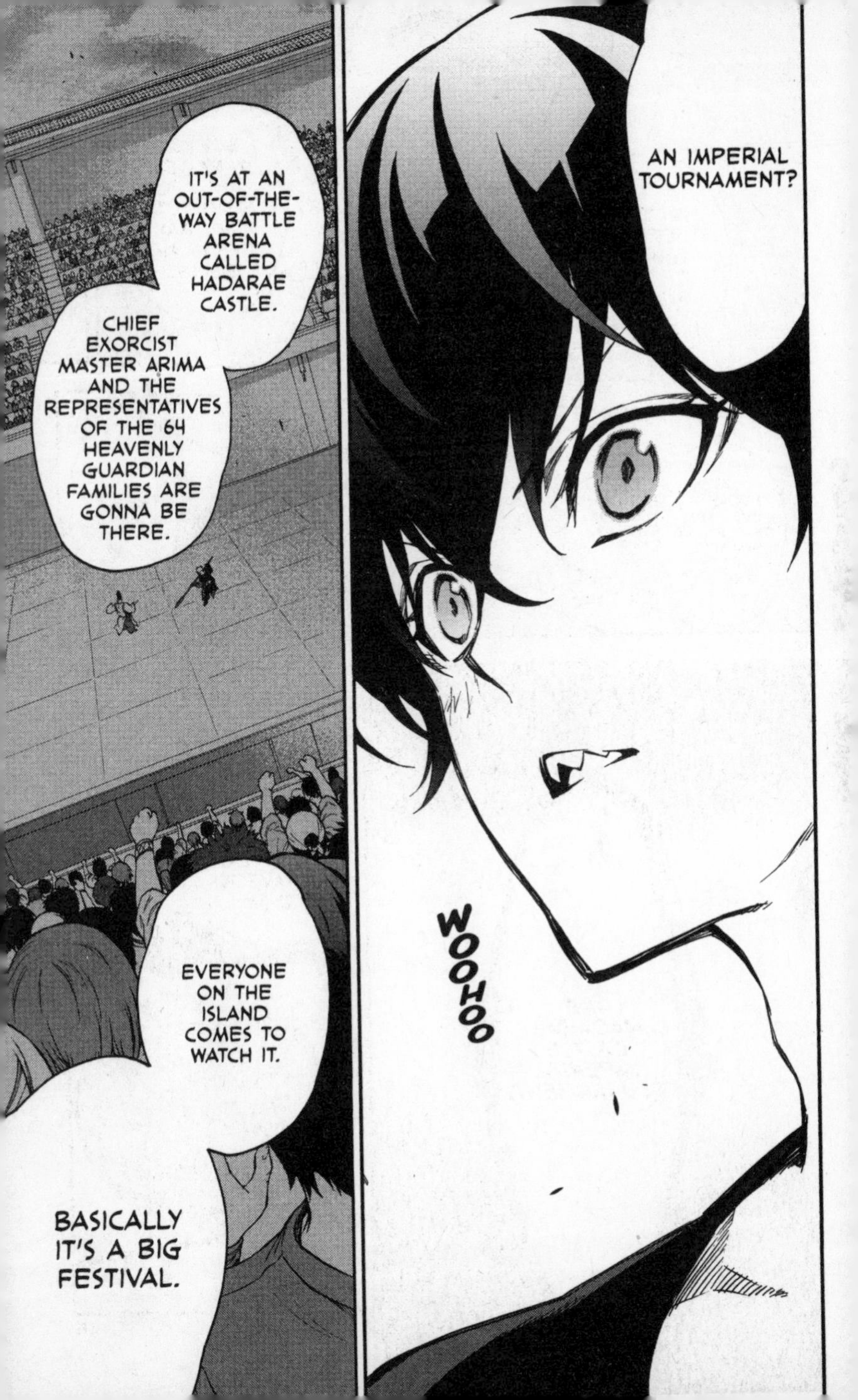
AN IMPERIAL TOURNAMENT?
WOOHOO
IT'S AT AN OUT-OF-THE-WAY BATTLE ARENA CALLED HADARAE CASTLE.
CHIEF EXORCIST MASTER ARIMA AND THE REPRESENTATIVES OF THE 64 HEAVENLY GUARDIAN FAMILIES ARE GONNA BE THERE.
EVERYONE ON THE ISLAND COMES TO WATCH IT.
BASICALLY IT'S A BIG FESTIVAL.

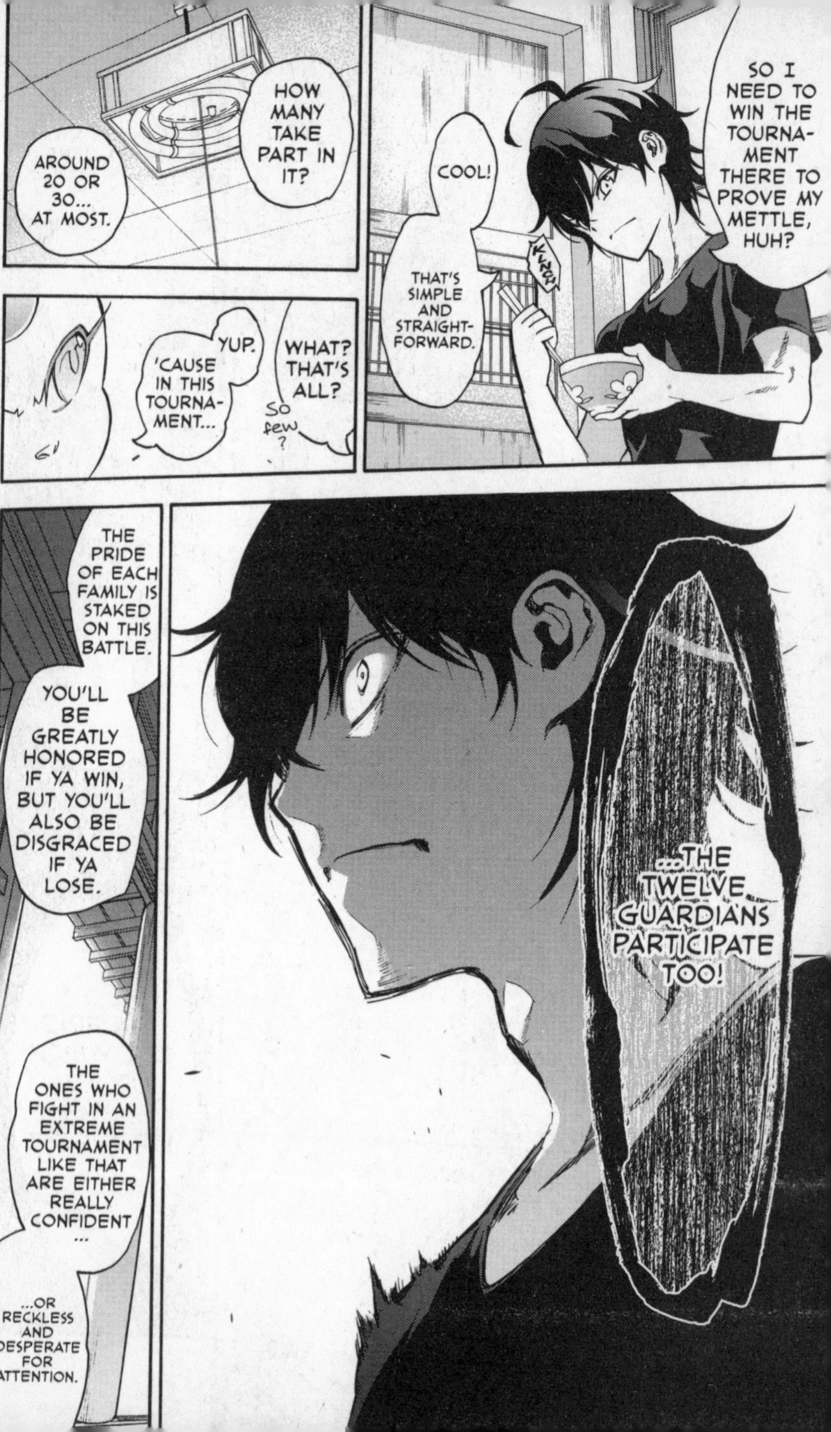
SO I NEED TO WIN THE TOURNAMENT THERE TO PROVE MY METTLE, HUH?
KLINCH
COOL!
THAT'S SIMPLE AND STRAIGHTFORWARD.
HOW MANY TAKE PART IN IT?
AROUND 20 OR 30... AT MOST.
WHAT? THAT'S ALL?
So few?
YUP. 'CAUSE IN THIS TOURNAMENT...
...THE TWELVE GUARDIANS PARTICIPATE TOO!
THE PRIDE OF EACH FAMILY IS STAKED ON THIS BATTLE.
YOU'LL BE GREATLY HONORED IF YA WIN, BUT YOU'LL ALSO BE DISGRACED IF YA LOSE.
THE ONES WHO FIGHT IN AN EXTREME TOURNAMENT LIKE THAT ARE EITHER REALLY CONFIDENT...
...OR RECKLESS AND DESPERATE FOR ATTENTION.

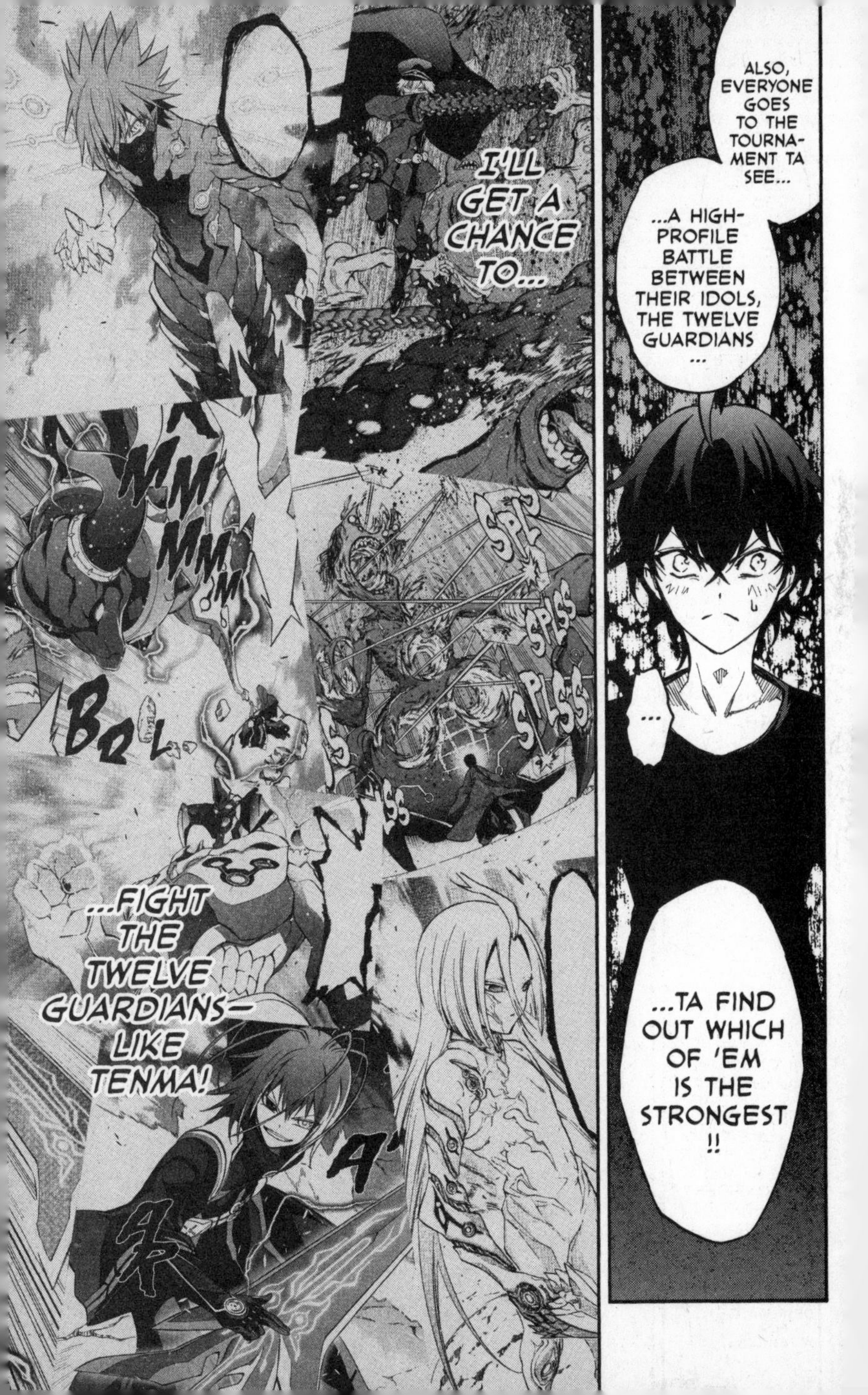
ALSO, EVERYONE GOES TO THE TOURNAMENT TA SEE...
...A HIGH-PROFILE BATTLE BETWEEN THEIR IDOLS, THE TWELVE GUARDIANS...
...
...TA FIND OUT WHICH OF 'EM IS THE STRONGEST!!
I'LL GET A CHANCE TO...
SPLSS
SPLSS
...FIGHT THE TWELVE GUARDIANS—LIKE TENMA!

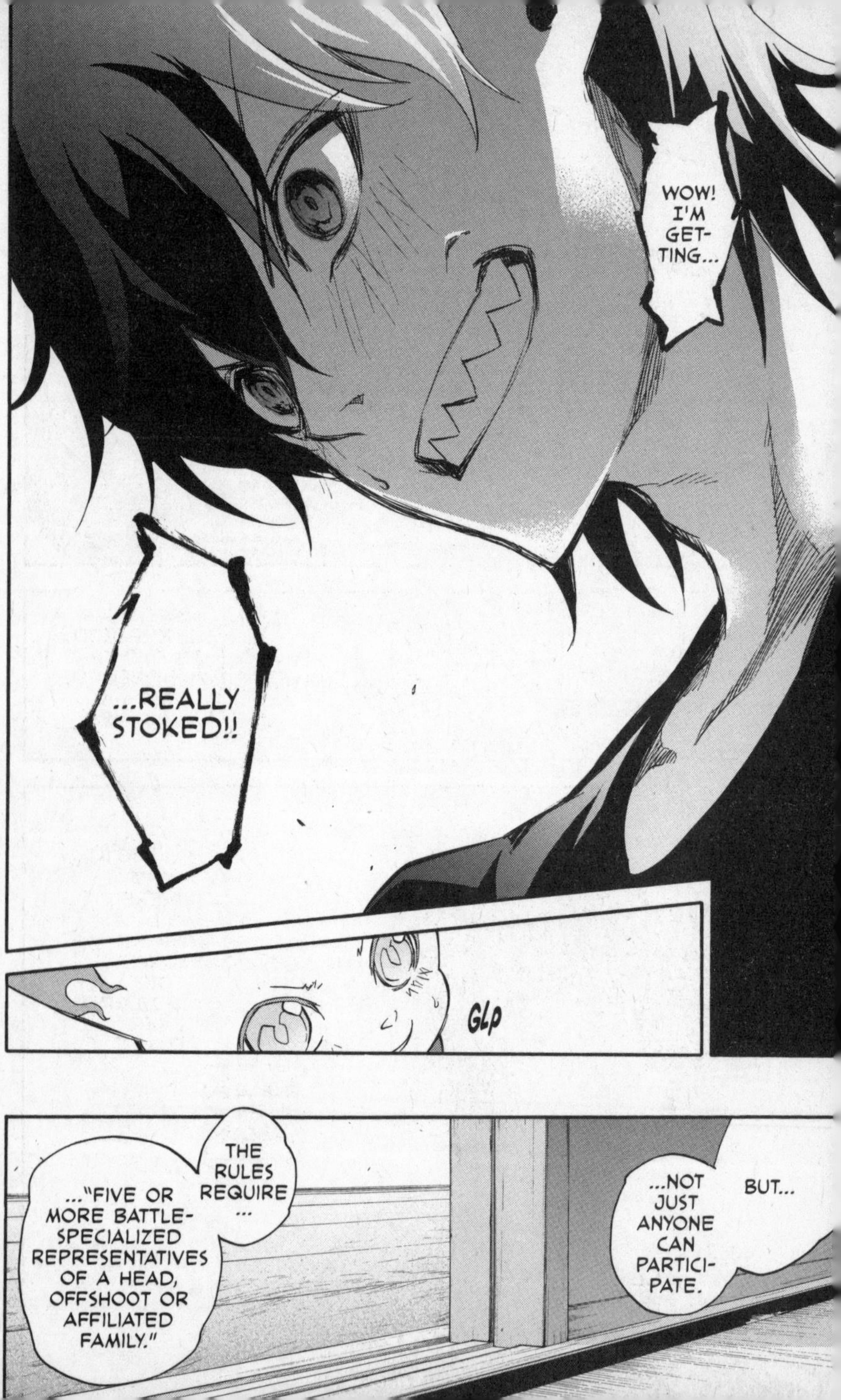
WOW! I'M GETTING...
...REALLY STOKED!!
GLP
BUT...
...NOT JUST ANYONE CAN PARTICIPATE.
THE RULES REQUIRE...
..."FIVE OR MORE BATTLE-SPECIALIZED REPRESENTATIVES OF A HEAD, OFFSHOOT OR AFFILIATED FAMILY."

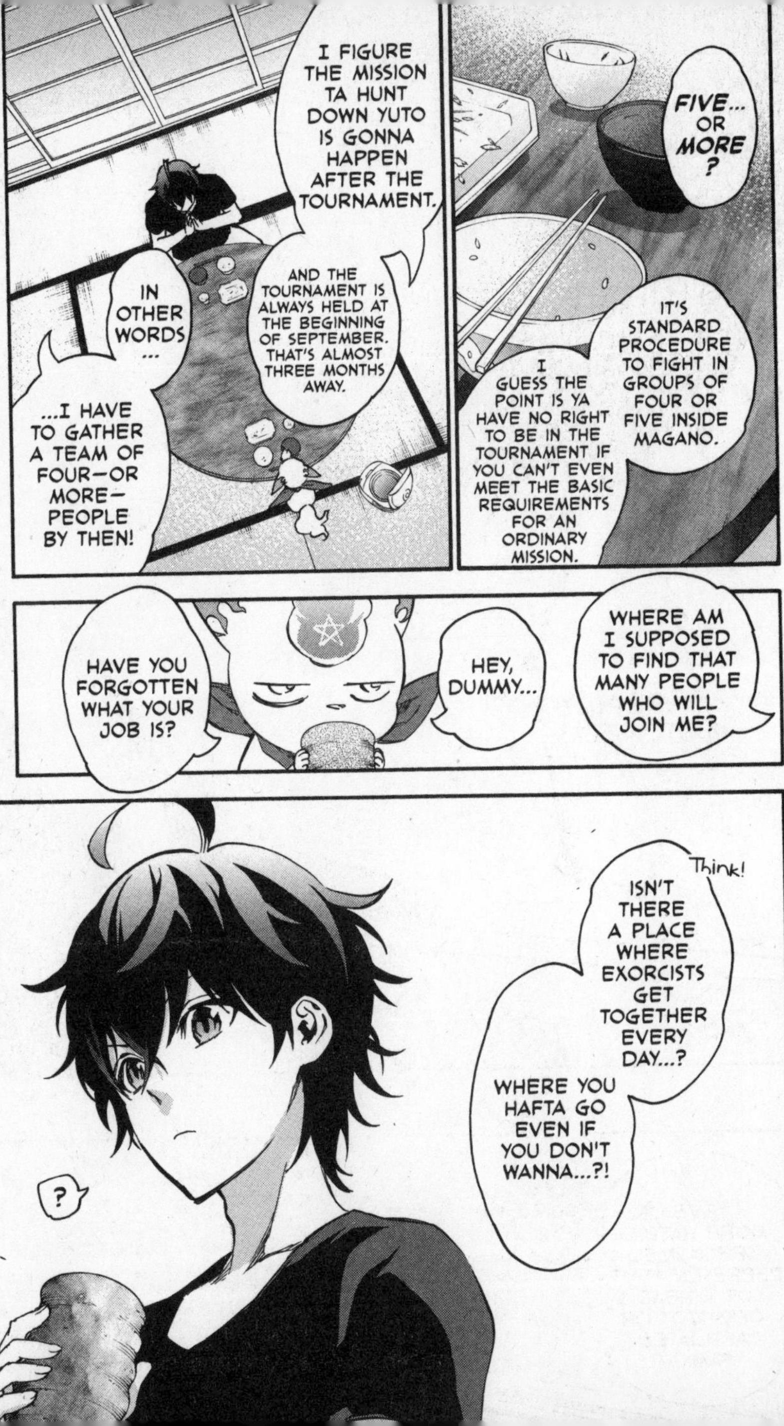
FIVE... OR MORE?
IT'S STANDARD PROCEDURE TO FIGHT IN GROUPS OF FOUR OR FIVE INSIDE MAGANO.
I GUESS THE POINT IS YA HAVE NO RIGHT TO BE IN THE TOURNAMENT IF YOU CAN'T EVEN MEET THE BASIC REQUIREMENTS FOR AN ORDINARY MISSION.
I FIGURE THE MISSION TA HUNT DOWN YUTO IS GONNA HAPPEN AFTER THE TOURNAMENT.
AND THE TOURNAMENT IS ALWAYS HELD AT THE BEGINNING OF SEPTEMBER. THAT'S ALMOST THREE MONTHS AWAY.
IN OTHER WORDS...
...I HAVE TO GATHER A TEAM OF FOUR—OR MORE—PEOPLE BY THEN!
WHERE AM I SUPPOSED TO FIND THAT MANY PEOPLE WHO WILL JOIN ME?
HEY, DUMMY...
HAVE YOU FORGOTTEN WHAT YOUR JOB IS?
Think!
ISN'T THERE A PLACE WHERE EXORCISTS GET TOGETHER EVERY DAY...?
WHERE YOU HAFTA GO EVEN IF YOU DON'T WANNA...?!
?

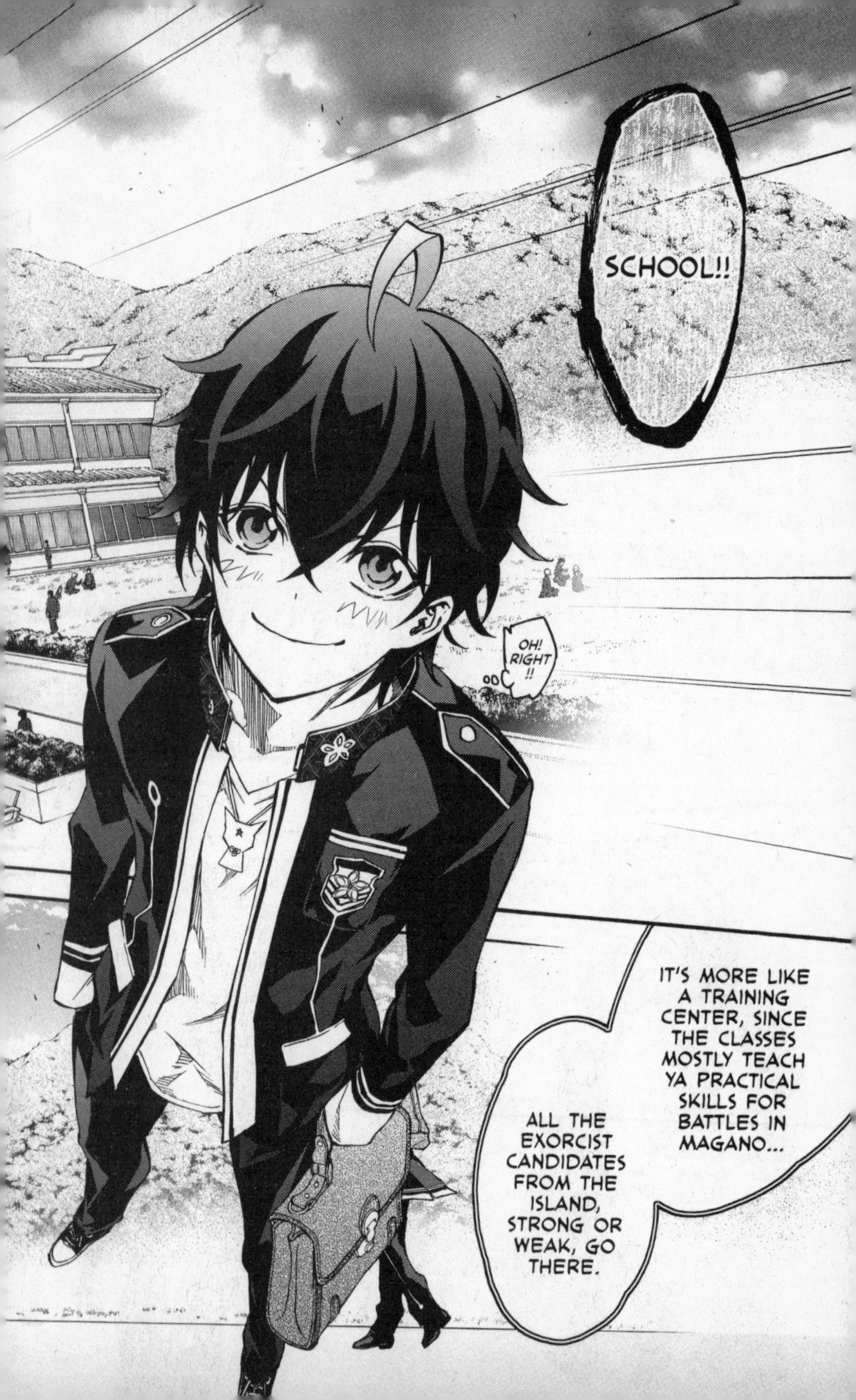
SCHOOL!!
OH! RIGHT !!
IT'S MORE LIKE A TRAINING CENTER, SINCE THE CLASSES MOSTLY TEACH YA PRACTICAL SKILLS FOR BATTLES IN MAGANO...
ALL THE EXORCIST CANDIDATES FROM THE ISLAND, STRONG OR WEAK, GO THERE.

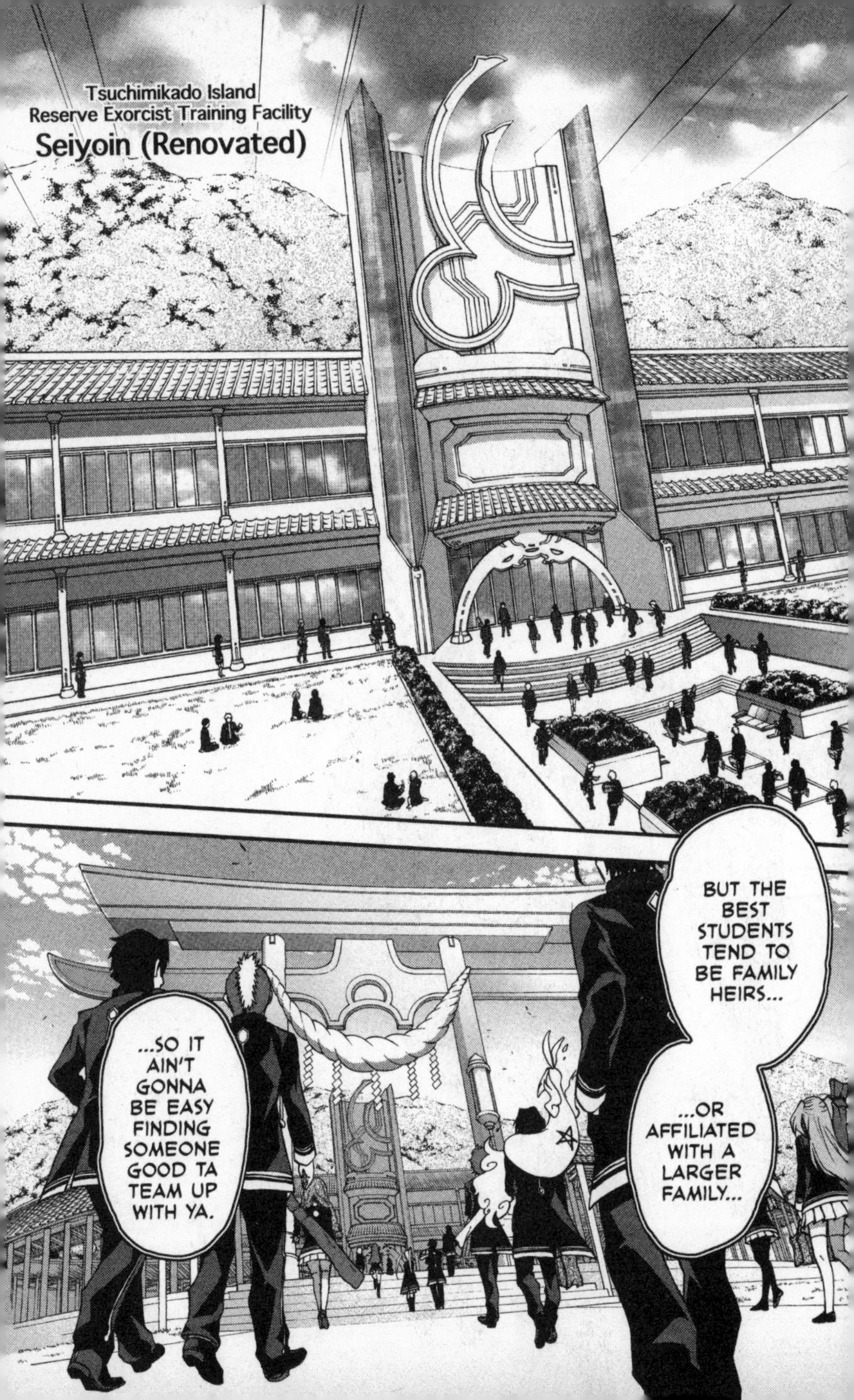
Tsuchimikado Island
Reserve Exorcist Training Facility
Seiyoin (Renovated)
BUT THE BEST STUDENTS TEND TO BE FAMILY HEIRS...
...OR AFFILIATED WITH A LARGER FAMILY...
...SO IT AIN'T GONNA BE EASY FINDING SOMEONE GOOD TA TEAM UP WITH YA.

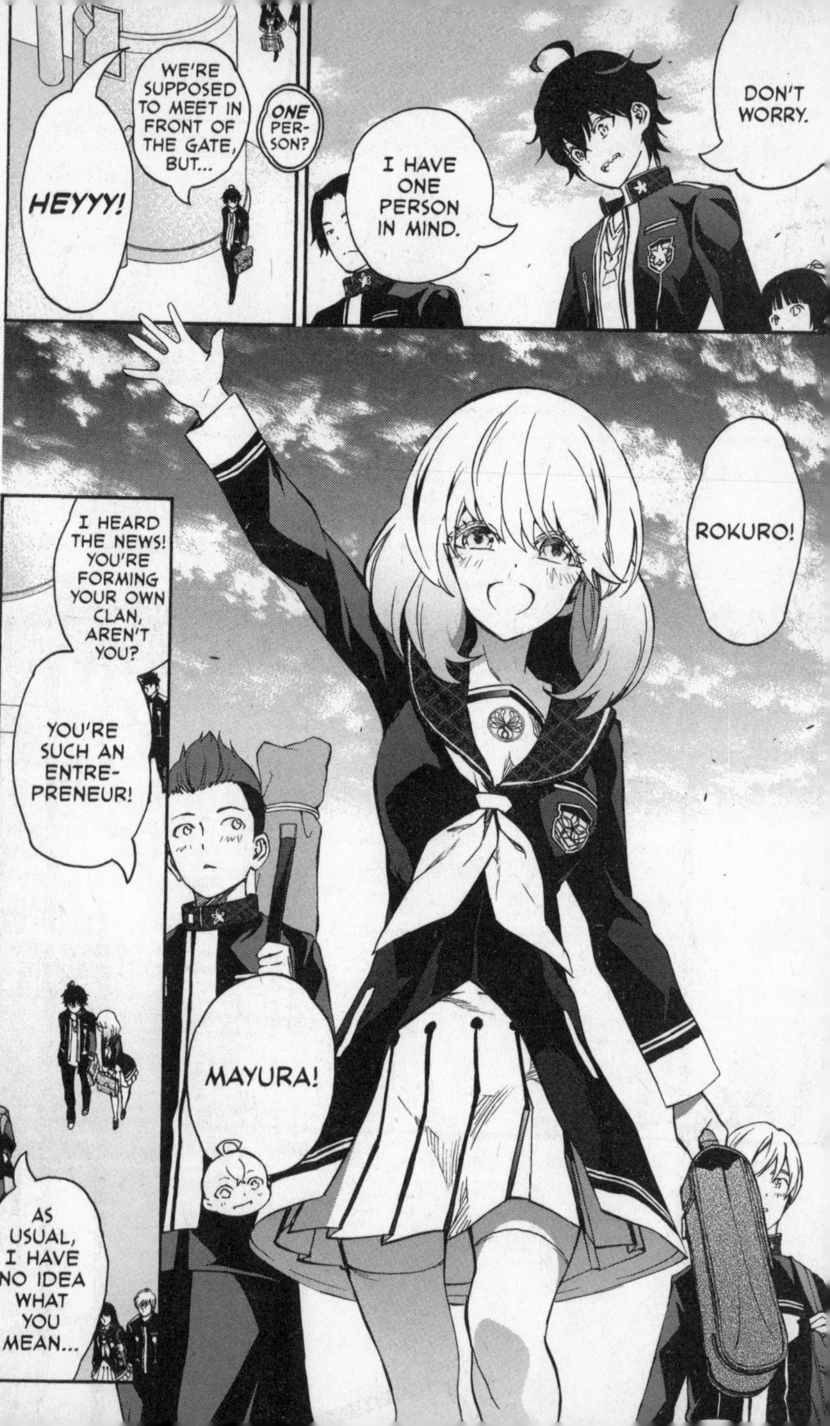
DON'T WORRY.
I HAVE ONE PERSON IN MIND.
ONE PERSON?
WE'RE SUPPOSED TO MEET IN FRONT OF THE GATE, BUT...
HEYYY!
ROKURO!
I HEARD THE NEWS! YOU'RE FORMING YOUR OWN CLAN, AREN'T YOU?
YOU'RE SUCH AN ENTRE-PRENEUR!
MAYURA!
AS USUAL, I HAVE NO IDEA WHAT YOU MEAN...

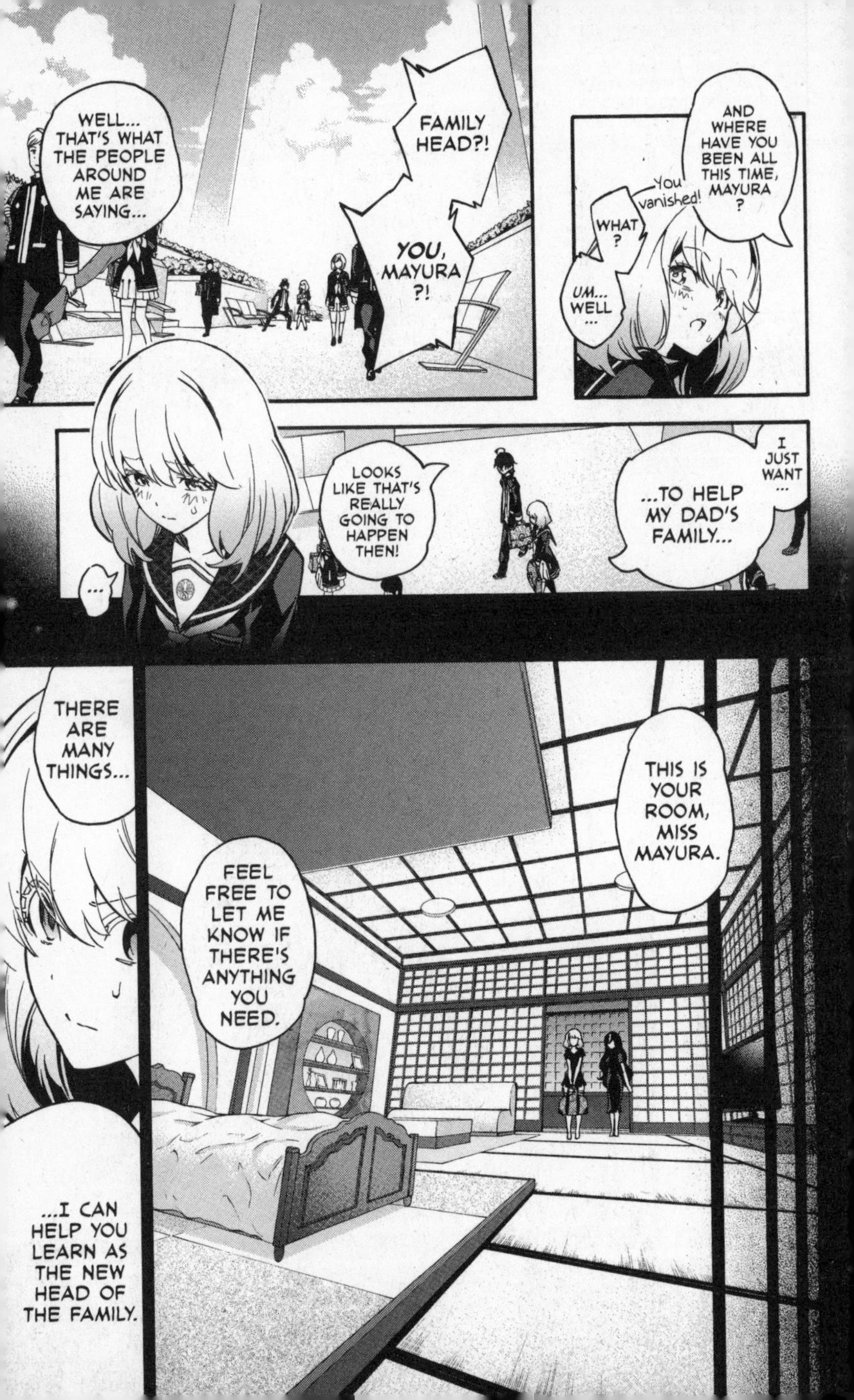
AND WHERE HAVE YOU BEEN ALL THIS TIME, MAYURA?
You vanished!
WHAT?
UM... WELL...
FAMILY HEAD?!
YOU, MAYURA?!
WELL... THAT'S WHAT THE PEOPLE AROUND ME ARE SAYING...
I JUST WANT...
...TO HELP MY DAD'S FAMILY...
LOOKS LIKE THAT'S REALLY GOING TO HAPPEN THEN!
...
THIS IS YOUR ROOM, MISS MAYURA.
FEEL FREE TO LET ME KNOW IF THERE'S ANYTHING YOU NEED.
THERE ARE MANY THINGS...
...I CAN HELP YOU LEARN AS THE NEW HEAD OF THE FAMILY.

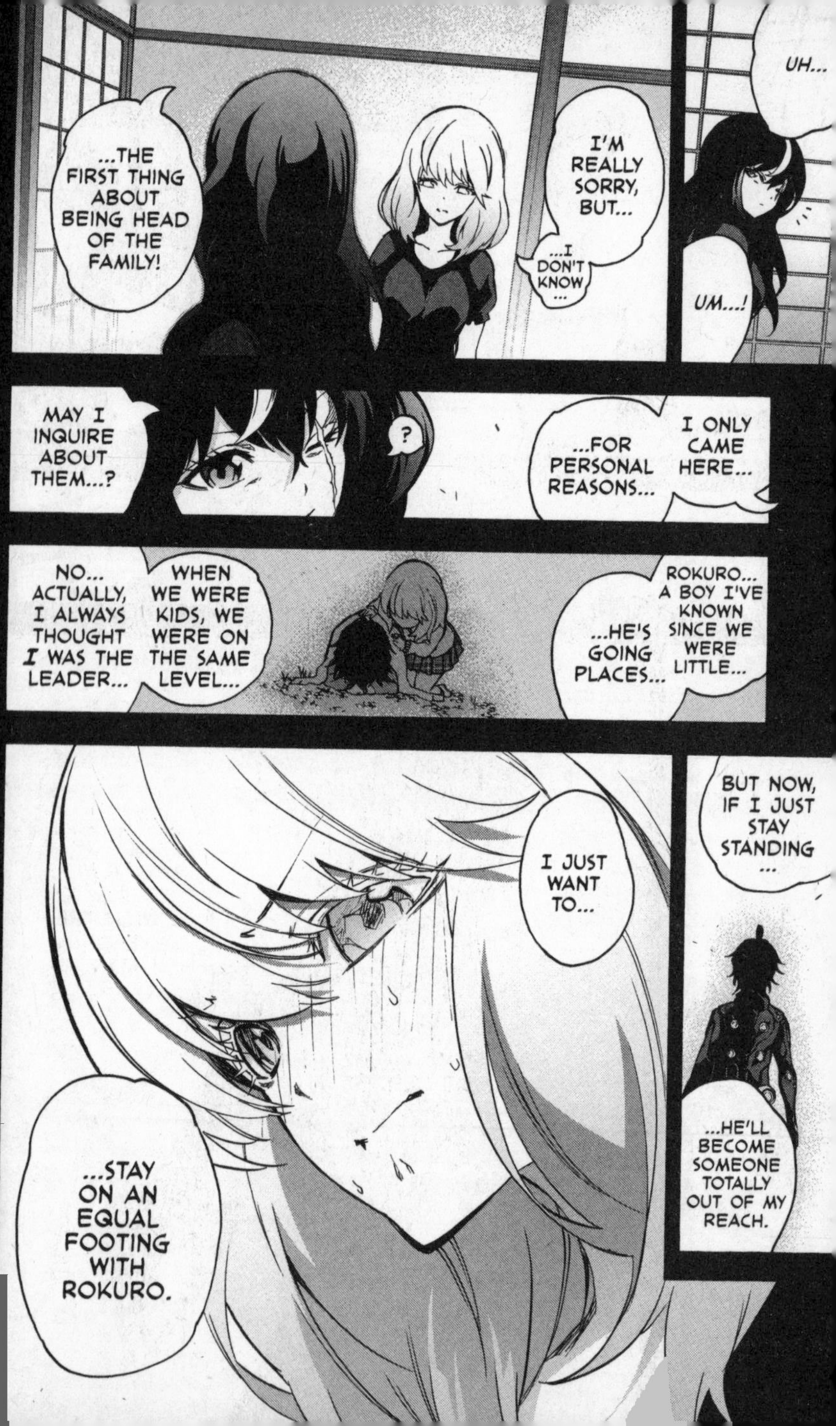
UH...
UM...!
I'M REALLY SORRY, BUT...
...I DON'T KNOW ...
...THE FIRST THING ABOUT BEING HEAD OF THE FAMILY!
I ONLY CAME HERE...
...FOR PERSONAL REASONS...
?
MAY I INQUIRE ABOUT THEM...?
ROKURO... A BOY I'VE KNOWN SINCE WE WERE LITTLE...
...HE'S GOING PLACES...
WHEN WE WERE KIDS, WE WERE ON THE SAME LEVEL...
NO... ACTUALLY, I ALWAYS THOUGHT *I* WAS THE LEADER...
BUT NOW, IF I JUST STAY STANDING ...
...HE'LL BECOME SOMEONE TOTALLY OUT OF MY REACH.
I JUST WANT TO...
...STAY ON AN EQUAL FOOTING WITH ROKURO.

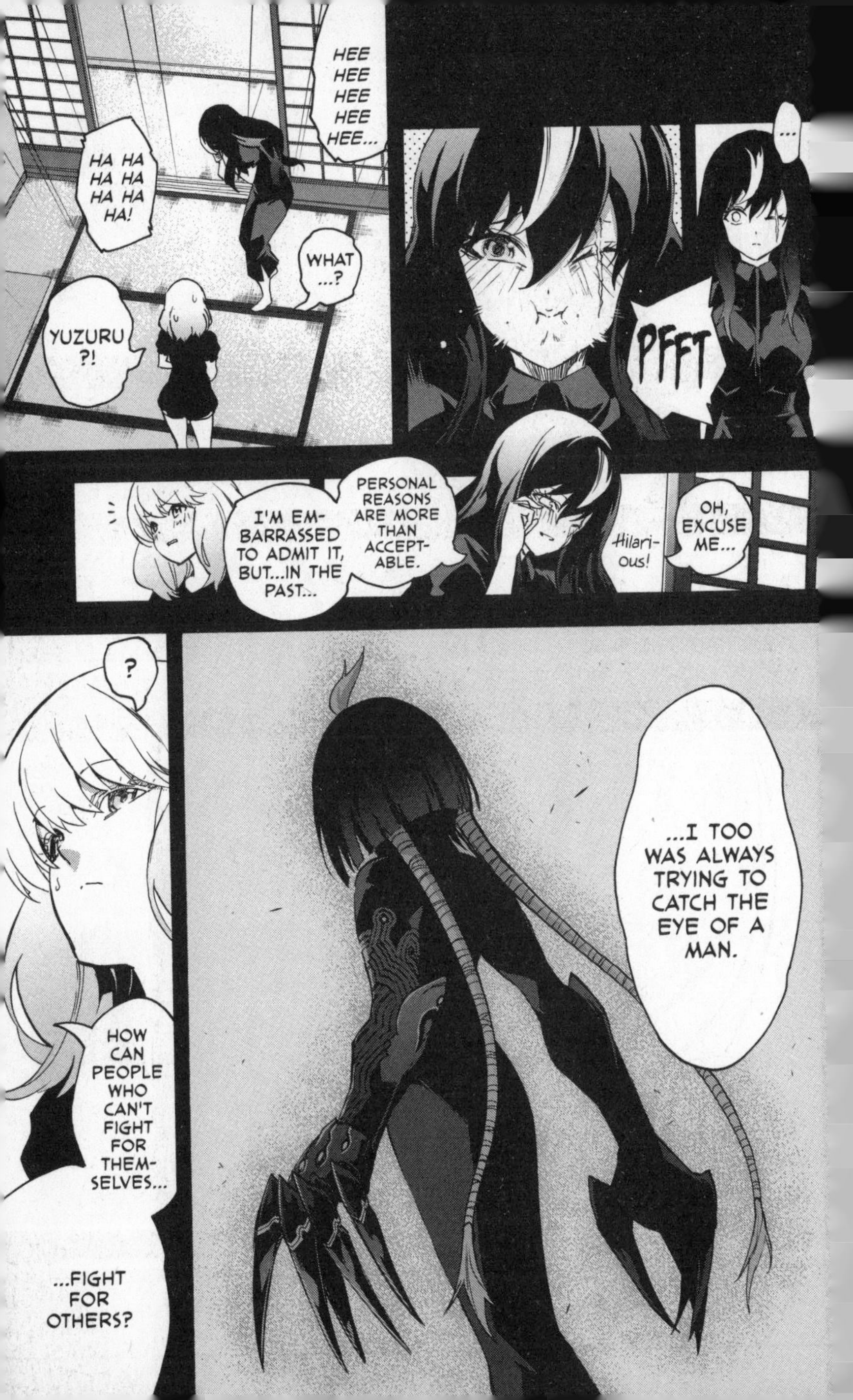
...
PFFT
HEE HEE HEE HEE HEE...
HA HA HA HA HA HA HA!
WHAT ...?
YUZURU ?!
OH, EXCUSE ME...
Hilari-ous!
PERSONAL REASONS ARE MORE THAN ACCEPT-ABLE.
I'M EM-BARRASSED TO ADMIT IT, BUT...IN THE PAST...
...I TOO WAS ALWAYS TRYING TO CATCH THE EYE OF A MAN.
?
HOW CAN PEOPLE WHO CAN'T FIGHT FOR THEM-SELVES...
...FIGHT FOR OTHERS?

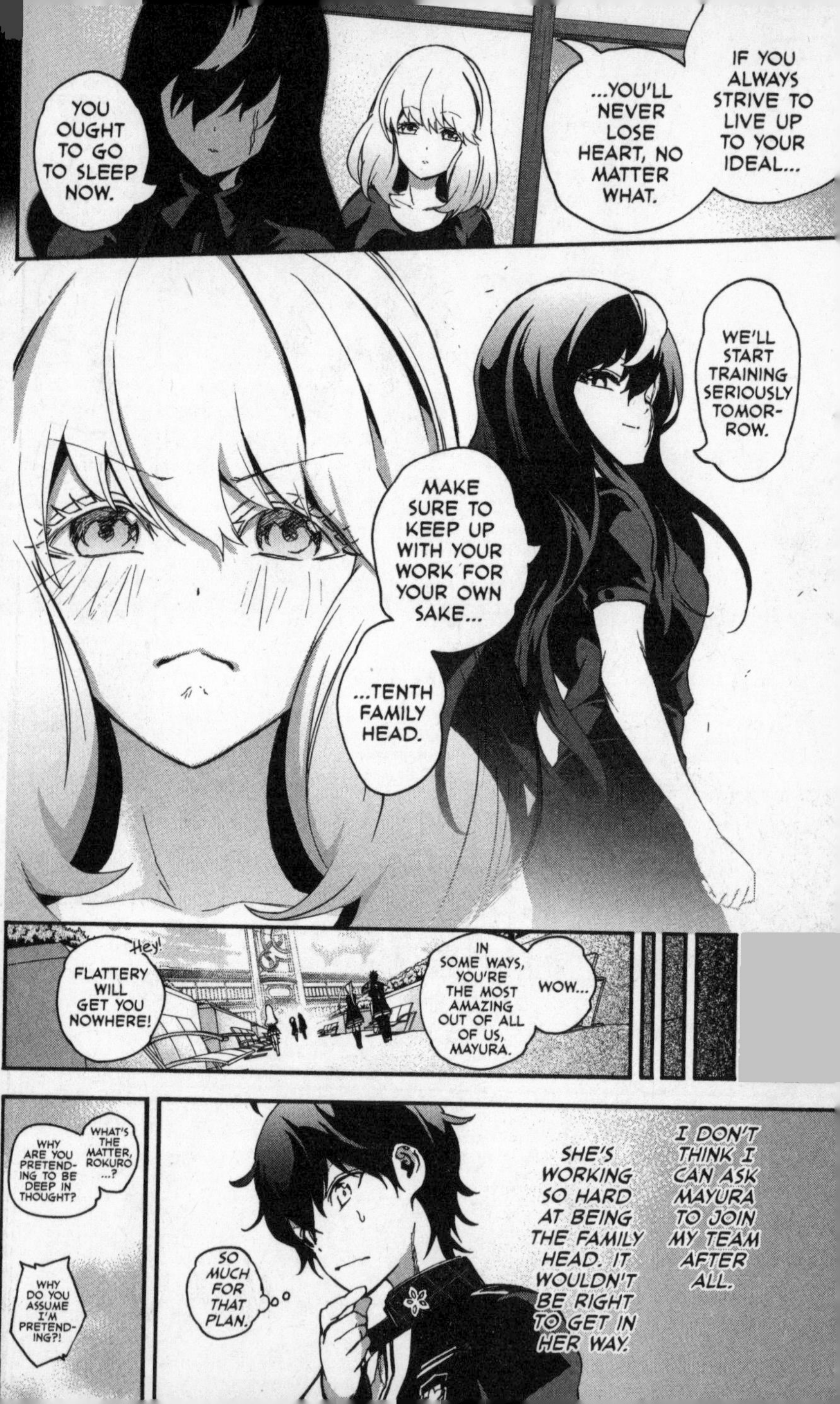
IF YOU ALWAYS STRIVE TO LIVE UP TO YOUR IDEAL...
...YOU'LL NEVER LOSE HEART, NO MATTER WHAT.
YOU OUGHT TO GO TO SLEEP NOW.
WE'LL START TRAINING SERIOUSLY TOMORROW.
MAKE SURE TO KEEP UP WITH YOUR WORK FOR YOUR OWN SAKE...
...TENTH FAMILY HEAD.
WOW...
IN SOME WAYS, YOU'RE THE MOST AMAZING OUT OF ALL OF US, MAYURA.
Hey!
FLATTERY WILL GET YOU NOWHERE!
I DON'T THINK I CAN ASK MAYURA TO JOIN MY TEAM AFTER ALL.
SHE'S WORKING SO HARD AT BEING THE FAMILY HEAD. IT WOULDN'T BE RIGHT TO GET IN HER WAY.
SO MUCH FOR THAT PLAN.
WHAT'S THE MATTER, ROKURO...?
WHY ARE YOU PRETENDING TO BE DEEP IN THOUGHT?
WHY DO YOU ASSUME I'M PRETENDING?!

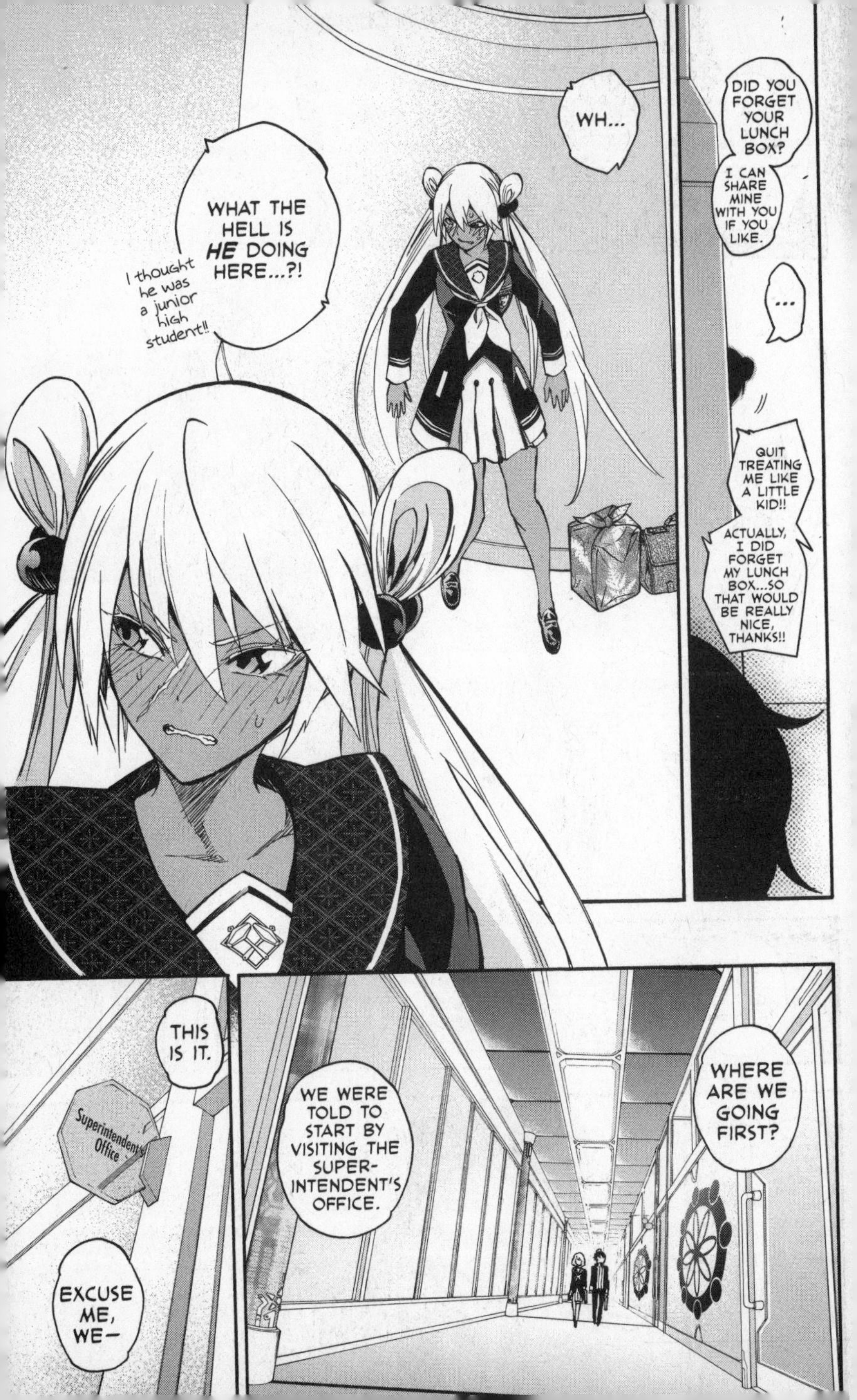
DID YOU FORGET YOUR LUNCH BOX?
I CAN SHARE MINE WITH YOU IF YOU LIKE.
...
QUIT TREATING ME LIKE A LITTLE KID!!
ACTUALLY, I DID FORGET MY LUNCH BOX...SO THAT WOULD BE REALLY NICE, THANKS!!
WH...
WHAT THE HELL IS *HE* DOING HERE...?!
I thought he was a junior high student!!
WHERE ARE WE GOING FIRST?
WE WERE TOLD TO START BY VISITING THE SUPER-INTENDENT'S OFFICE.
THIS IS IT.
Superintendent's Office
EXCUSE ME, WE—

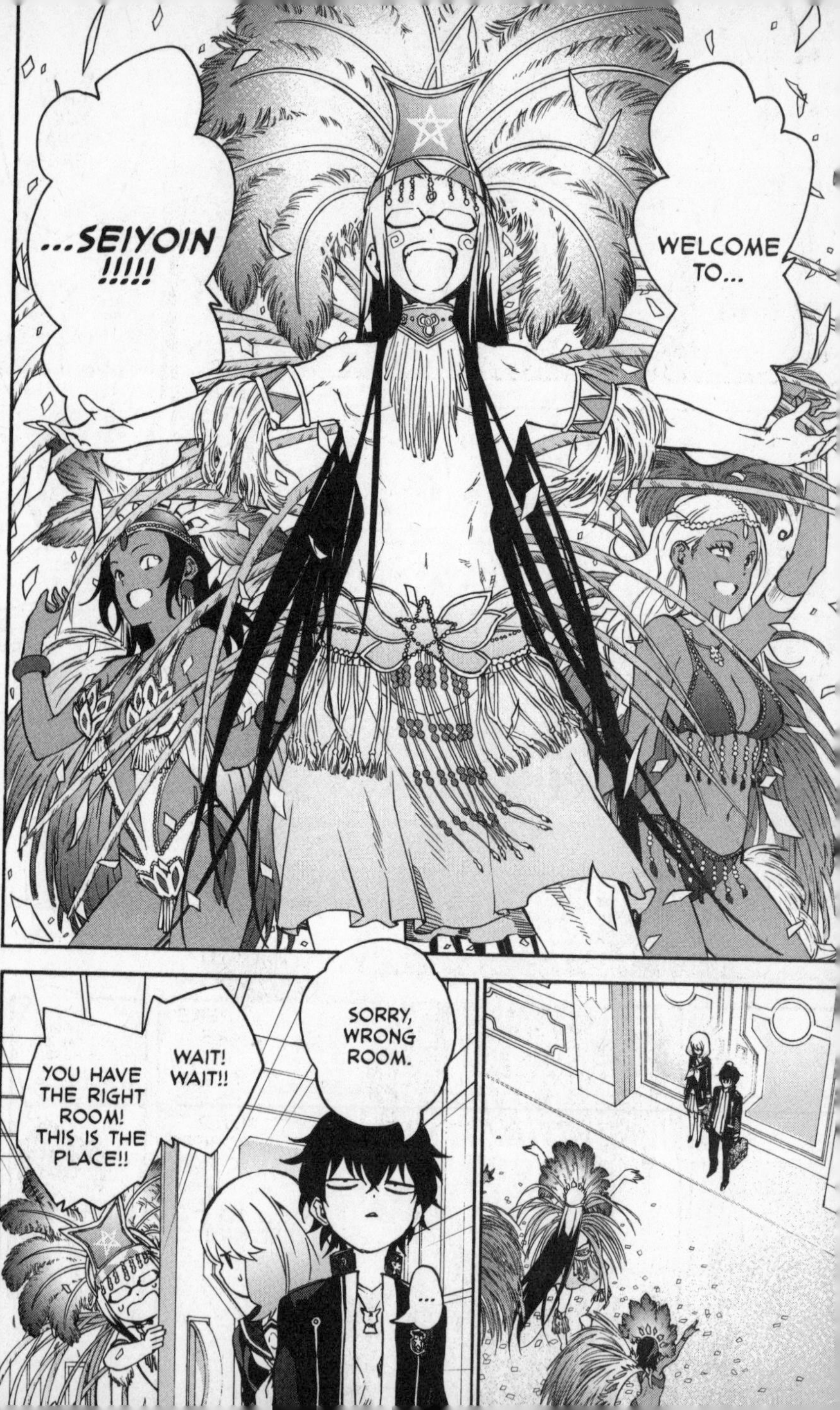
WELCOME TO...
...SEIYOIN !!!!!
SORRY, WRONG ROOM.
WAIT! WAIT!!
YOU HAVE THE RIGHT ROOM! THIS IS THE PLACE!!
...

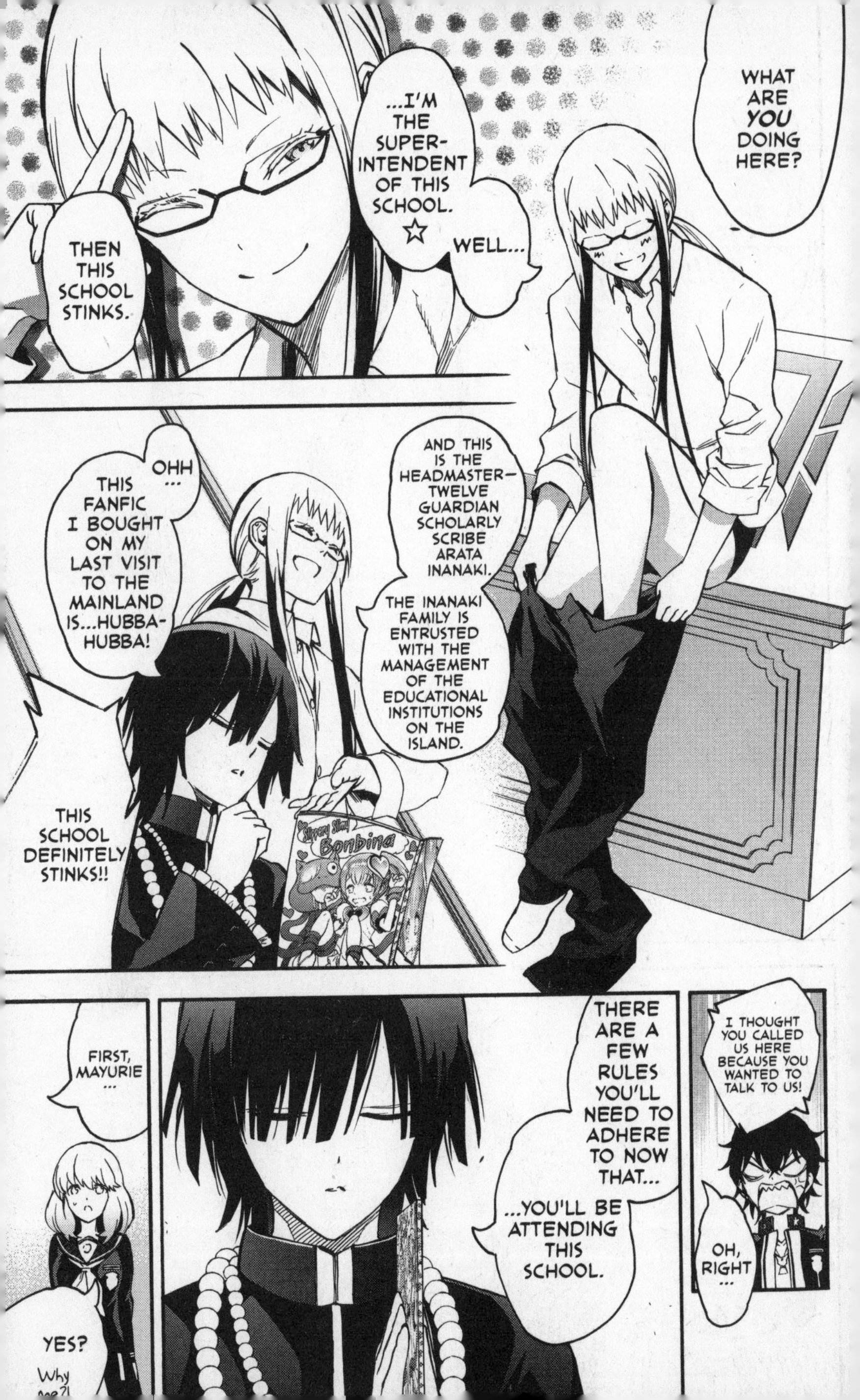

WHAT ARE YOU DOING HERE?
WELL...
...I'M THE SUPER-INTENDENT OF THIS SCHOOL. ☆
THEN THIS SCHOOL STINKS.
AND THIS IS THE HEADMASTER—TWELVE GUARDIAN SCHOLARLY SCRIBE ARATA INANAKI.
THE INANAKI FAMILY IS ENTRUSTED WITH THE MANAGEMENT OF THE EDUCATIONAL INSTITUTIONS ON THE ISLAND.
OHH... THIS FANFIC I BOUGHT ON MY LAST VISIT TO THE MAINLAND IS...HUBBA-HUBBA!
Slippery Slimy Bonbina
THIS SCHOOL DEFINITELY STINKS!!
I THOUGHT YOU CALLED US HERE BECAUSE YOU WANTED TO TALK TO US!
OH, RIGHT...
THERE ARE A FEW RULES YOU'LL NEED TO ADHERE TO NOW THAT...
...YOU'LL BE ATTENDING THIS SCHOOL.
FIRST, MAYURIE...
YES?
Why

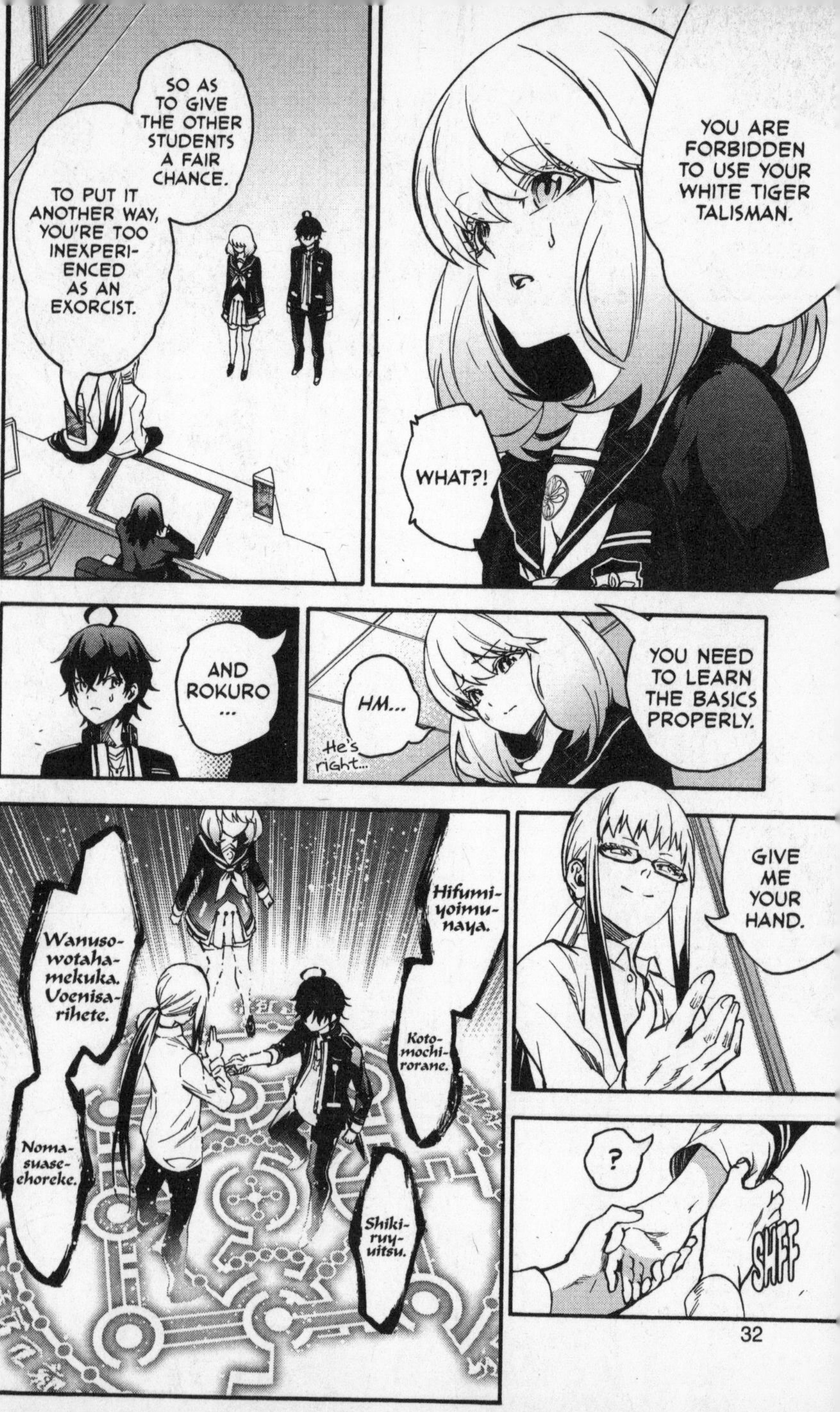

YOU ARE FORBIDDEN TO USE YOUR WHITE TIGER TALISMAN.
WHAT?!
SO AS TO GIVE THE OTHER STUDENTS A FAIR CHANCE.
TO PUT IT ANOTHER WAY, YOU'RE TOO INEXPERI-ENCED AS AN EXORCIST.
YOU NEED TO LEARN THE BASICS PROPERLY.
HM...
He's right...
AND ROKURO...
GIVE ME YOUR HAND.
?
SHFF
Hifumi-yoimu-naya.
Koto-mochi-rorane.
Wanuso-wotaha-mekuka. Voenisa-rihete.
Noma-suase-ehoreke.
Shiki-ruy-uitsu.

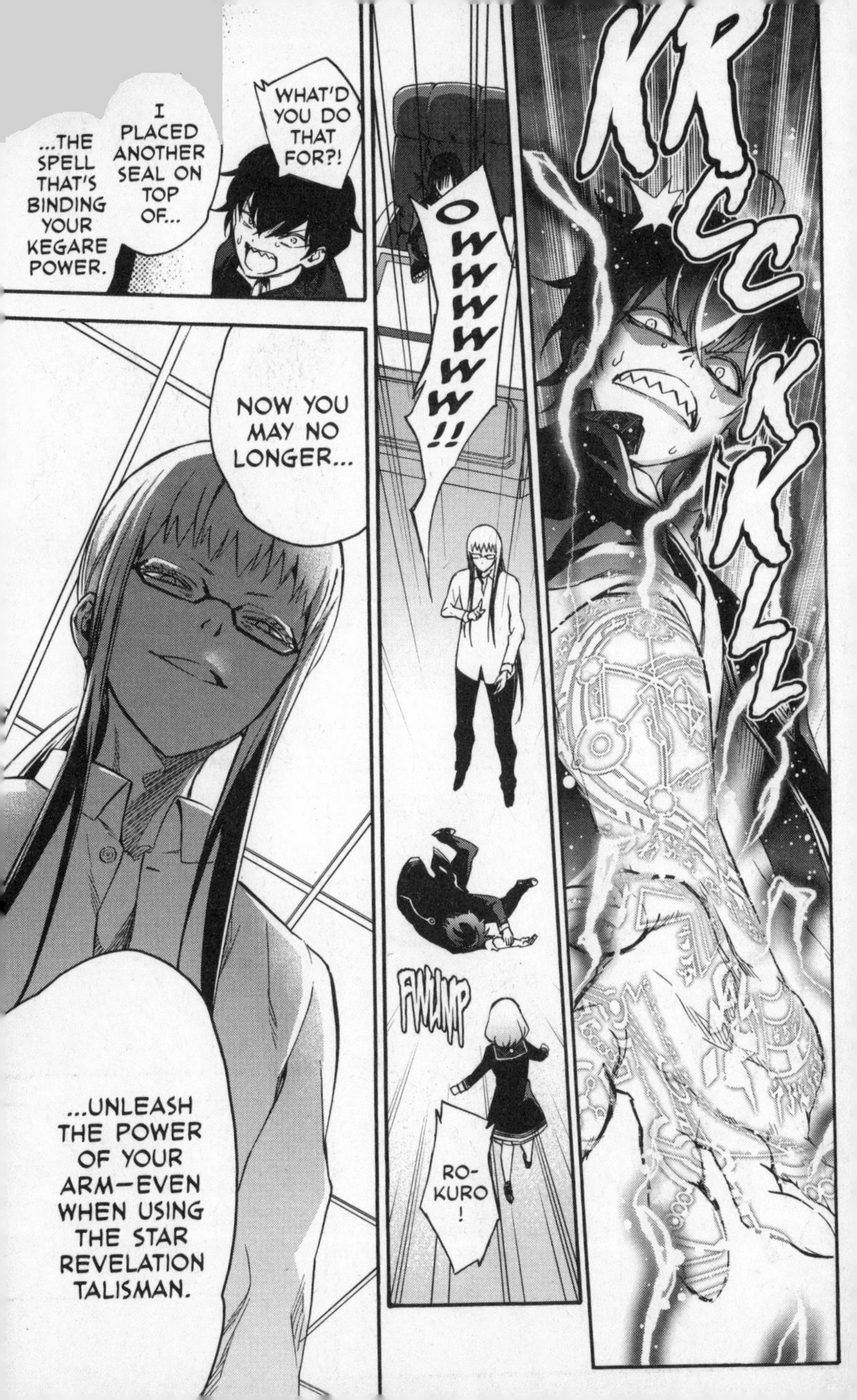
KRCCKKLZ
OWWWWWW!!
FWUMP
RO-KURO!
WHAT'D YOU DO THAT FOR?!
I PLACED ANOTHER SEAL ON TOP OF...
...THE SPELL THAT'S BINDING YOUR KEGARE POWER.
NOW YOU MAY NO LONGER...
...UNLEASH THE POWER OF YOUR ARM—EVEN WHEN USING THE STAR REVELATION TALISMAN.

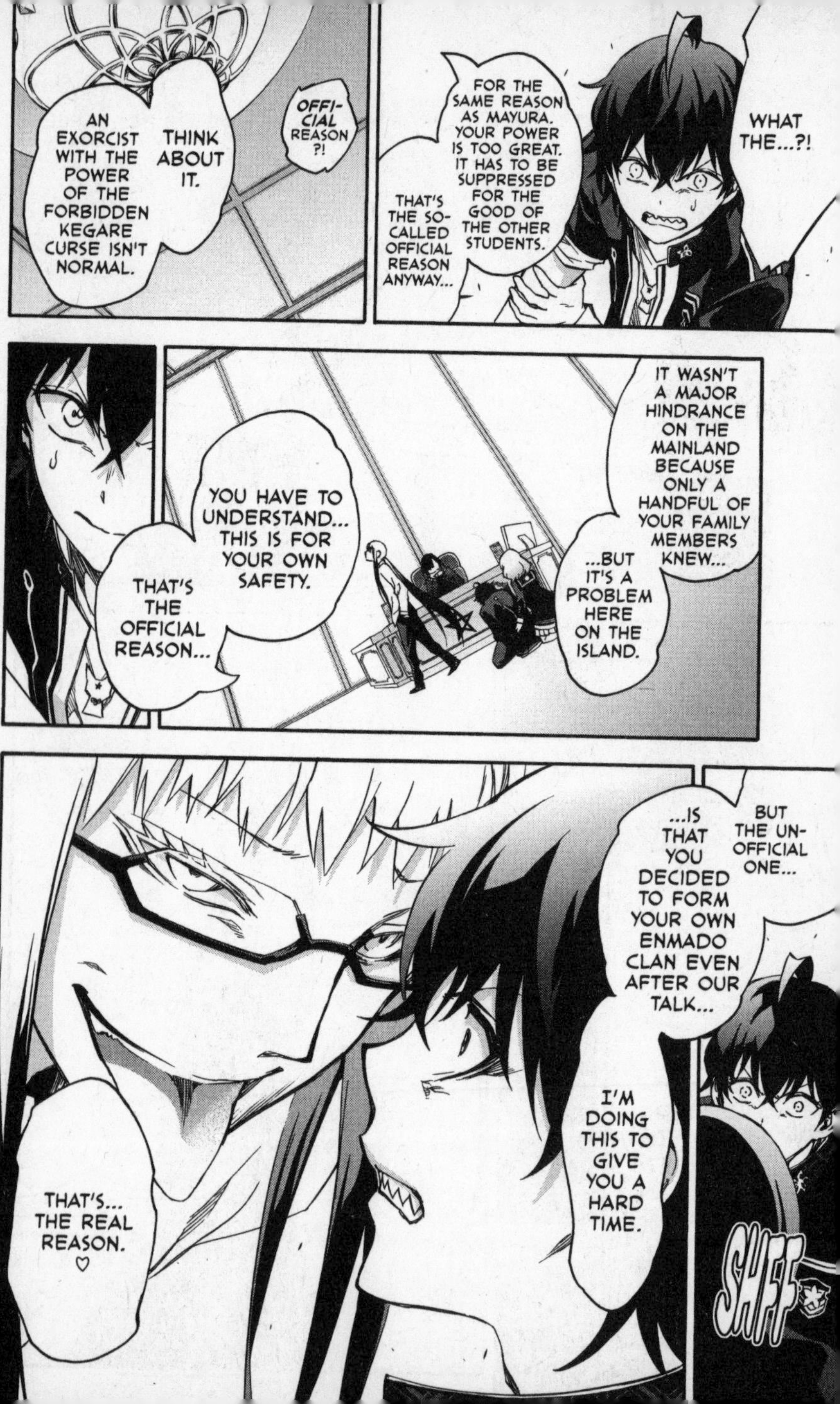
WHAT THE...?!
FOR THE SAME REASON AS MAYURA. YOUR POWER IS TOO GREAT. IT HAS TO BE SUPPRESSED FOR THE GOOD OF THE OTHER STUDENTS.
THAT'S THE SO-CALLED OFFICIAL REASON ANYWAY...
OFFI-CIAL REASON?!
THINK ABOUT IT.
AN EXORCIST WITH THE POWER OF THE FORBIDDEN KEGARE CURSE ISN'T NORMAL.
IT WASN'T A MAJOR HINDRANCE ON THE MAINLAND BECAUSE ONLY A HANDFUL OF YOUR FAMILY MEMBERS KNEW...
...BUT IT'S A PROBLEM HERE ON THE ISLAND.
YOU HAVE TO UNDERSTAND... THIS IS FOR YOUR OWN SAFETY.
THAT'S THE OFFICIAL REASON...
BUT THE UN-OFFICIAL ONE...
...IS THAT YOU DECIDED TO FORM YOUR OWN ENMADO CLAN EVEN AFTER OUR TALK...
SHFF
I'M DOING THIS TO GIVE YOU A HARD TIME.
THAT'S... THE REAL REASON. ♡

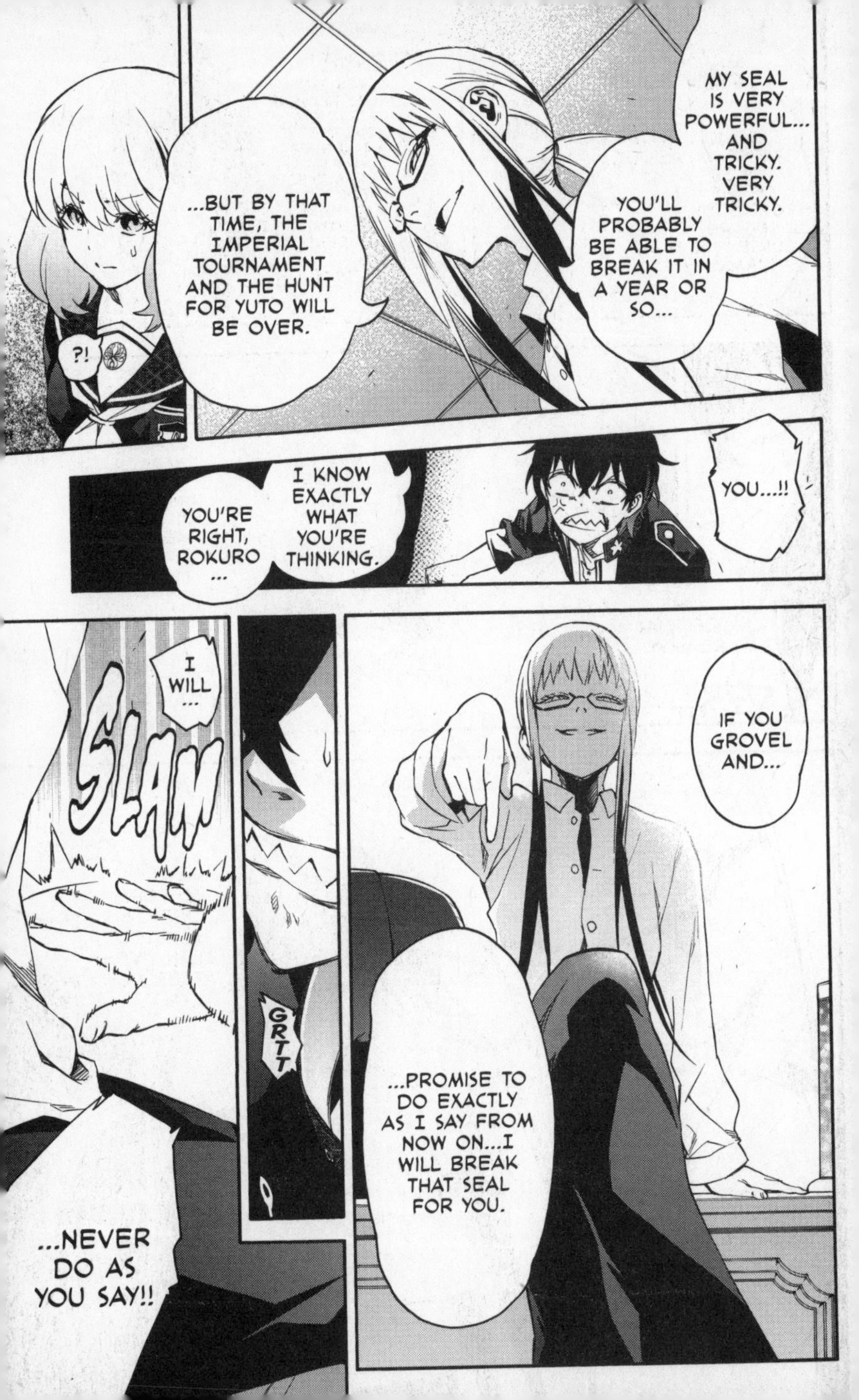
MY SEAL IS VERY POWERFUL... AND TRICKY. VERY TRICKY.
YOU'LL PROBABLY BE ABLE TO BREAK IT IN A YEAR OR SO...
...BUT BY THAT TIME, THE IMPERIAL TOURNAMENT AND THE HUNT FOR YUTO WILL BE OVER.
?!
YOU...!!
I KNOW EXACTLY WHAT YOU'RE THINKING.
YOU'RE RIGHT, ROKURO...
IF YOU GROVEL AND...
...PROMISE TO DO EXACTLY AS I SAY FROM NOW ON...I WILL BREAK THAT SEAL FOR YOU.
GRTT
I WILL...
SLAM
...NEVER DO AS YOU SAY!!

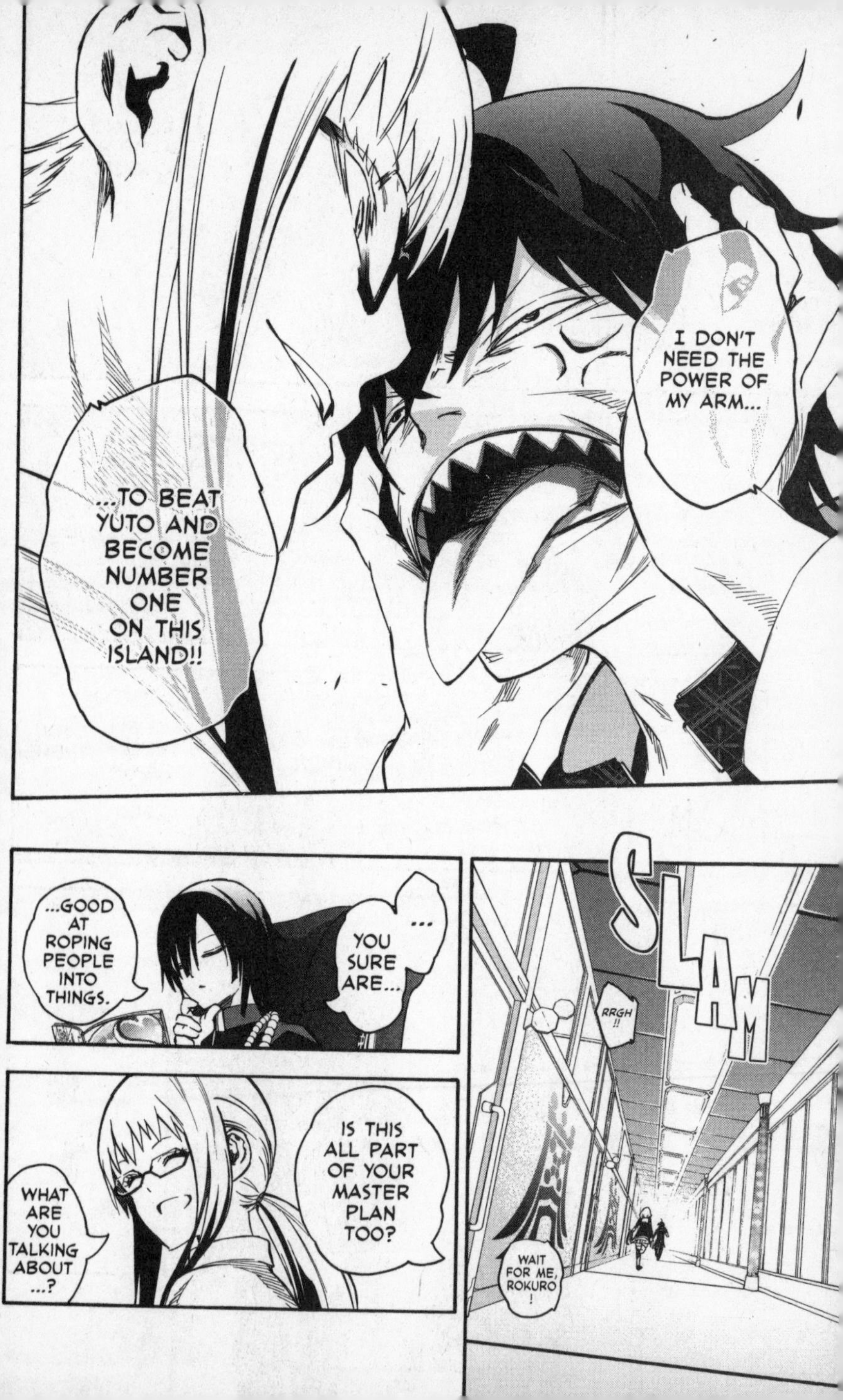
I DON'T NEED THE POWER OF MY ARM...
...TO BEAT YUTO AND BECOME NUMBER ONE ON THIS ISLAND!!
SLAM
RRGH!!
WAIT FOR ME, ROKURO!
... YOU SURE ARE...
...GOOD AT ROPING PEOPLE INTO THINGS.
IS THIS ALL PART OF YOUR MASTER PLAN TOO?
WHAT ARE YOU TALKING ABOUT ...?

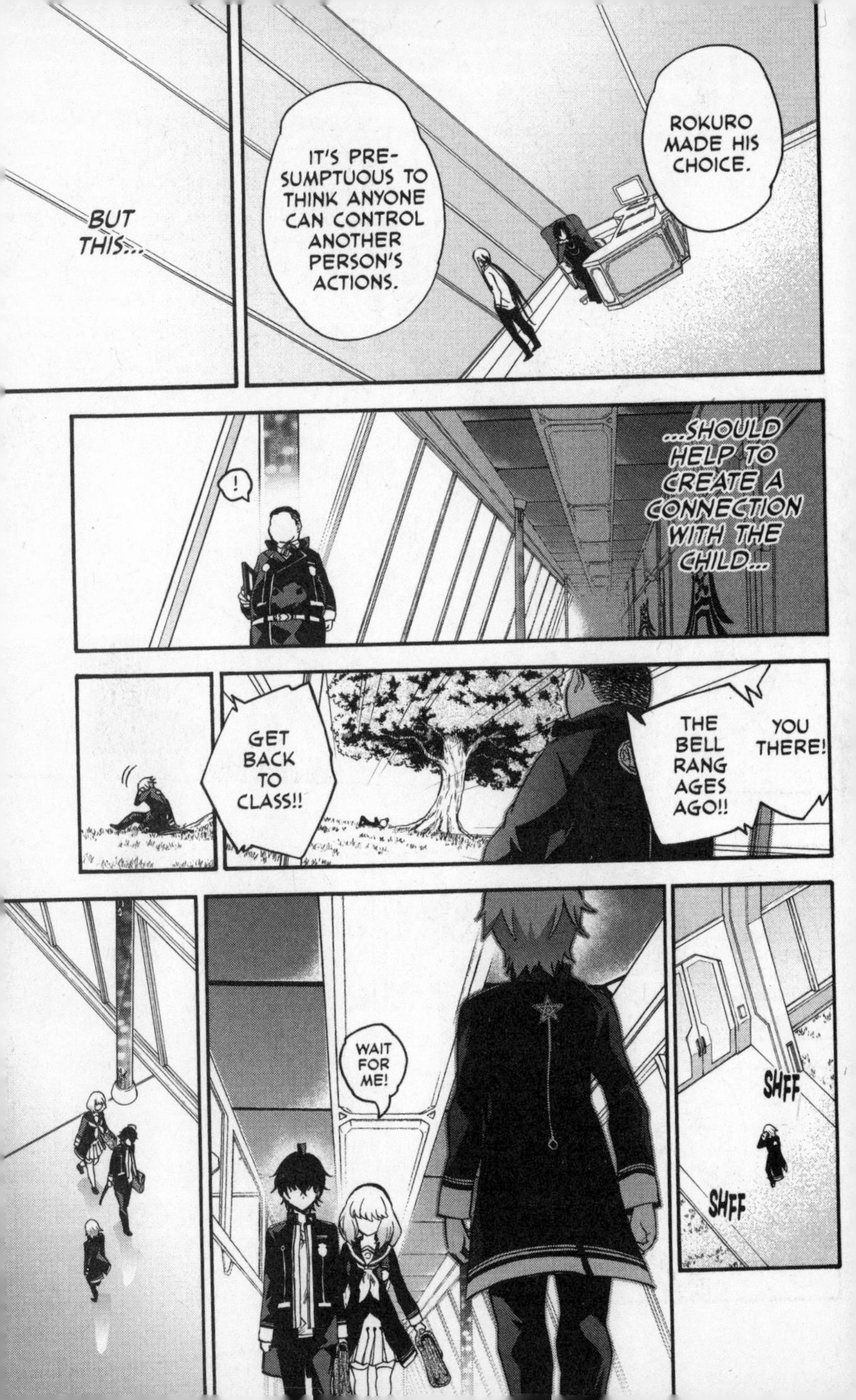
ROKURO MADE HIS CHOICE.
IT'S PRE-SUMPTUOUS TO THINK ANYONE CAN CONTROL ANOTHER PERSON'S ACTIONS.
BUT THIS...
...SHOULD HELP TO CREATE A CONNECTION WITH THE CHILD...
!
YOU THERE!
THE BELL RANG AGES AGO!!
GET BACK TO CLASS!!
SHFF
SHFF
WAIT FOR ME!

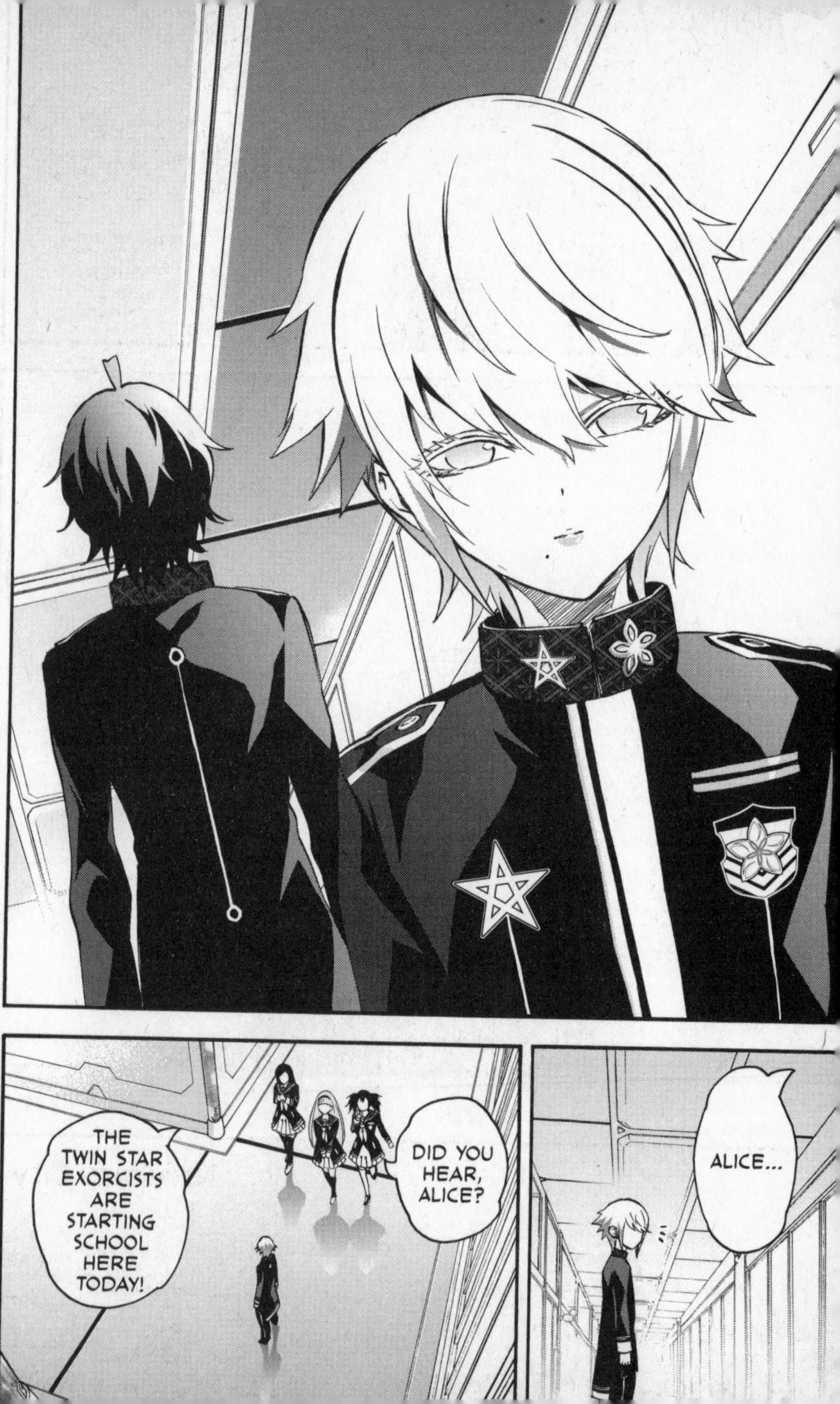
ALICE...
DID YOU HEAR, ALICE?
THE TWIN STAR EXORCISTS ARE STARTING SCHOOL HERE TODAY!

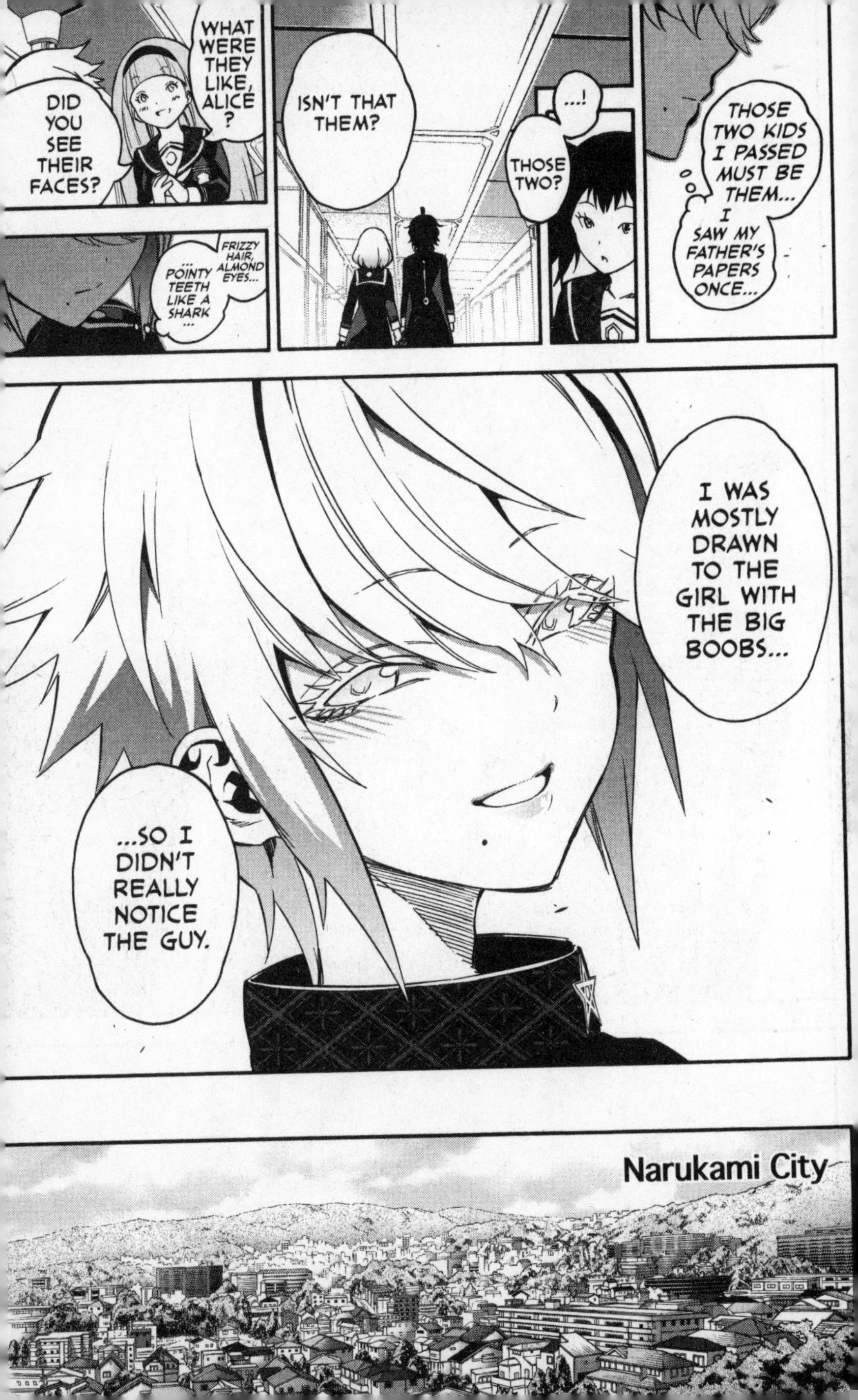
THOSE TWO KIDS I PASSED MUST BE THEM...
I SAW MY FATHER'S PAPERS ONCE...
...!
THOSE TWO?
ISN'T THAT THEM?
WHAT WERE THEY LIKE, ALICE?
DID YOU SEE THEIR FACES?
FRIZZY HAIR, ALMOND EYES...
...POINTY TEETH LIKE A SHARK...
I WAS MOSTLY DRAWN TO THE GIRL WITH THE BIG BOOBS...
...SO I DIDN'T REALLY NOTICE THE GUY.
Narukami City

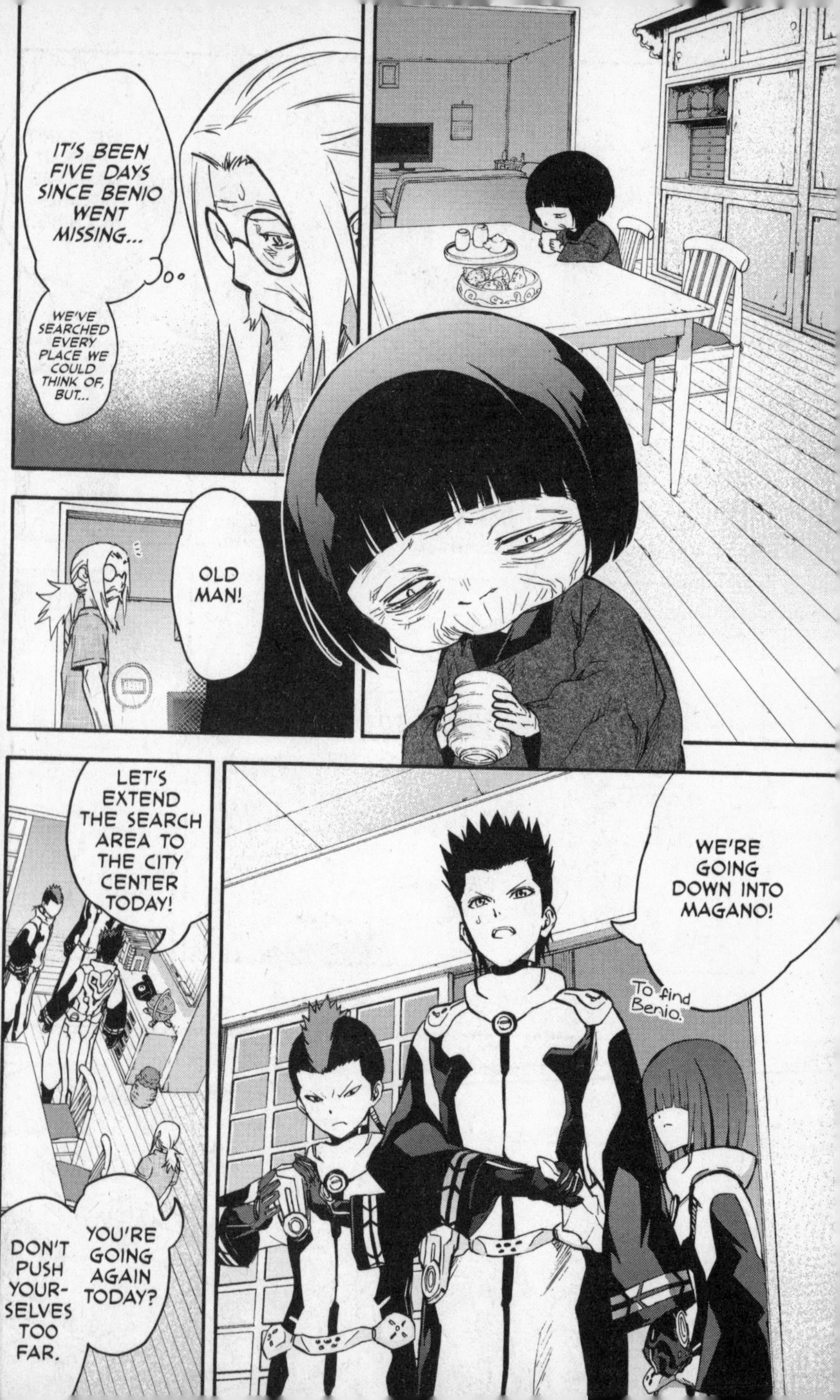
IT'S BEEN FIVE DAYS SINCE BENIO WENT MISSING...
WE'VE SEARCHED EVERY PLACE WE COULD THINK OF, BUT...
OLD MAN!
WE'RE GOING DOWN INTO MAGANO!
To find Benio.
LET'S EXTEND THE SEARCH AREA TO THE CITY CENTER TODAY!
YOU'RE GOING AGAIN TODAY?
DON'T PUSH YOUR-SELVES TOO FAR.

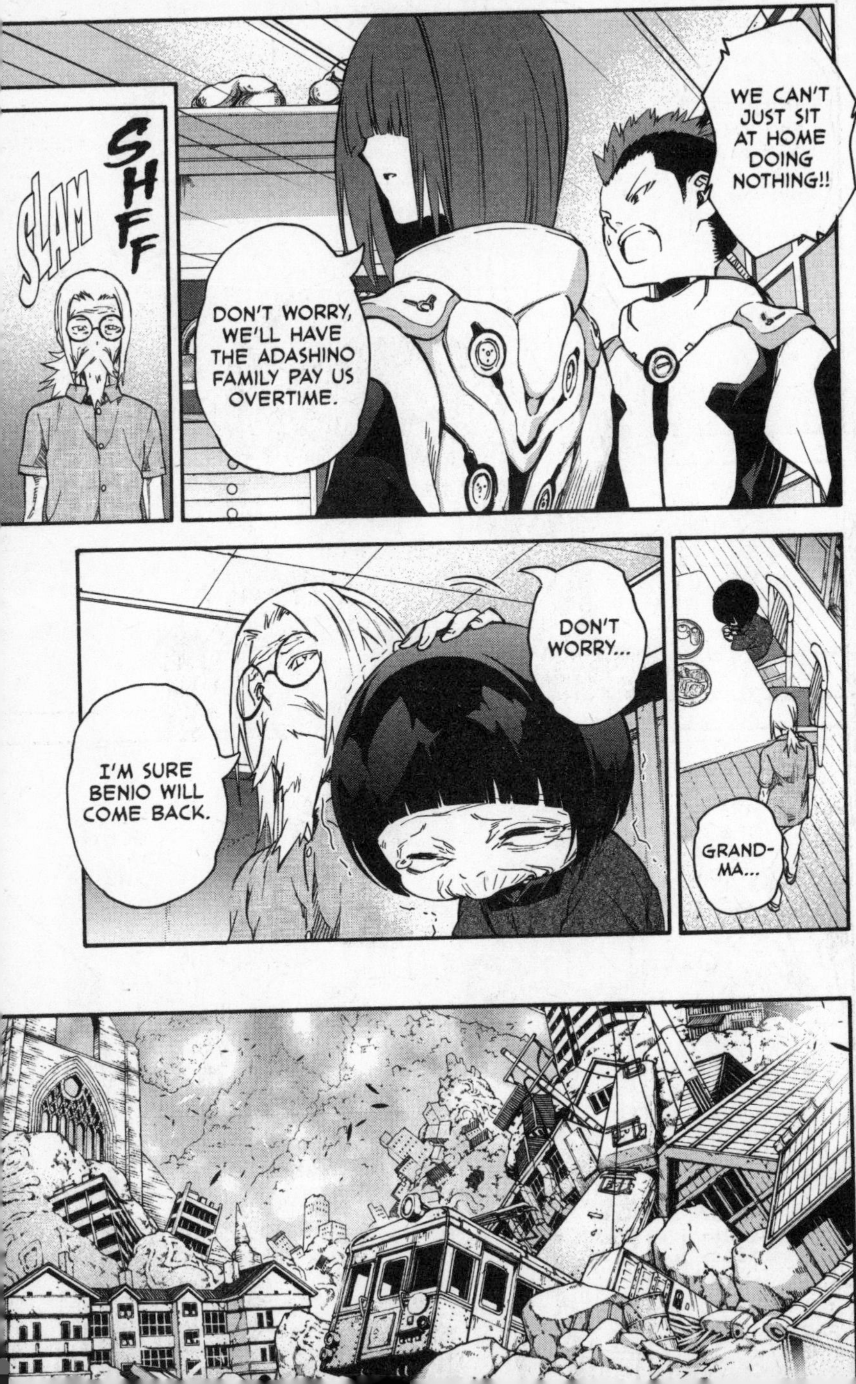
WE CAN'T JUST SIT AT HOME DOING NOTHING!!
DON'T WORRY, WE'LL HAVE THE ADASHINO FAMILY PAY US OVERTIME.
SHFF
SLAM
GRAND-MA...
DON'T WORRY...
I'M SURE BENIO WILL COME BACK.

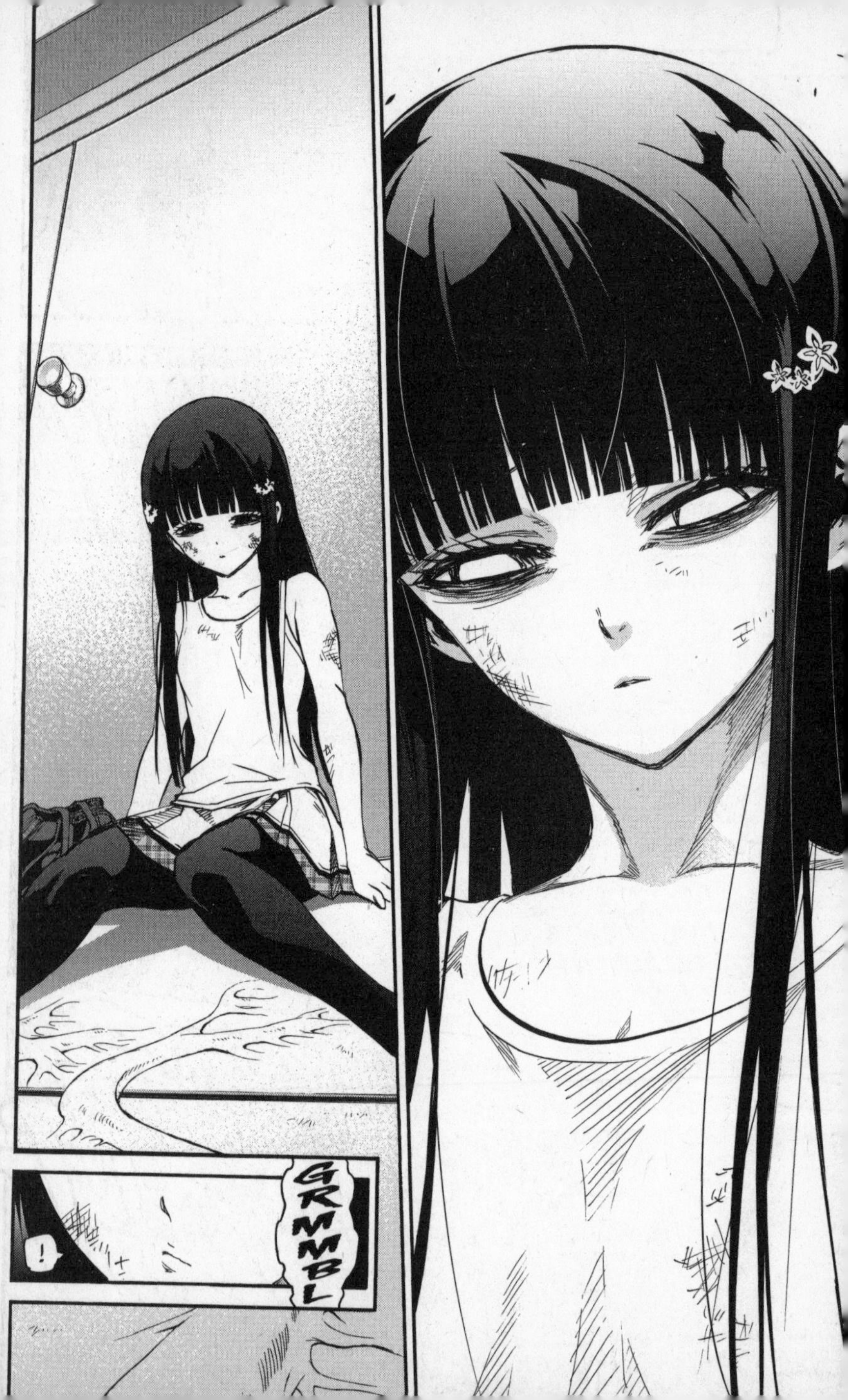
GRMMMBL
!

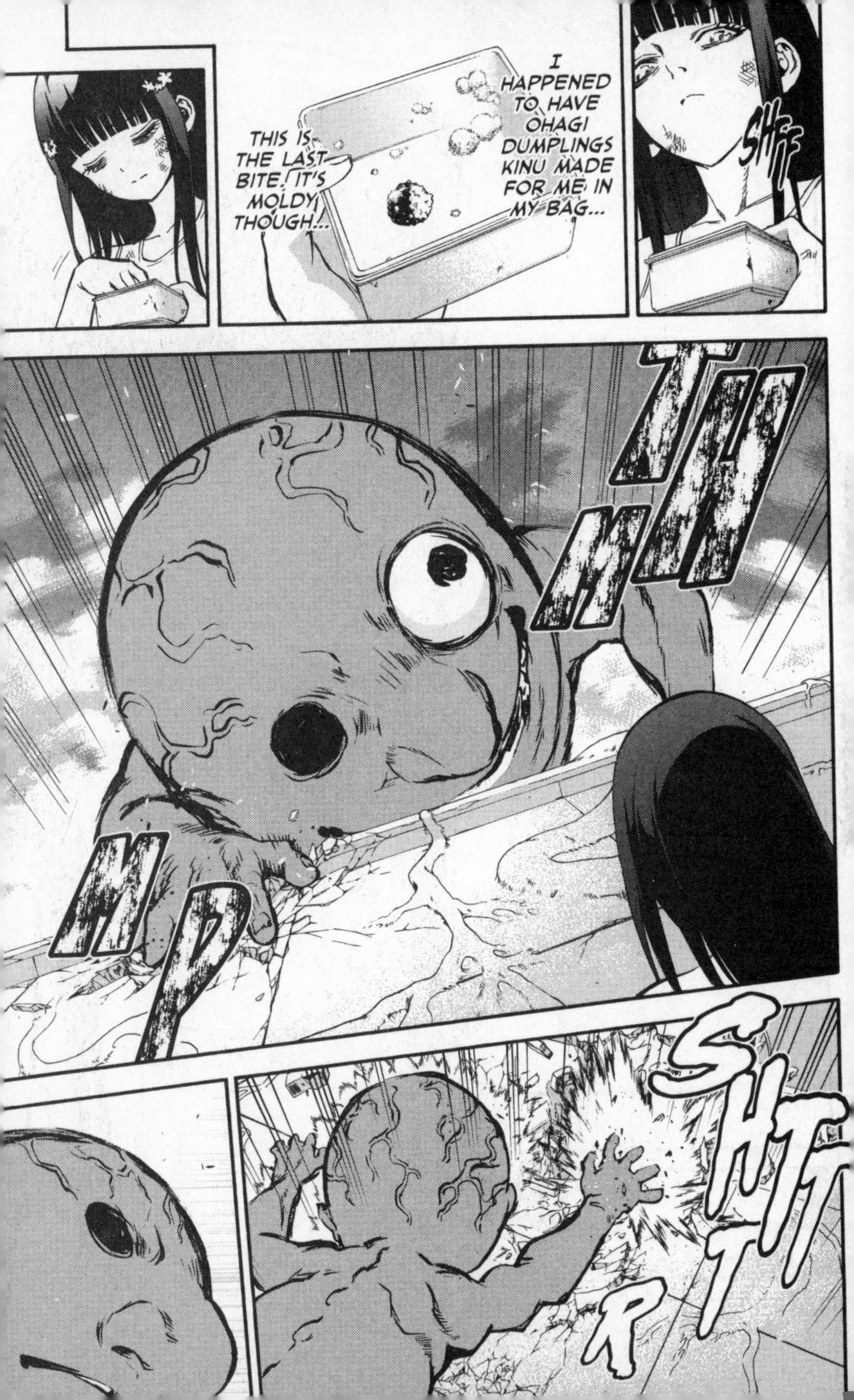
SHIF
I HAPPENED TO HAVE OHAGI DUMPLINGS KINU MADE FOR ME IN MY BAG...
THIS IS THE LAST BITE. IT'S MOLDY THOUGH...
THMM
MP
SHTT
R

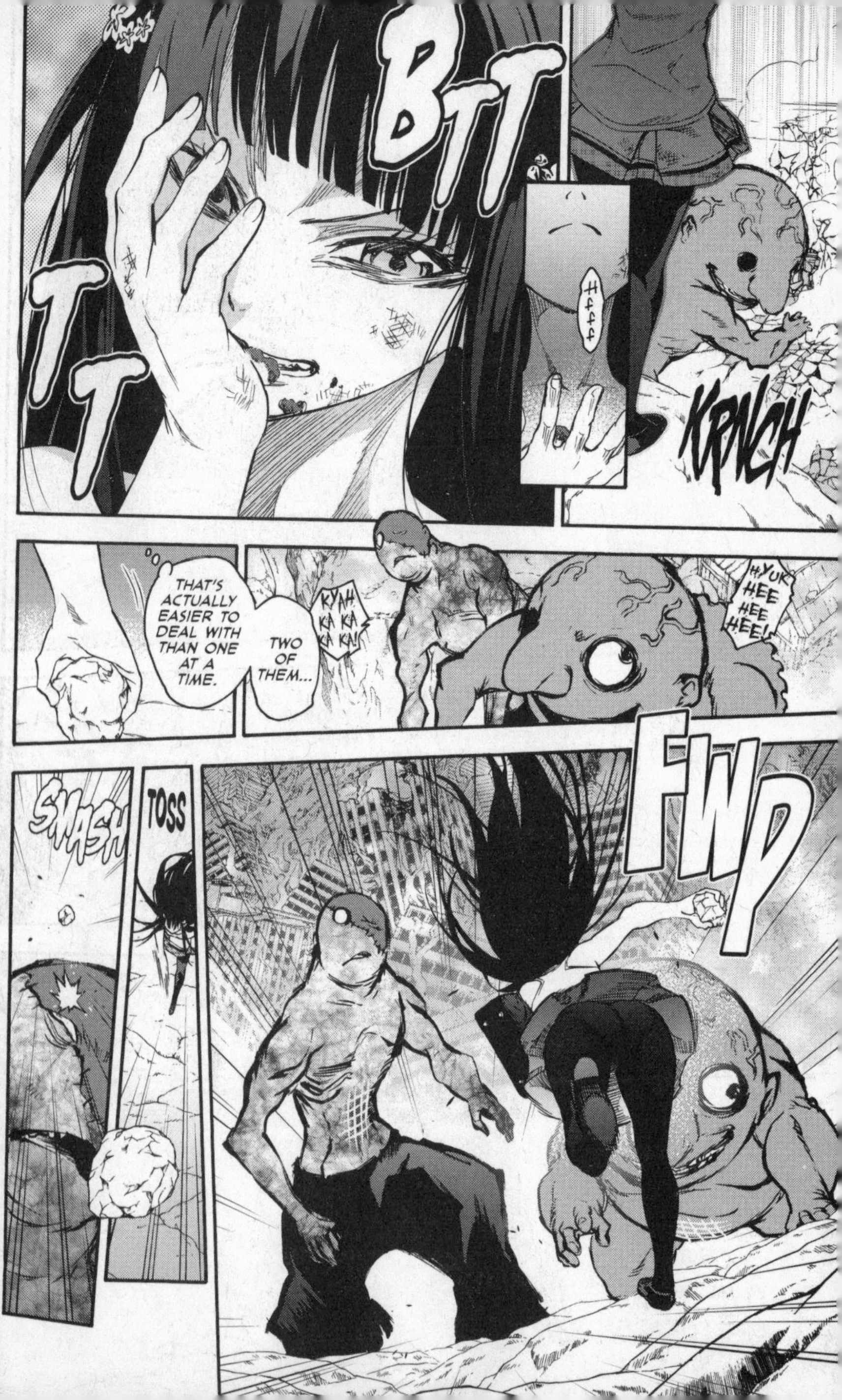
KRNCH
Hfff
BTT
TT
HYUK HEE HEE HEE!
KYAH KA KA KA!
TWO OF THEM...
THAT'S ACTUALLY EASIER TO DEAL WITH THAN ONE AT A TIME.
FWD
TOSS
SMASH

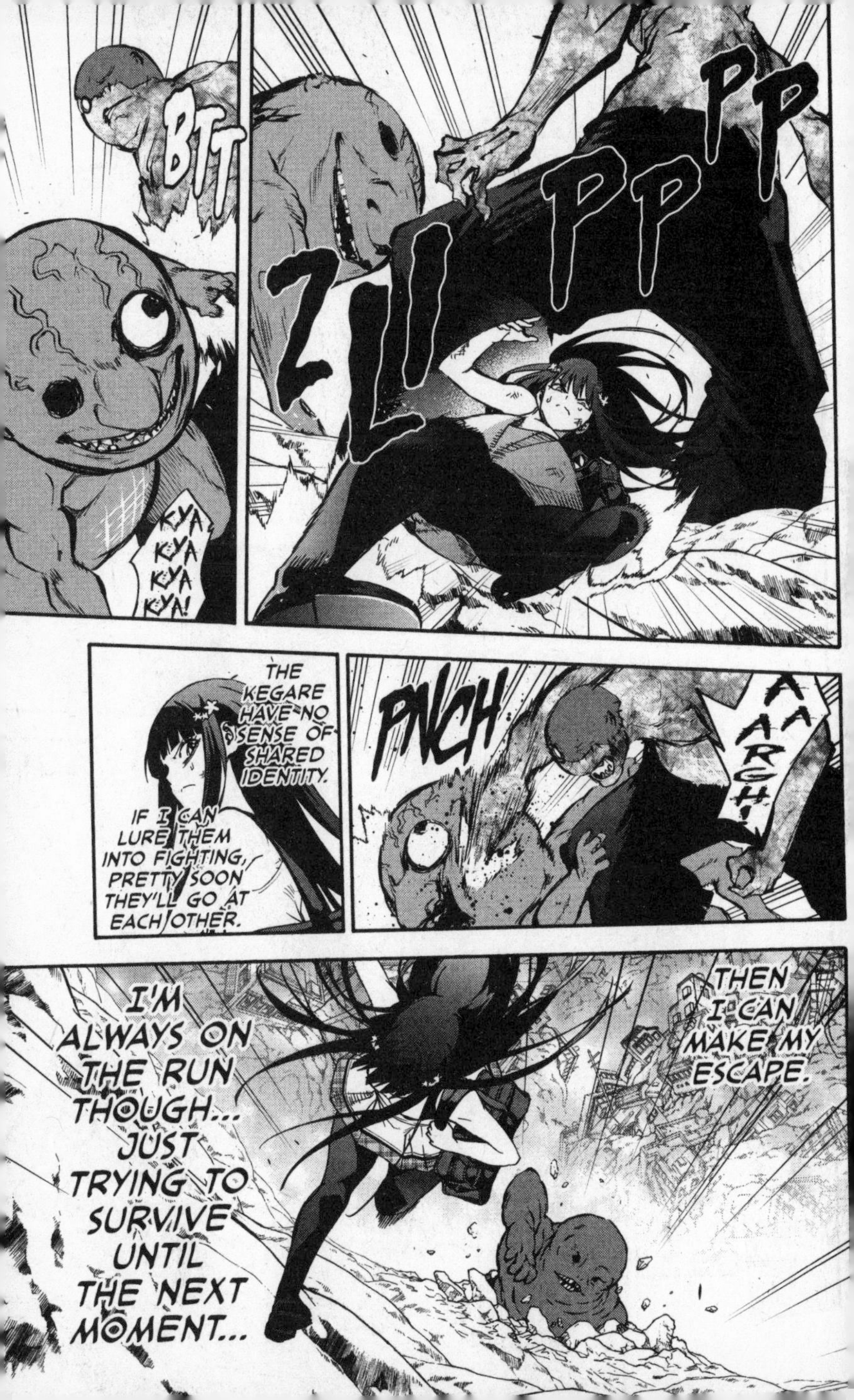
ZIIPPPPP
BTT
KYA KYA KYA KYA!
AAARGH!!
PNCH
THE KEGARE HAVE NO SENSE OF SHARED IDENTITY.
IF I CAN LURE THEM INTO FIGHTING, PRETTY SOON THEY'LL GO AT EACH OTHER.
THEN I CAN MAKE MY ESCAPE.
I'M ALWAYS ON THE RUN THOUGH... JUST TRYING TO SURVIVE UNTIL THE NEXT MOMENT...

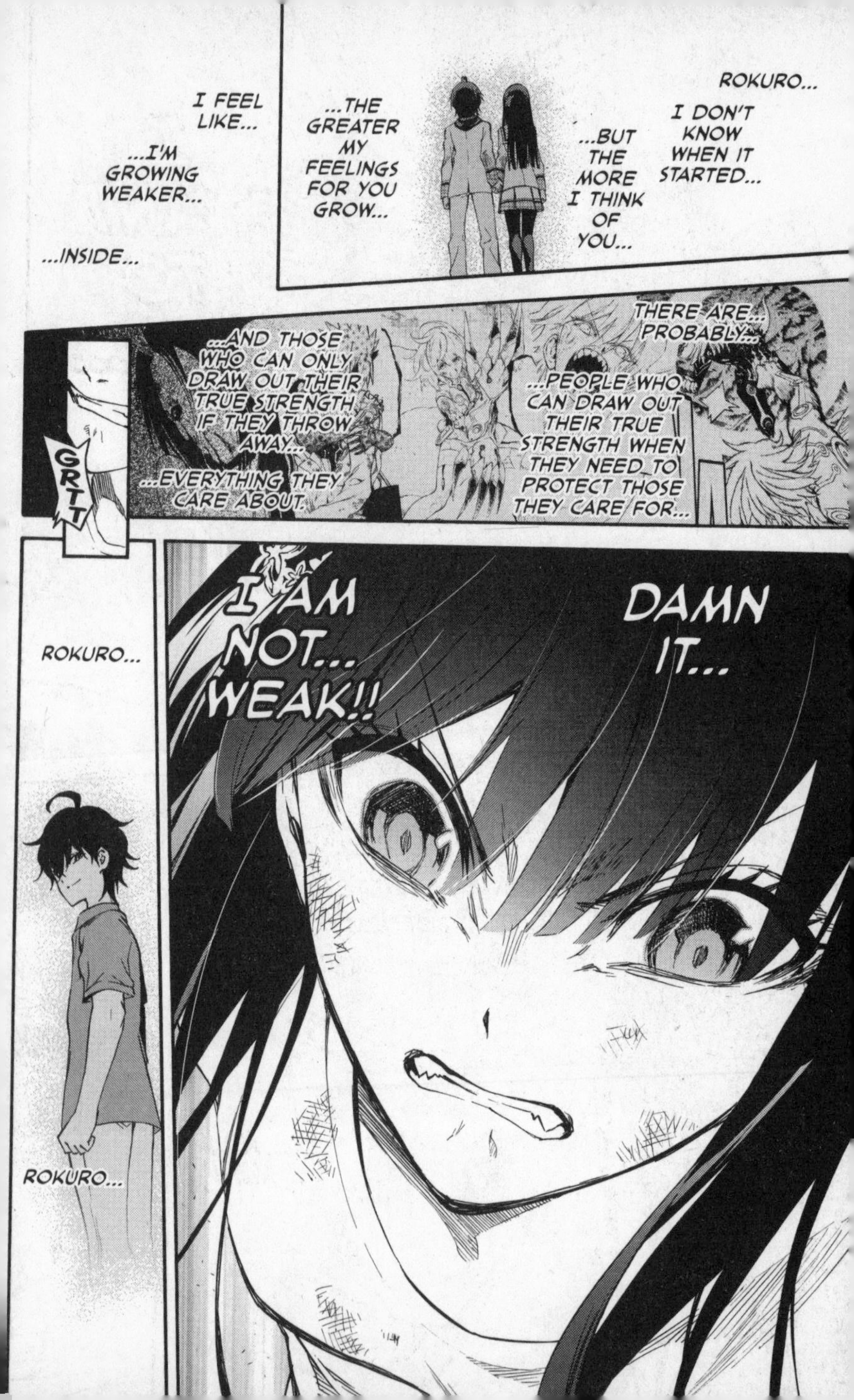
ROKURO...
I DON'T KNOW WHEN IT STARTED...
...BUT THE MORE I THINK OF YOU...
...THE GREATER MY FEELINGS FOR YOU GROW...
I FEEL LIKE...
...I'M GROWING WEAKER...
...INSIDE...
THERE ARE... PROBABLY...
...PEOPLE WHO CAN DRAW OUT THEIR TRUE STRENGTH WHEN THEY NEED TO PROTECT THOSE THEY CARE FOR...
...AND THOSE WHO CAN ONLY DRAW OUT THEIR TRUE STRENGTH IF THEY THROW AWAY...
...EVERYTHING THEY CARE ABOUT.
GRTT
DAMN IT...
I AM NOT... WEAK!!
ROKURO...
ROKURO...

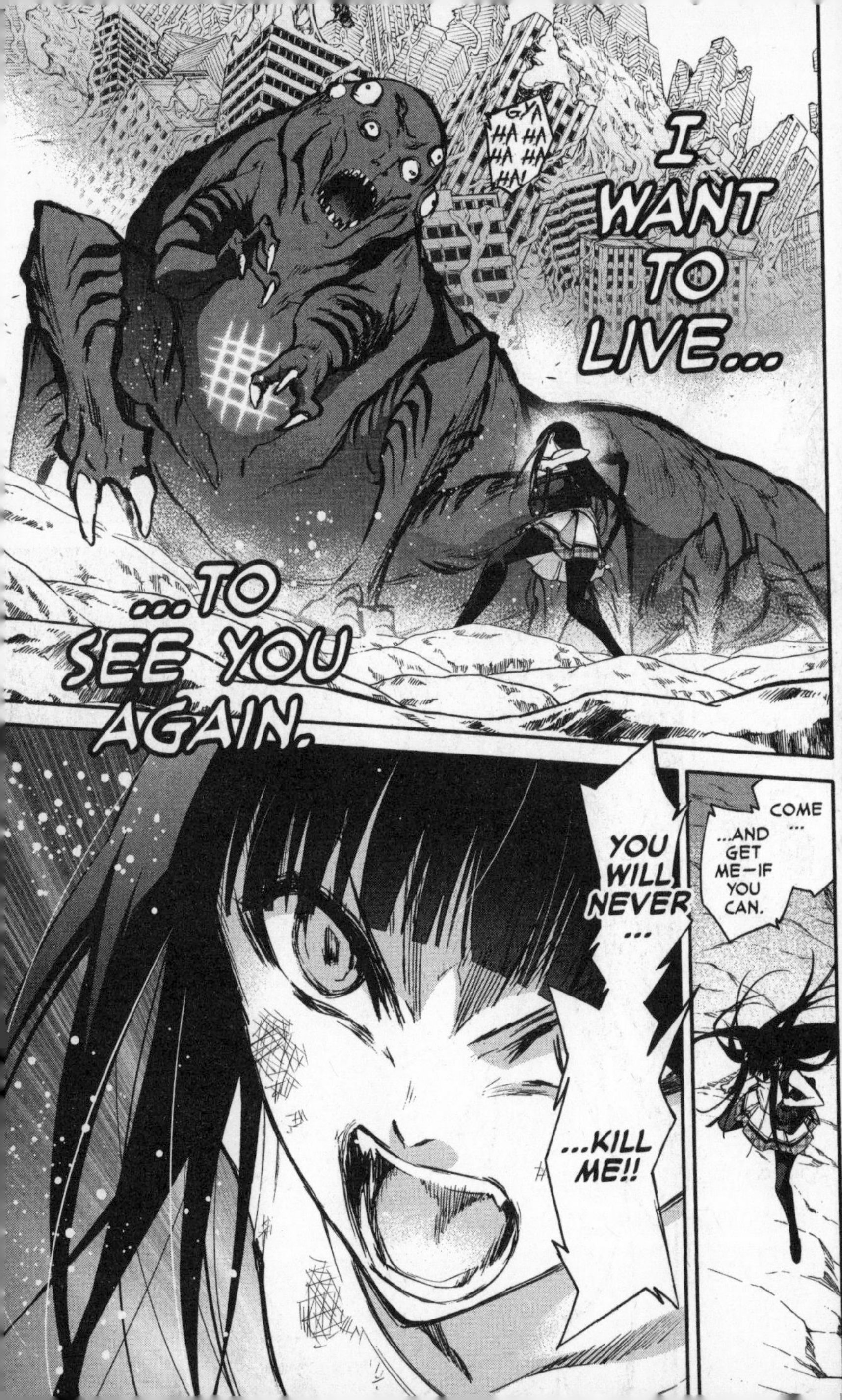
I WANT TO LIVE...
GYA HA HA HA HA HA!
...TO SEE YOU AGAIN.
COME...
...AND GET ME—IF YOU CAN.
YOU WILL NEVER...
...KILL ME!!

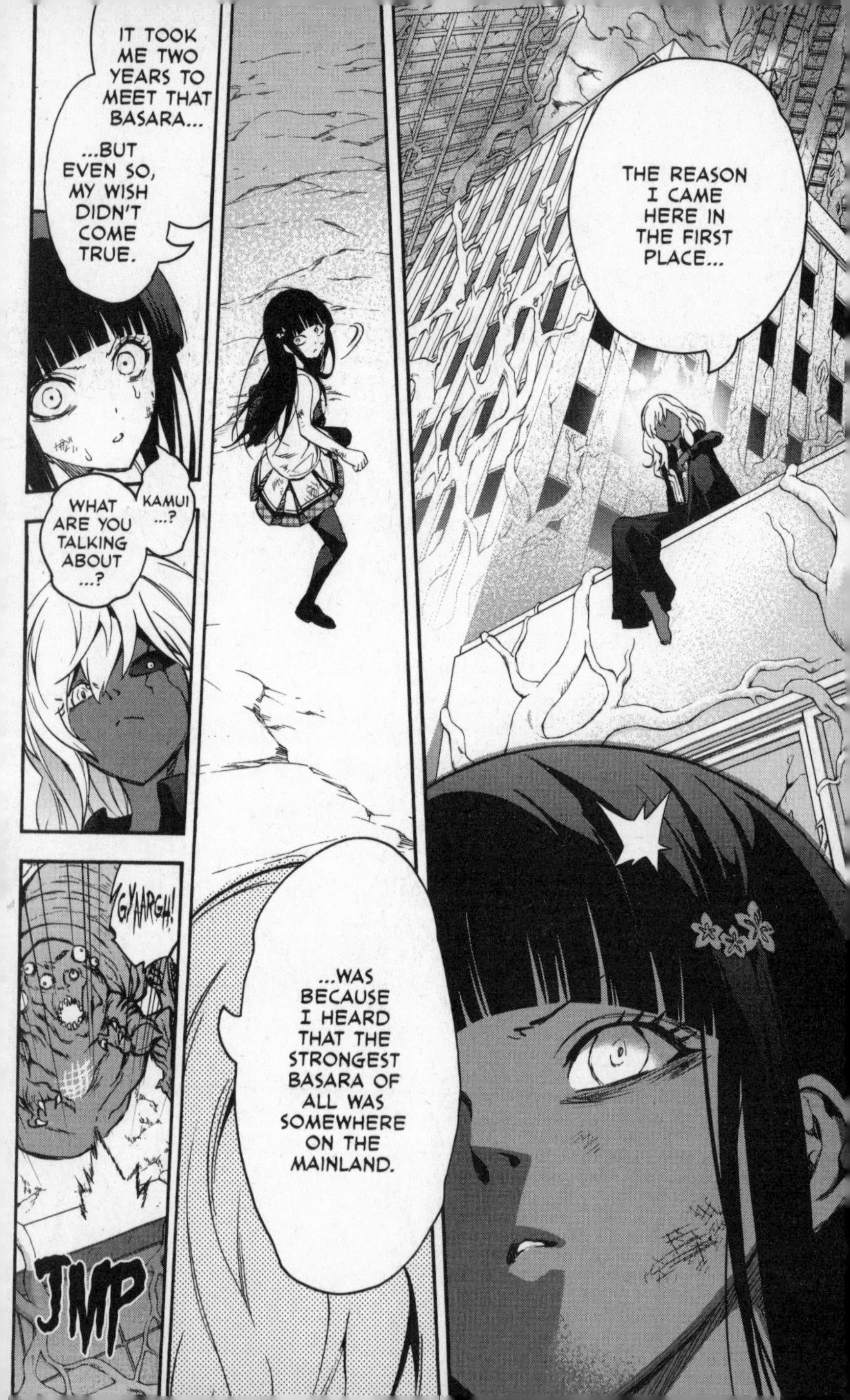
THE REASON I CAME HERE IN THE FIRST PLACE...
...WAS BECAUSE I HEARD THAT THE STRONGEST BASARA OF ALL WAS SOMEWHERE ON THE MAINLAND.
IT TOOK ME TWO YEARS TO MEET THAT BASARA...
...BUT EVEN SO, MY WISH DIDN'T COME TRUE.
KAMUI ...?
WHAT ARE YOU TALKING ABOUT ...?
GYAARGH!
JMP

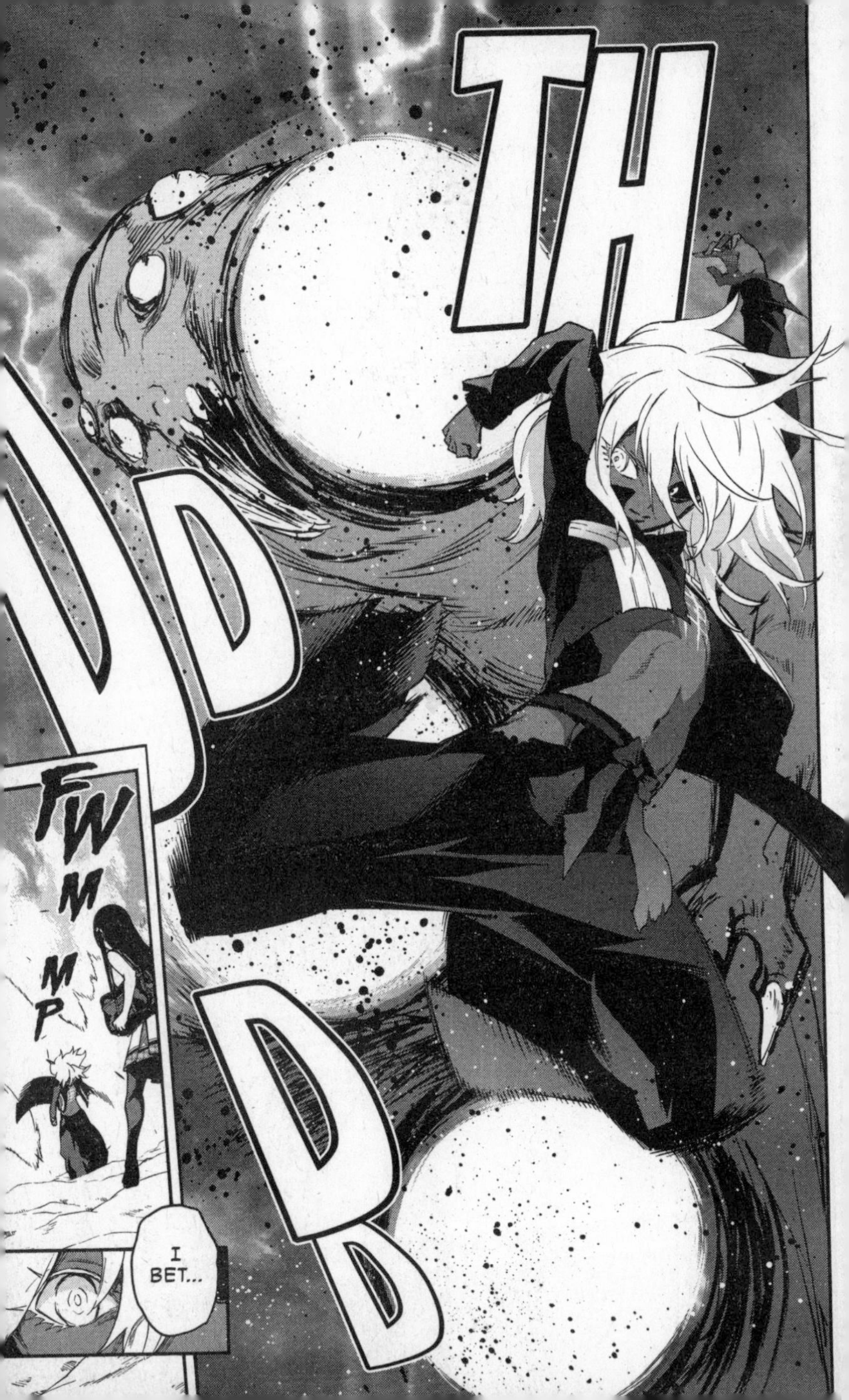
THUDD
FWMMP
I BET...

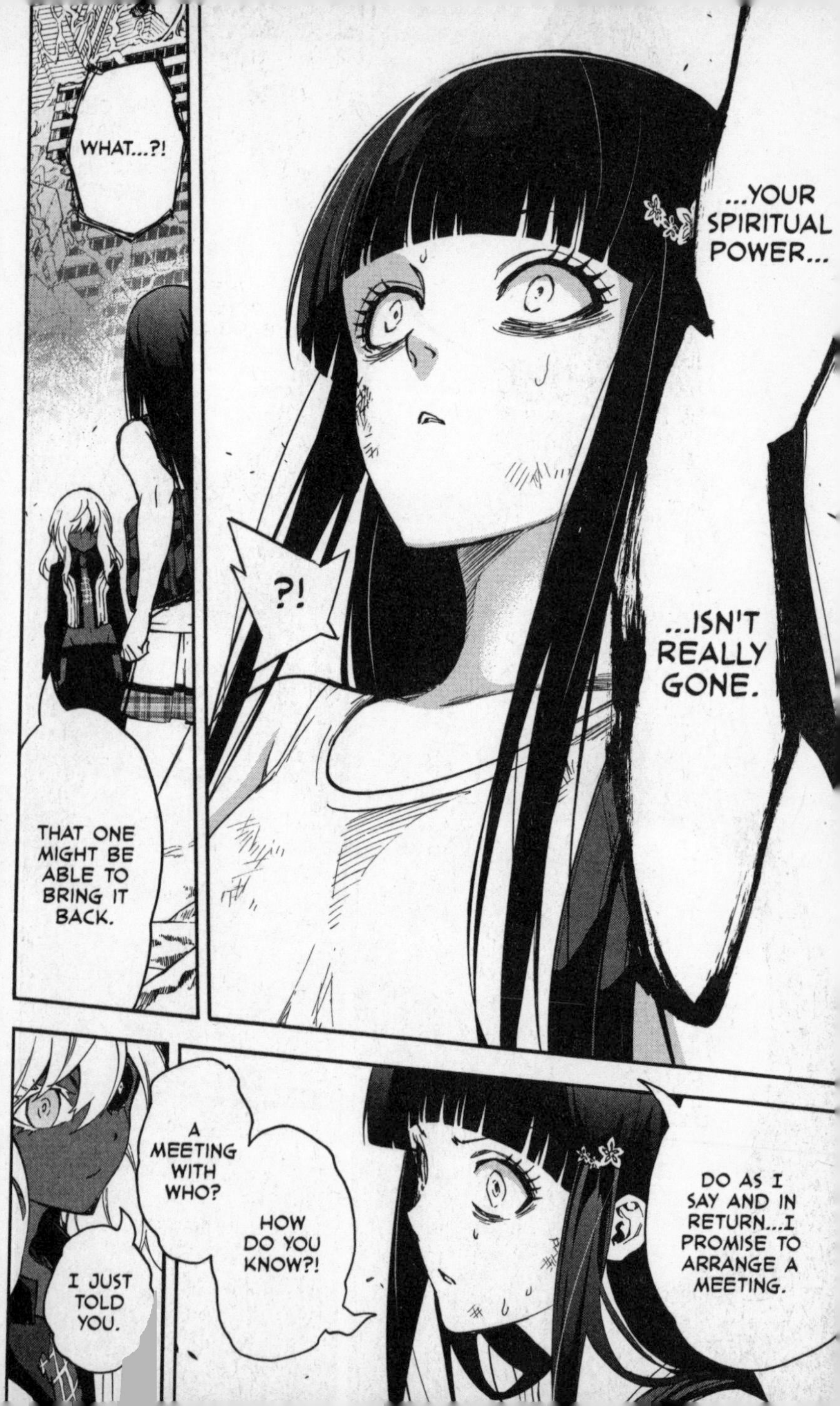
...YOUR SPIRITUAL POWER...
...ISN'T REALLY GONE.
?!
WHAT...?!
THAT ONE MIGHT BE ABLE TO BRING IT BACK.
DO AS I SAY AND IN RETURN...I PROMISE TO ARRANGE A MEETING.
A MEETING WITH WHO?
HOW DO YOU KNOW?!
I JUST TOLD YOU.

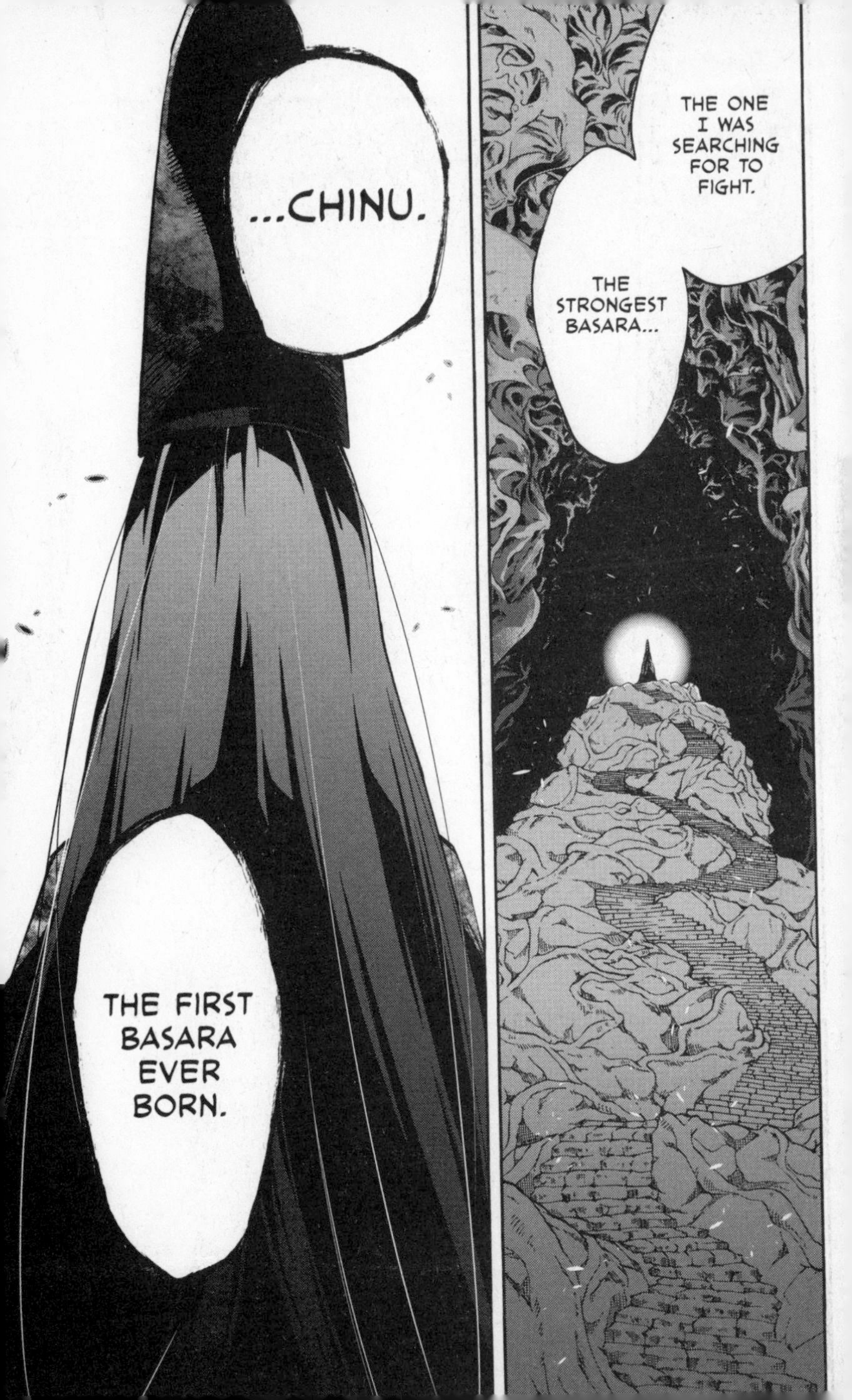
THE ONE I WAS SEARCHING FOR TO FIGHT.
THE STRONGEST BASARA...
...CHINU.
THE FIRST BASARA EVER BORN.

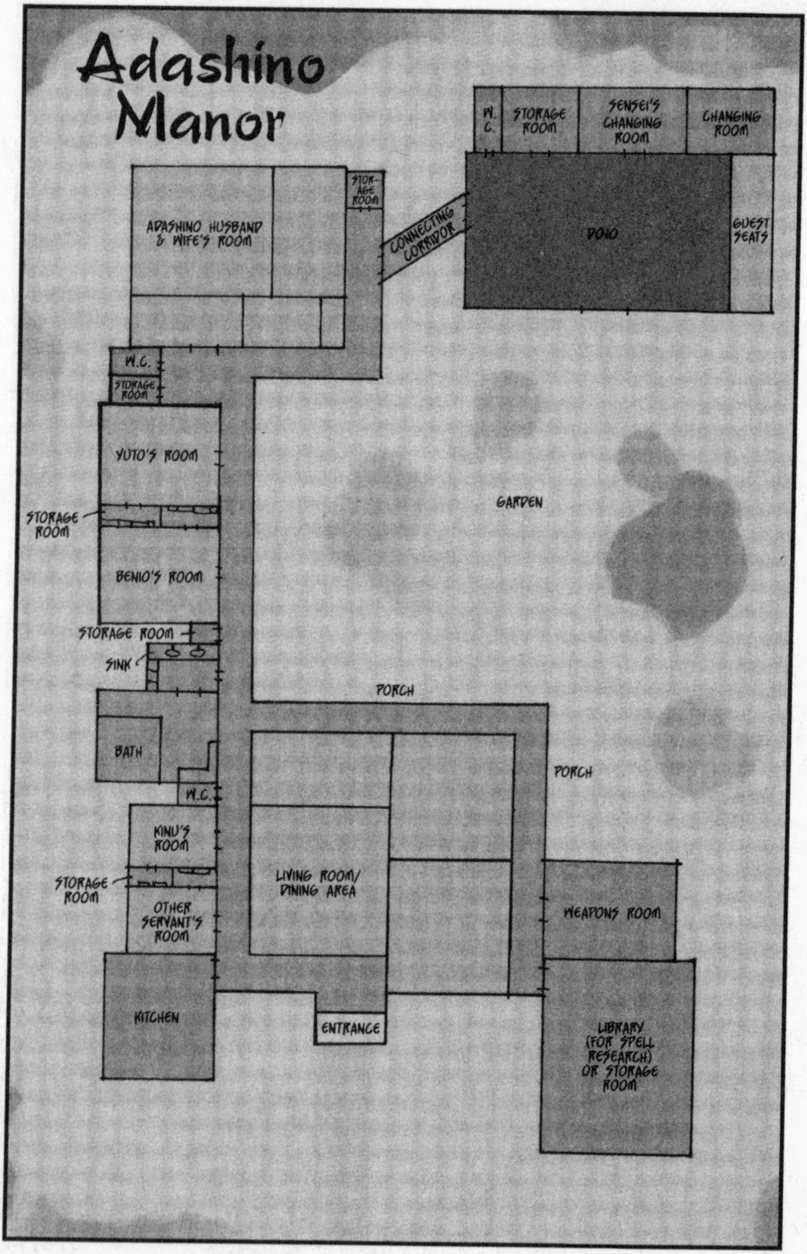
Adashino Manor
W.C.
STORAGE ROOM
SENSEI'S CHANGING ROOM
CHANGING ROOM
STORAGE ROOM
ADASHINO HUSBAND & WIFE'S ROOM
CONNECTING CORRIDOR
DOJO
GUEST SEATS
W.C.
STORAGE ROOM
YUTO'S ROOM
STORAGE ROOM
GARDEN
BENIO'S ROOM
STORAGE ROOM
SINK
PORCH
BATH
PORCH
W.C.
KINU'S ROOM
STORAGE ROOM
LIVING ROOM/ DINING AREA
OTHER SERVANT'S ROOM
WEAPONS ROOM
KITCHEN
ENTRANCE
LIBRARY (FOR SPELL RESEARCH) OR STORAGE ROOM

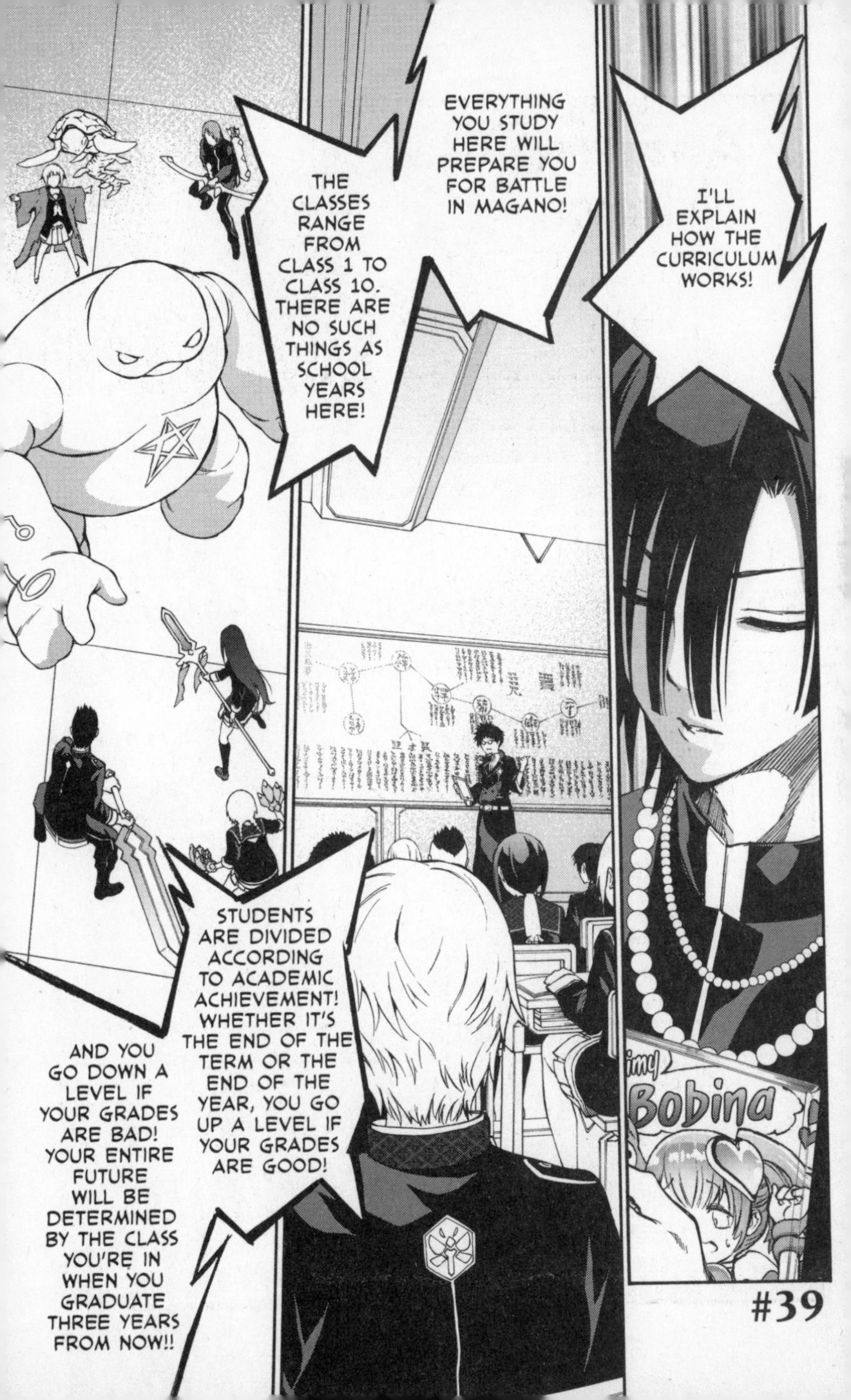
I'LL EXPLAIN HOW THE CURRICULUM WORKS!
EVERYTHING YOU STUDY HERE WILL PREPARE YOU FOR BATTLE IN MAGANO!
THE CLASSES RANGE FROM CLASS 1 TO CLASS 10. THERE ARE NO SUCH THINGS AS SCHOOL YEARS HERE!
Bobina
STUDENTS ARE DIVIDED ACCORDING TO ACADEMIC ACHIEVEMENT! WHETHER IT'S THE END OF THE TERM OR THE END OF THE YEAR, YOU GO UP A LEVEL IF YOUR GRADES ARE GOOD!
AND YOU GO DOWN A LEVEL IF YOUR GRADES ARE BAD! YOUR ENTIRE FUTURE WILL BE DETERMINED BY THE CLASS YOU'RE IN WHEN YOU GRADUATE THREE YEARS FROM NOW!!

#39

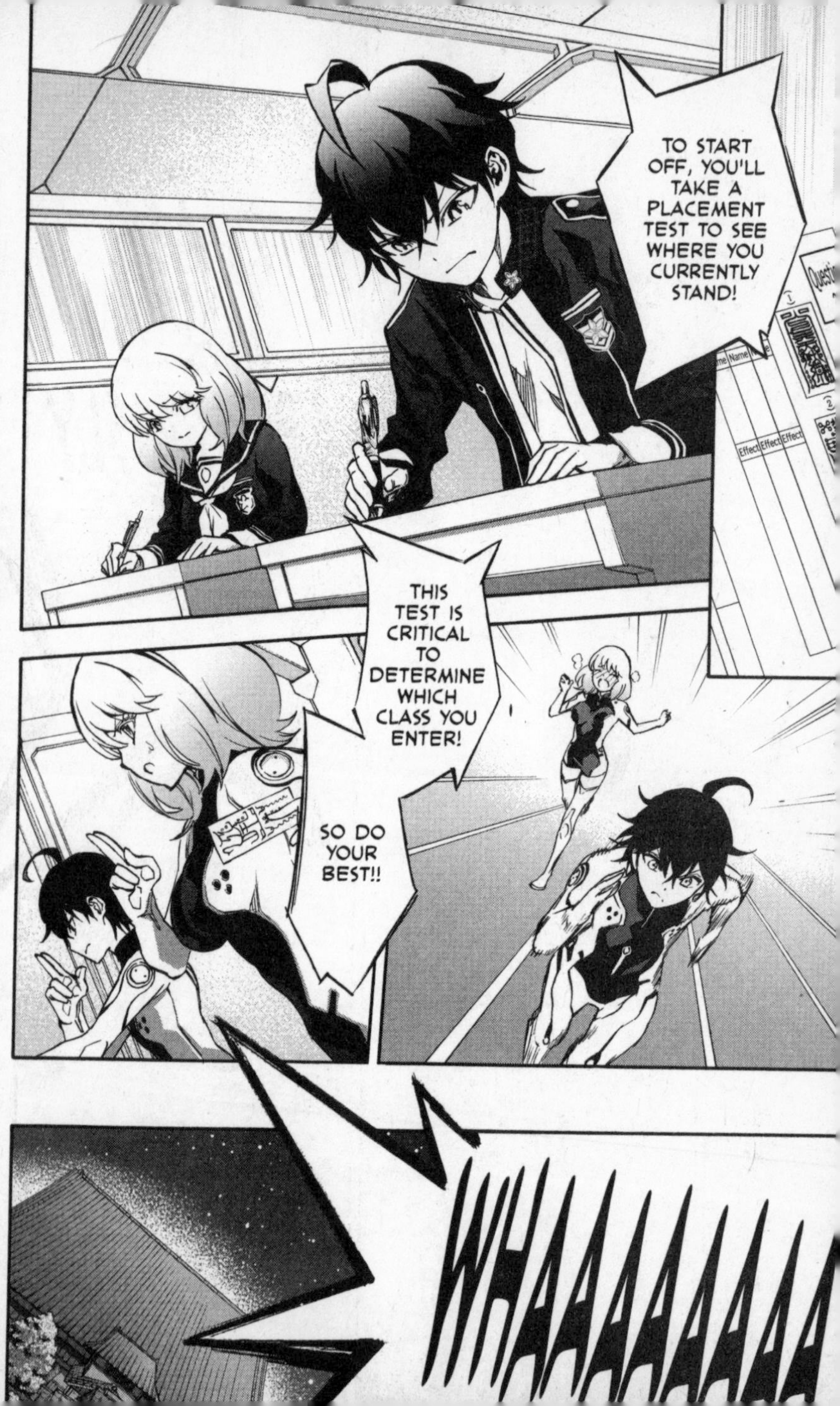
TO START OFF, YOU'LL TAKE A PLACEMENT TEST TO SEE WHERE YOU CURRENTLY STAND!
THIS TEST IS CRITICAL TO DETERMINE WHICH CLASS YOU ENTER!
SO DO YOUR BEST!!
WHAAAAAAAA

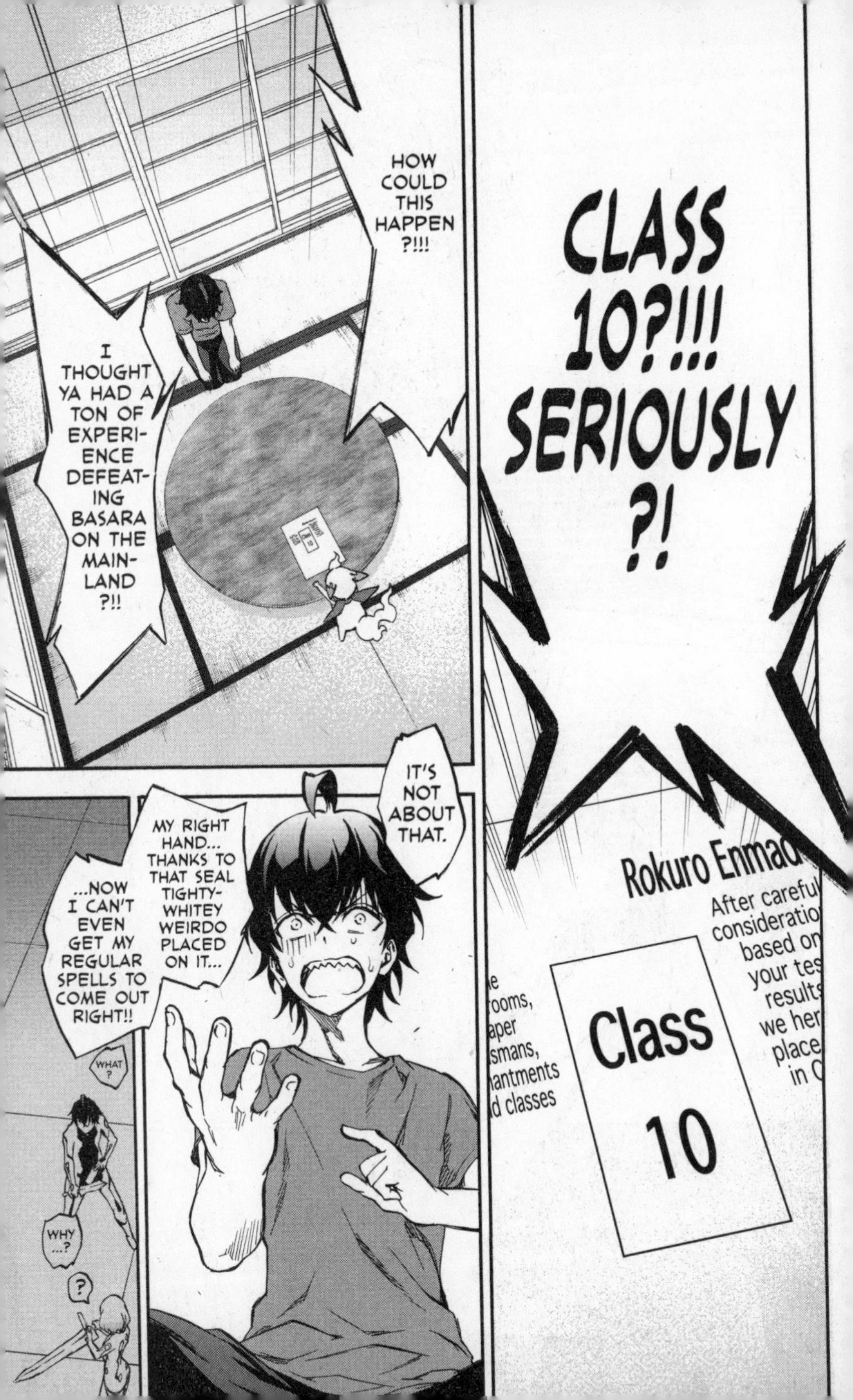
CLASS 10?!!! SERIOUSLY ?!
Rokuro Enmad
After careful consideratio based on your tes results we her place in C
Class 10
HOW COULD THIS HAPPEN ?!!!
I THOUGHT YA HAD A TON OF EXPERI-ENCE DEFEAT-ING BASARA ON THE MAIN-LAND ?!!
IT'S NOT ABOUT THAT.
MY RIGHT HAND... THANKS TO THAT SEAL TIGHTY-WHITEY WEIRDO PLACED ON IT...
...NOW I CAN'T EVEN GET MY REGULAR SPELLS TO COME OUT RIGHT!!
WHAT ?
WHY ...?
?

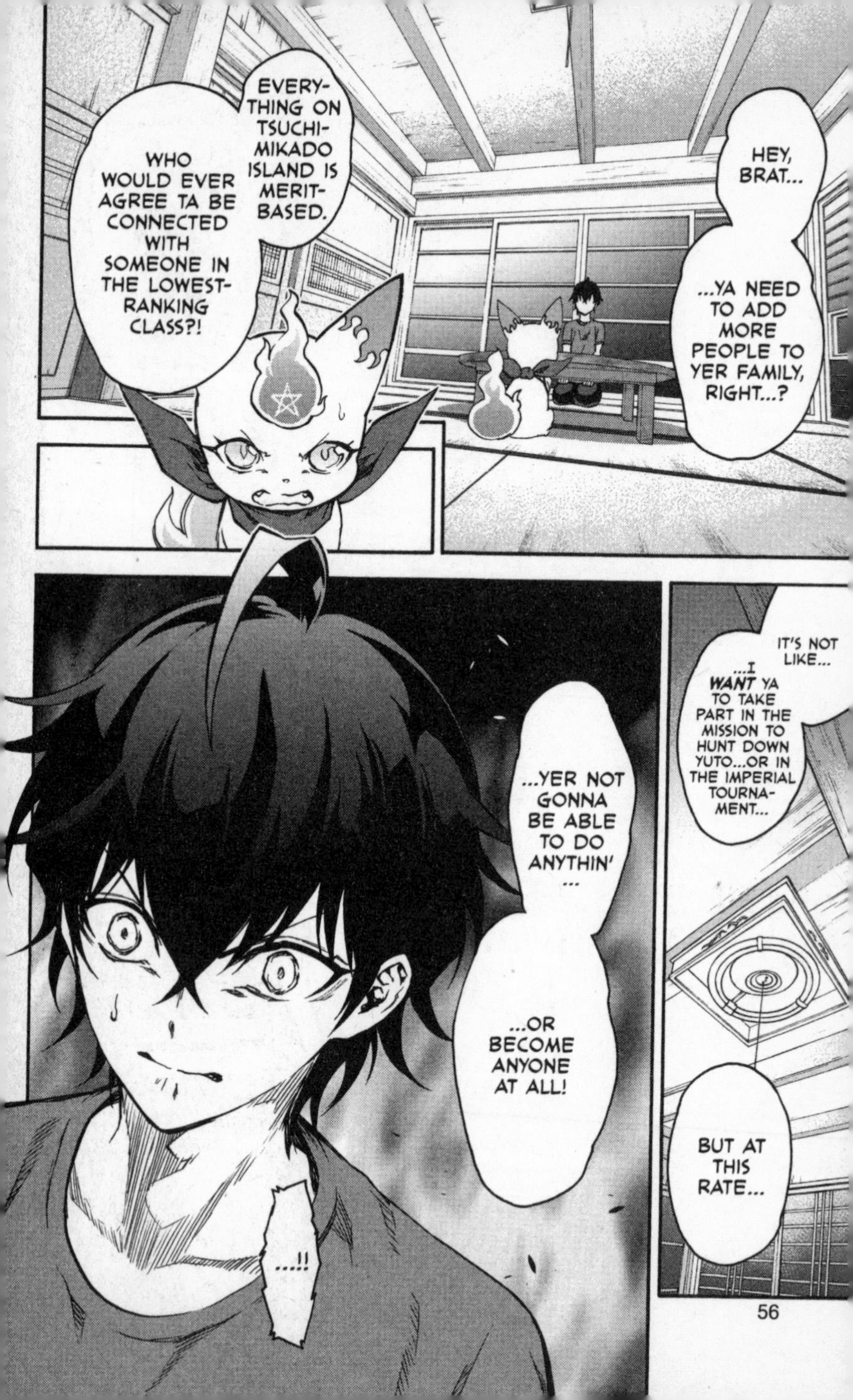
HEY, BRAT...
...YA NEED TO ADD MORE PEOPLE TO YER FAMILY, RIGHT...?
EVERY-THING ON TSUCHI-MIKADO ISLAND IS MERIT-BASED.
WHO WOULD EVER AGREE TA BE CONNECTED WITH SOMEONE IN THE LOWEST-RANKING CLASS?!
IT'S NOT LIKE...
...I *WANT* YA TO TAKE PART IN THE MISSION TO HUNT DOWN YUTO...OR IN THE IMPERIAL TOURNA-MENT...
BUT AT THIS RATE...
...YER NOT GONNA BE ABLE TO DO ANYTHIN' ...
...OR BECOME ANYONE AT ALL!
...!!

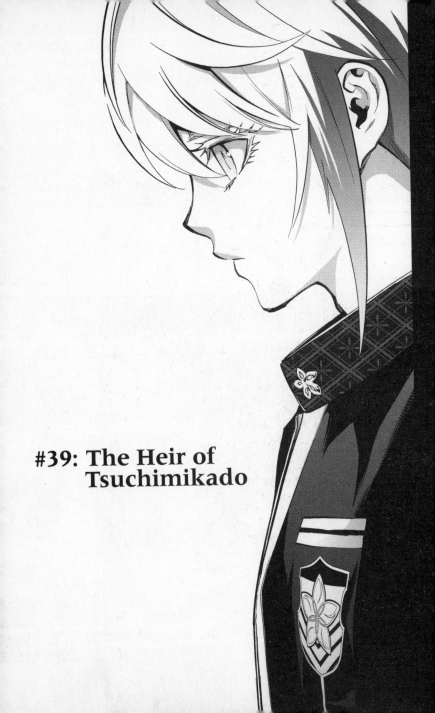

# #39: The Heir of Tsuchimikado

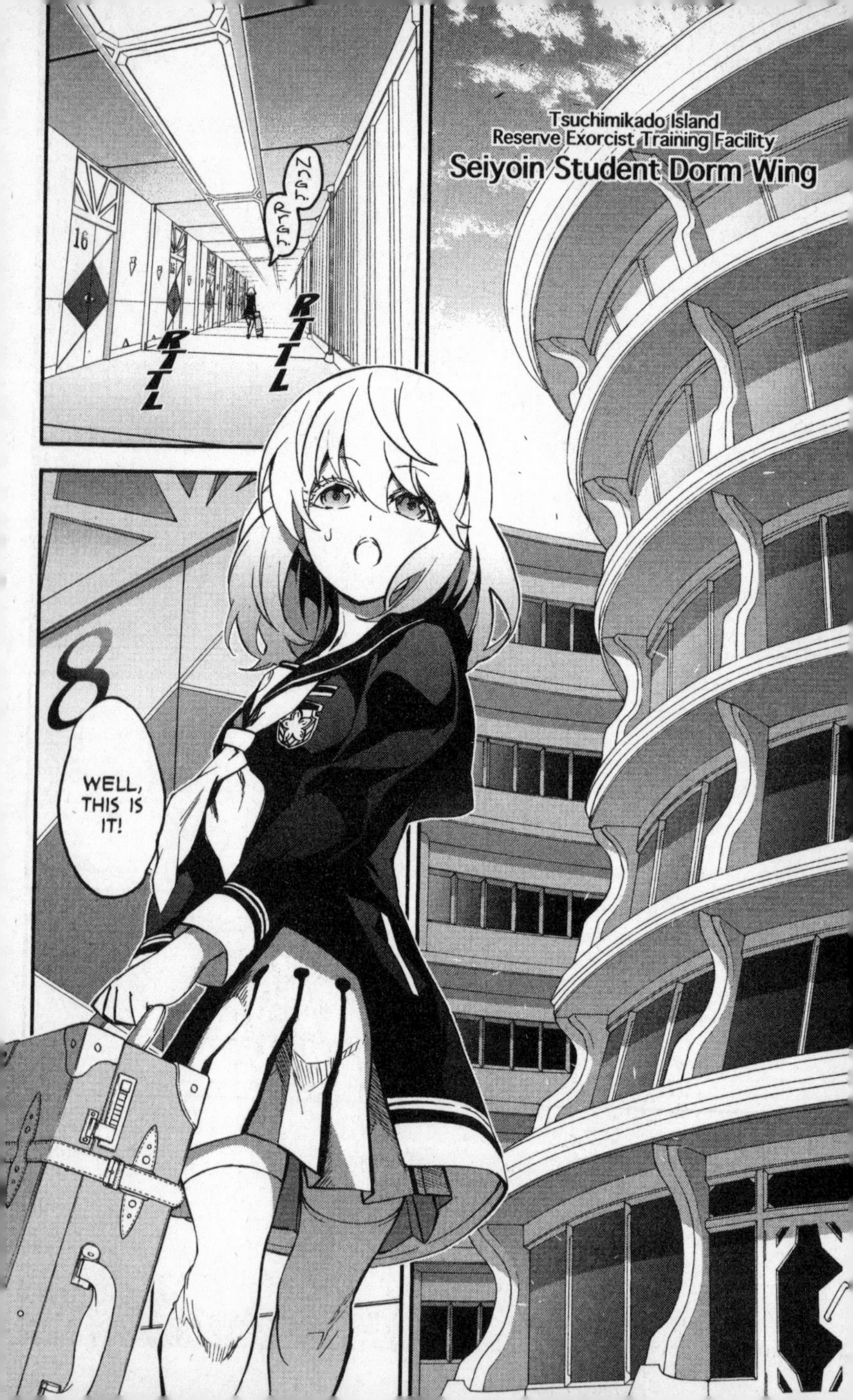
Tsuchimikado Island
Reserve Exorcist Training Facility
Seiyoin Student Dorm Wing
Nngh. Rrgh.
RTTL
RTTL
WELL, THIS IS IT!

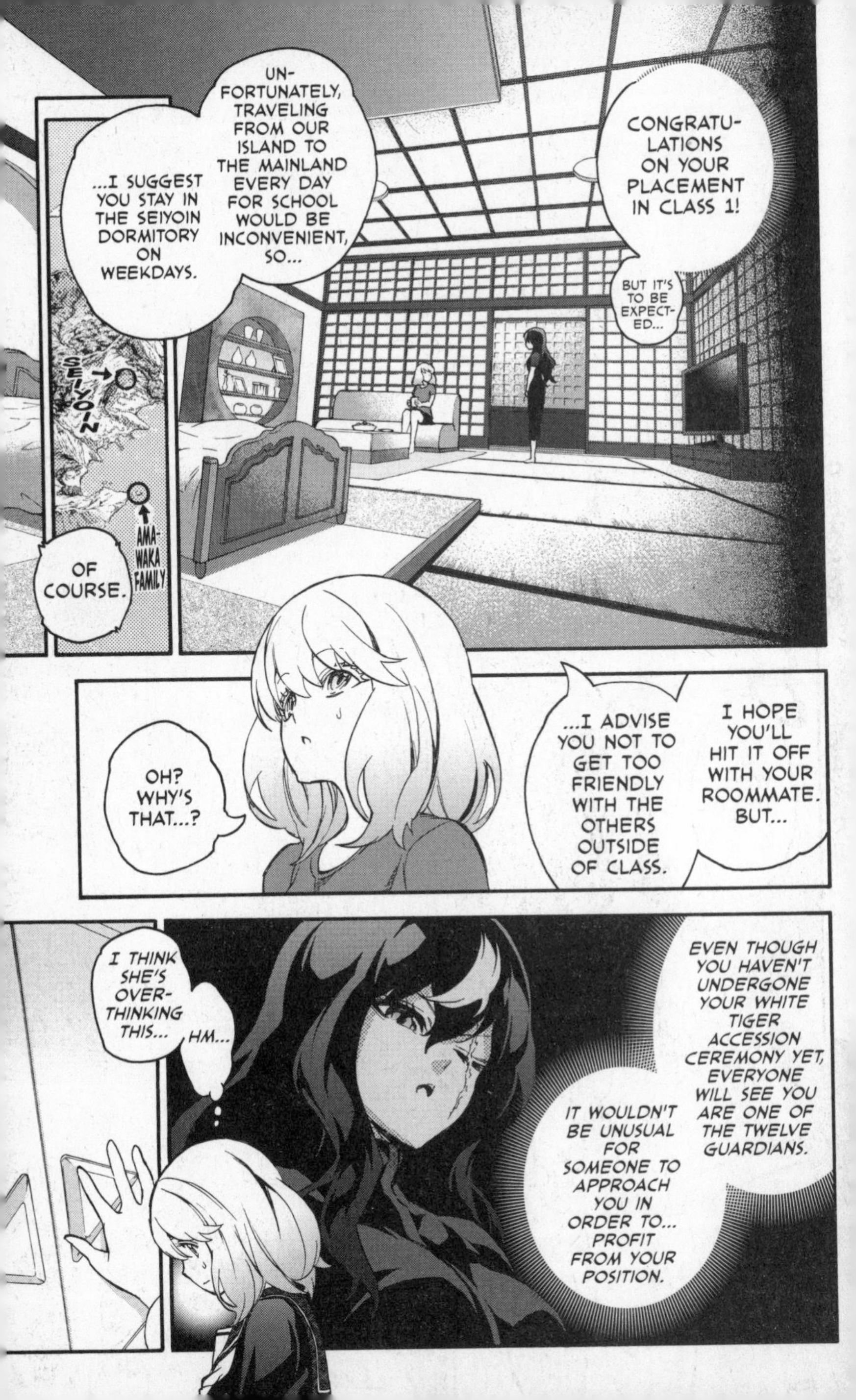
CONGRATULATIONS ON YOUR PLACEMENT IN CLASS 1!
BUT IT'S TO BE EXPECTED...
UNFORTUNATELY, TRAVELING FROM OUR ISLAND TO THE MAINLAND EVERY DAY FOR SCHOOL WOULD BE INCONVENIENT, SO...
...I SUGGEST YOU STAY IN THE SEIYOIN DORMITORY ON WEEKDAYS.
SEIYOIN
AMAWAKA FAMILY
OF COURSE.
I HOPE YOU'LL HIT IT OFF WITH YOUR ROOMMATE. BUT...
...I ADVISE YOU NOT TO GET TOO FRIENDLY WITH THE OTHERS OUTSIDE OF CLASS.
OH? WHY'S THAT...?
EVEN THOUGH YOU HAVEN'T UNDERGONE YOUR WHITE TIGER ACCESSION CEREMONY YET, EVERYONE WILL SEE YOU ARE ONE OF THE TWELVE GUARDIANS.
IT WOULDN'T BE UNUSUAL FOR SOMEONE TO APPROACH YOU IN ORDER TO... PROFIT FROM YOUR POSITION.
HM...
I THINK SHE'S OVERTHINKING THIS...

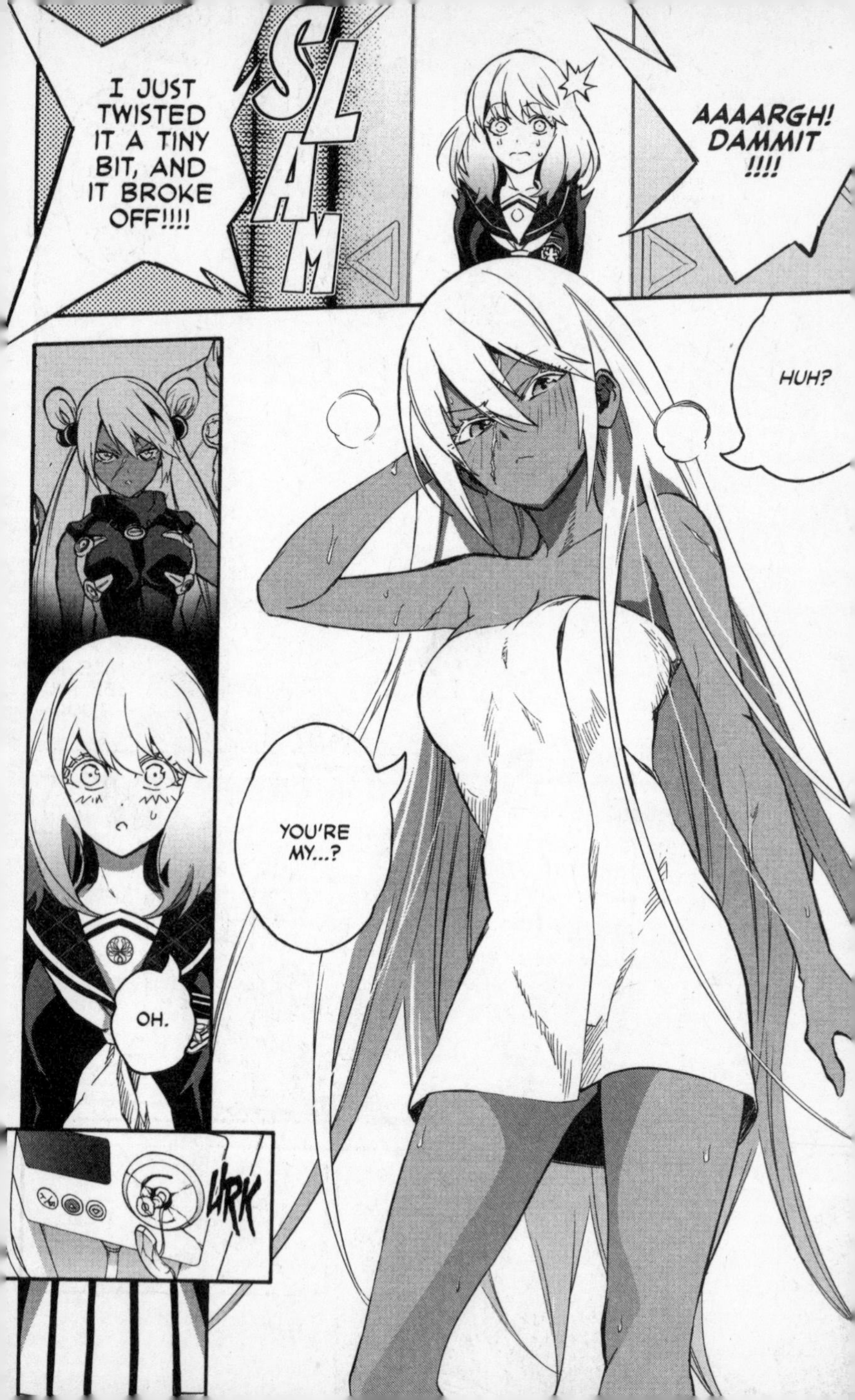
AAAARGH! DAMMIT!!!!
SLAM
I JUST TWISTED IT A TINY BIT, AND IT BROKE OFF!!!!
HUH?
YOU'RE MY...?
OH.
URK

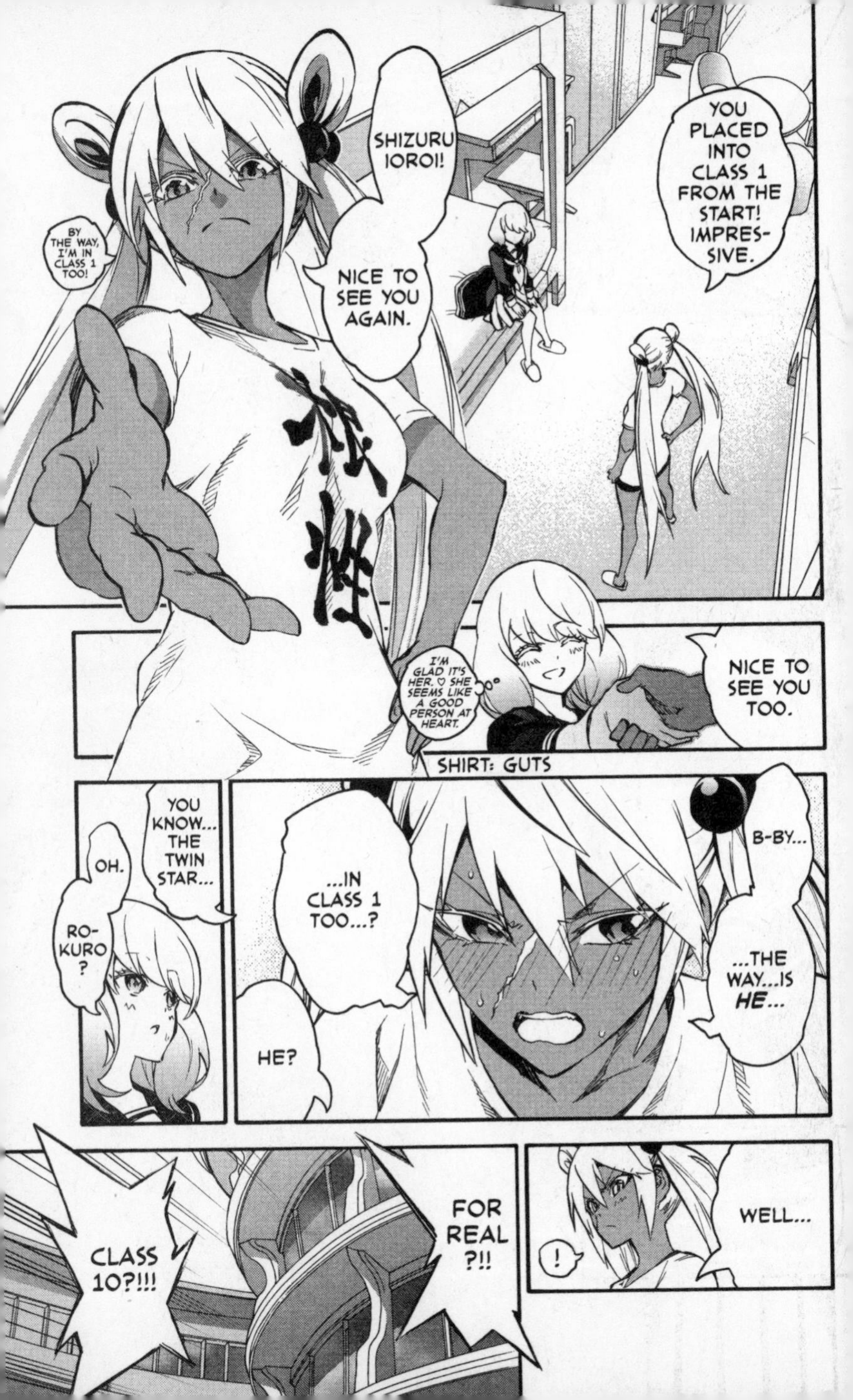
YOU PLACED INTO CLASS 1 FROM THE START! IMPRESSIVE.
SHIZURU IOROI!
NICE TO SEE YOU AGAIN.
BY THE WAY, I'M IN CLASS 1 TOO!
NICE TO SEE YOU TOO.
I'M GLAD IT'S HER. ♡ SHE SEEMS LIKE A GOOD PERSON AT HEART.
SHIRT: GUTS
B-BY...
...THE WAY...IS *HE*...
...IN CLASS 1 TOO...?
HE?
YOU KNOW... THE TWIN STAR...
OH.
RO-KURO?
WELL...
!
FOR REAL?!!
CLASS 10?!!!

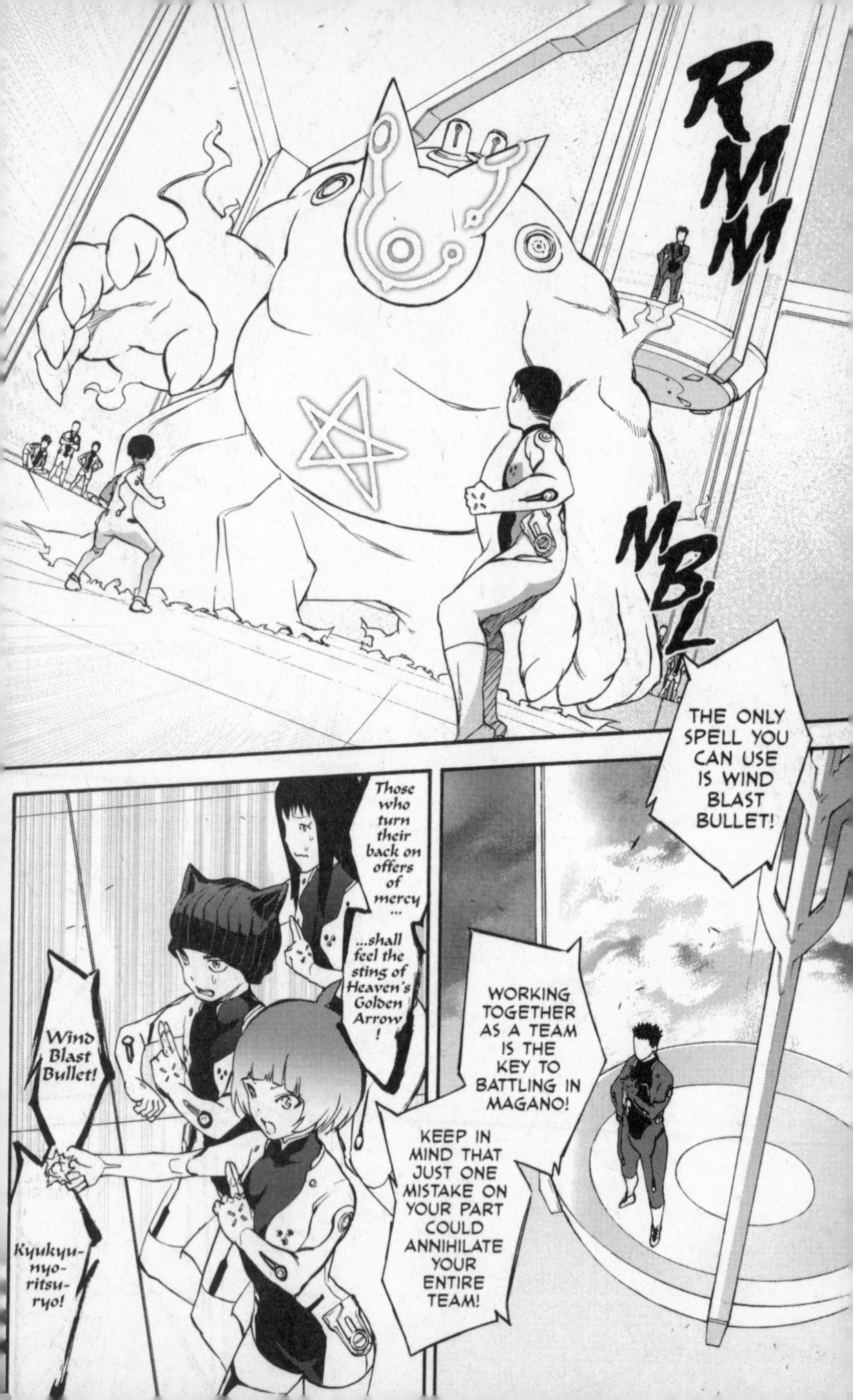
RMMMBL
THE ONLY SPELL YOU CAN USE IS WIND BLAST BULLET!
WORKING TOGETHER AS A TEAM IS THE KEY TO BATTLING IN MAGANO!
KEEP IN MIND THAT JUST ONE MISTAKE ON YOUR PART COULD ANNIHILATE YOUR ENTIRE TEAM!
Those who turn their back on offers of mercy...
...shall feel the sting of Heaven's Golden Arrow!
Wind Blast Bullet!
Kyukyu-nyo-ritsu-ryo!

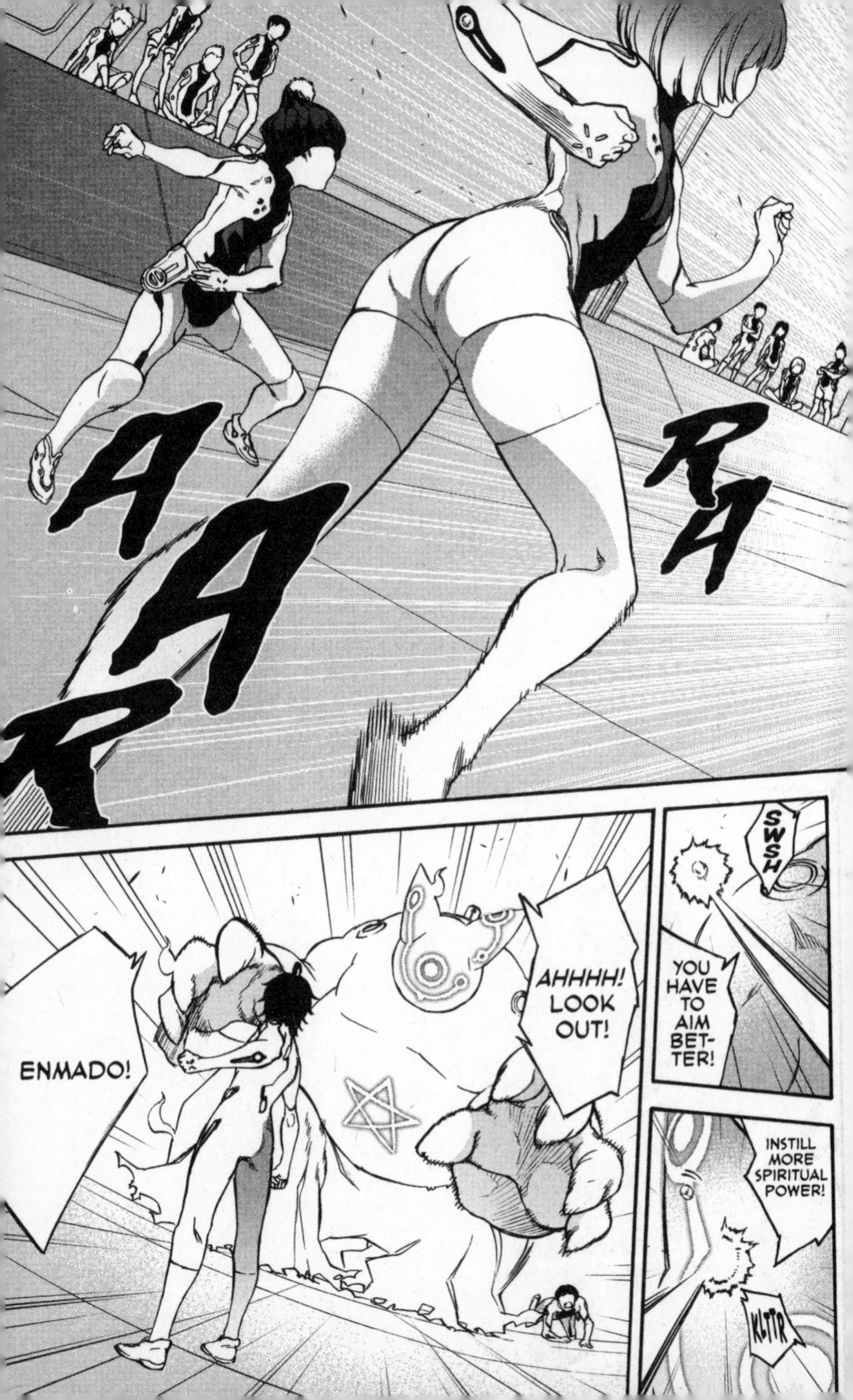
RAAAR
SWSH
YOU HAVE TO AIM BET-TER!
INSTILL MORE SPIRITUAL POWER!
KLTTR
AHHHH! LOOK OUT!
ENMADO!

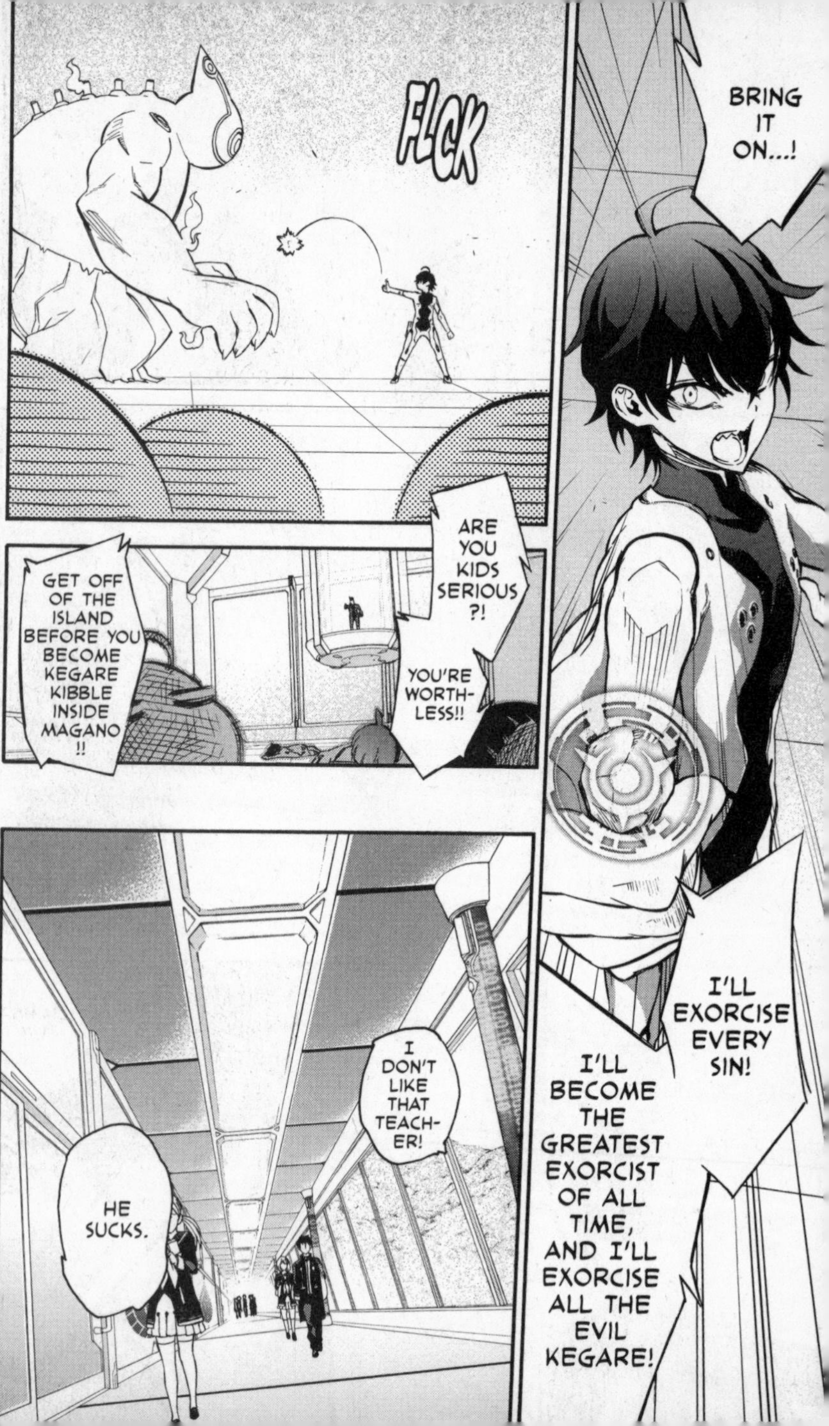
BRING IT ON...!
I'LL EXORCISE EVERY SIN!
I'LL BECOME THE GREATEST EXORCIST OF ALL TIME, AND I'LL EXORCISE ALL THE EVIL KEGARE!
FLCK
ARE YOU KIDS SERIOUS?!
YOU'RE WORTHLESS!!
GET OFF OF THE ISLAND BEFORE YOU BECOME KEGARE KIBBLE INSIDE MAGANO!!
I DON'T LIKE THAT TEACHER!
HE SUCKS.

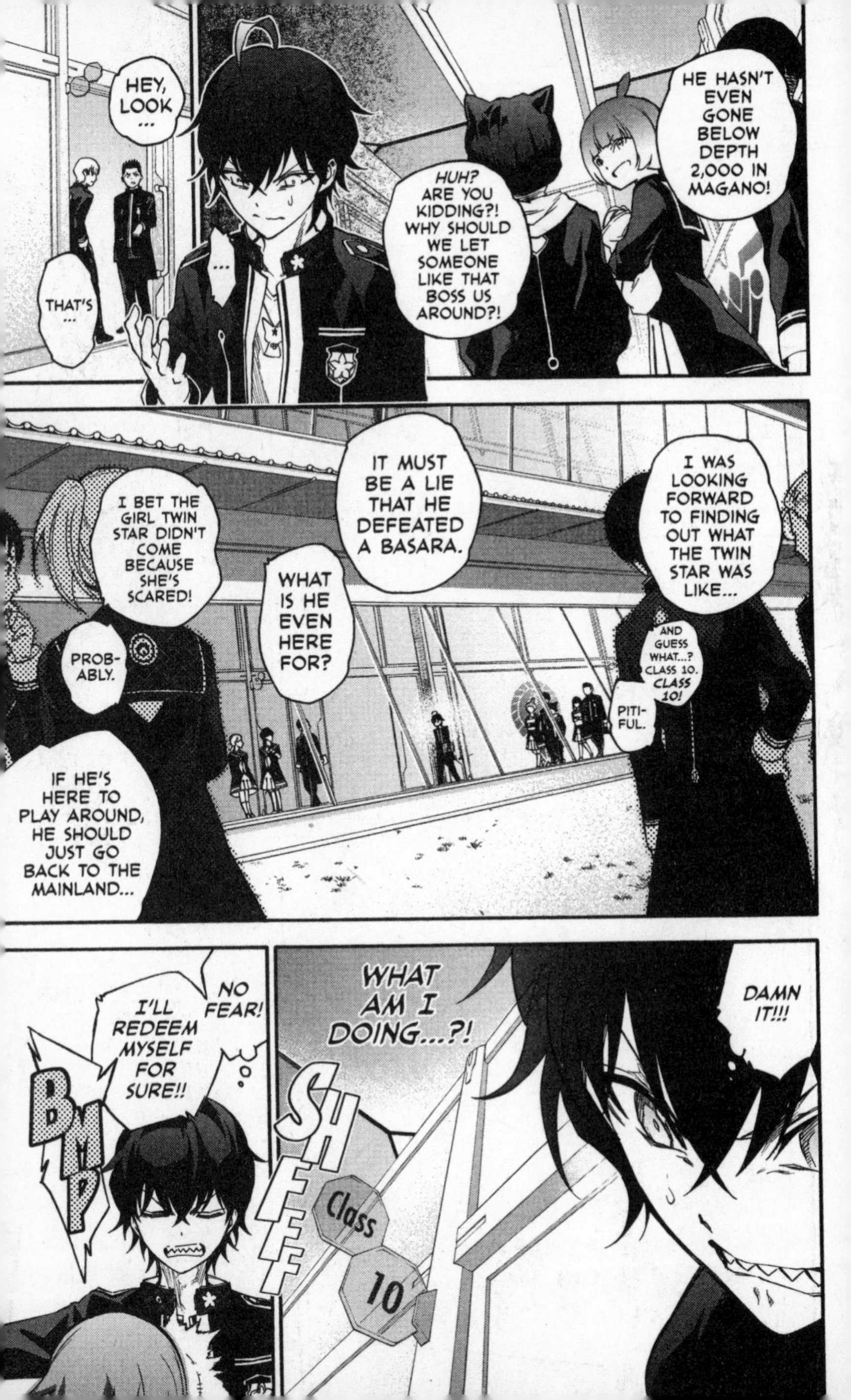
HE HASN'T EVEN GONE BELOW DEPTH 2,000 IN MAGANO!
HUH? ARE YOU KIDDING?! WHY SHOULD WE LET SOMEONE LIKE THAT BOSS US AROUND?!
HEY, LOOK...
...
THAT'S...
I WAS LOOKING FORWARD TO FINDING OUT WHAT THE TWIN STAR WAS LIKE...
AND GUESS WHAT...? CLASS 10. CLASS 10!
PITIFUL.
IT MUST BE A LIE THAT HE DEFEATED A BASARA.
WHAT IS HE EVEN HERE FOR?
I BET THE GIRL TWIN STAR DIDN'T COME BECAUSE SHE'S SCARED!
PROB-ABLY.
IF HE'S HERE TO PLAY AROUND, HE SHOULD JUST GO BACK TO THE MAINLAND...
DAMN IT!!!
WHAT AM I DOING...?!
SHFFFF
Class
10
NO FEAR!
I'LL REDEEM MYSELF FOR SURE!!
BMP

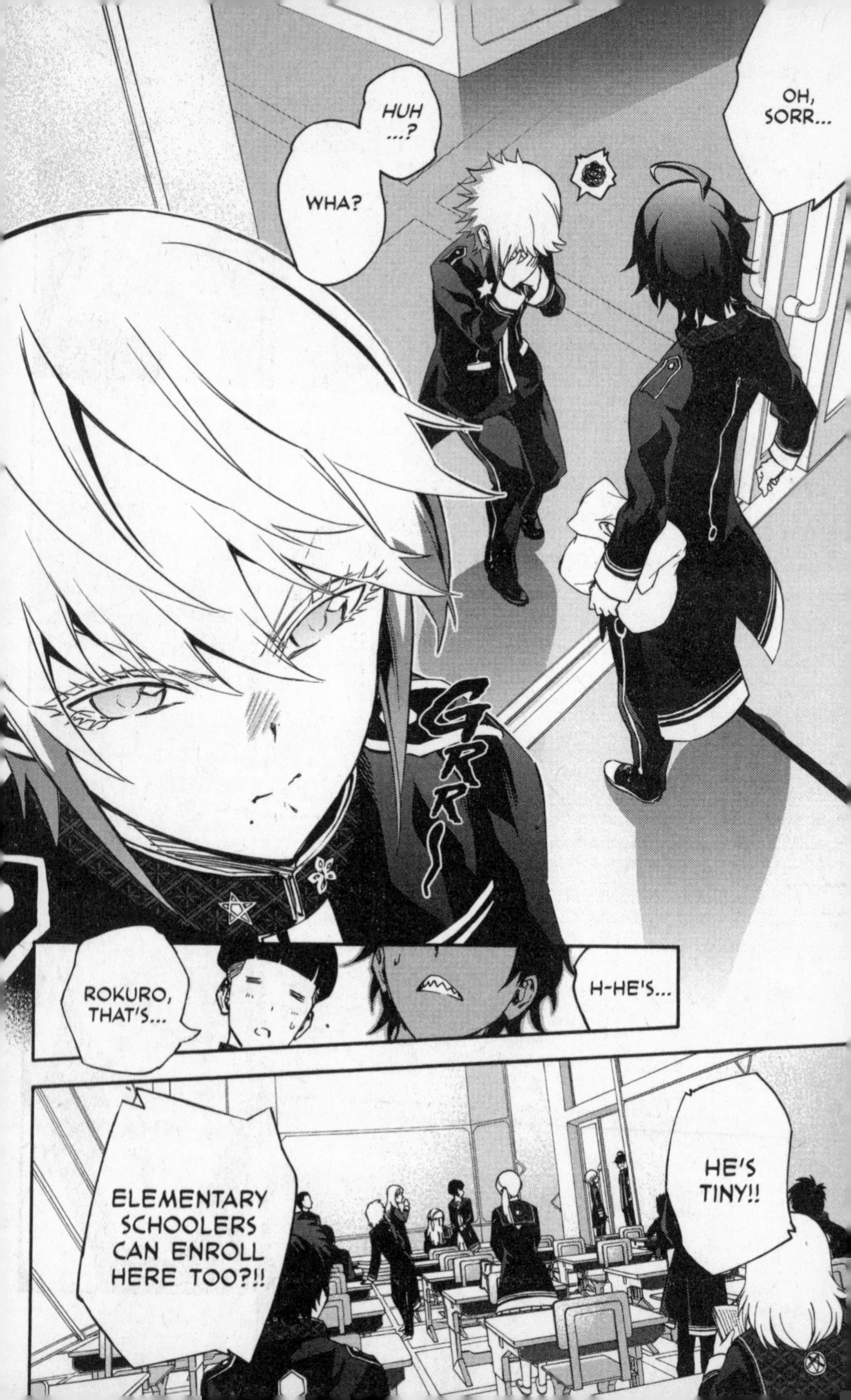
OH, SORR...
HUH ...?
WHA?
GRR
H-HE'S...
ROKURO, THAT'S...
HE'S TINY!!
ELEMENTARY SCHOOLERS CAN ENROLL HERE TOO?!!

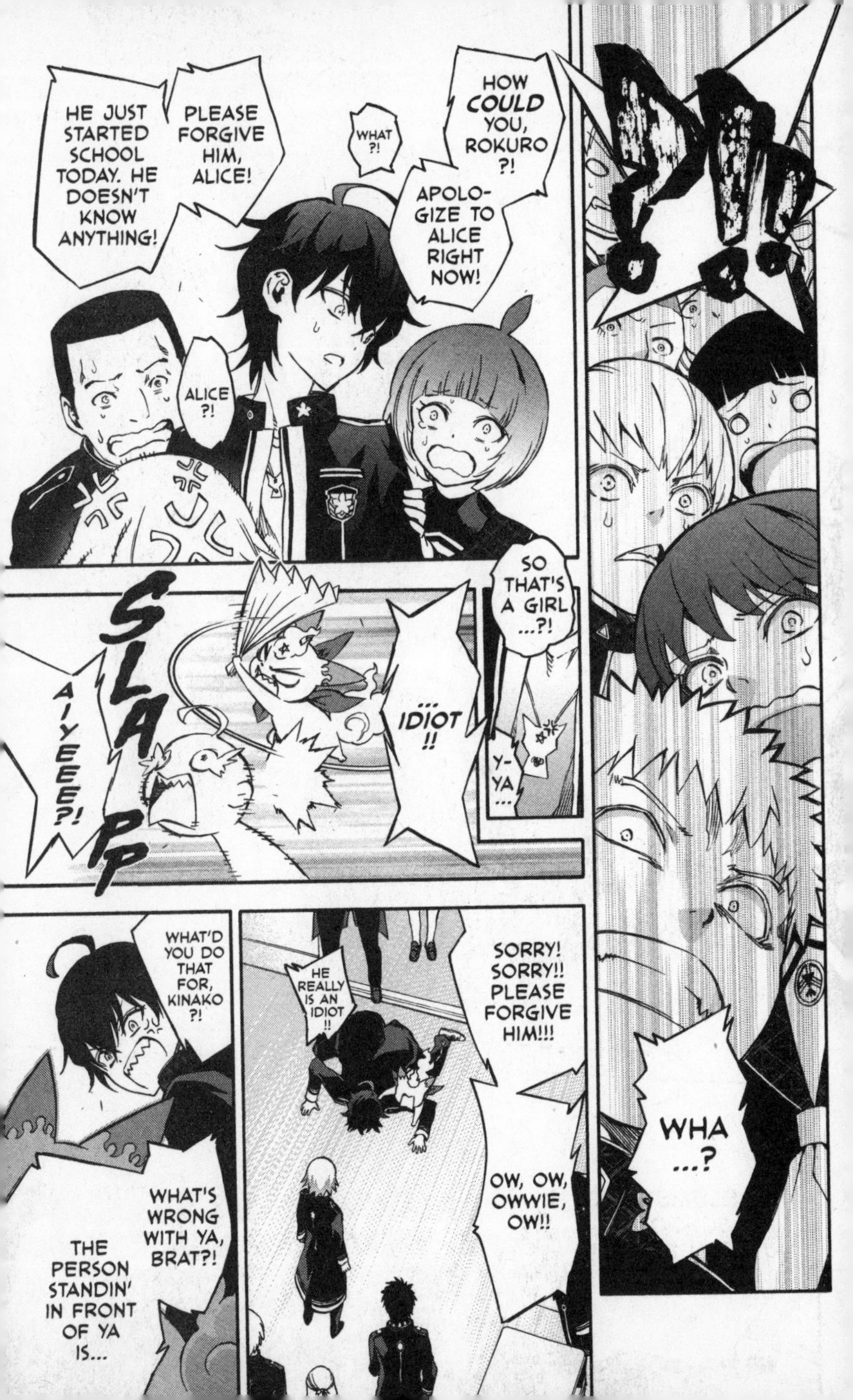
?!
WHA ...?
HOW COULD YOU, ROKURO ?!
WHAT ?!
APOLOGIZE TO ALICE RIGHT NOW!
PLEASE FORGIVE HIM, ALICE!
HE JUST STARTED SCHOOL TODAY. HE DOESN'T KNOW ANYTHING!
ALICE ?!
SO THAT'S A GIRL ...?!
Y-YA ...
...IDIOT !!
SLAPP
AIYEEE?!
SORRY! SORRY!! PLEASE FORGIVE HIM!!!
HE REALLY IS AN IDIOT !!
OW, OW, OWWIE, OW!!
WHAT'D YOU DO THAT FOR, KINAKO ?!
WHAT'S WRONG WITH YA, BRAT?!
THE PERSON STANDIN' IN FRONT OF YA IS...

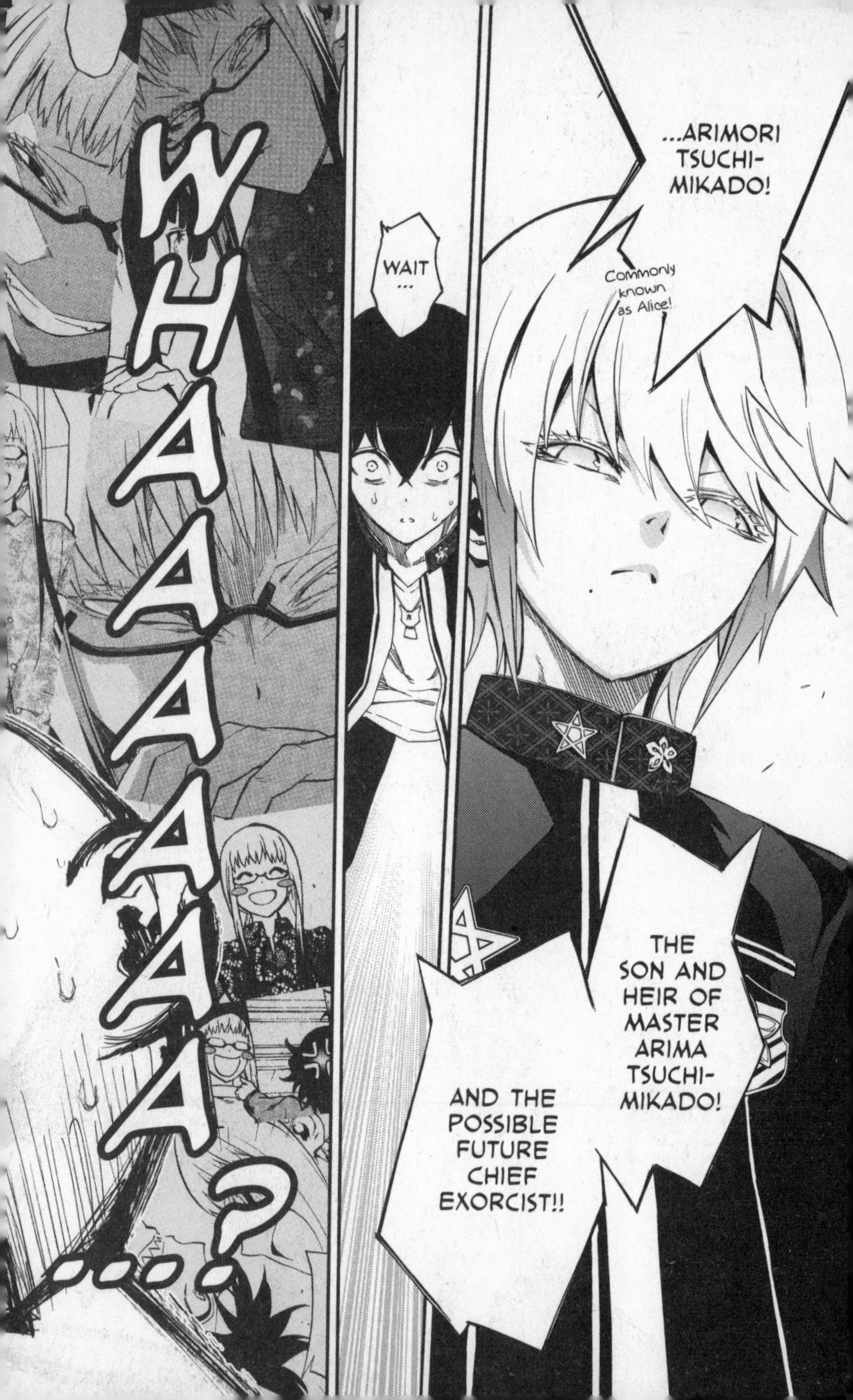
...ARIMORI TSUCHI-MIKADO!
Commonly known as Alice!
WAIT ...
THE SON AND HEIR OF MASTER ARIMA TSUCHI-MIKADO!
AND THE POSSIBLE FUTURE CHIEF EXORCIST!!
WHAAAAAA...?

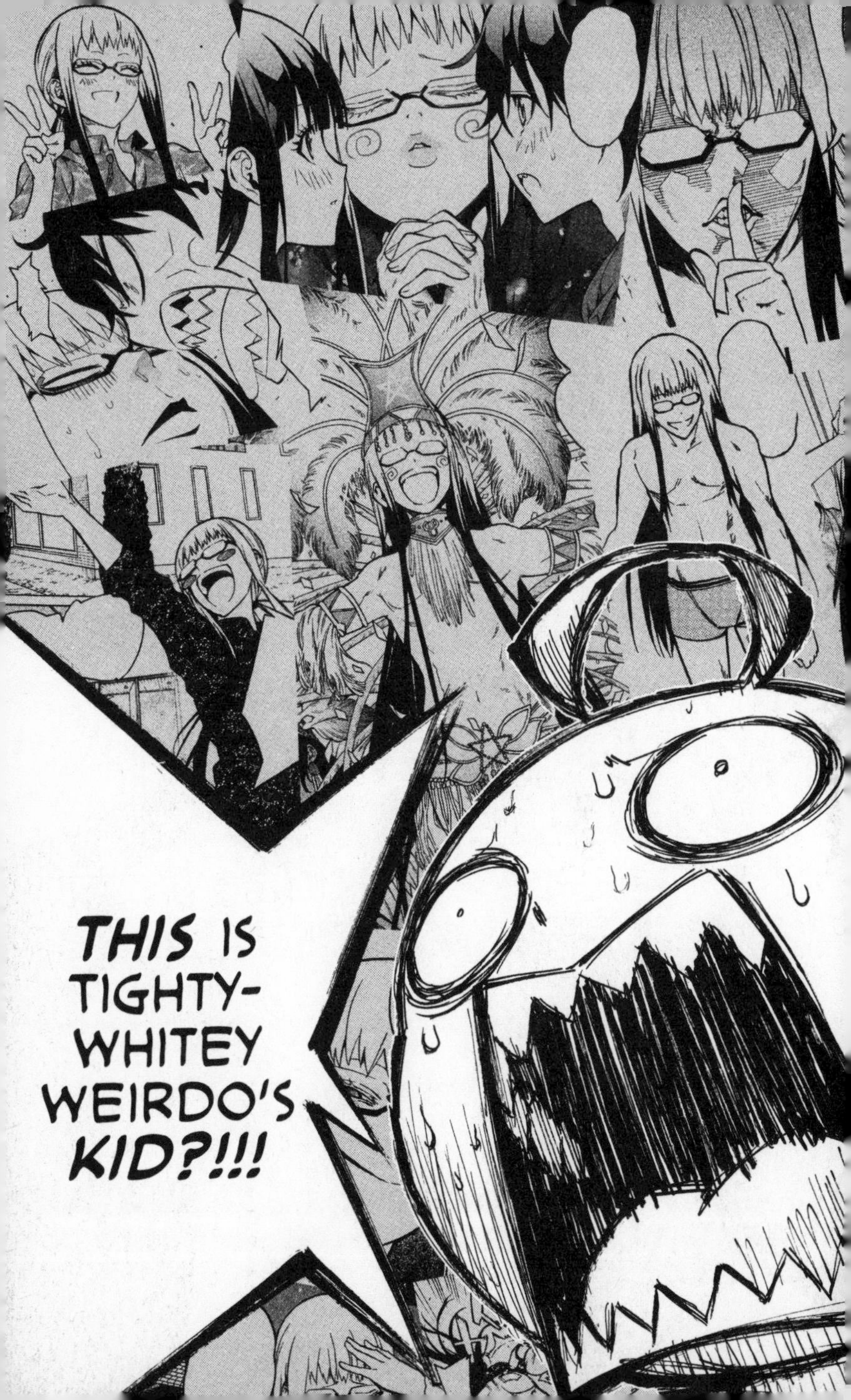
THIS IS TIGHTY-WHITEY WEIRDO'S KID?!!!

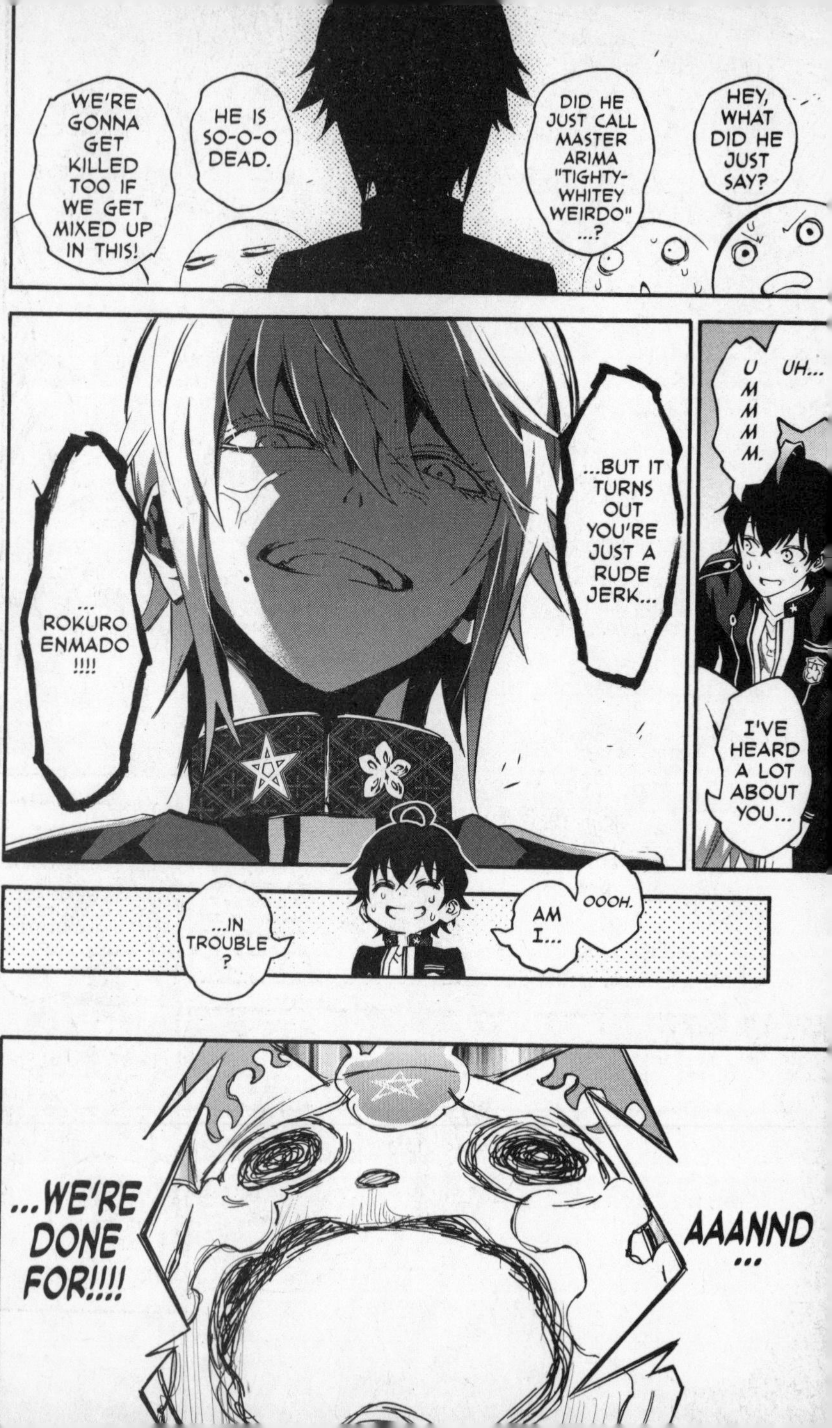
HEY, WHAT DID HE JUST SAY?
DID HE JUST CALL MASTER ARIMA "TIGHTY-WHITEY WEIRDO" ...?
HE IS SO-O-O DEAD.
WE'RE GONNA GET KILLED TOO IF WE GET MIXED UP IN THIS!
UH...
UMMMMM.
I'VE HEARD A LOT ABOUT YOU...
...BUT IT TURNS OUT YOU'RE JUST A RUDE JERK...
... ROKURO ENMADO !!!!
OOOH.
AM I...
...IN TROUBLE ?
AAANND ...
...WE'RE DONE FOR!!!!

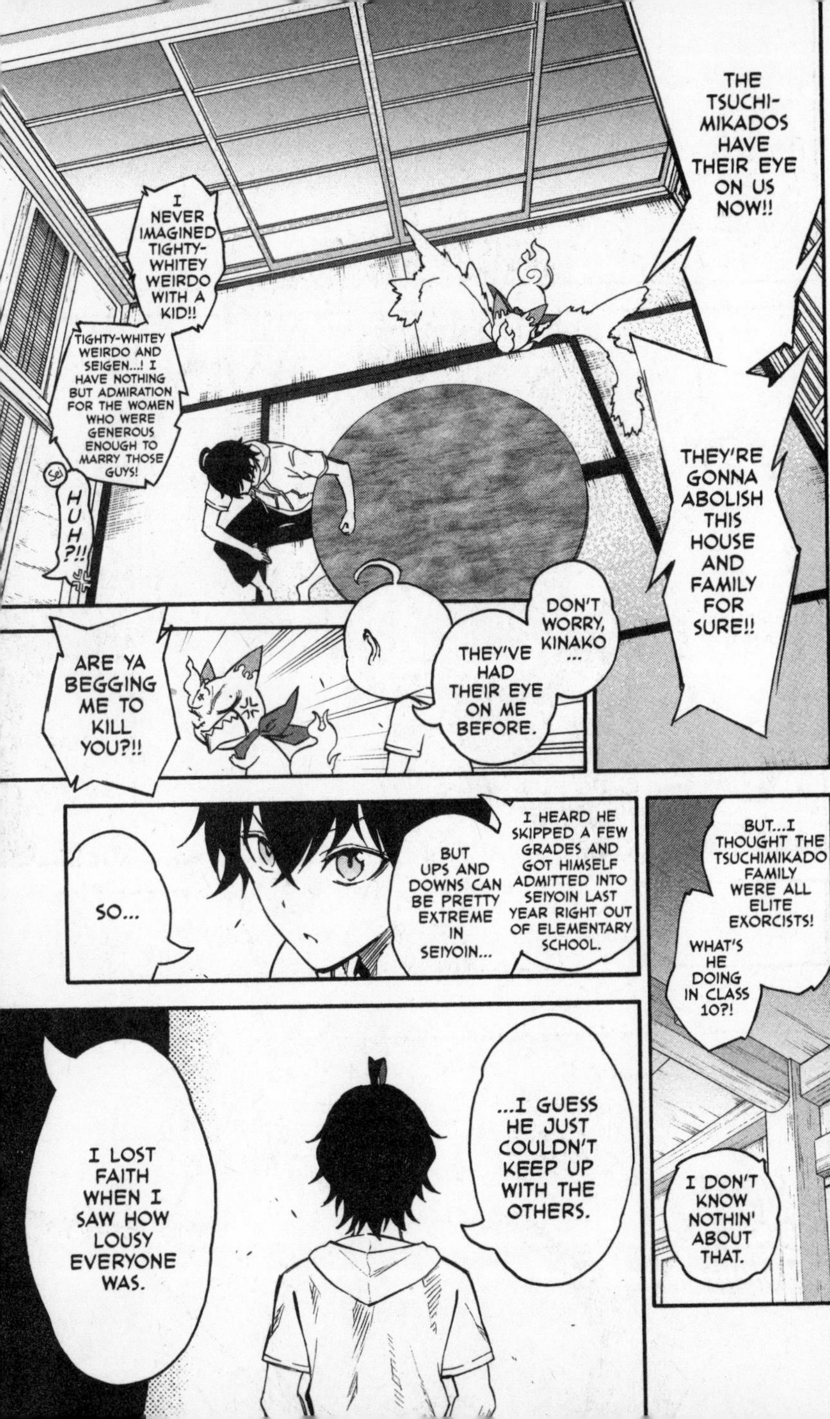
THE TSUCHI-MIKADOS HAVE THEIR EYE ON US NOW!!
THEY'RE GONNA ABOLISH THIS HOUSE AND FAMILY FOR SURE!!
I NEVER IMAGINED TIGHTY-WHITEY WEIRDO WITH A KID!!
TIGHTY-WHITEY WEIRDO AND SEIGEN...! I HAVE NOTHING BUT ADMIRATION FOR THE WOMEN WHO WERE GENEROUS ENOUGH TO MARRY THOSE GUYS!
Sei
HUH?!!
DON'T WORRY, KINAKO...
THEY'VE HAD THEIR EYE ON ME BEFORE.
ARE YA BEGGING ME TO KILL YOU?!!
BUT...I THOUGHT THE TSUCHIMIKADO FAMILY WERE ALL ELITE EXORCISTS!
WHAT'S HE DOING IN CLASS 10?!
I DON'T KNOW NOTHIN' ABOUT THAT.
I HEARD HE SKIPPED A FEW GRADES AND GOT HIMSELF ADMITTED INTO SEIYOIN LAST YEAR RIGHT OUT OF ELEMENTARY SCHOOL.
BUT UPS AND DOWNS CAN BE PRETTY EXTREME IN SEIYOIN...
SO...
...I GUESS HE JUST COULDN'T KEEP UP WITH THE OTHERS.
I LOST FAITH WHEN I SAW HOW LOUSY EVERYONE WAS.

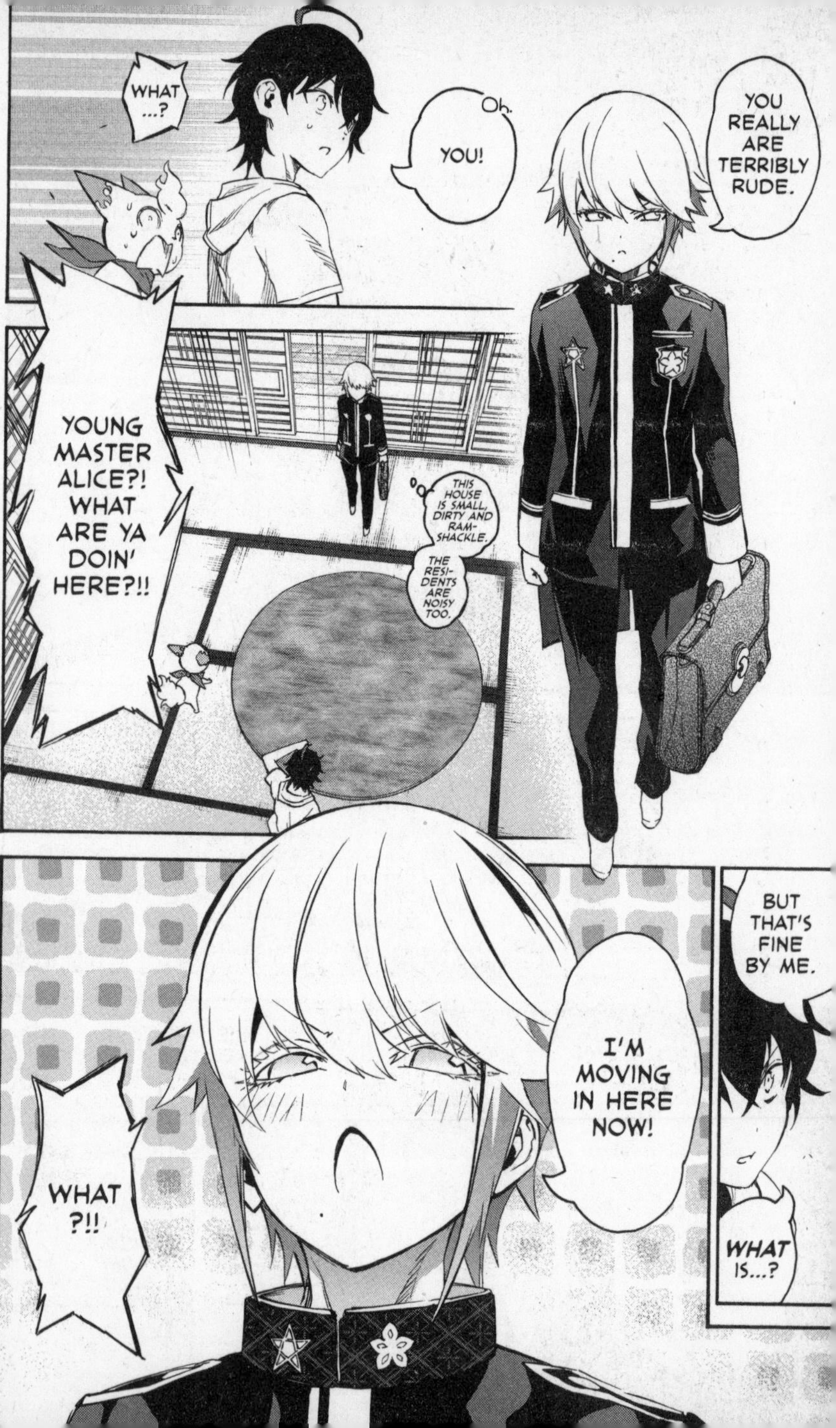

YOU REALLY ARE TERRIBLY RUDE.
Oh.
YOU!
WHAT ...?
YOUNG MASTER ALICE?! WHAT ARE YA DOIN' HERE?!!
THIS HOUSE IS SMALL, DIRTY AND RAM-SHACKLE.
THE RESI-DENTS ARE NOISY TOO.
BUT THAT'S FINE BY ME.
WHAT IS...?
I'M MOVING IN HERE NOW!
WHAT ?!!

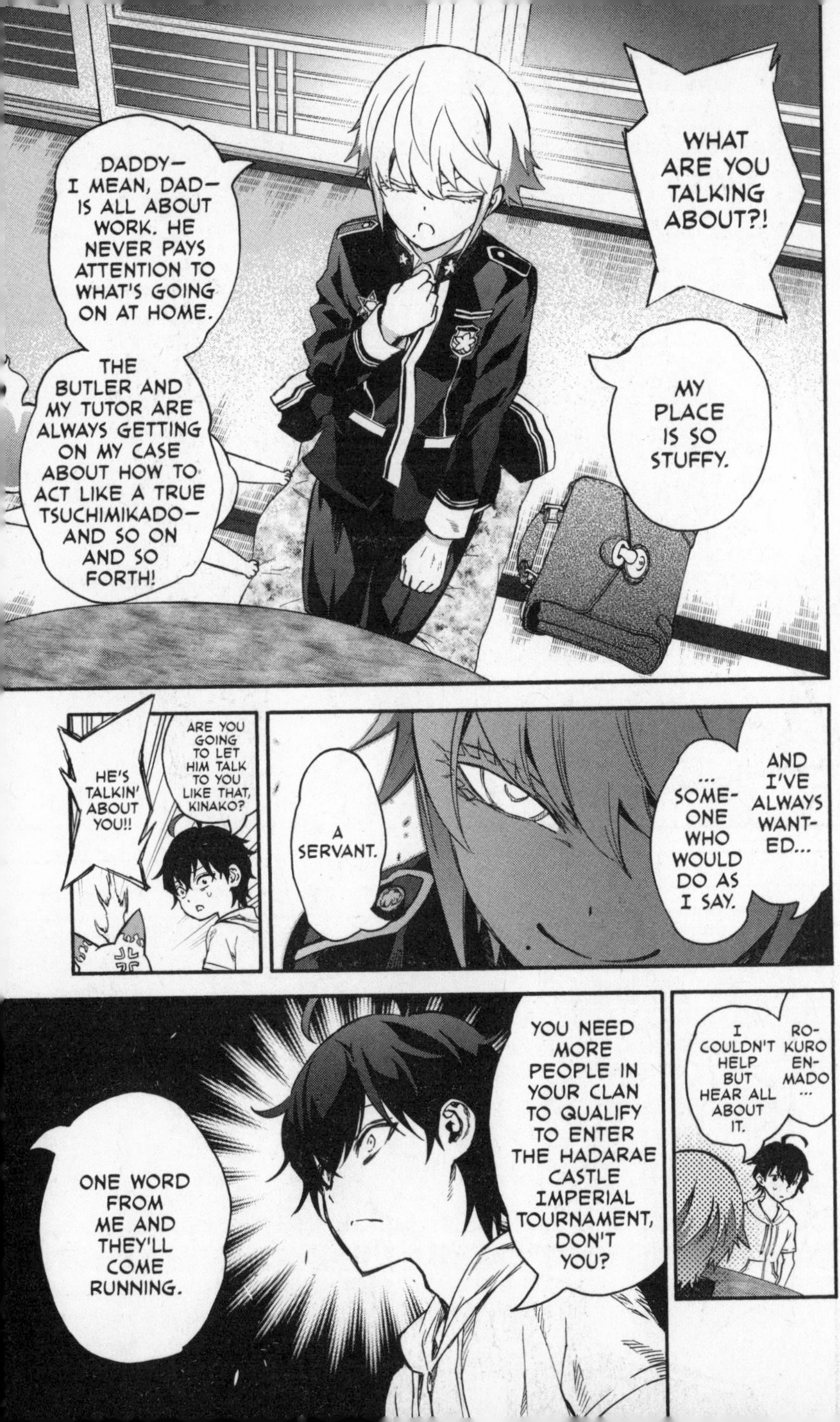
WHAT ARE YOU TALKING ABOUT?!
MY PLACE IS SO STUFFY.
DADDY—I MEAN, DAD—IS ALL ABOUT WORK. HE NEVER PAYS ATTENTION TO WHAT'S GOING ON AT HOME.
THE BUTLER AND MY TUTOR ARE ALWAYS GETTING ON MY CASE ABOUT HOW TO ACT LIKE A TRUE TSUCHIMIKADO—AND SO ON AND SO FORTH!
AND I'VE ALWAYS WANTED...
...SOMEONE WHO WOULD DO AS I SAY.
A SERVANT.
ARE YOU GOING TO LET HIM TALK TO YOU LIKE THAT, KINAKO?
HE'S TALKIN' ABOUT YOU!!
ROKURO ENMADO...
I COULDN'T HELP BUT HEAR ALL ABOUT IT.
YOU NEED MORE PEOPLE IN YOUR CLAN TO QUALIFY TO ENTER THE HADARAE CASTLE IMPERIAL TOURNAMENT, DON'T YOU?
ONE WORD FROM ME AND THEY'LL COME RUNNING.

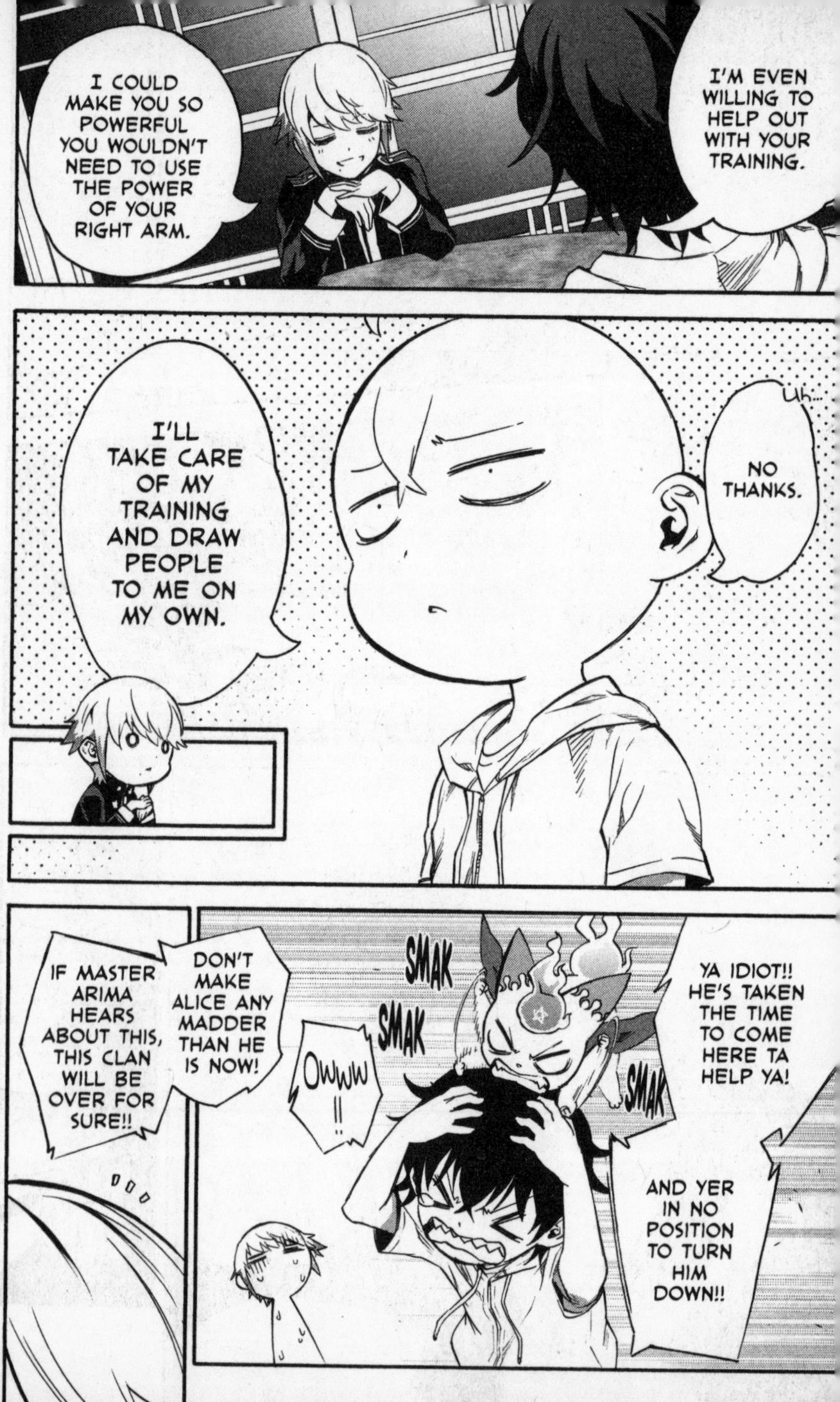
I'M EVEN WILLING TO HELP OUT WITH YOUR TRAINING.
I COULD MAKE YOU SO POWERFUL YOU WOULDN'T NEED TO USE THE POWER OF YOUR RIGHT ARM.
Uh...
NO THANKS.
I'LL TAKE CARE OF MY TRAINING AND DRAW PEOPLE TO ME ON MY OWN.
YA IDIOT!! HE'S TAKEN THE TIME TO COME HERE TA HELP YA!
SMAK
SMAK
SMAK
Owww!!
AND YER IN NO POSITION TO TURN HIM DOWN!!
DON'T MAKE ALICE ANY MADDER THAN HE IS NOW!
IF MASTER ARIMA HEARS ABOUT THIS, THIS CLAN WILL BE OVER FOR SURE!!

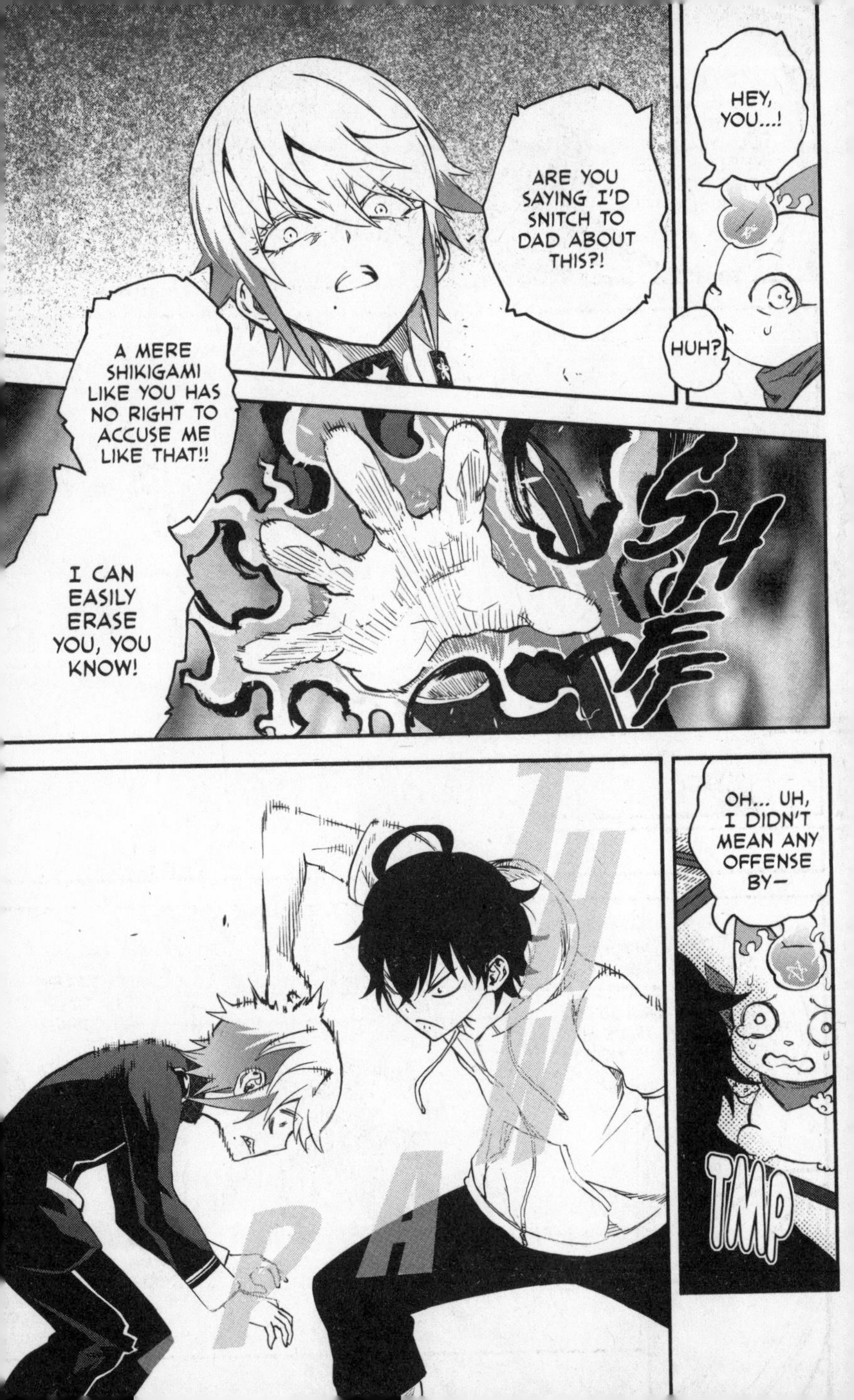
HEY, YOU...!
HUH?
ARE YOU SAYING I'D SNITCH TO DAD ABOUT THIS?!
A MERE SHIKIGAMI LIKE YOU HAS NO RIGHT TO ACCUSE ME LIKE THAT!!
I CAN EASILY ERASE YOU, YOU KNOW!
OH... UH, I DIDN'T MEAN ANY OFFENSE BY—
TMP

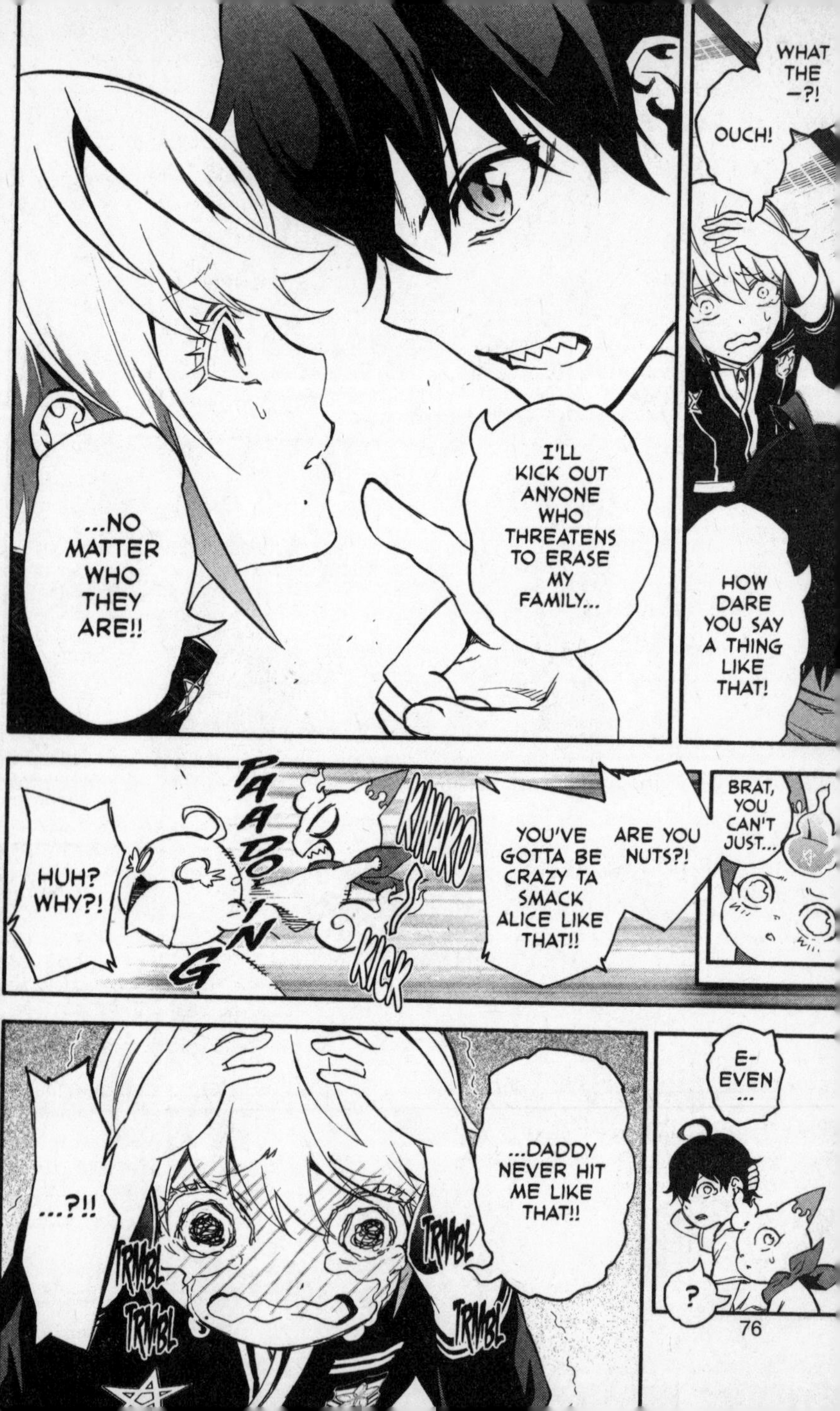
WHAT THE —?!
OUCH!
HOW DARE YOU SAY A THING LIKE THAT!
I'LL KICK OUT ANYONE WHO THREATENS TO ERASE MY FAMILY...
...NO MATTER WHO THEY ARE!!
BRAT, YOU CAN'T JUST...
ARE YOU NUTS?!
YOU'VE GOTTA BE CRAZY TA SMACK ALICE LIKE THAT!!
KINAKO
KICK
PAADOING
HUH? WHY?!
E-EVEN...
?
...DADDY NEVER HIT ME LIKE THAT!!
TRMBL
TRMBL
TRMBL
TRMBL
...?!!

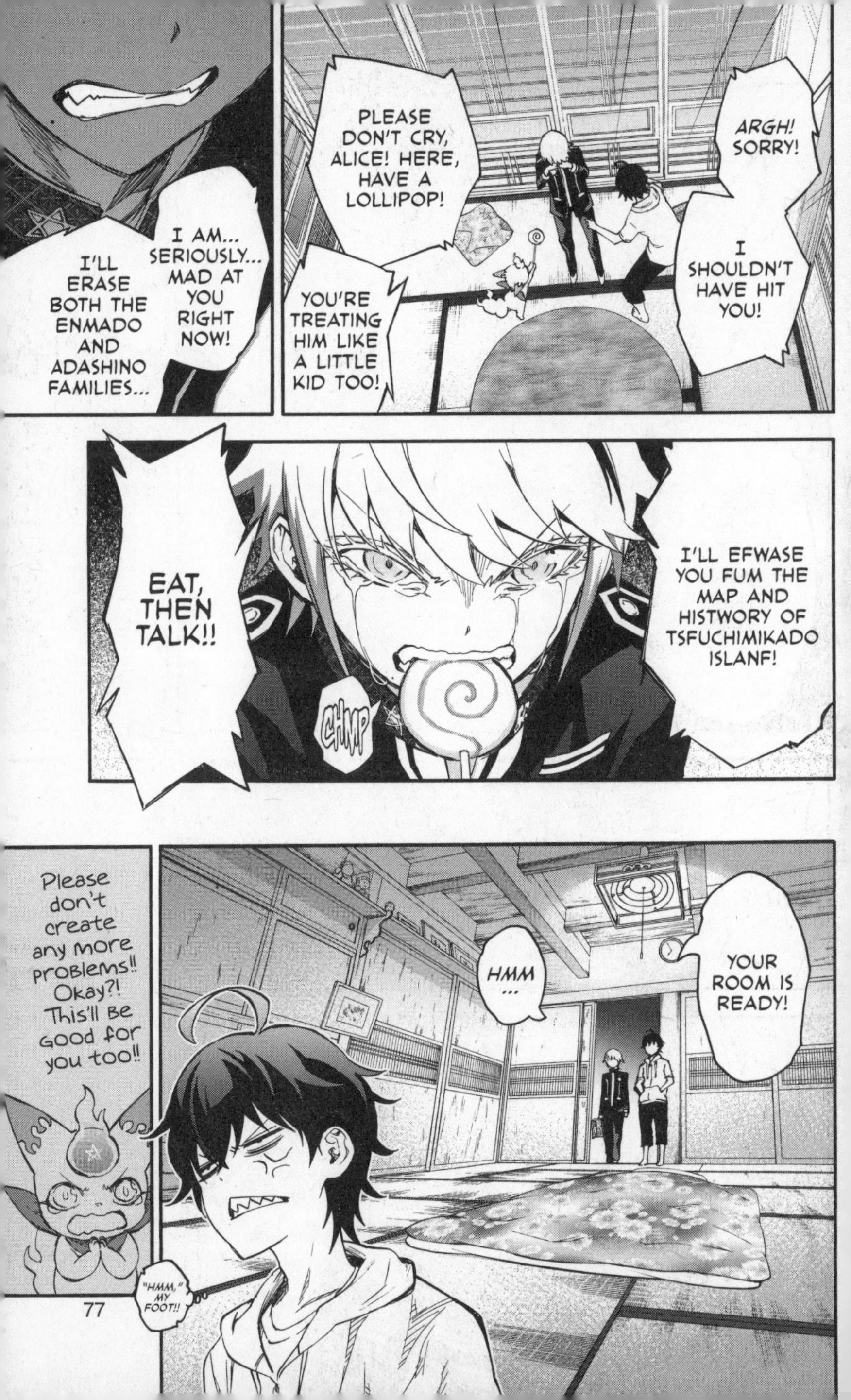
ARGH! SORRY!
PLEASE DON'T CRY, ALICE! HERE, HAVE A LOLLIPOP!
I SHOULDN'T HAVE HIT YOU!
YOU'RE TREATING HIM LIKE A LITTLE KID TOO!
I AM... SERIOUSLY... MAD AT YOU RIGHT NOW!
I'LL ERASE BOTH THE ENMADO AND ADASHINO FAMILIES...
I'LL EFWASE YOU FUM THE MAP AND HISTWORY OF TSFUCHIMIKADO ISLANF!
CHMP
EAT, THEN TALK!!
YOUR ROOM IS READY!
HMM...
"HMM," MY FOOT!!
Please don't create any more problems!! Okay?! This'll be good for you too!!

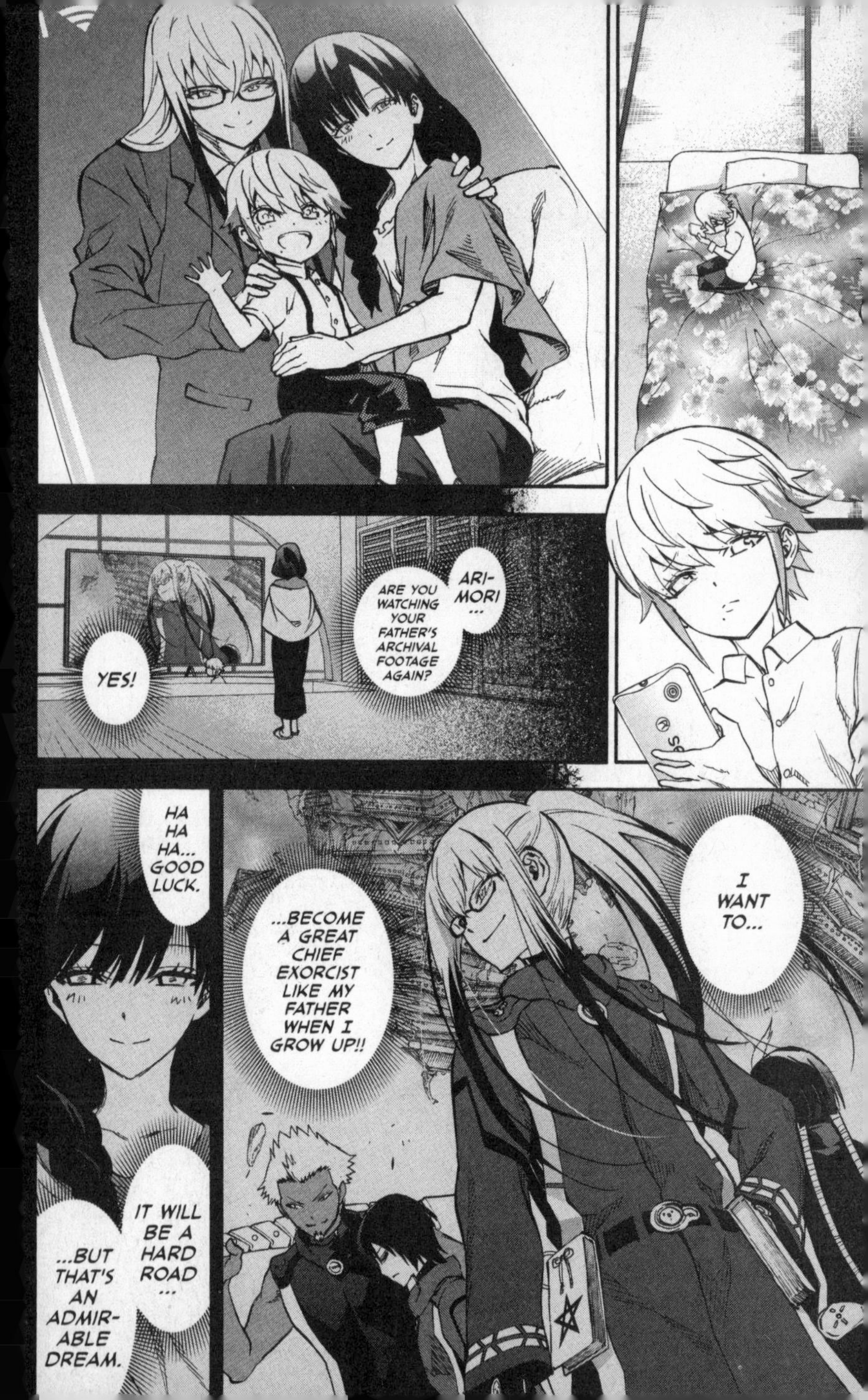
ARI-MORI...
ARE YOU WATCHING YOUR FATHER'S ARCHIVAL FOOTAGE AGAIN?
YES!
I WANT TO...
...BECOME A GREAT CHIEF EXORCIST LIKE MY FATHER WHEN I GROW UP!!
HA HA HA... GOOD LUCK.
IT WILL BE A HARD ROAD...
...BUT THAT'S AN ADMIRABLE DREAM.

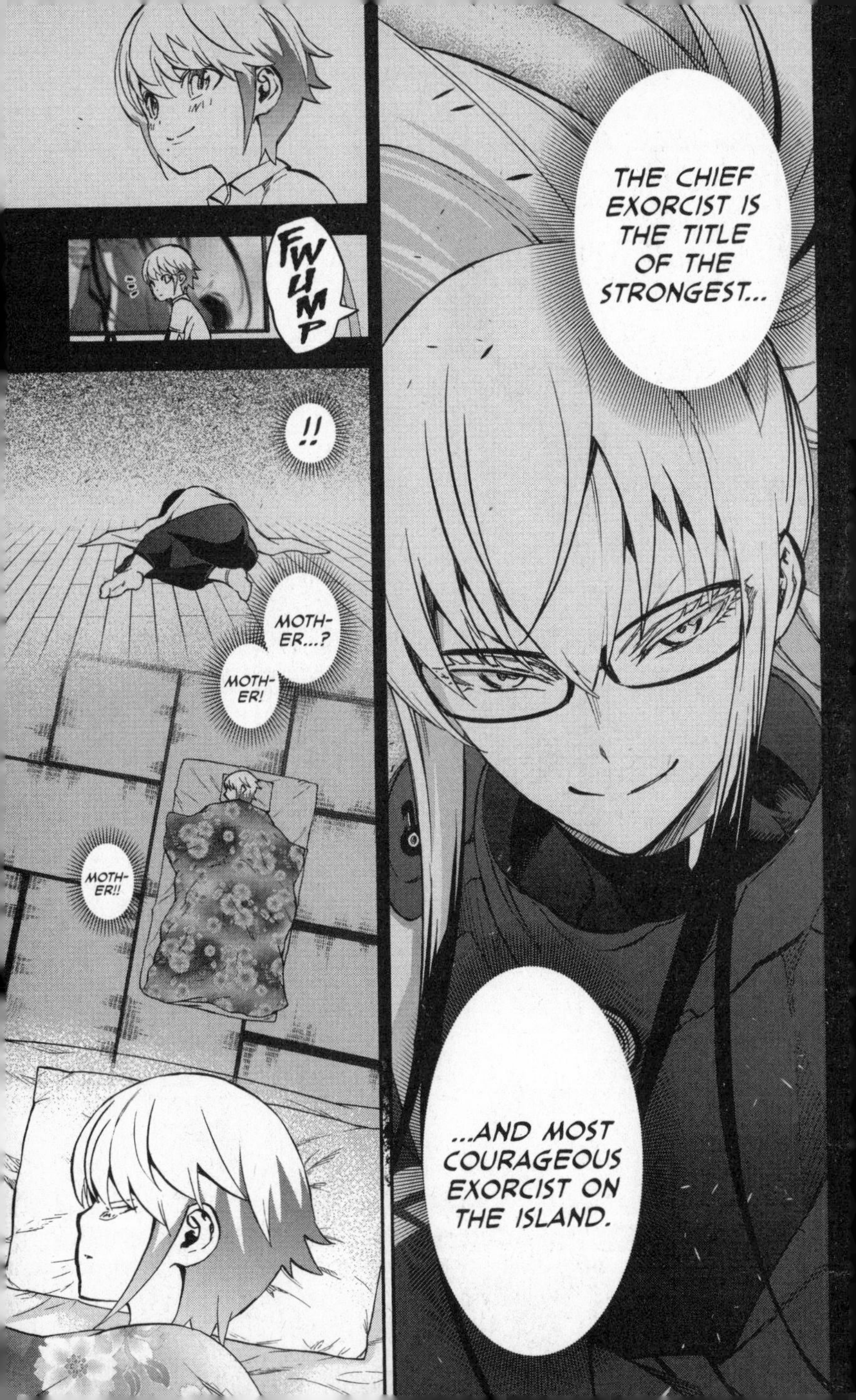
THE CHIEF EXORCIST IS THE TITLE OF THE STRONGEST...
...AND MOST COURAGEOUS EXORCIST ON THE ISLAND.
FWUMP
!!
MOTH-ER...?
MOTH-ER!
MOTH-ER!!

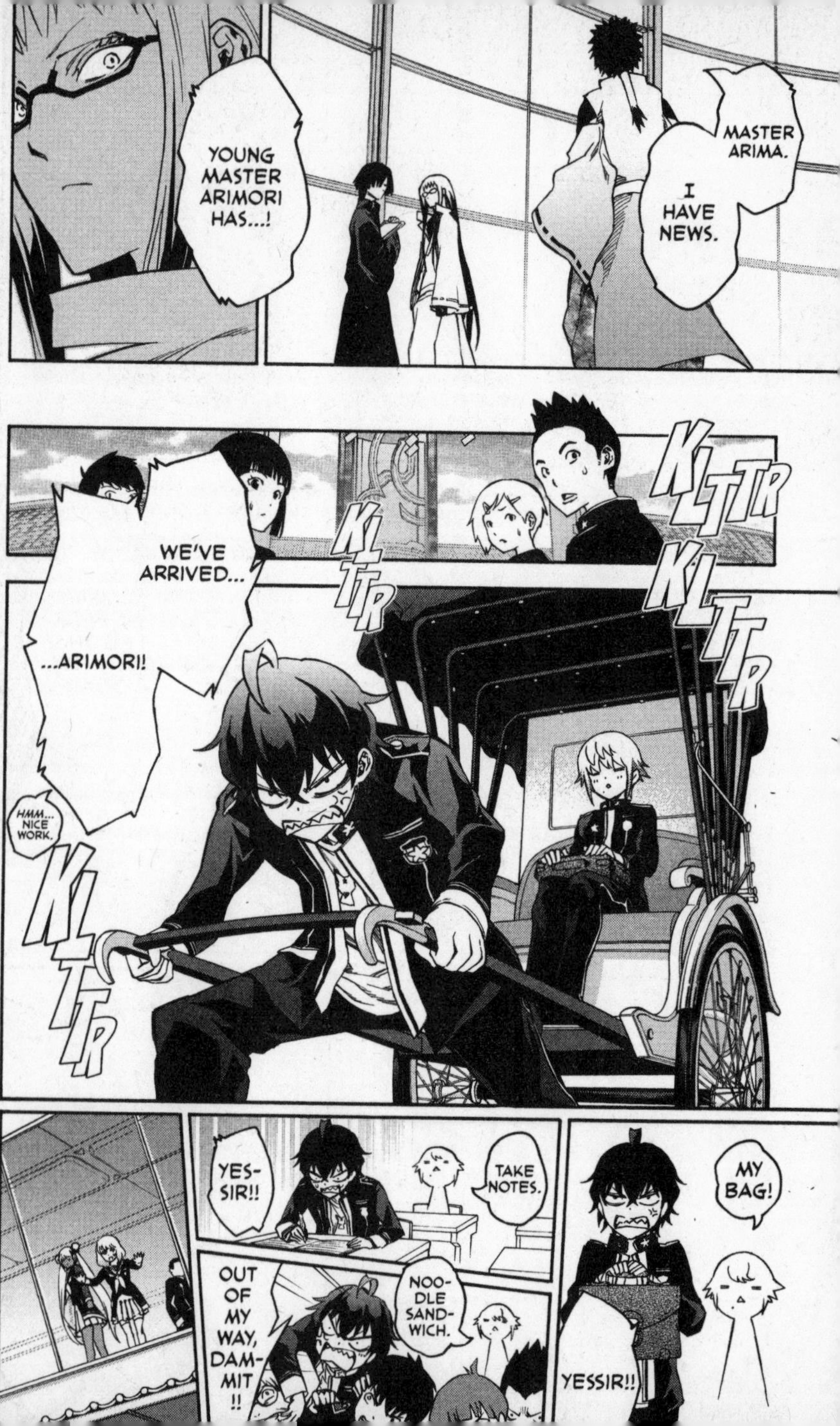
MASTER ARIMA.
I HAVE NEWS.
YOUNG MASTER ARIMORI HAS...!
KLTTR
KLTTR
WE'VE ARRIVED...
...ARIMORI!
KLTTR
HMM... NICE WORK.
KLTTR
MY BAG!
YESSIR!!
TAKE NOTES.
YES-SIR!!
NOO-DLE SAND-WICH.
OUT OF MY WAY, DAM-MIT!!

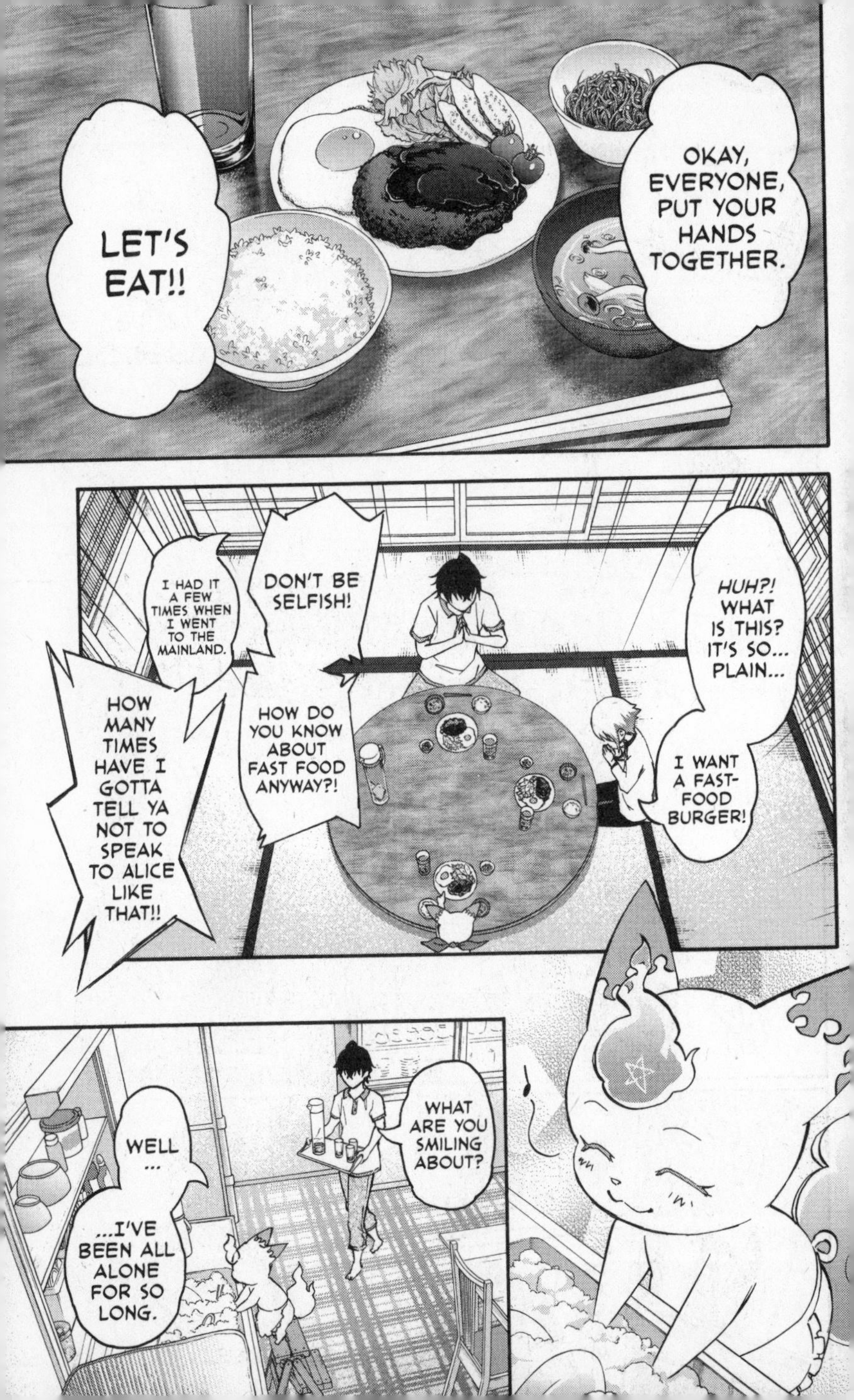
OKAY, EVERYONE, PUT YOUR HANDS TOGETHER.
LET'S EAT!!
*HUH?!* WHAT IS THIS? IT'S SO... PLAIN...
I WANT A FAST-FOOD BURGER!
DON'T BE SELFISH!
HOW DO YOU KNOW ABOUT FAST FOOD ANYWAY?!
I HAD IT A FEW TIMES WHEN I WENT TO THE MAINLAND.
HOW MANY TIMES HAVE I GOTTA TELL YA NOT TO SPEAK TO ALICE LIKE THAT!!
WHAT ARE YOU SMILING ABOUT?
WELL...
...I'VE BEEN ALL ALONE FOR SO LONG.

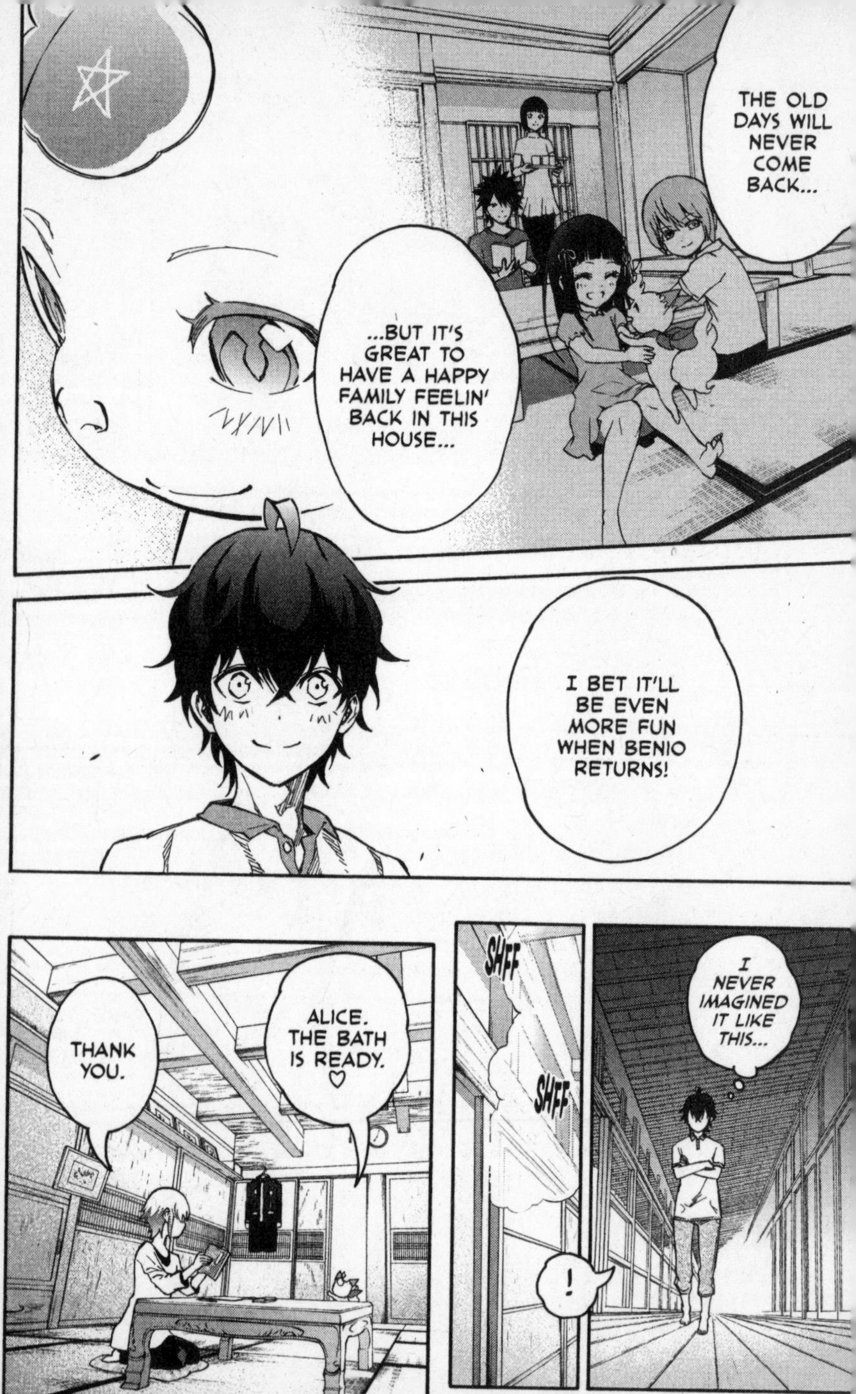
THE OLD DAYS WILL NEVER COME BACK...
...BUT IT'S GREAT TO HAVE A HAPPY FAMILY FEELIN' BACK IN THIS HOUSE...
I BET IT'LL BE EVEN MORE FUN WHEN BENIO RETURNS!
I NEVER IMAGINED IT LIKE THIS...
SHFF
SHFF
!
ALICE. THE BATH IS READY. ♡
THANK YOU.

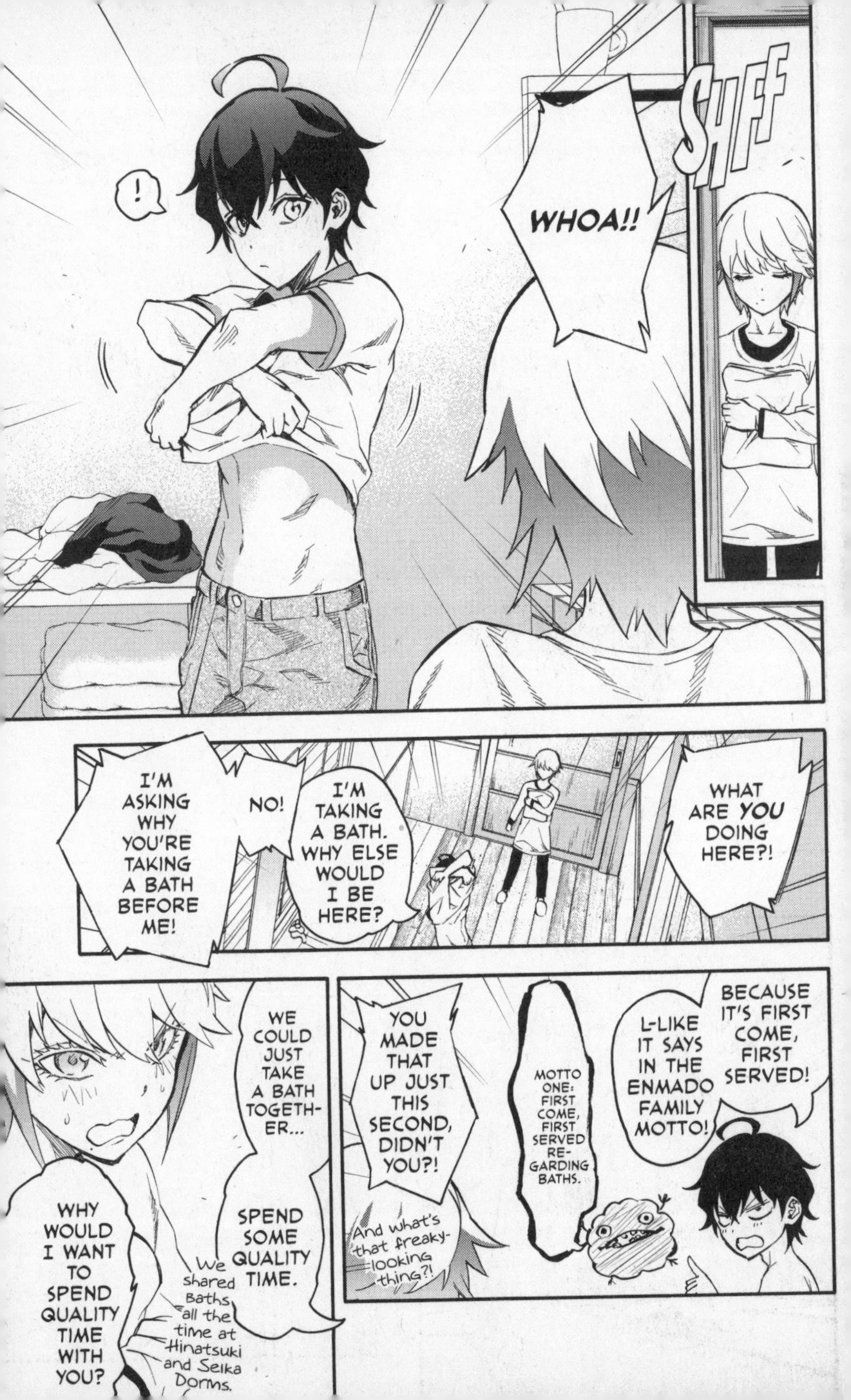
SHFF
WHOA!!
!
WHAT ARE YOU DOING HERE?!
I'M TAKING A BATH. WHY ELSE WOULD I BE HERE?
NO!
I'M ASKING WHY YOU'RE TAKING A BATH BEFORE ME!
BECAUSE IT'S FIRST COME, FIRST SERVED!
L-LIKE IT SAYS IN THE ENMADO FAMILY MOTTO!
MOTTO ONE: FIRST COME, FIRST SERVED REGARDING BATHS.
YOU MADE THAT UP JUST THIS SECOND, DIDN'T YOU?!
And what's that freaky-looking thing?!
WE COULD JUST TAKE A BATH TOGETHER...
SPEND SOME QUALITY TIME.
We shared Baths all the time at Hinatsuki and Seika Dorms.
WHY WOULD I WANT TO SPEND QUALITY TIME WITH YOU?

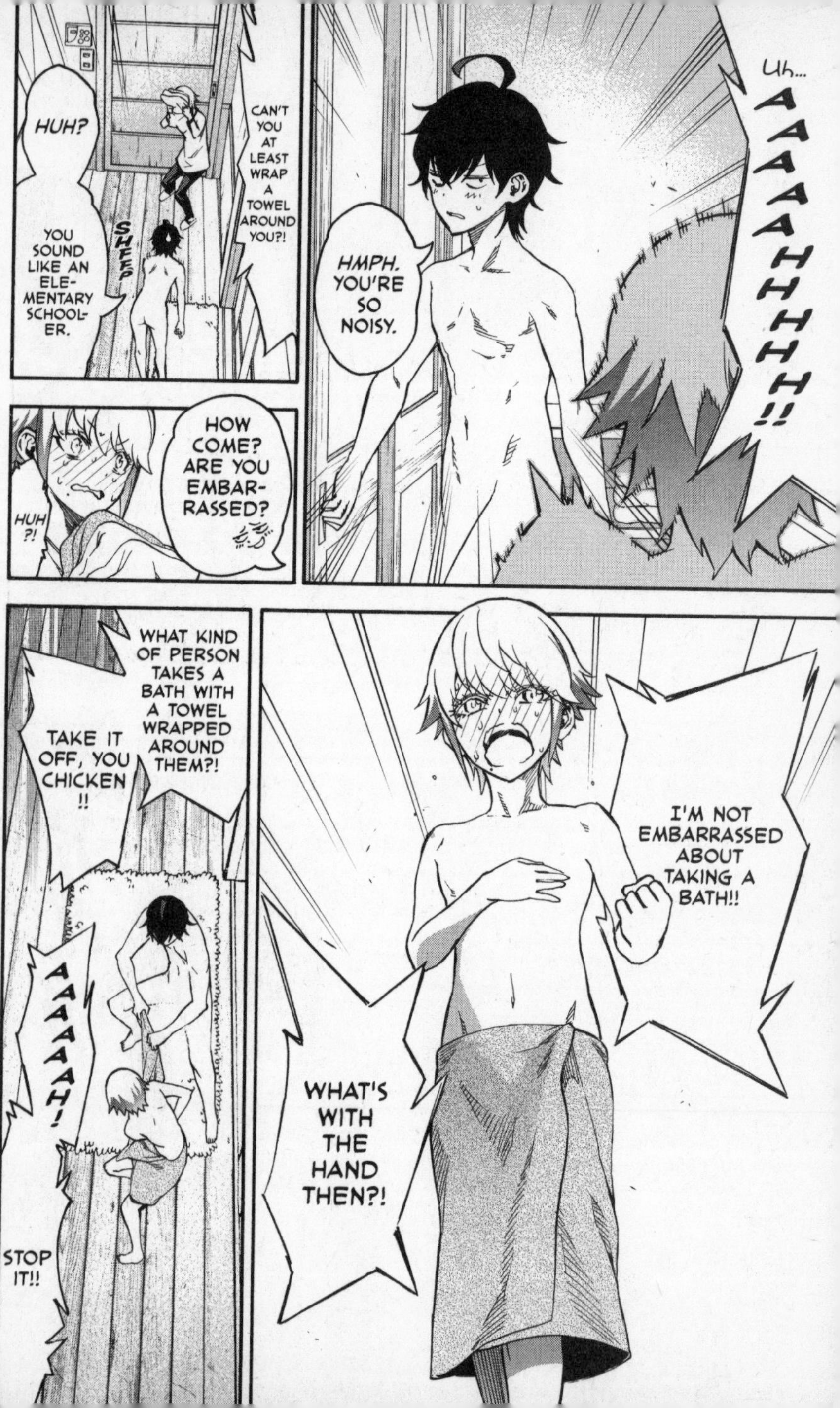
Uh...
AAAAAHHHHH!!
HMPH. YOU'RE SO NOISY.
CAN'T YOU AT LEAST WRAP A TOWEL AROUND YOU?!
HUH?
SHFFP
YOU SOUND LIKE AN ELEMENTARY SCHOOLER.
HOW COME? ARE YOU EMBARRASSED?
HUH?!
I'M NOT EMBARRASSED ABOUT TAKING A BATH!!
WHAT'S WITH THE HAND THEN?!
WHAT KIND OF PERSON TAKES A BATH WITH A TOWEL WRAPPED AROUND THEM?!
TAKE IT OFF, YOU CHICKEN!!
AAAAAAH!
STOP IT!!

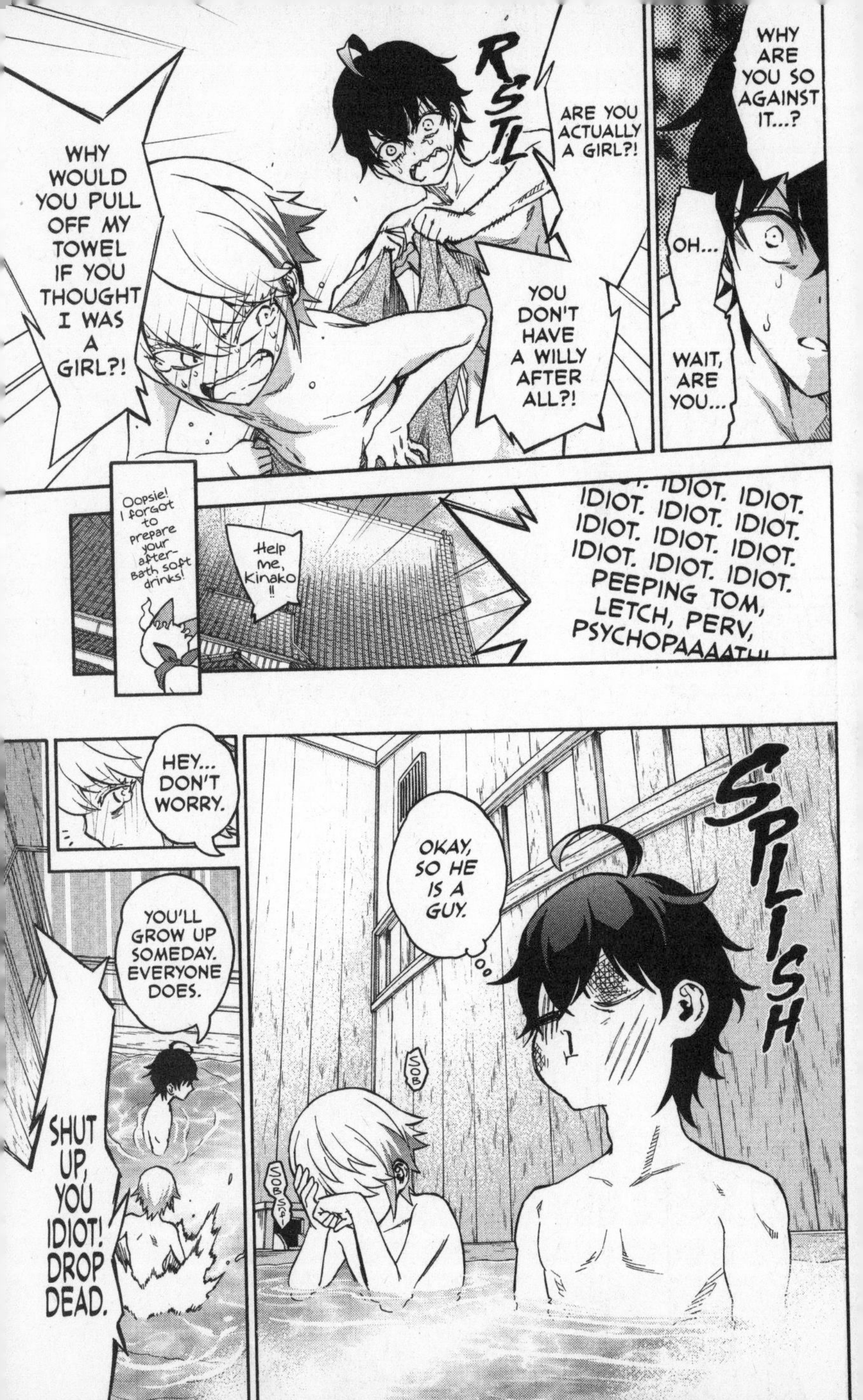

WHY ARE YOU SO AGAINST IT...?
OH...
WAIT, ARE YOU...
RSTL
ARE YOU ACTUALLY A GIRL?!
YOU DON'T HAVE A WILLY AFTER ALL?!
WHY WOULD YOU PULL OFF MY TOWEL IF YOU THOUGHT I WAS A GIRL?!
IDIOT. IDIOT. IDIOT. IDIOT. IDIOT. IDIOT. IDIOT. IDIOT. IDIOT. IDIOT. IDIOT. IDIOT. IDIOT. PEEPING TOM, LETCH, PERV, PSYCHOPAAAATH
Help me, Kinako!!
Oopsie! I forgot to prepare your after-bath soft drinks!
SPLISH
OKAY, SO HE IS A GUY.
SOB
SOB
HEY... DON'T WORRY.
YOU'LL GROW UP SOMEDAY. EVERYONE DOES.
SHUT UP, YOU IDIOT! DROP DEAD.

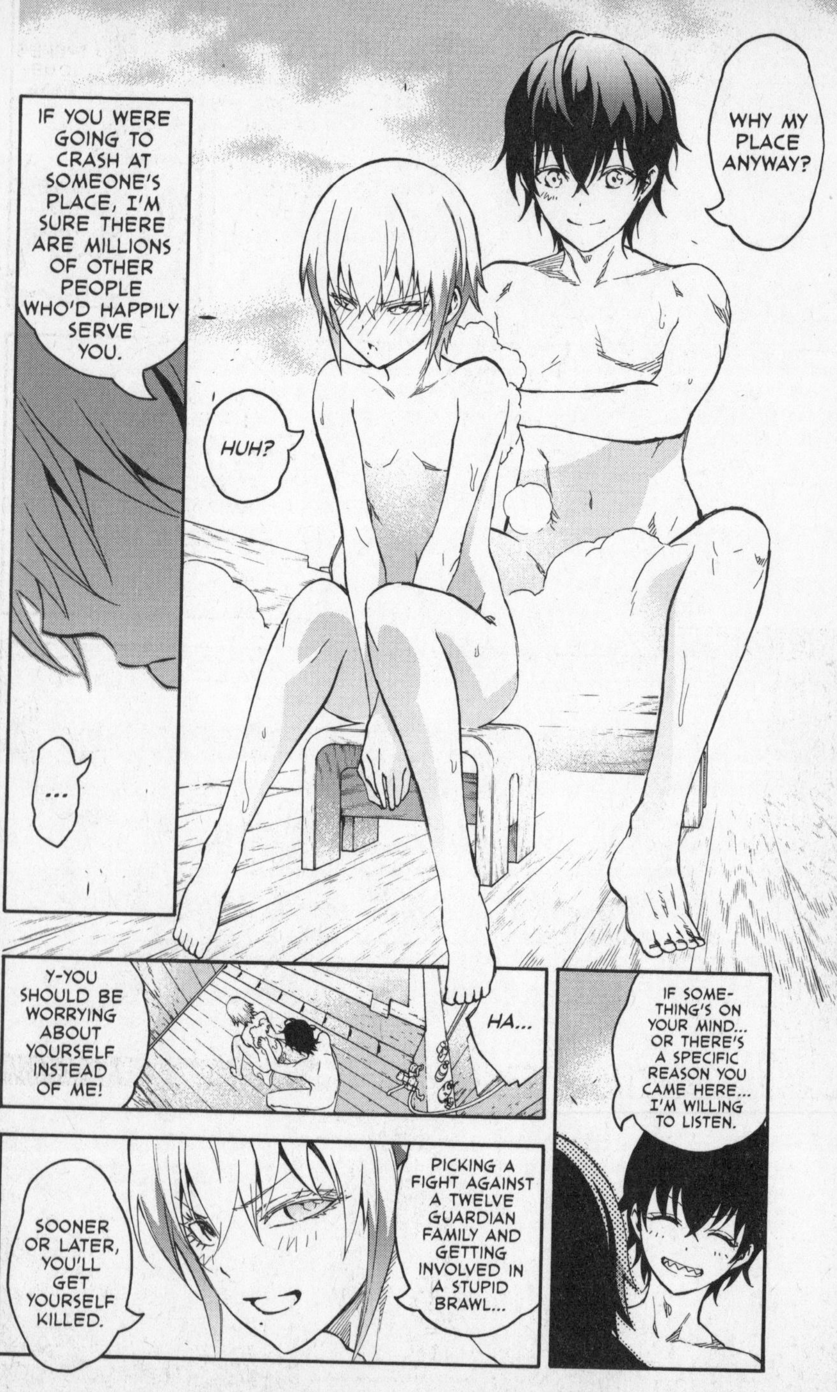
WHY MY PLACE ANYWAY?
HUH?
IF YOU WERE GOING TO CRASH AT SOMEONE'S PLACE, I'M SURE THERE ARE MILLIONS OF OTHER PEOPLE WHO'D HAPPILY SERVE YOU.
...
IF SOMETHING'S ON YOUR MIND... OR THERE'S A SPECIFIC REASON YOU CAME HERE... I'M WILLING TO LISTEN.
HA...
Y-YOU SHOULD BE WORRYING ABOUT YOURSELF INSTEAD OF ME!
PICKING A FIGHT AGAINST A TWELVE GUARDIAN FAMILY AND GETTING INVOLVED IN A STUPID BRAWL...
SOONER OR LATER, YOU'LL GET YOURSELF KILLED.

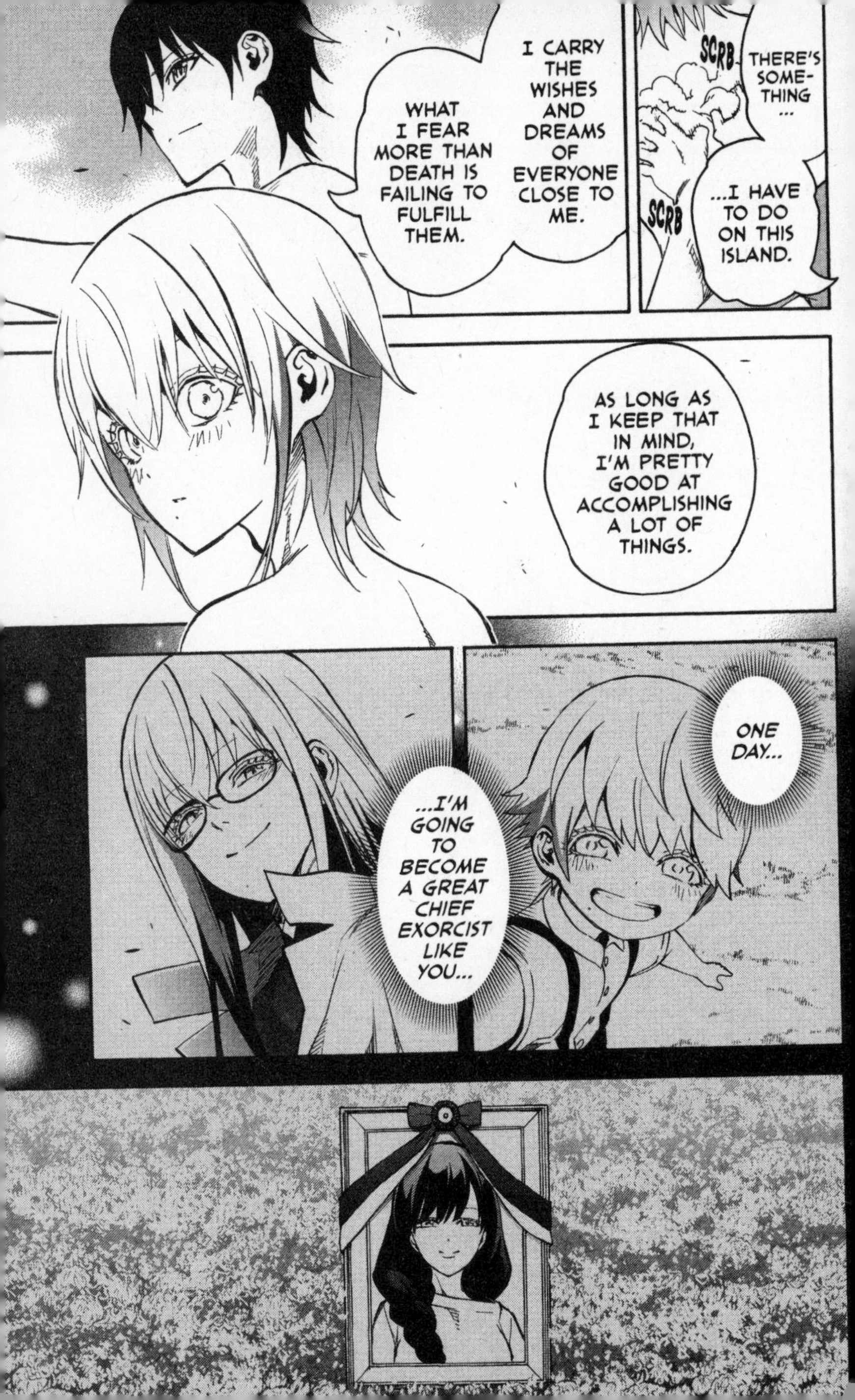
SCRB
THERE'S SOMETHING...
SCRB
...I HAVE TO DO ON THIS ISLAND.
I CARRY THE WISHES AND DREAMS OF EVERYONE CLOSE TO ME.
WHAT I FEAR MORE THAN DEATH IS FAILING TO FULFILL THEM.
AS LONG AS I KEEP THAT IN MIND, I'M PRETTY GOOD AT ACCOMPLISHING A LOT OF THINGS.
ONE DAY...
...I'M GOING TO BECOME A GREAT CHIEF EXORCIST LIKE YOU...

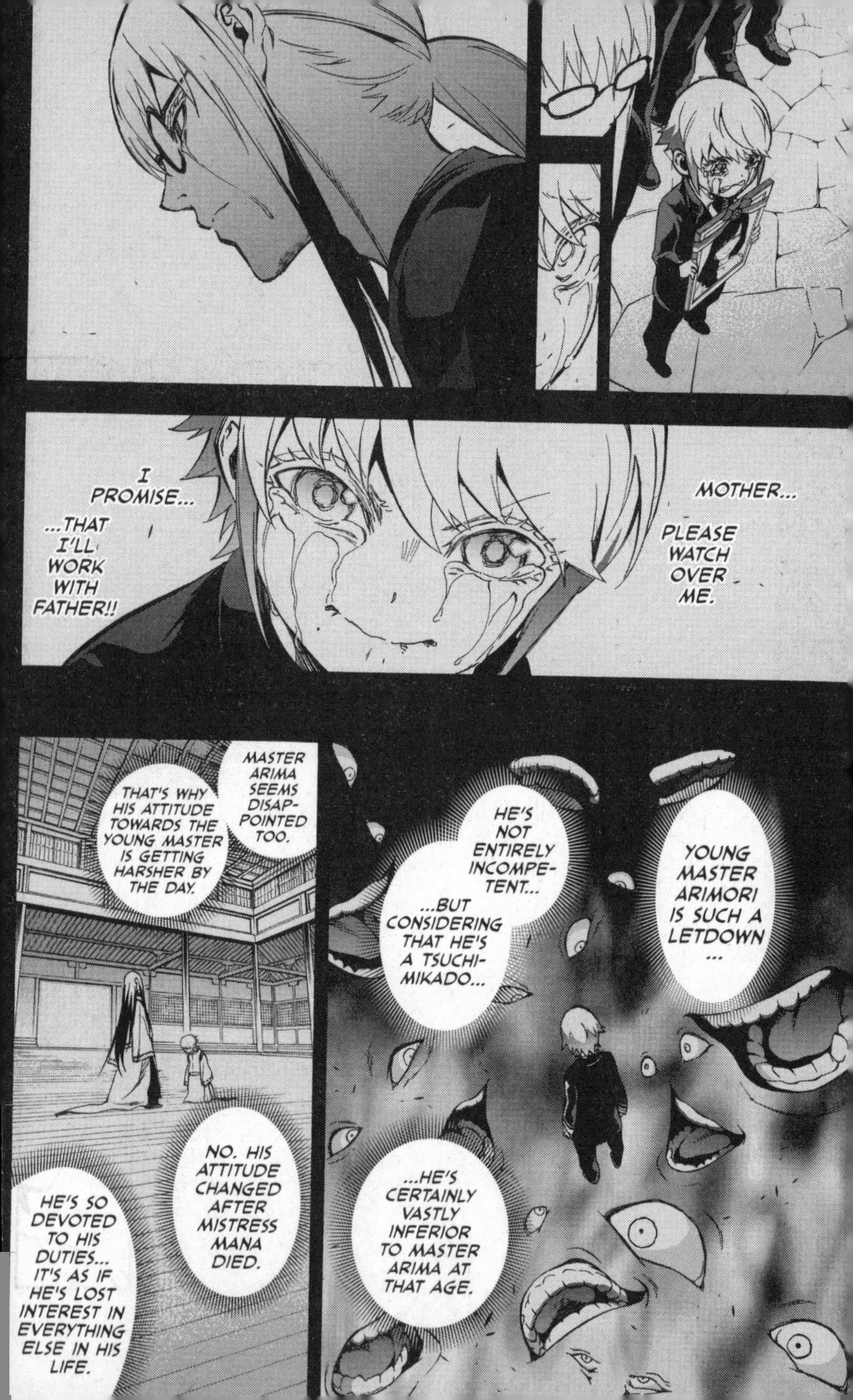
MOTHER...
PLEASE WATCH OVER ME.
I PROMISE...
...THAT I'LL WORK WITH FATHER!!
YOUNG MASTER ARIMORI IS SUCH A LETDOWN...
HE'S NOT ENTIRELY INCOMPETENT...
...BUT CONSIDERING THAT HE'S A TSUCHIMIKADO...
...HE'S CERTAINLY VASTLY INFERIOR TO MASTER ARIMA AT THAT AGE.
MASTER ARIMA SEEMS DISAPPOINTED TOO.
THAT'S WHY HIS ATTITUDE TOWARDS THE YOUNG MASTER IS GETTING HARSHER BY THE DAY.
NO. HIS ATTITUDE CHANGED AFTER MISTRESS MANA DIED.
HE'S SO DEVOTED TO HIS DUTIES... IT'S AS IF HE'S LOST INTEREST IN EVERYTHING ELSE IN HIS LIFE.

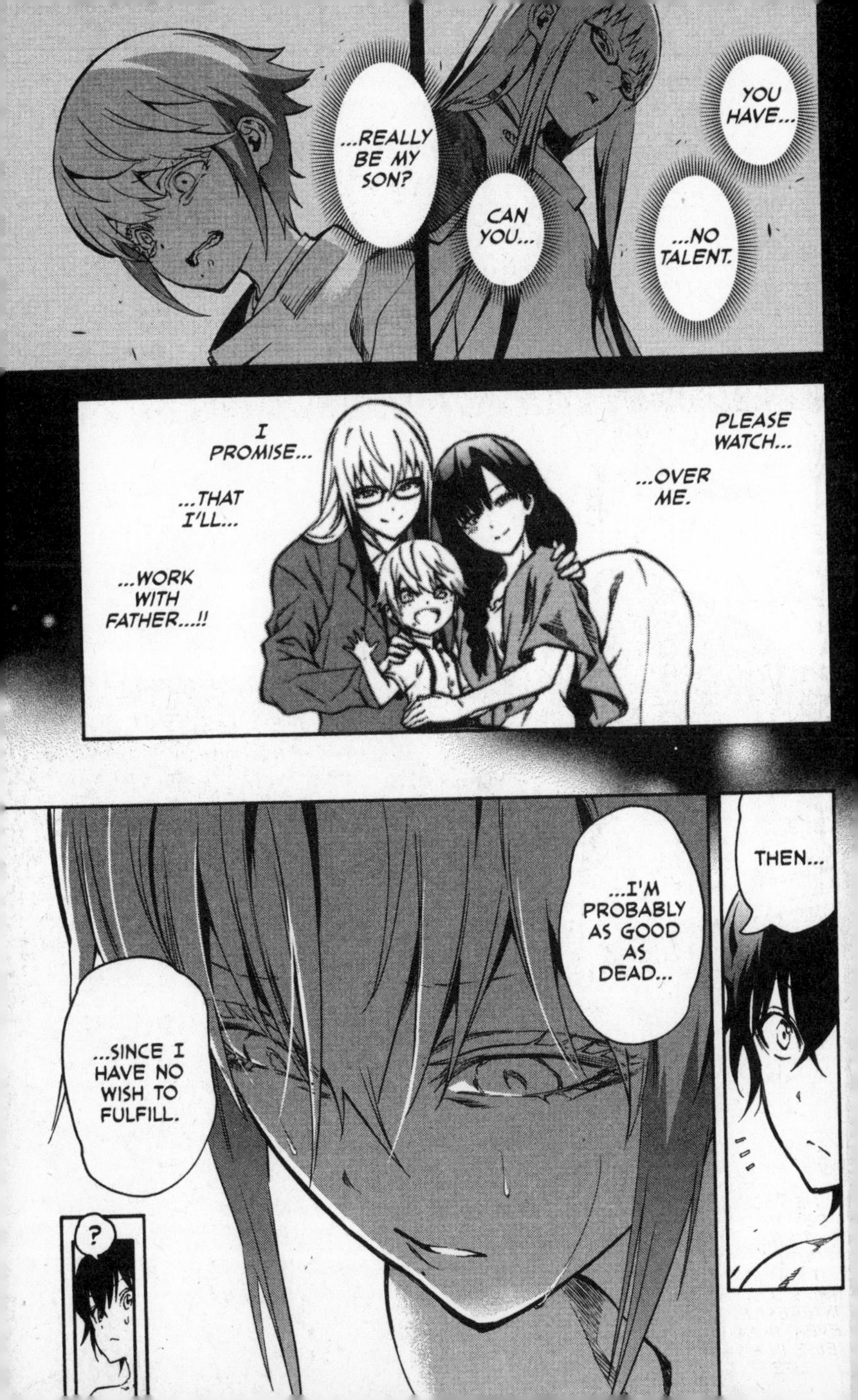
YOU HAVE...
...NO TALENT.
CAN YOU...
...REALLY BE MY SON?
PLEASE WATCH...
...OVER ME.
I PROMISE...
...THAT I'LL...
...WORK WITH FATHER...!!
THEN...
...I'M PROBABLY AS GOOD AS DEAD...
...SINCE I HAVE NO WISH TO FULFILL.
?

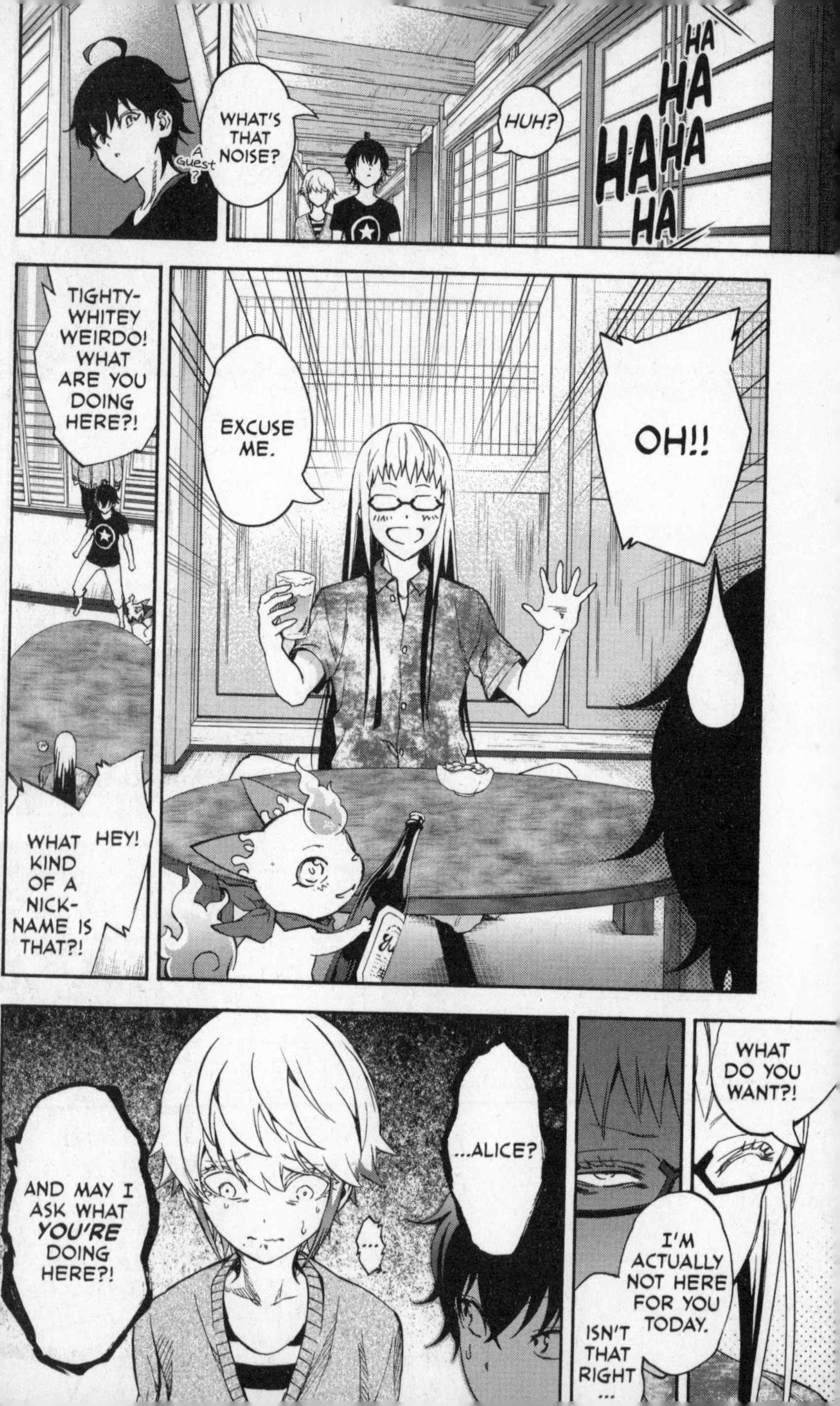
HA HA HAHA HAHA HA
HUH?
WHAT'S THAT NOISE?
A Guest?
OH!!
EXCUSE ME.
TIGHTY-WHITEY WEIRDO! WHAT ARE YOU DOING HERE?!
HEY! WHAT KIND OF A NICK-NAME IS THAT?!
WHAT DO YOU WANT?!
I'M ACTUALLY NOT HERE FOR YOU TODAY.
ISN'T THAT RIGHT ...
...ALICE?
AND MAY I ASK WHAT YOU'RE DOING HERE?!
...

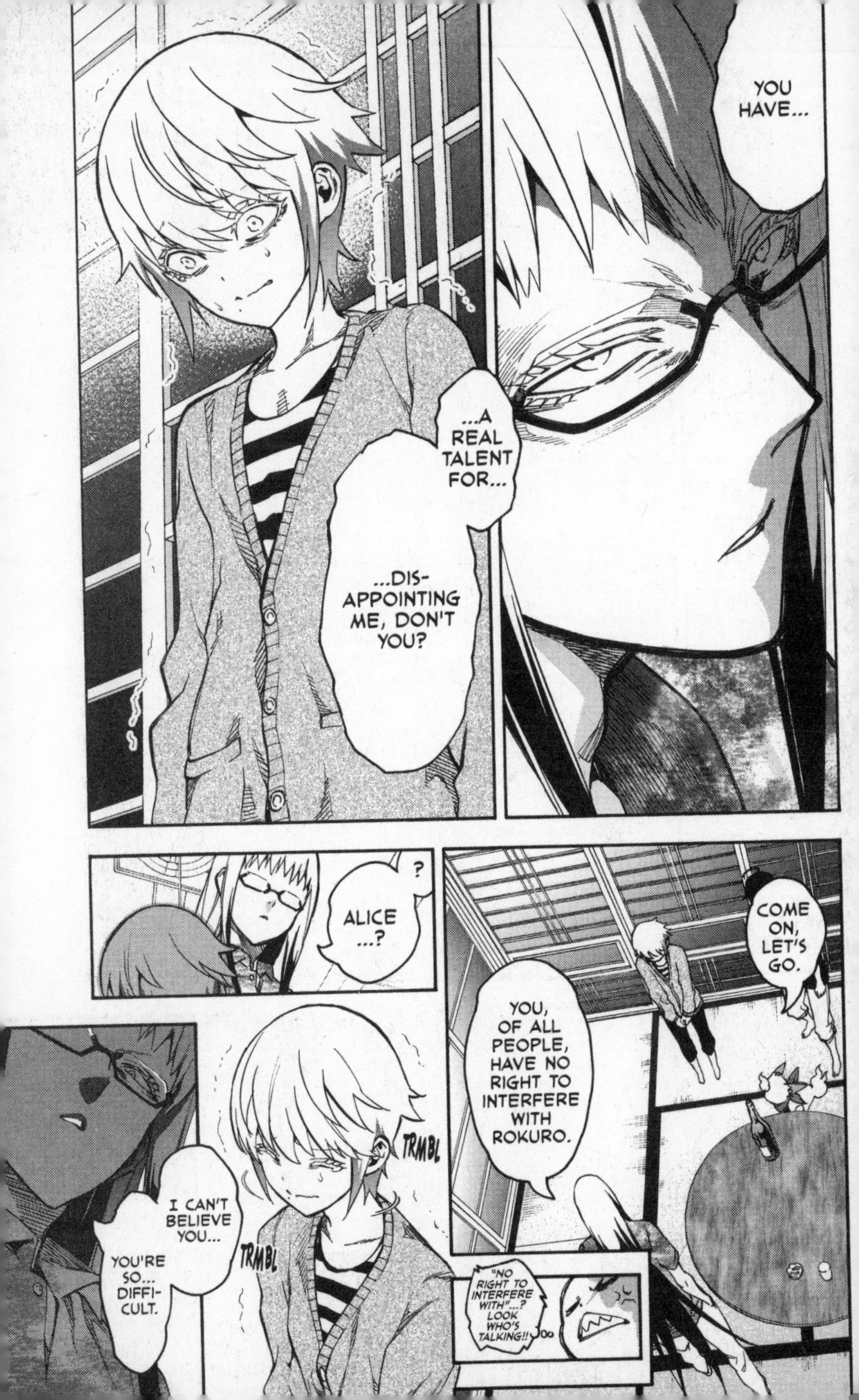
YOU HAVE...
...A REAL TALENT FOR...
...DIS-APPOINTING ME, DON'T YOU?
COME ON, LET'S GO.
YOU, OF ALL PEOPLE, HAVE NO RIGHT TO INTERFERE WITH ROKURO.
?
ALICE ...?
TRMBL
I CAN'T BELIEVE YOU...
YOU'RE SO... DIFFI-CULT.
TRMBL
"NO RIGHT TO INTERFERE WITH"...? LOOK WHO'S TALKING!!

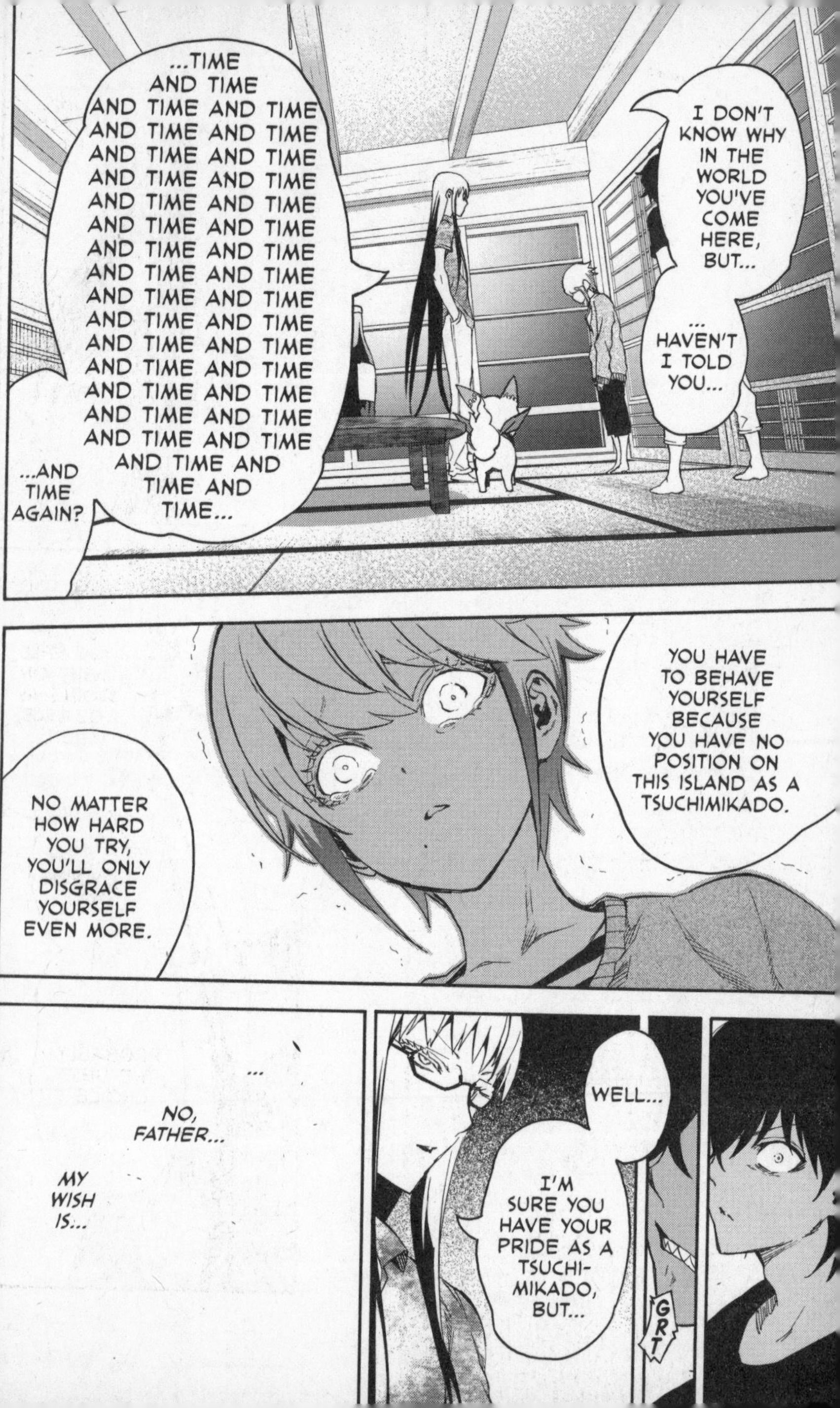
I DON'T KNOW WHY IN THE WORLD YOU'VE COME HERE, BUT...
...HAVEN'T I TOLD YOU...
...TIME AND TIME AND TIME AND TIME AND TIME AND TIME AND TIME AND TIME AND TIME AND TIME AND TIME AND TIME AND TIME AND TIME AND TIME AND TIME AND TIME AND TIME AND TIME AND TIME AND TIME AND TIME AND TIME AND TIME AND TIME AND TIME AND TIME AND TIME AND TIME AND TIME AND TIME AND TIME AND TIME AND TIME AND TIME...
...AND TIME AGAIN?
YOU HAVE TO BEHAVE YOURSELF BECAUSE YOU HAVE NO POSITION ON THIS ISLAND AS A TSUCHIMIKADO.
NO MATTER HOW HARD YOU TRY, YOU'LL ONLY DISGRACE YOURSELF EVEN MORE.
WELL...
I'M SURE YOU HAVE YOUR PRIDE AS A TSUCHI-MIKADO, BUT...
GRT
...
NO, FATHER...
MY WISH IS...

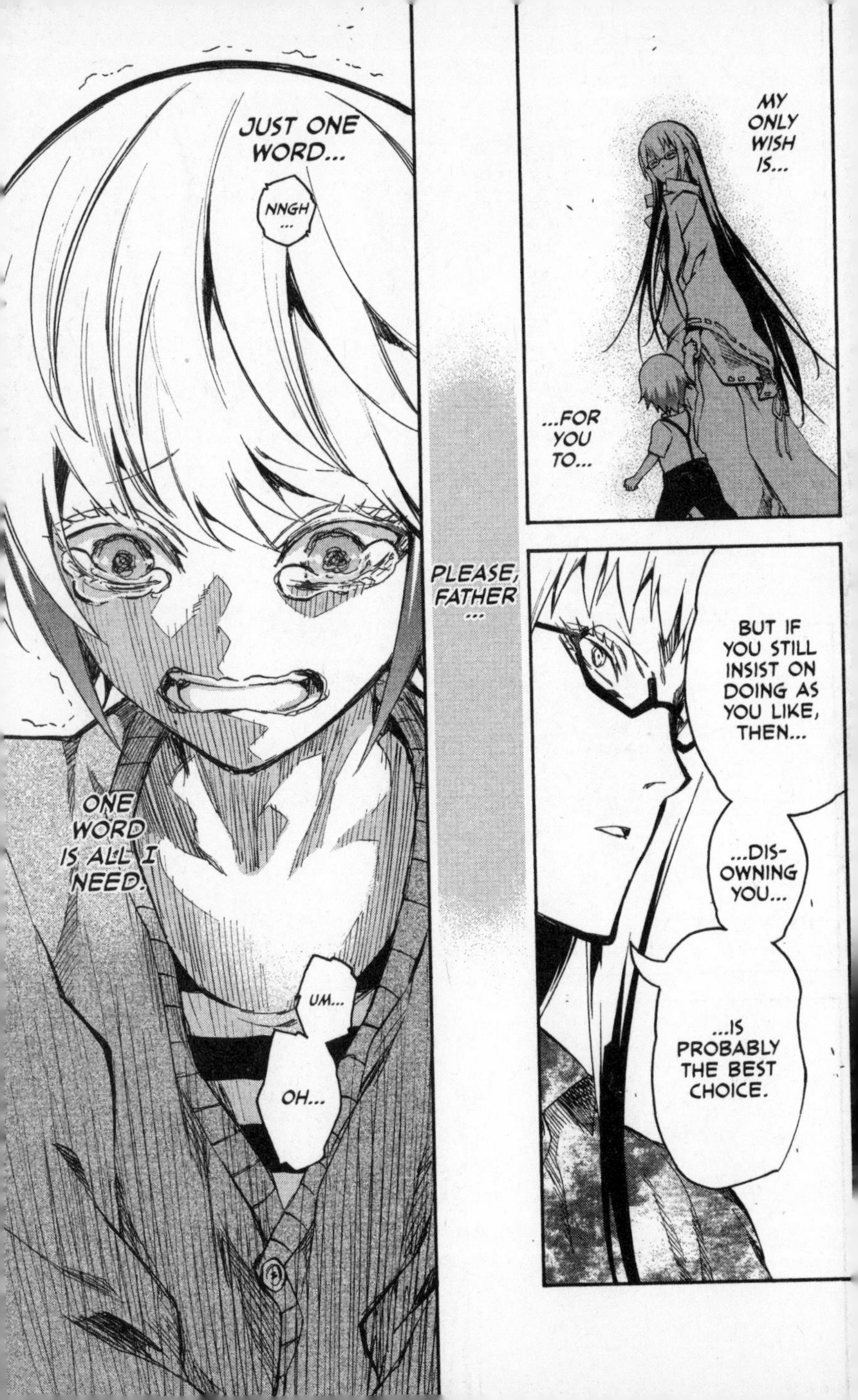
MY ONLY WISH IS...
...FOR YOU TO...
BUT IF YOU STILL INSIST ON DOING AS YOU LIKE, THEN...
...DIS-OWNING YOU...
...IS PROBABLY THE BEST CHOICE.
PLEASE, FATHER...
JUST ONE WORD...
NNGH...
ONE WORD IS ALL I NEED.
UM...
OH...

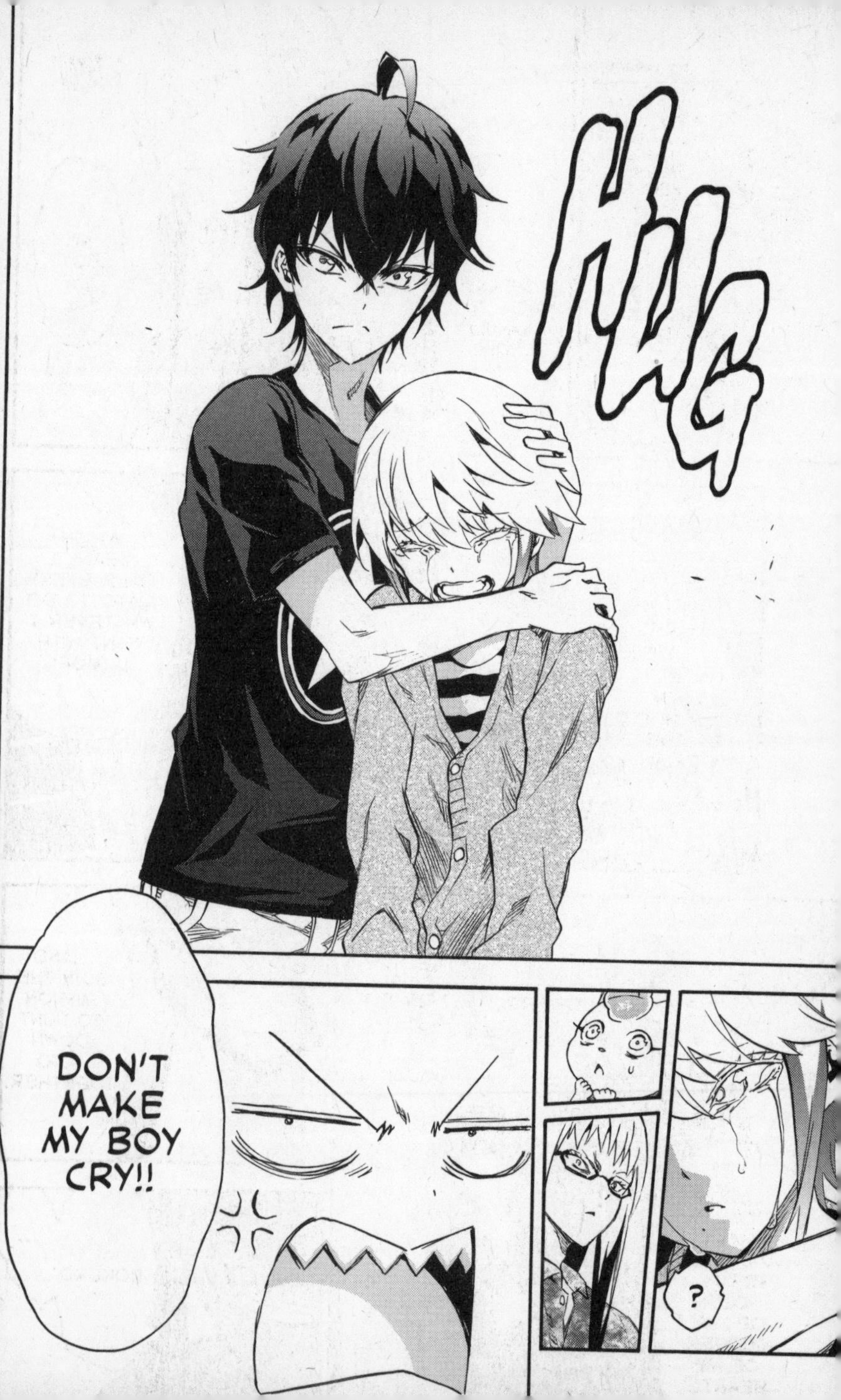
HUG
?
DON'T MAKE MY BOY CRY!!

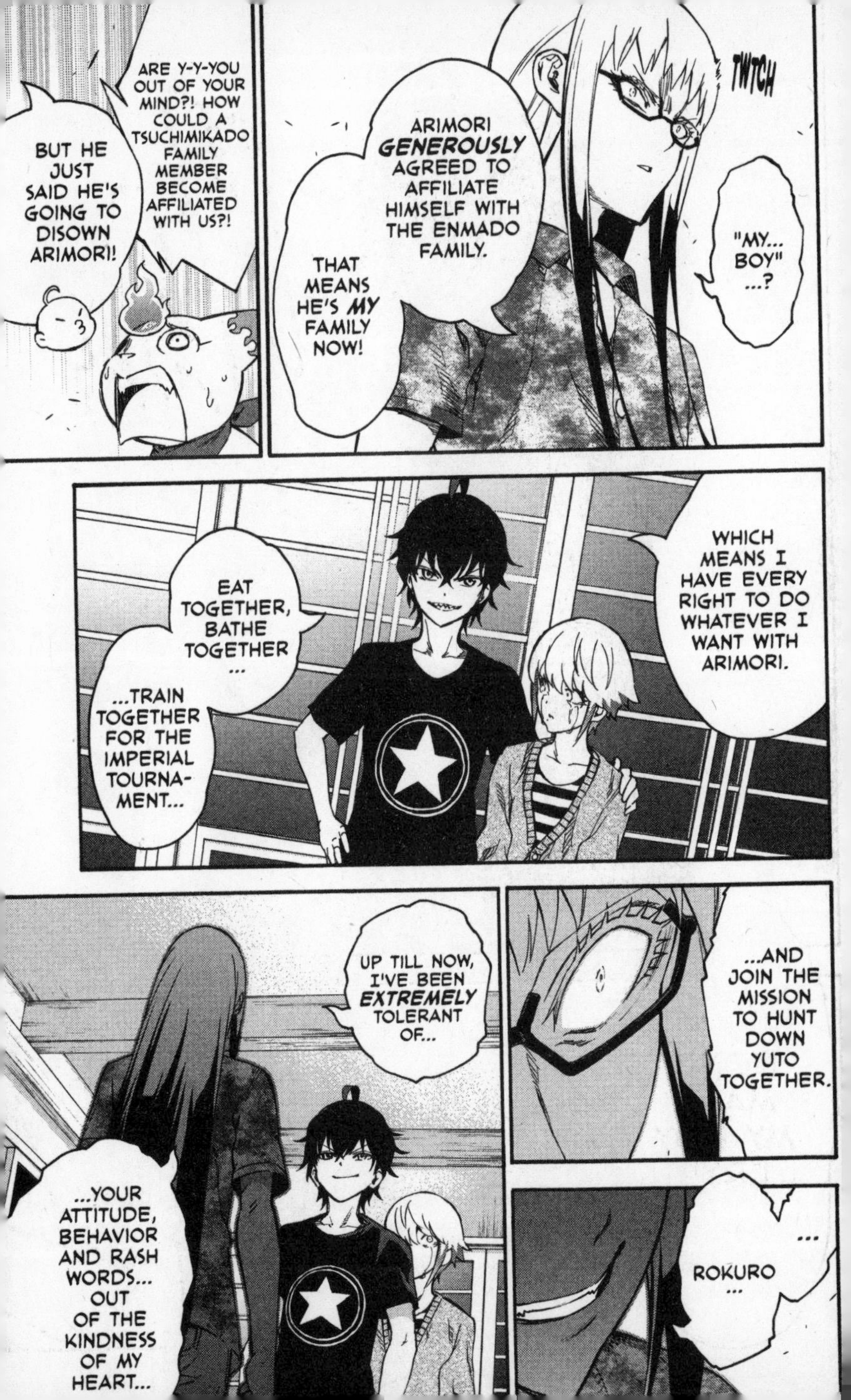
TWTCH
"MY... BOY" ...?
ARIMORI *GENEROUSLY* AGREED TO AFFILIATE HIMSELF WITH THE ENMADO FAMILY.
THAT MEANS HE'S *MY* FAMILY NOW!
ARE Y-Y-YOU OUT OF YOUR MIND?! HOW COULD A TSUCHIMIKADO FAMILY MEMBER BECOME AFFILIATED WITH US?!
BUT HE JUST SAID HE'S GOING TO DISOWN ARIMORI!
WHICH MEANS I HAVE EVERY RIGHT TO DO WHATEVER I WANT WITH ARIMORI.
EAT TOGETHER, BATHE TOGETHER...
...TRAIN TOGETHER FOR THE IMPERIAL TOURNA-MENT...
...AND JOIN THE MISSION TO HUNT DOWN YUTO TOGETHER.
... ROKURO ...
UP TILL NOW, I'VE BEEN *EXTREMELY* TOLERANT OF...
...YOUR ATTITUDE, BEHAVIOR AND RASH WORDS... OUT OF THE KINDNESS OF MY HEART...

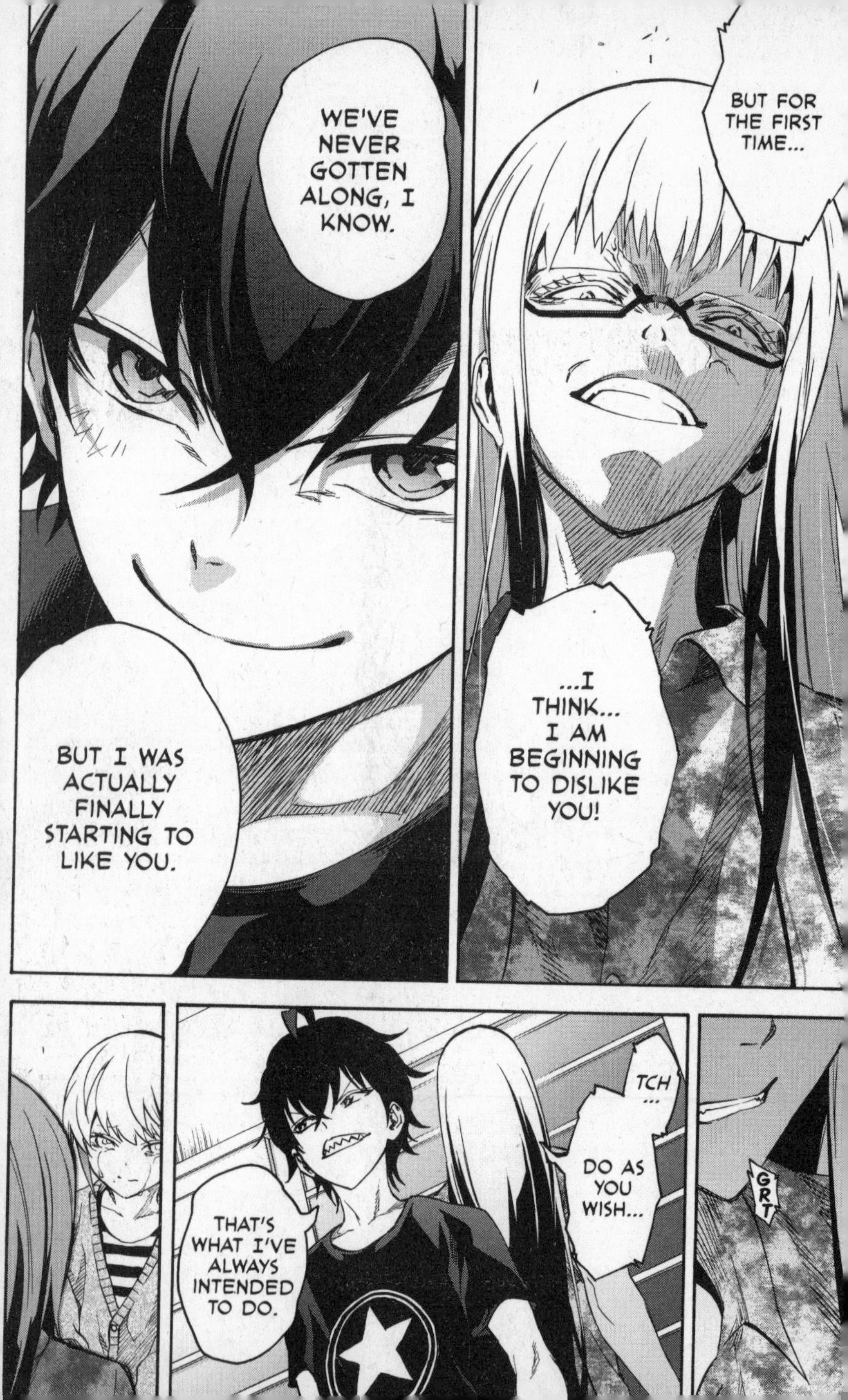
BUT FOR THE FIRST TIME...
...I THINK... I AM BEGINNING TO DISLIKE YOU!
WE'VE NEVER GOTTEN ALONG, I KNOW.
BUT I WAS ACTUALLY FINALLY STARTING TO LIKE YOU.
GRT
TCH...
DO AS YOU WISH...
THAT'S WHAT I'VE ALWAYS INTENDED TO DO.

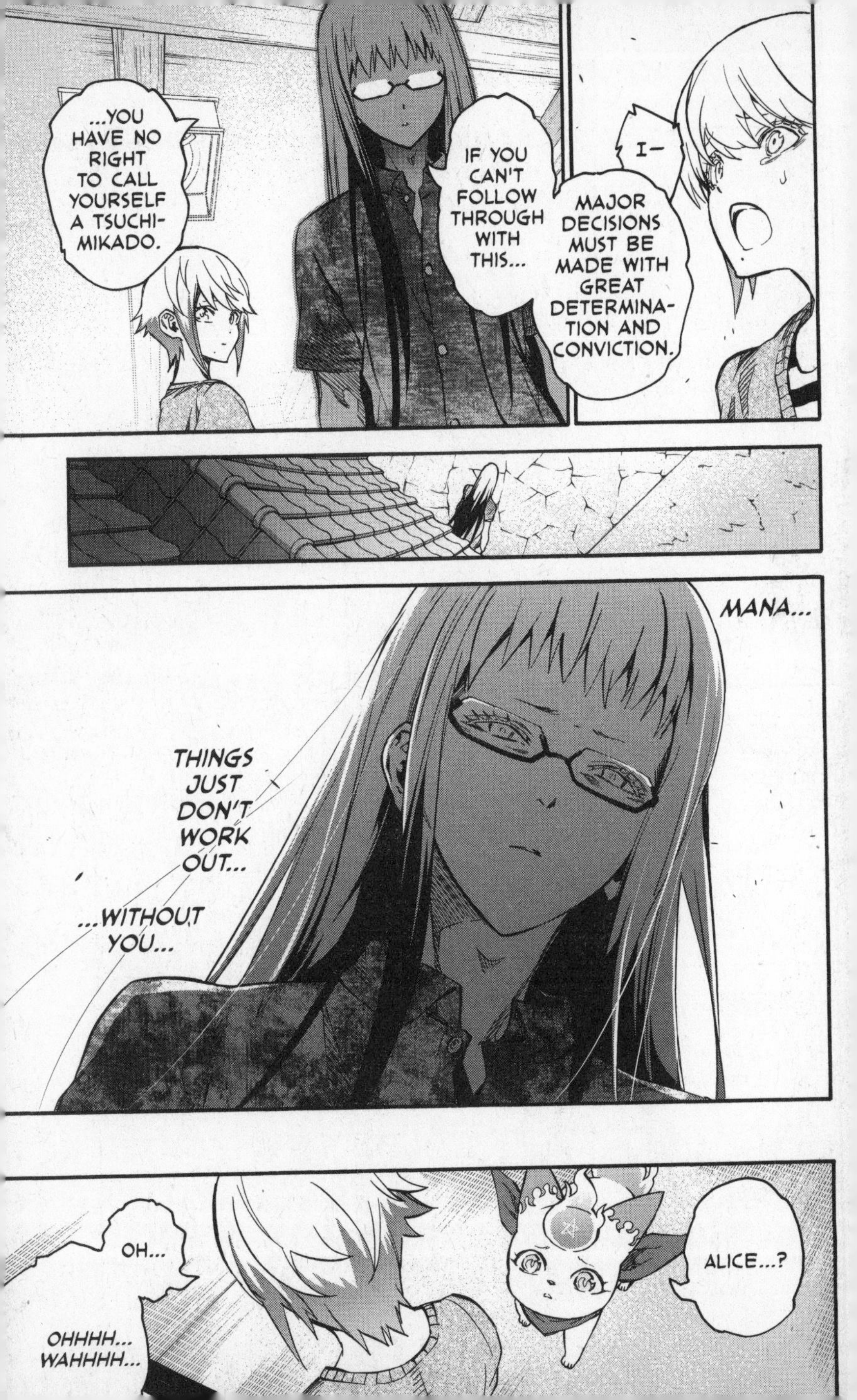
I—
MAJOR DECISIONS MUST BE MADE WITH GREAT DETERMINATION AND CONVICTION.
IF YOU CAN'T FOLLOW THROUGH WITH THIS...
...YOU HAVE NO RIGHT TO CALL YOURSELF A TSUCHIMIKADO.
MANA...
THINGS JUST DON'T WORK OUT...
...WITHOUT YOU...
ALICE...?
OH...
OHHHH... WAHHHH...

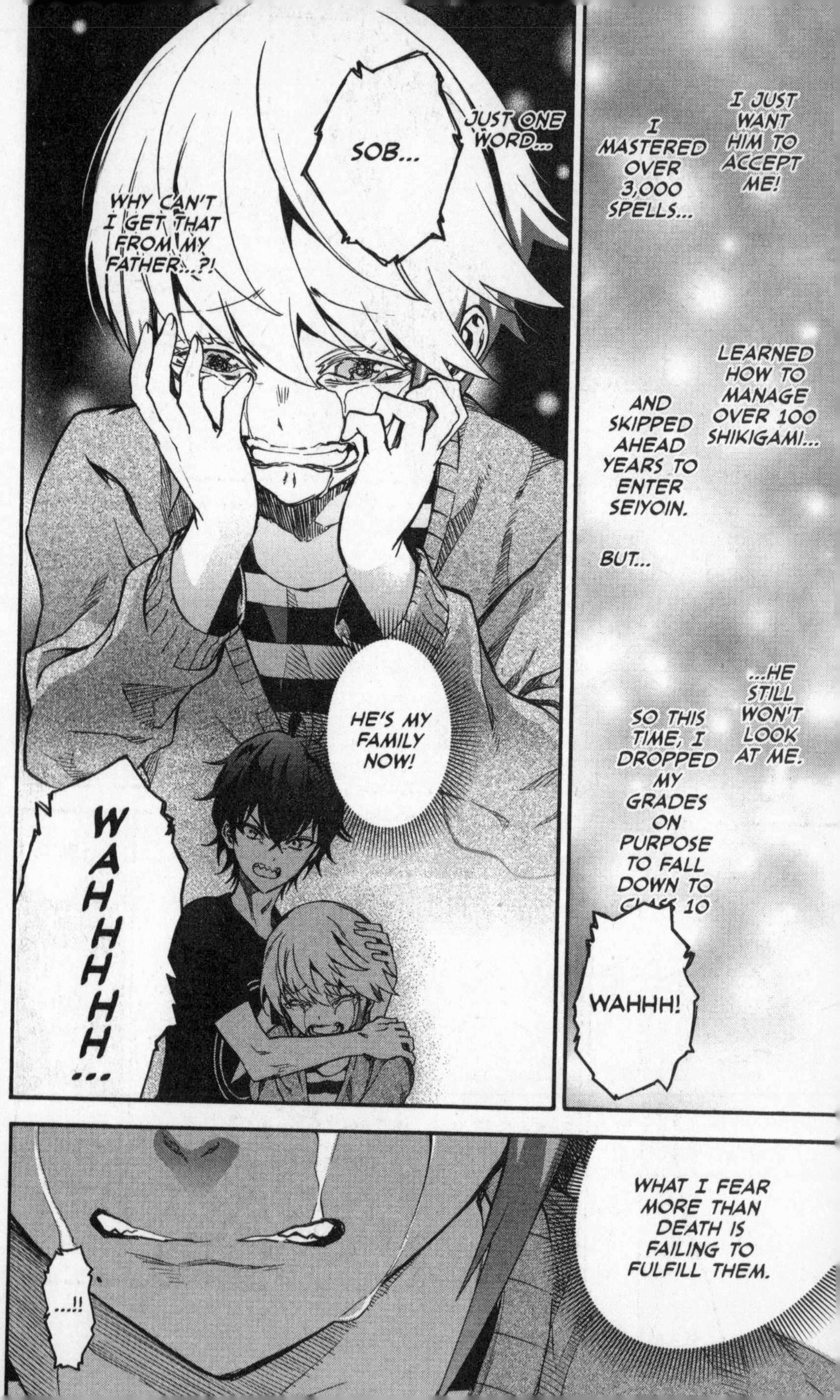
I JUST WANT HIM TO ACCEPT ME!
I MASTERED OVER 3,000 SPELLS...
LEARNED HOW TO MANAGE OVER 100 SHIKIGAMI...
AND SKIPPED AHEAD YEARS TO ENTER SEIYOIN.
BUT...
...HE STILL WON'T LOOK AT ME.
SO THIS TIME, I DROPPED MY GRADES ON PURPOSE TO FALL DOWN TO CLASS 10
WAHHH!
JUST ONE WORD...
SOB...
WHY CAN'T I GET THAT FROM MY FATHER...?!
HE'S MY FAMILY NOW!
WAHHHHH...
WHAT I FEAR MORE THAN DEATH IS FAILING TO FULFILL THEM.
...!!

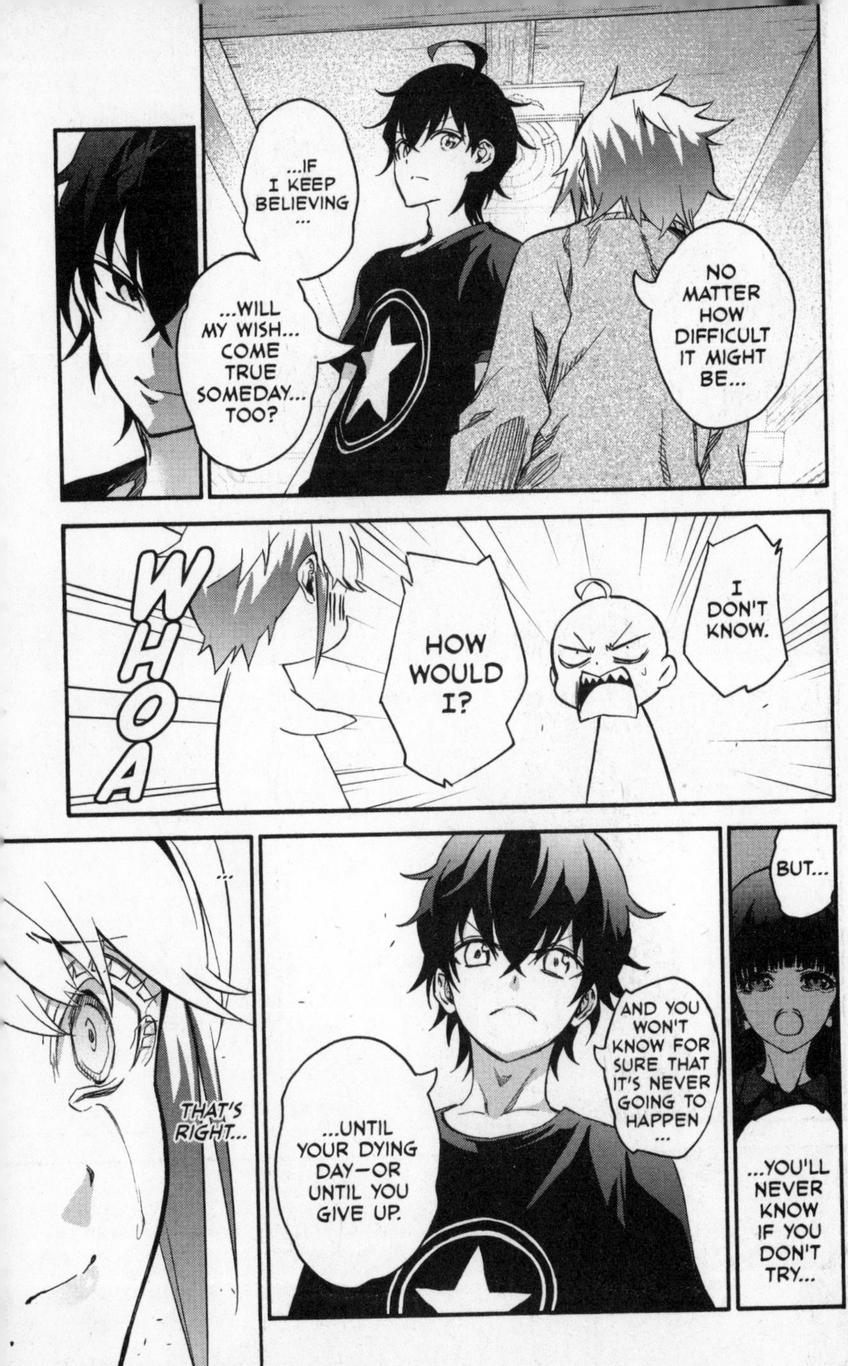

NO MATTER HOW DIFFICULT IT MIGHT BE...
...IF I KEEP BELIEVING...
...WILL MY WISH... COME TRUE SOMEDAY... TOO?
I DON'T KNOW.
HOW WOULD I?
WHOA
BUT...
...YOU'LL NEVER KNOW IF YOU DON'T TRY...
AND YOU WON'T KNOW FOR SURE THAT IT'S NEVER GOING TO HAPPEN...
...UNTIL YOUR DYING DAY—OR UNTIL YOU GIVE UP.
...
THAT'S RIGHT...

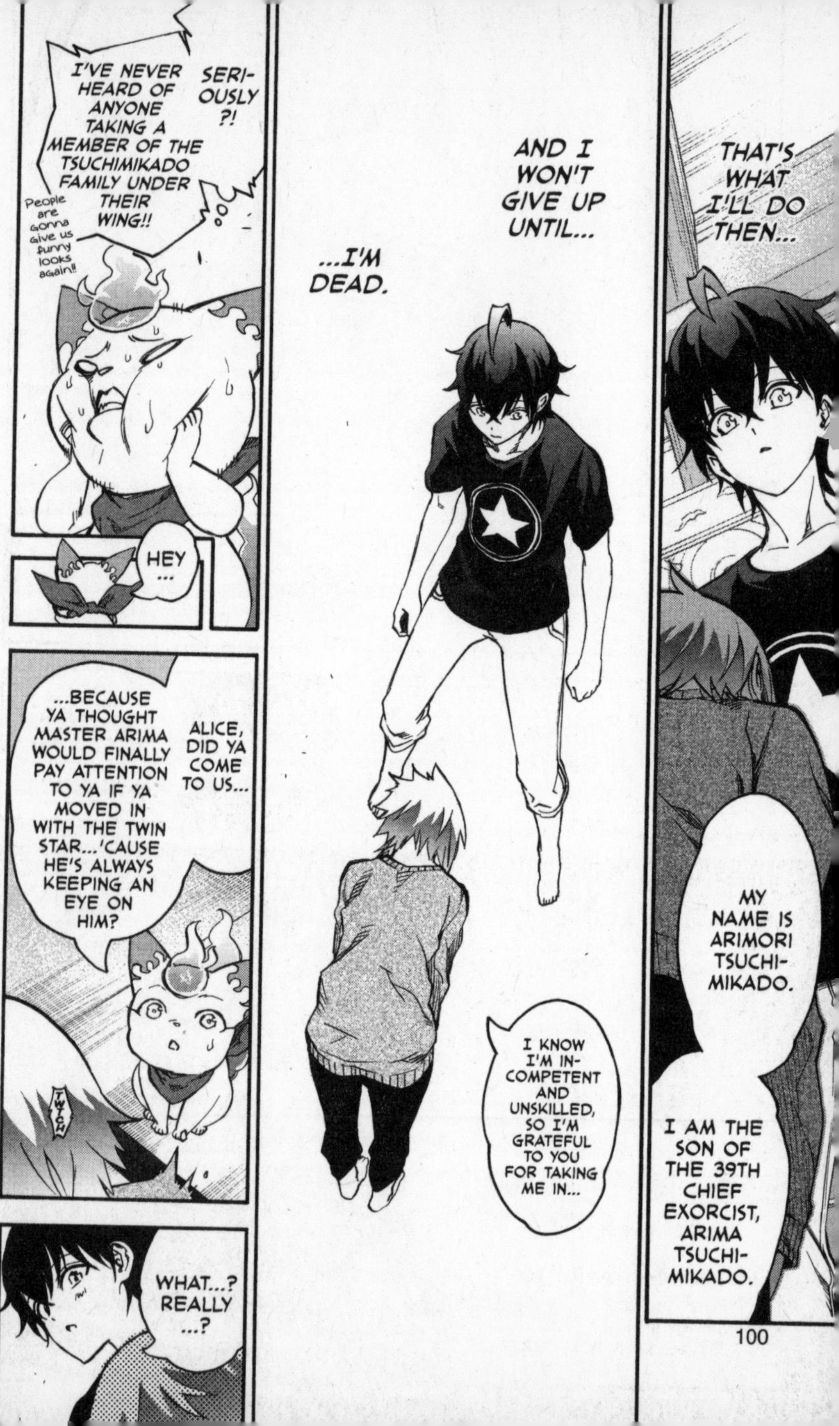
THAT'S WHAT I'LL DO THEN...
MY NAME IS ARIMORI TSUCHIMIKADO.
I AM THE SON OF THE 39TH CHIEF EXORCIST, ARIMA TSUCHIMIKADO.
AND I WON'T GIVE UP UNTIL...
...I'M DEAD.
I KNOW I'M INCOMPETENT AND UNSKILLED, SO I'M GRATEFUL TO YOU FOR TAKING ME IN...
SERIOUSLY?!
I'VE NEVER HEARD OF ANYONE TAKING A MEMBER OF THE TSUCHIMIKADO FAMILY UNDER THEIR WING!!
People are gonna give us funny looks again!!
HEY...
ALICE, DID YA COME TO US...
...BECAUSE YA THOUGHT MASTER ARIMA WOULD FINALLY PAY ATTENTION TO YA IF YA MOVED IN WITH THE TWIN STAR...'CAUSE HE'S ALWAYS KEEPING AN EYE ON HIM?
TWITCH
WHAT...? REALLY...?

·····!!!

WHO ARE YOU CALLING A DADDY'S BOY?!

HEY !!

I DON'T WANT TO TURN INTO A DADDY'S BOY LIKE HIM.

MAYBE I SHOULDN'T LET HIM STAY IN MY HOUSE.

YOU JERK !!

HE JUST NEEDS TIME FOR THINGS TO GROW, THAT'S ALL...

OH, HE'S A BOY ALL RIGHT.

YA REALLY ARE SO CUTE, ALICE. I CAN'T HELP THINKIN' THAT YER ACTUALLY A GIRL.

**Enmado Family Roster**
Family Head: 1
Shikigami: 1
Affiliated Member (Lodger): 1

# Qnyoritsuro!

Question Corner

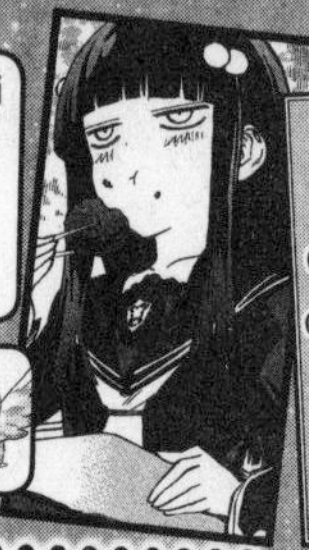

**Q** Benio loves ohagi dumplings, but does she like *yatsuhashi* as well?
(From Kinako Adashino)

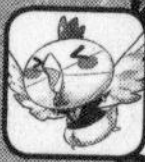

**A** She does.

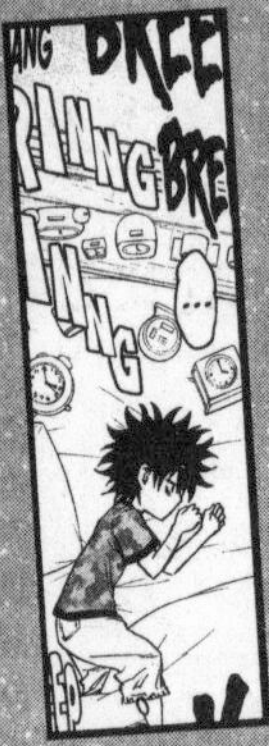

**Q** Why are there so many clocks in Rokuro's room?
(From Ohagi Dumpling Lover)

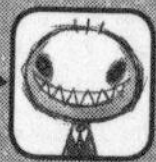

**A** He can't wake up with just a couple of alarm clocks, so he started buying more of them, to the point where people began to think his hobby was alarm clock collecting.

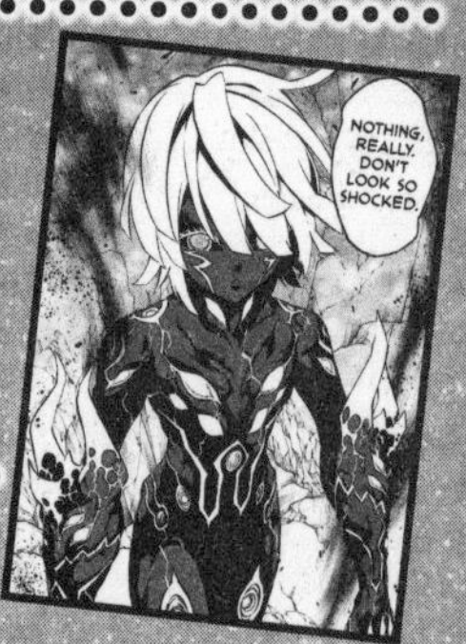
NOTHING, REALLY. DON'T LOOK SO SHOCKED.

**Q** Which character was the most difficult to draw?
(From Cheese)

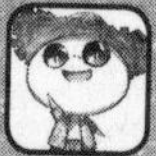

**A** Yuto in his Dark Embryo form. I'm amazed that the anime staff managed to animate him...!

**Q** A Basara appeared in the novel *Twin Star Exorcists: Heavenly Bond of the Young Tiger*. Could you tell me her name and what she looks like? (Personally, I think her name is Chikura, which, by the way, is located near Minamiboso City.)
(From Reito Oyama)

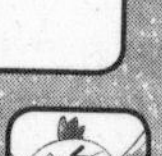

**A** Something like this... I borrowed the name you came up with.

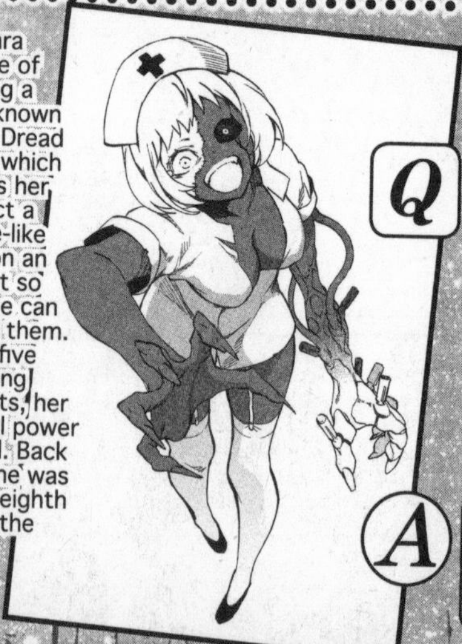

A Basara capable of wielding a curse known as the Dread Curse, which enables her to inflict a zombie-like state on an exorcist so that she can control them. Of the five ying-yang elements, her spiritual power is Metal. Back then, she was ranked eighth among the Basara.

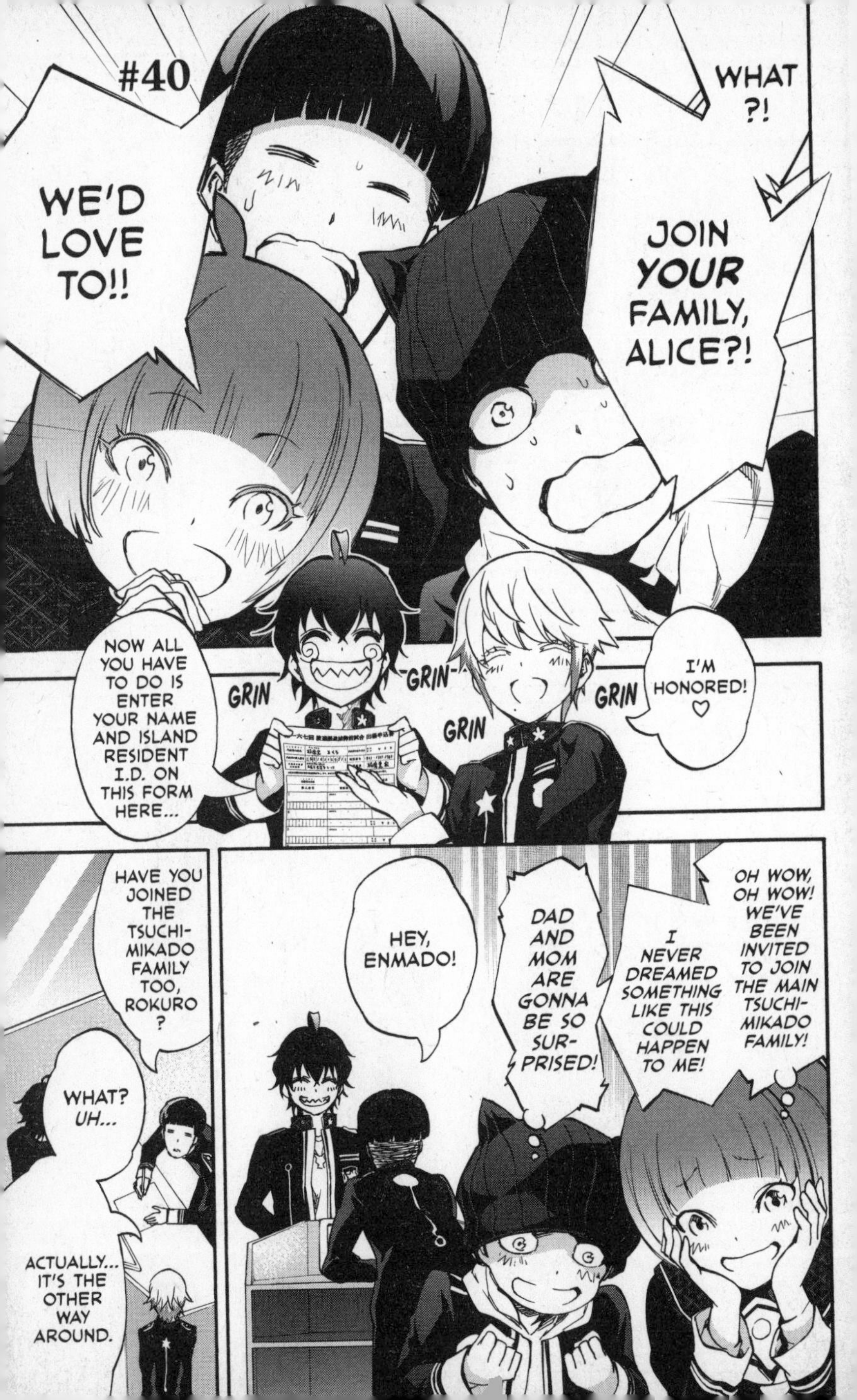
#40
WHAT ?!
JOIN YOUR FAMILY, ALICE?!
WE'D LOVE TO!!
I'M HONORED! ♡
GRIN
GRIN
-GRIN-
GRIN
NOW ALL YOU HAVE TO DO IS ENTER YOUR NAME AND ISLAND RESIDENT I.D. ON THIS FORM HERE...
OH WOW, OH WOW! WE'VE BEEN INVITED TO JOIN THE MAIN TSUCHI-MIKADO FAMILY!
I NEVER DREAMED SOMETHING LIKE THIS COULD HAPPEN TO ME!
DAD AND MOM ARE GONNA BE SO SUR-PRISED!
HEY, ENMADO!
HAVE YOU JOINED THE TSUCHI-MIKADO FAMILY TOO, ROKURO ?
WHAT? UH...
ACTUALLY... IT'S THE OTHER WAY AROUND.

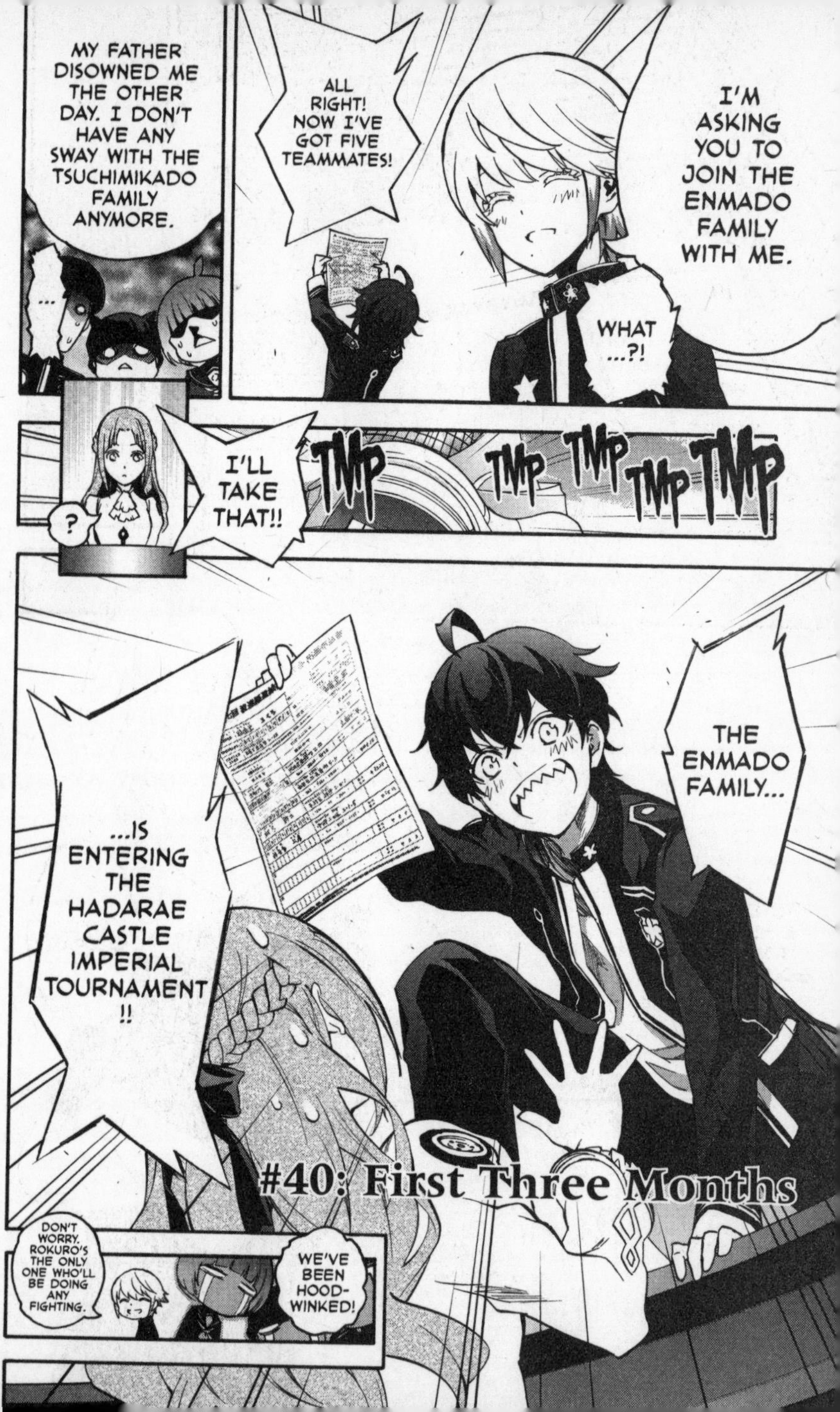
I'M ASKING YOU TO JOIN THE ENMADO FAMILY WITH ME.
WHAT ...?!
ALL RIGHT! NOW I'VE GOT FIVE TEAMMATES!
MY FATHER DISOWNED ME THE OTHER DAY. I DON'T HAVE ANY SWAY WITH THE TSUCHIMIKADO FAMILY ANYMORE.
...
TMP TMP TMP TMP TMP
I'LL TAKE THAT!!
?
THE ENMADO FAMILY...
...IS ENTERING THE HADARAE CASTLE IMPERIAL TOURNAMENT!!
#40: First Three Months
WE'VE BEEN HOOD-WINKED!
DON'T WORRY. ROKURO'S THE ONLY ONE WHO'LL BE DOING ANY FIGHTING.

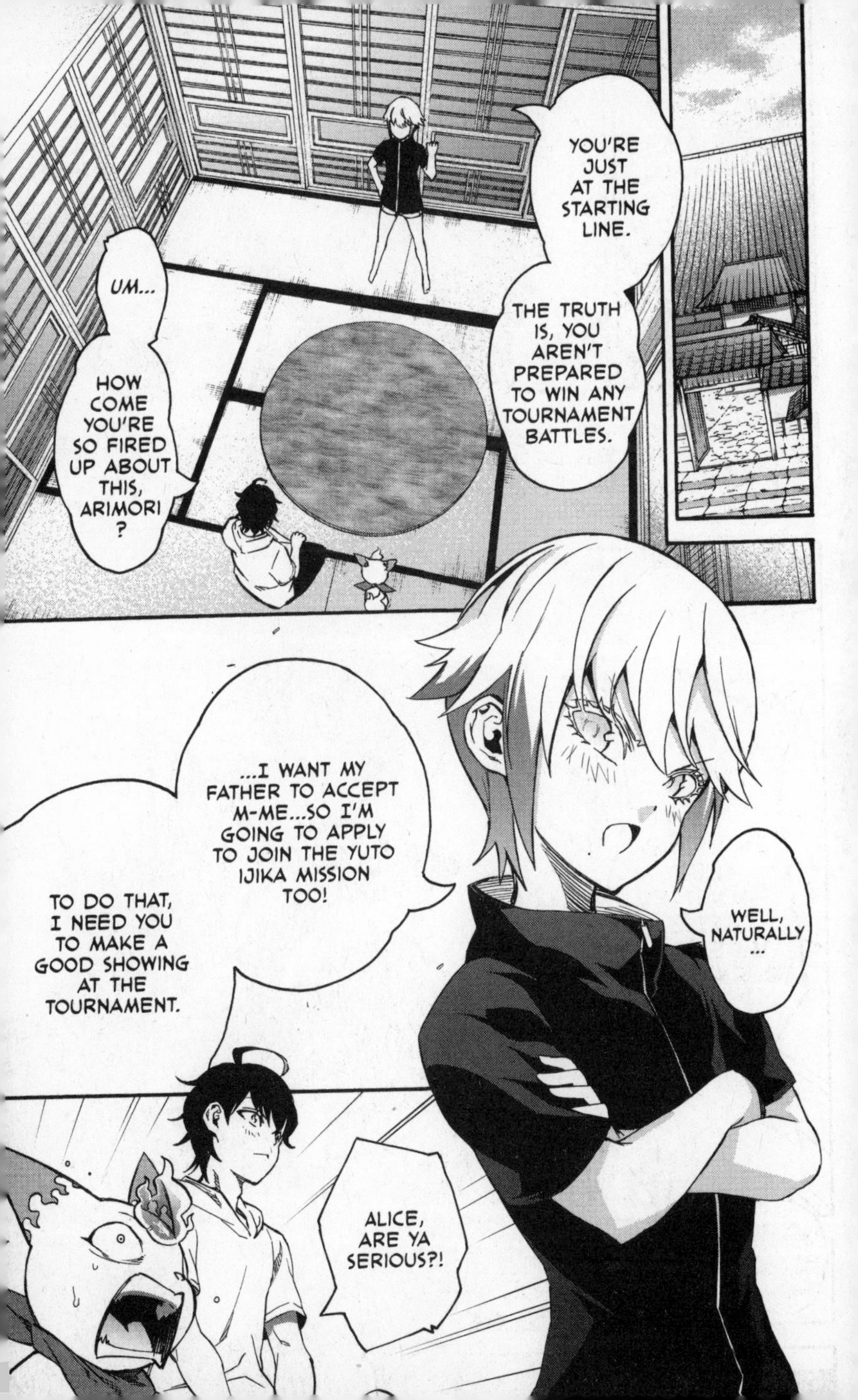
YOU'RE JUST AT THE STARTING LINE.
THE TRUTH IS, YOU AREN'T PREPARED TO WIN ANY TOURNAMENT BATTLES.
UM...
HOW COME YOU'RE SO FIRED UP ABOUT THIS, ARIMORI?
WELL, NATURALLY...
...I WANT MY FATHER TO ACCEPT M-ME...SO I'M GOING TO APPLY TO JOIN THE YUTO IJIKA MISSION TOO!
TO DO THAT, I NEED YOU TO MAKE A GOOD SHOWING AT THE TOURNAMENT.
ALICE, ARE YA SERIOUS?!

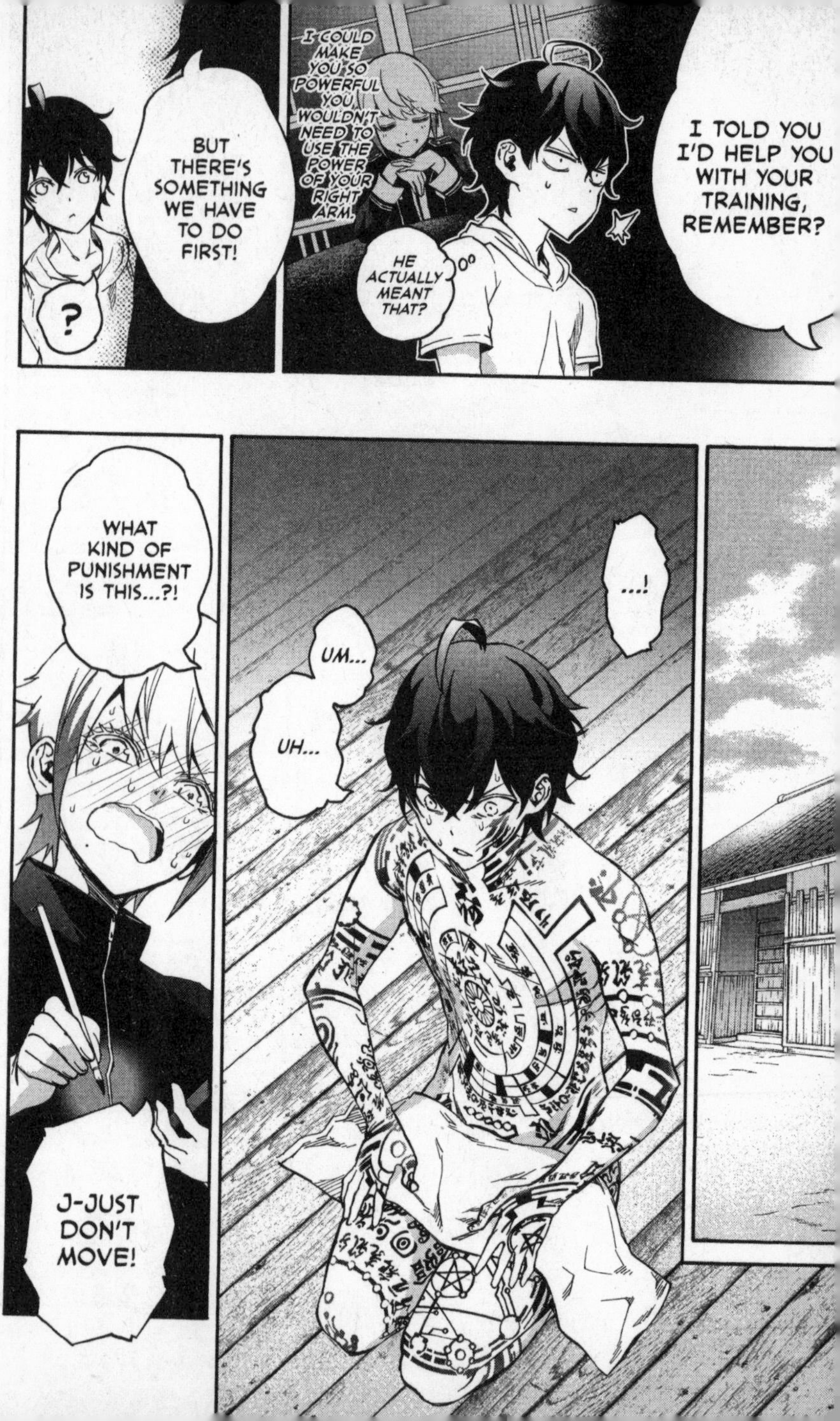
I TOLD YOU I'D HELP YOU WITH YOUR TRAINING, REMEMBER?
I COULD MAKE YOU SO POWERFUL YOU WOULDN'T NEED TO USE THE POWER OF YOUR RIGHT ARM.
HE ACTUALLY MEANT THAT?
BUT THERE'S SOMETHING WE HAVE TO DO FIRST!
?
...!
UM...
UH...
WHAT KIND OF PUNISHMENT IS THIS...?!
J-JUST DON'T MOVE!

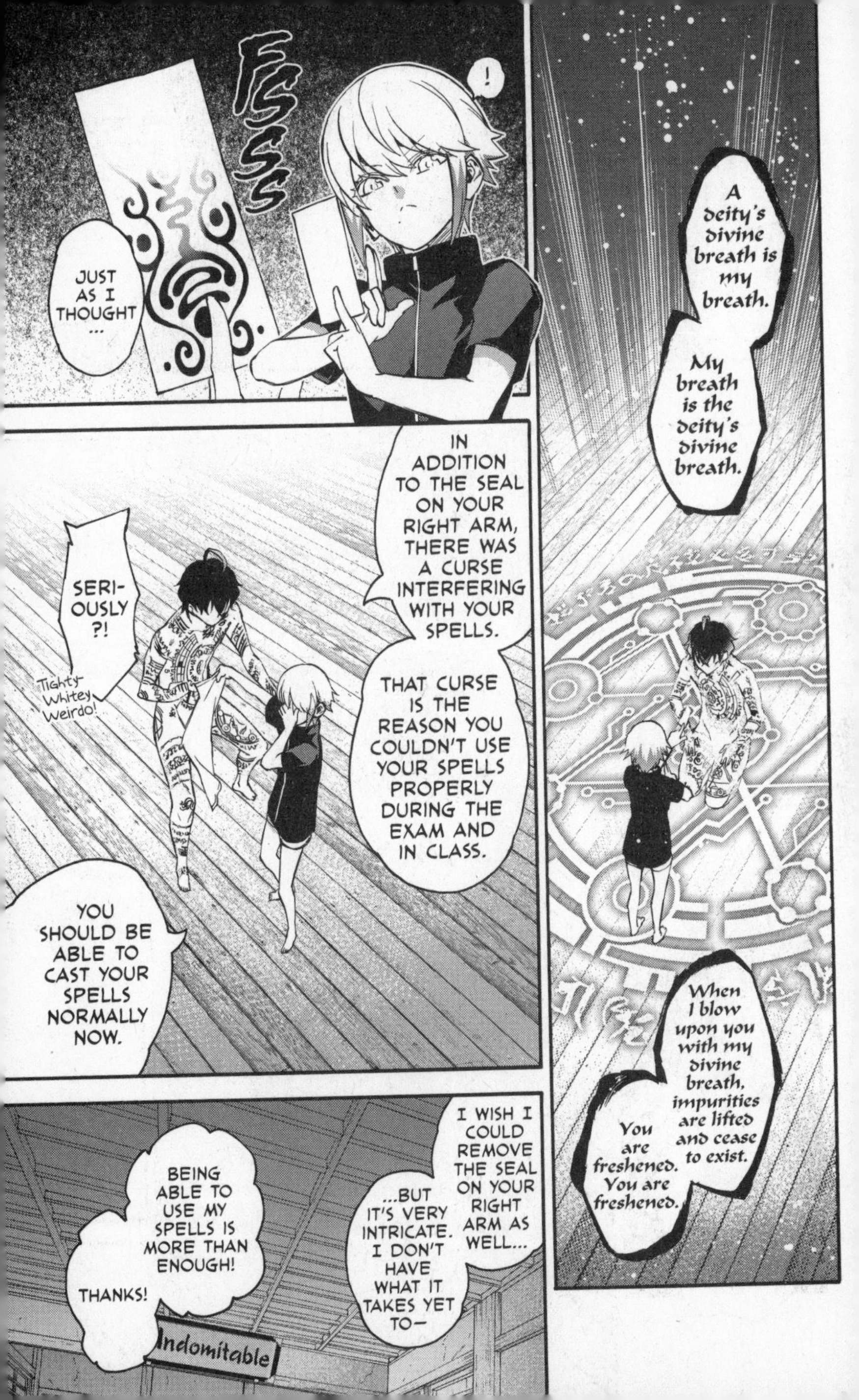
A deity's divine breath is my breath.
My breath is the deity's divine breath.
When I blow upon you with my divine breath, impurities are lifted and cease to exist.
You are freshened. You are freshened.
FSSS
!
JUST AS I THOUGHT...
IN ADDITION TO THE SEAL ON YOUR RIGHT ARM, THERE WAS A CURSE INTERFERING WITH YOUR SPELLS.
THAT CURSE IS THE REASON YOU COULDN'T USE YOUR SPELLS PROPERLY DURING THE EXAM AND IN CLASS.
SERIOUSLY?!
Tighty-Whitey Weirdo!
YOU SHOULD BE ABLE TO CAST YOUR SPELLS NORMALLY NOW.
I WISH I COULD REMOVE THE SEAL ON YOUR RIGHT ARM AS WELL...
...BUT IT'S VERY INTRICATE. I DON'T HAVE WHAT IT TAKES YET TO—
BEING ABLE TO USE MY SPELLS IS MORE THAN ENOUGH!
THANKS!
Indomitable

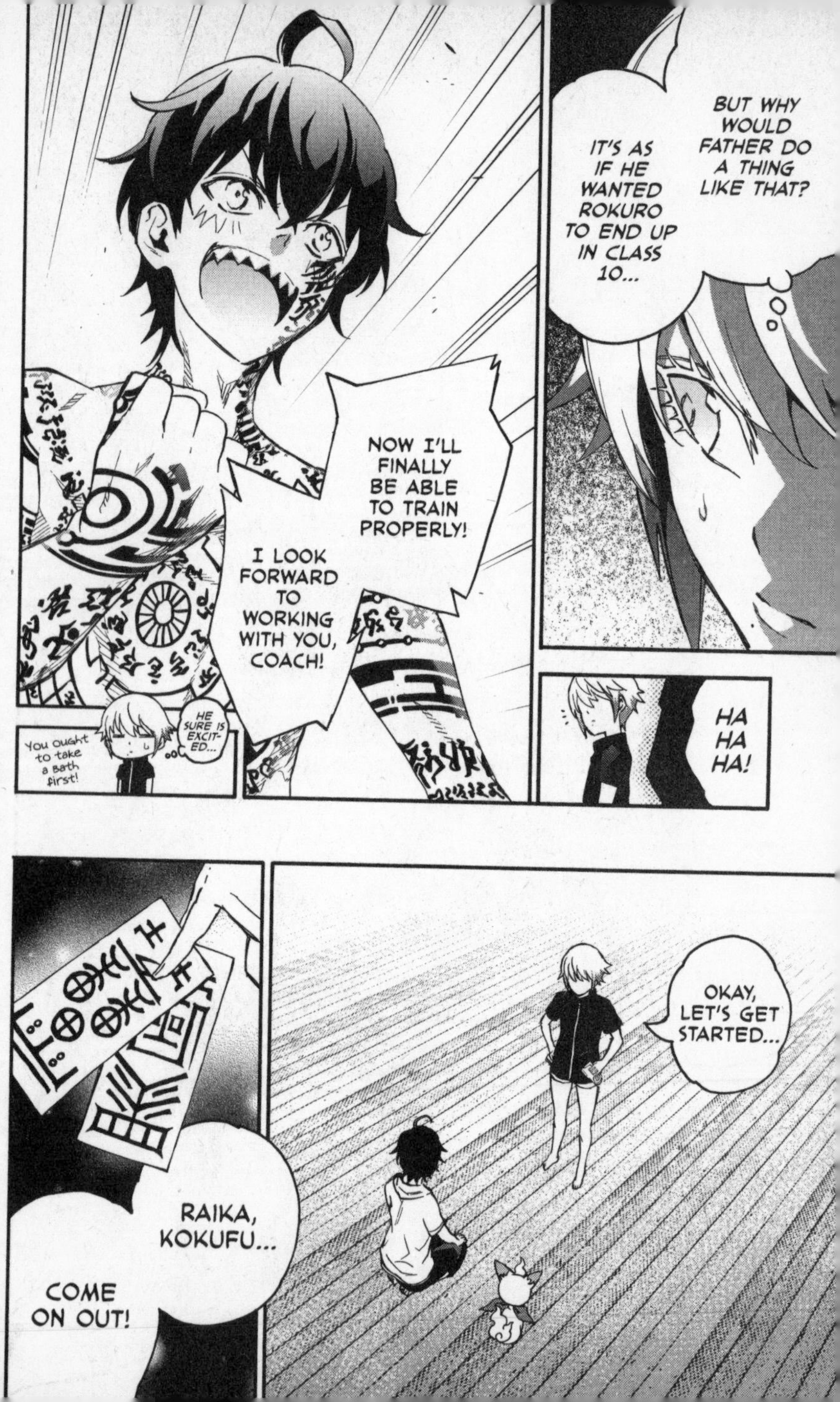
BUT WHY WOULD FATHER DO A THING LIKE THAT?
IT'S AS IF HE WANTED ROKURO TO END UP IN CLASS 10...
HA HA HA!
NOW I'LL FINALLY BE ABLE TO TRAIN PROPERLY!
I LOOK FORWARD TO WORKING WITH YOU, COACH!
HE SURE IS EXCITED...
You ought to take a bath first!
OKAY, LET'S GET STARTED...
RAIKA, KOKUFU...
COME ON OUT!

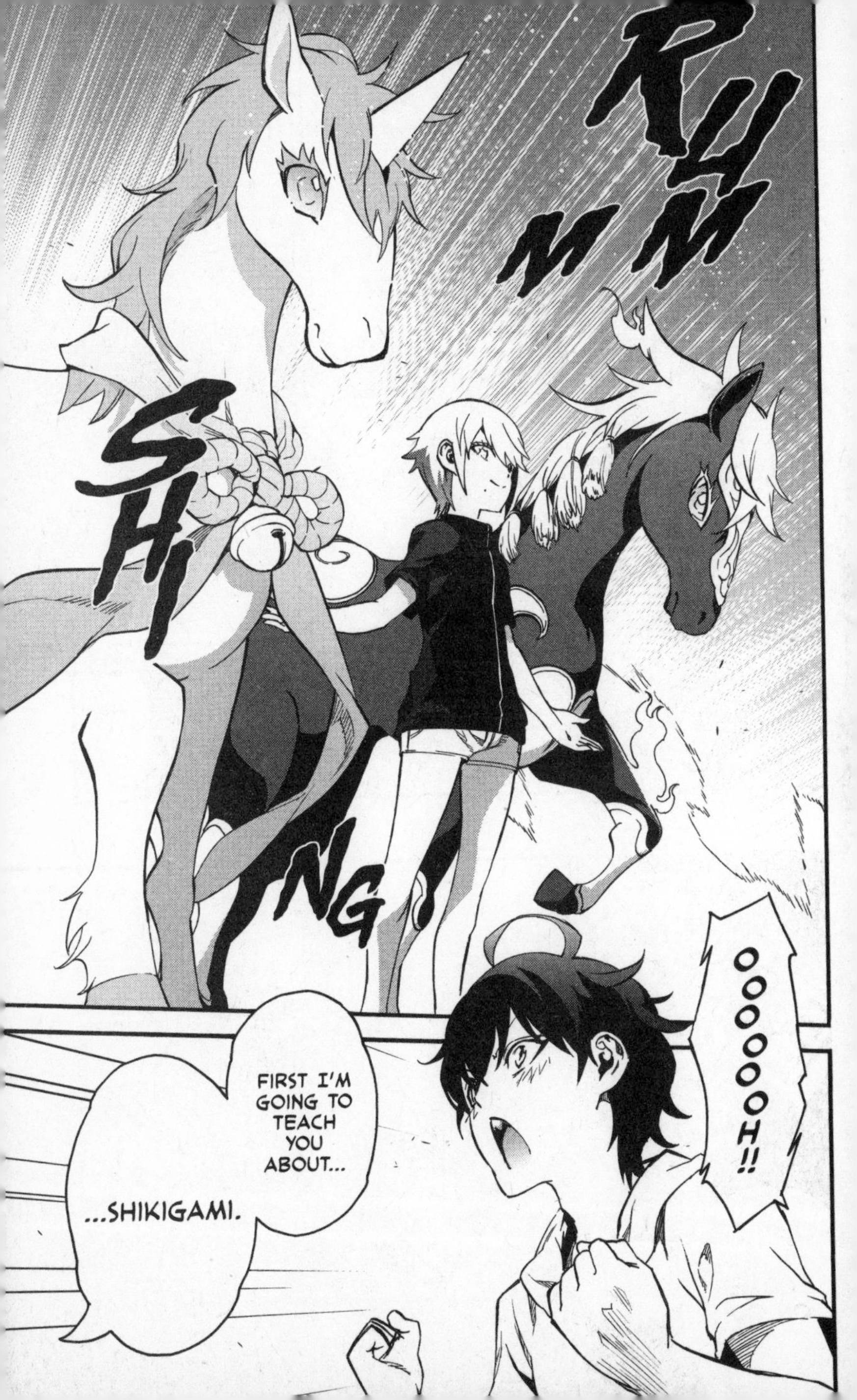
RUMMM
SHING
OOOOOOOH!!
FIRST I'M GOING TO TEACH YOU ABOUT...
...SHIKIGAMI.

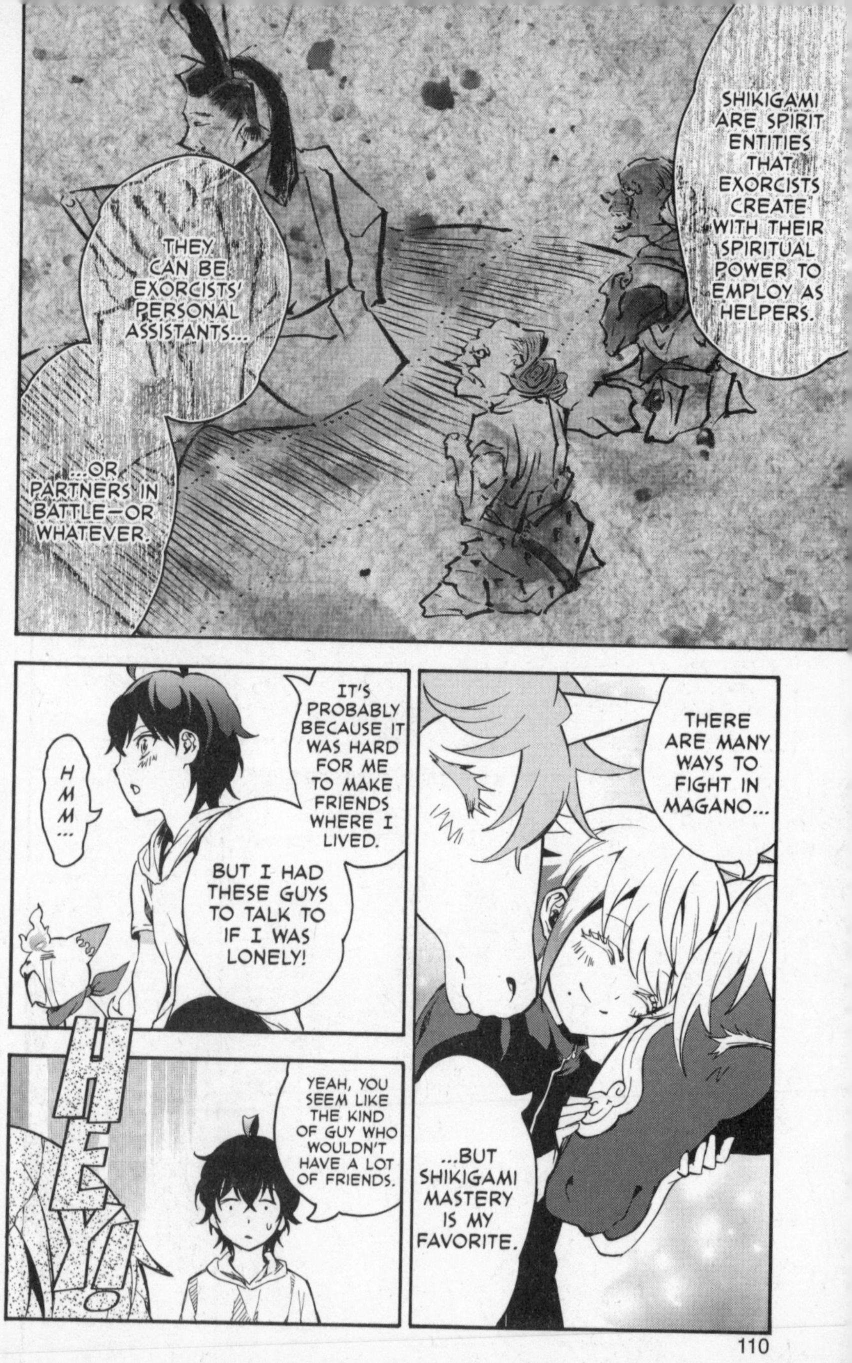
SHIKIGAMI ARE SPIRIT ENTITIES THAT EXORCISTS CREATE WITH THEIR SPIRITUAL POWER TO EMPLOY AS HELPERS.
THEY CAN BE EXORCISTS' PERSONAL ASSISTANTS...
...OR PARTNERS IN BATTLE—OR WHATEVER.
THERE ARE MANY WAYS TO FIGHT IN MAGANO...
...BUT SHIKIGAMI MASTERY IS MY FAVORITE.
IT'S PROBABLY BECAUSE IT WAS HARD FOR ME TO MAKE FRIENDS WHERE I LIVED.
BUT I HAD THESE GUYS TO TALK TO IF I WAS LONELY!
HMMM...
YEAH, YOU SEEM LIKE THE KIND OF GUY WHO WOULDN'T HAVE A LOT OF FRIENDS.
HEY!

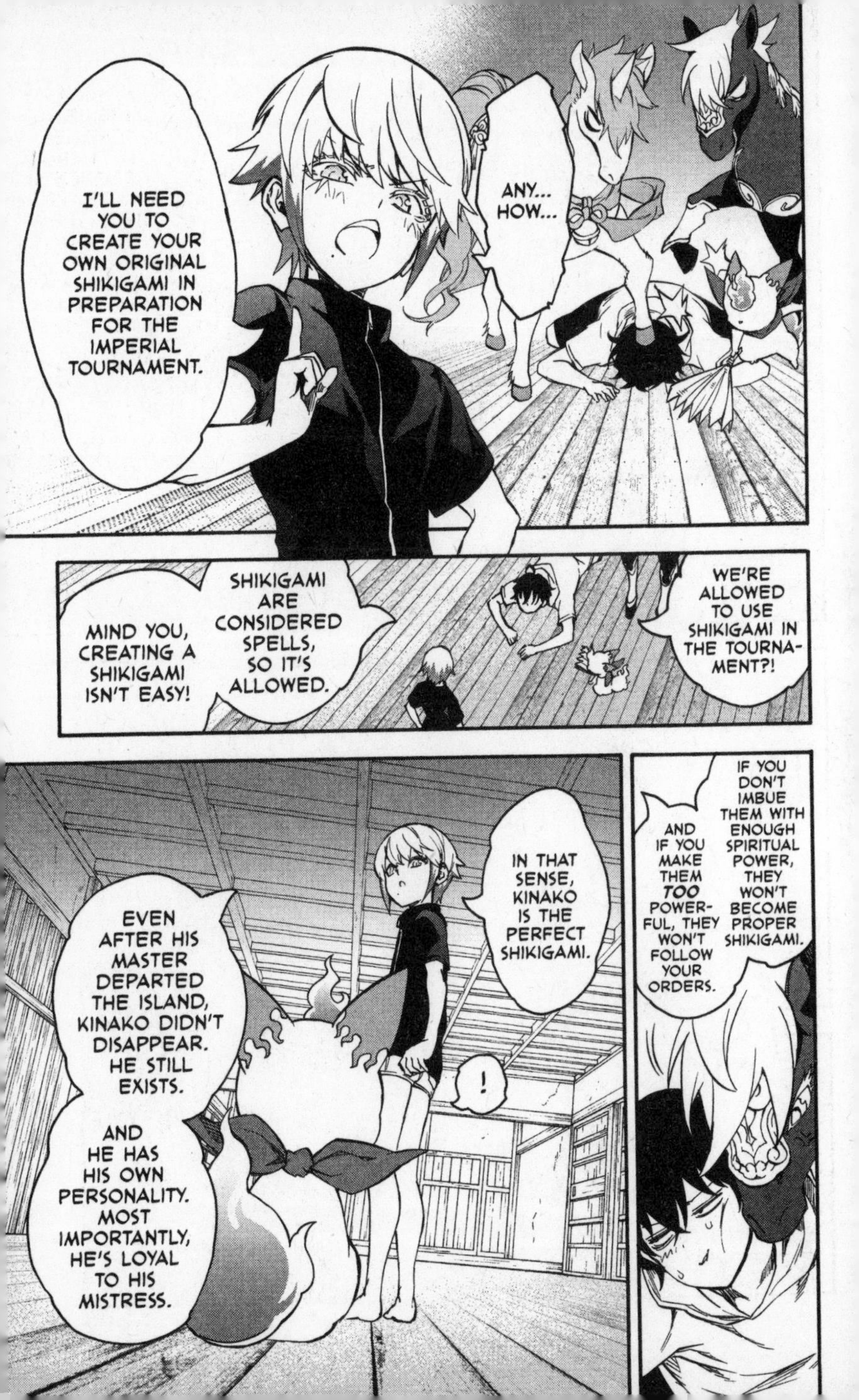
ANY... HOW...
I'LL NEED YOU TO CREATE YOUR OWN ORIGINAL SHIKIGAMI IN PREPARATION FOR THE IMPERIAL TOURNAMENT.
WE'RE ALLOWED TO USE SHIKIGAMI IN THE TOURNA-MENT?!
SHIKIGAMI ARE CONSIDERED SPELLS, SO IT'S ALLOWED.
MIND YOU, CREATING A SHIKIGAMI ISN'T EASY!
IF YOU DON'T IMBUE THEM WITH ENOUGH SPIRITUAL POWER, THEY WON'T BECOME PROPER SHIKIGAMI.
AND IF YOU MAKE THEM *TOO* POWER-FUL, THEY WON'T FOLLOW YOUR ORDERS.
IN THAT SENSE, KINAKO IS THE PERFECT SHIKIGAMI.
!
EVEN AFTER HIS MASTER DEPARTED THE ISLAND, KINAKO DIDN'T DISAPPEAR. HE STILL EXISTS.
AND HE HAS HIS OWN PERSONALITY. MOST IMPORTANTLY, HE'S LOYAL TO HIS MISTRESS.

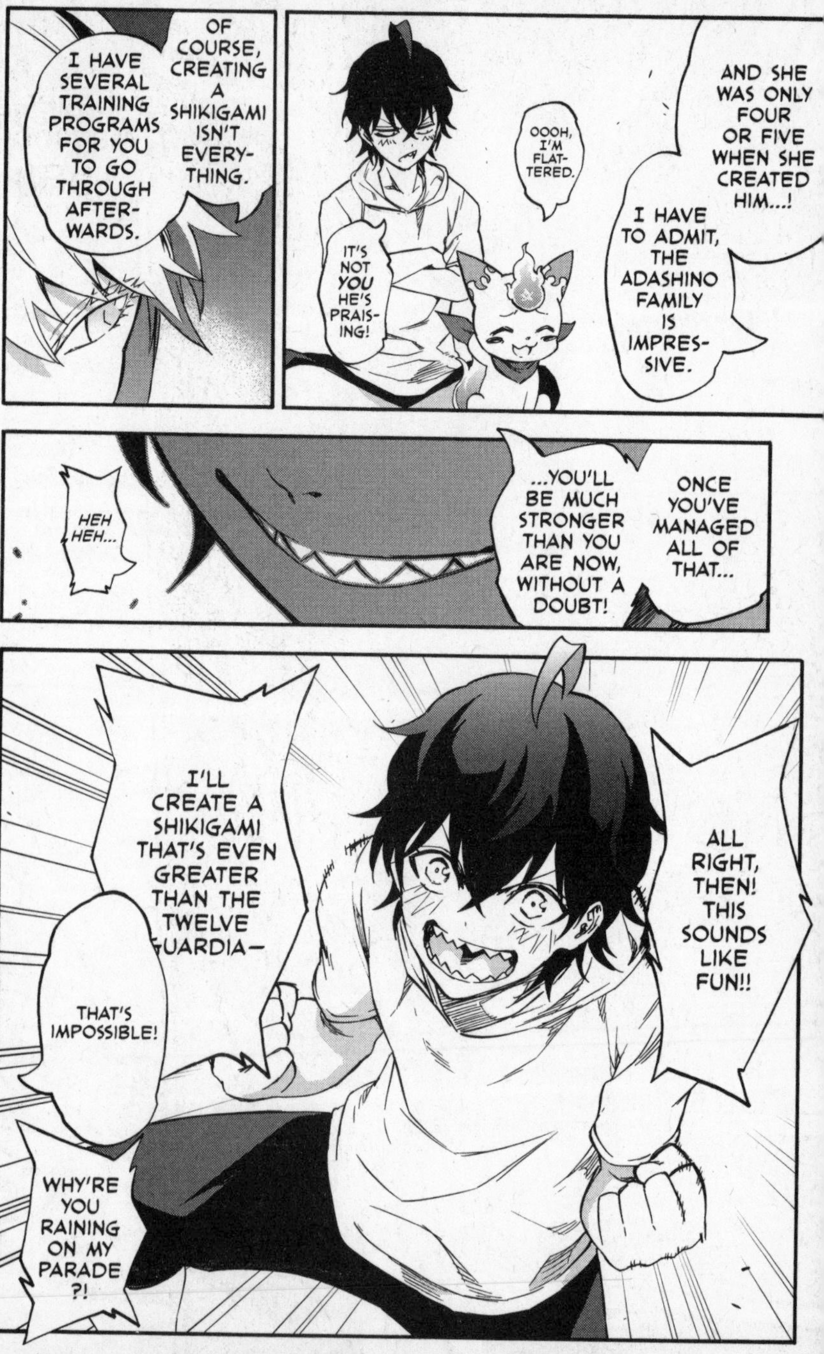
AND SHE WAS ONLY FOUR OR FIVE WHEN SHE CREATED HIM...!
I HAVE TO ADMIT, THE ADASHINO FAMILY IS IMPRESSIVE.
OOOH, I'M FLATTERED.
IT'S NOT *YOU* HE'S PRAISING!
OF COURSE, CREATING A SHIKIGAMI ISN'T EVERYTHING.
I HAVE SEVERAL TRAINING PROGRAMS FOR YOU TO GO THROUGH AFTERWARDS.
ONCE YOU'VE MANAGED ALL OF THAT...
...YOU'LL BE MUCH STRONGER THAN YOU ARE NOW, WITHOUT A DOUBT!
HEH HEH...
ALL RIGHT, THEN! THIS SOUNDS LIKE FUN!!
I'LL CREATE A SHIKIGAMI THAT'S EVEN GREATER THAN THE TWELVE GUARDIA—
THAT'S IMPOSSIBLE!
WHY'RE YOU RAINING ON MY PARADE?!

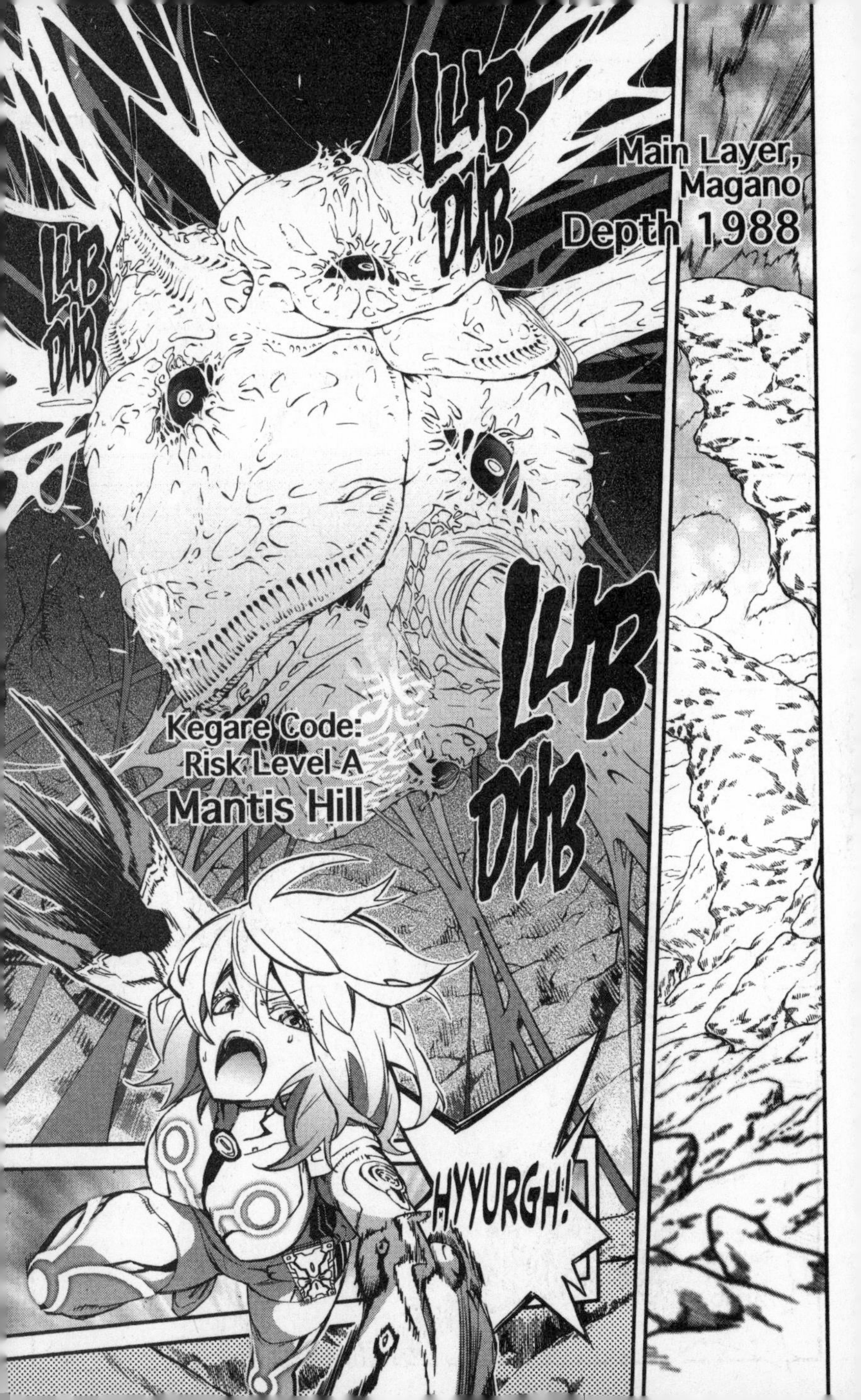
Main Layer, Magano
Depth 1988
LUB DUB
LUB DUB
LUB DUB
Kegare Code: Risk Level A
Mantis Hill
HYYURGH!

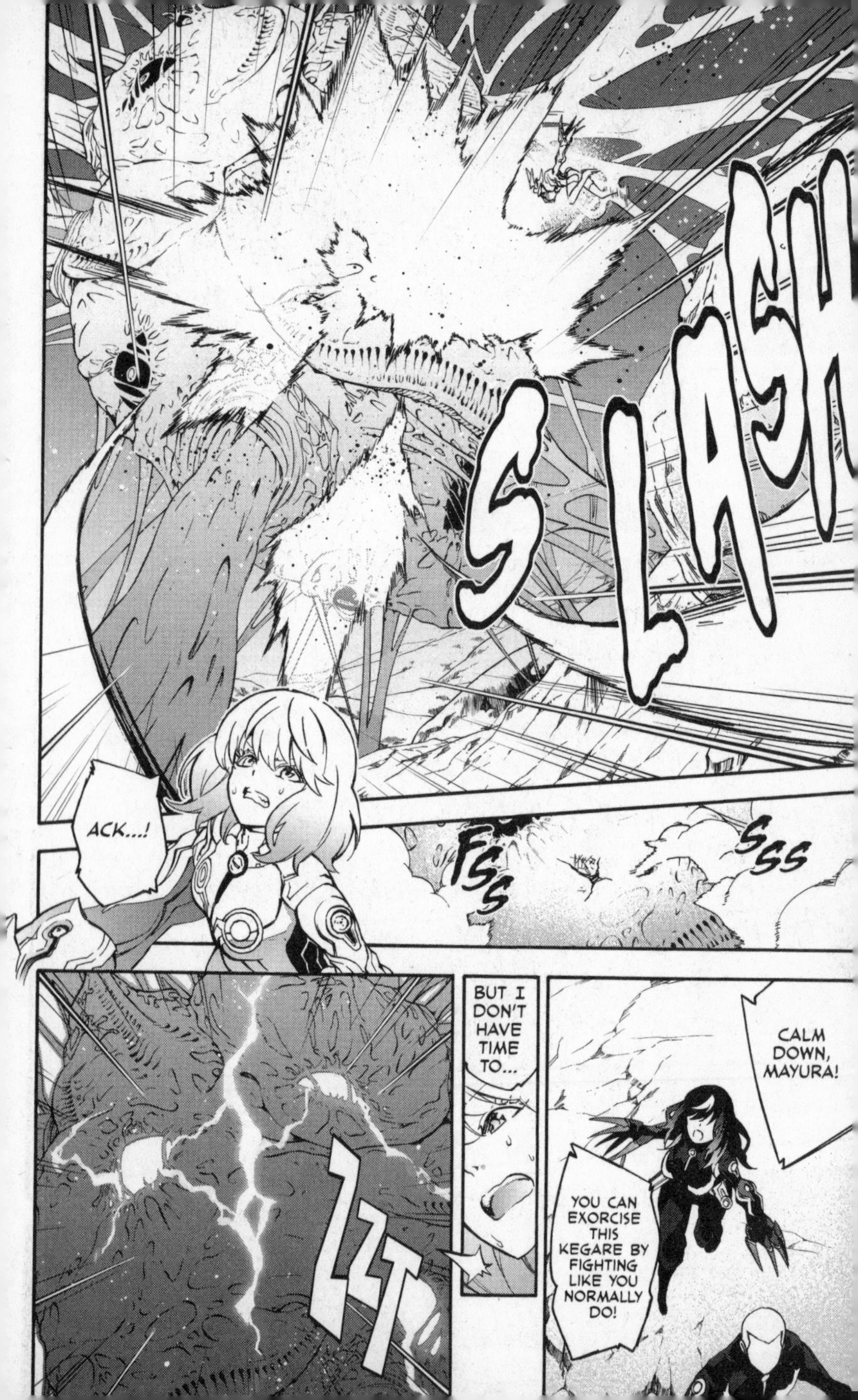
SLASH
ACK...!
SSS
FSS
CALM DOWN, MAYURA!
YOU CAN EXORCISE THIS KEGARE BY FIGHTING LIKE YOU NORMALLY DO!
BUT I DON'T HAVE TIME TO...
ZZT

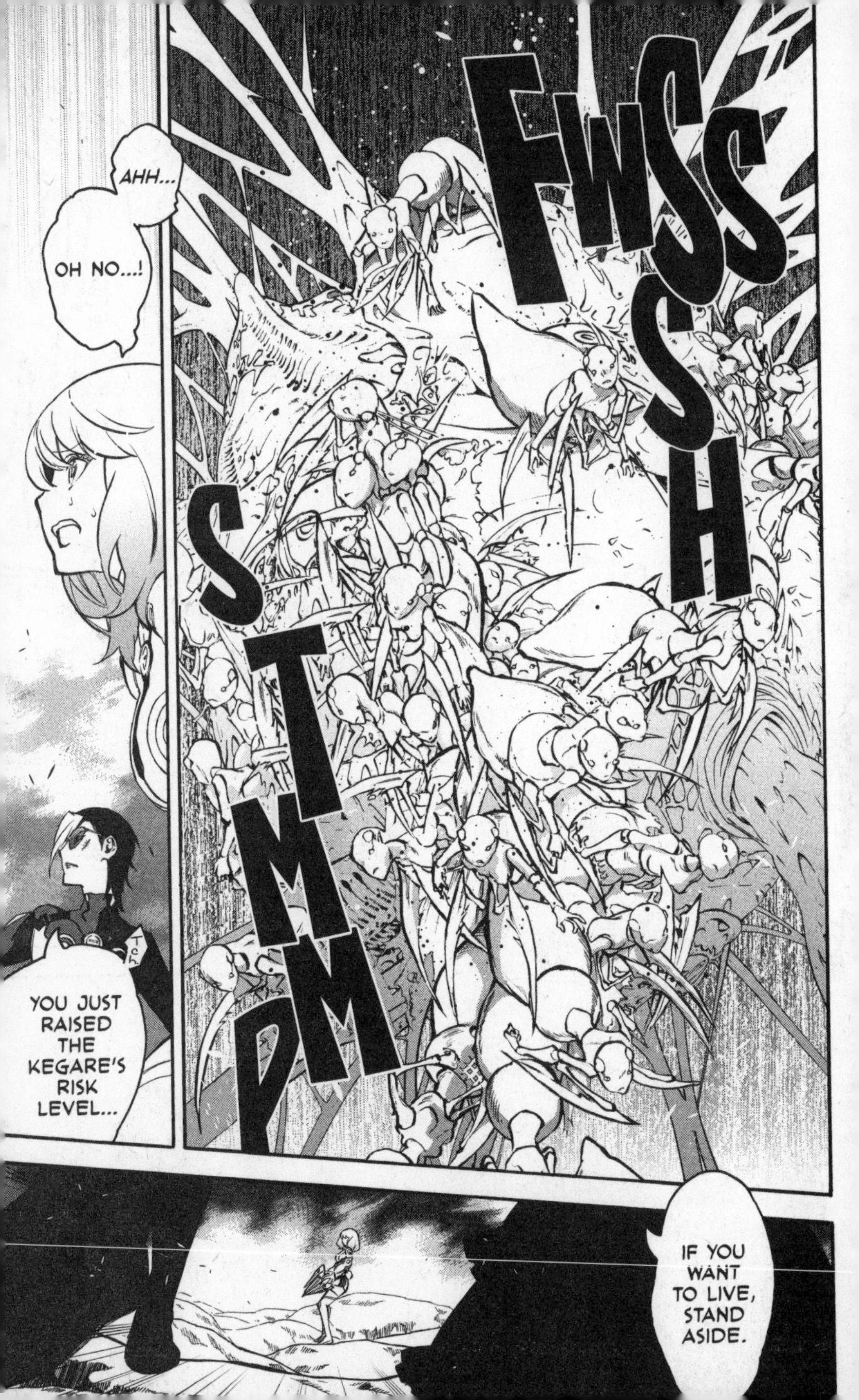
FWSSSH
STMMP
AHH...
OH NO...!
Tch
YOU JUST RAISED THE KEGARE'S RISK LEVEL...
IF YOU WANT TO LIVE, STAND ASIDE.

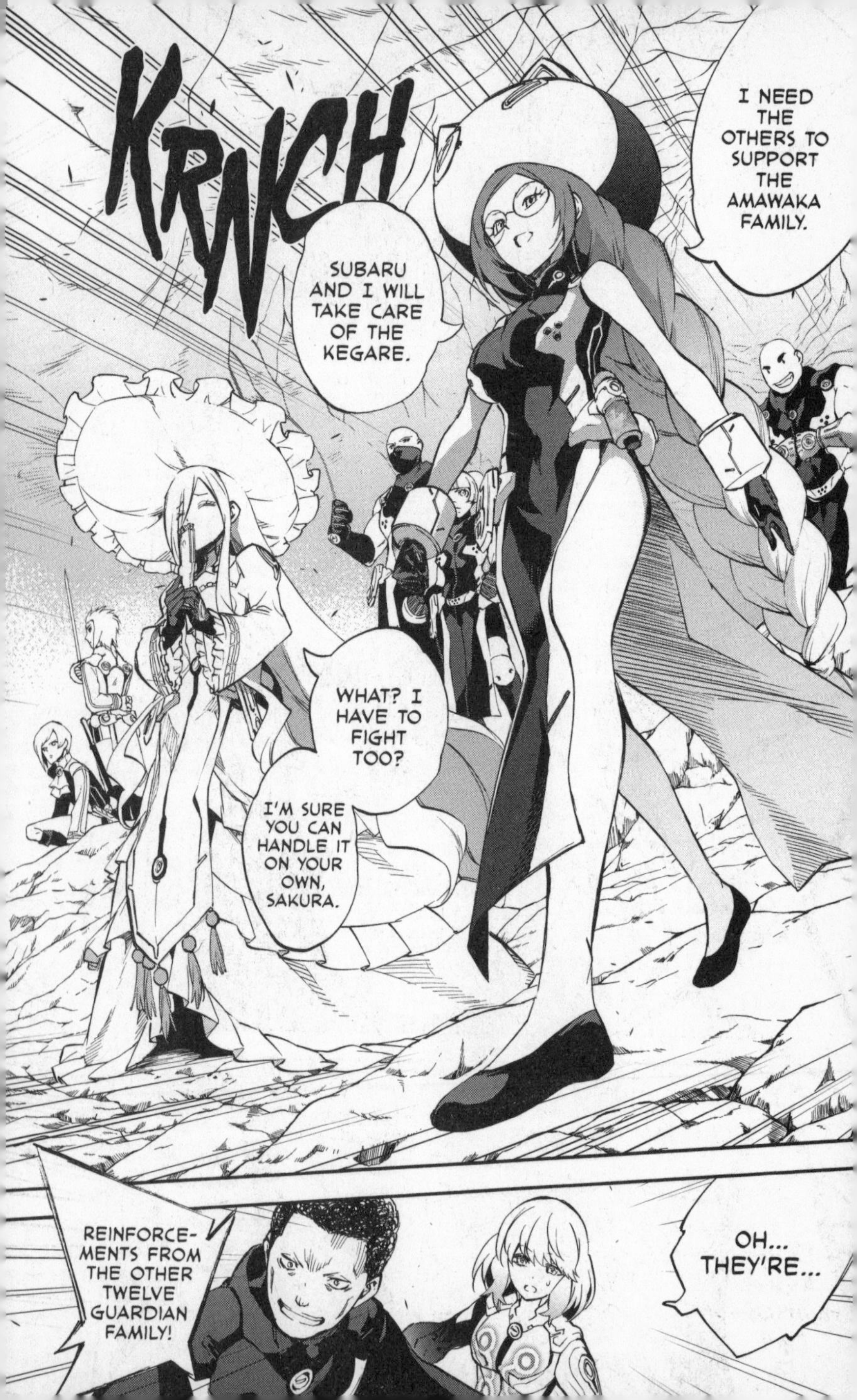
I NEED THE OTHERS TO SUPPORT THE AMAWAKA FAMILY.
KRNCH
SUBARU AND I WILL TAKE CARE OF THE KEGARE.
WHAT? I HAVE TO FIGHT TOO?
I'M SURE YOU CAN HANDLE IT ON YOUR OWN, SAKURA.
OH... THEY'RE...
REINFORCE-MENTS FROM THE OTHER TWELVE GUARDIAN FAMILY!

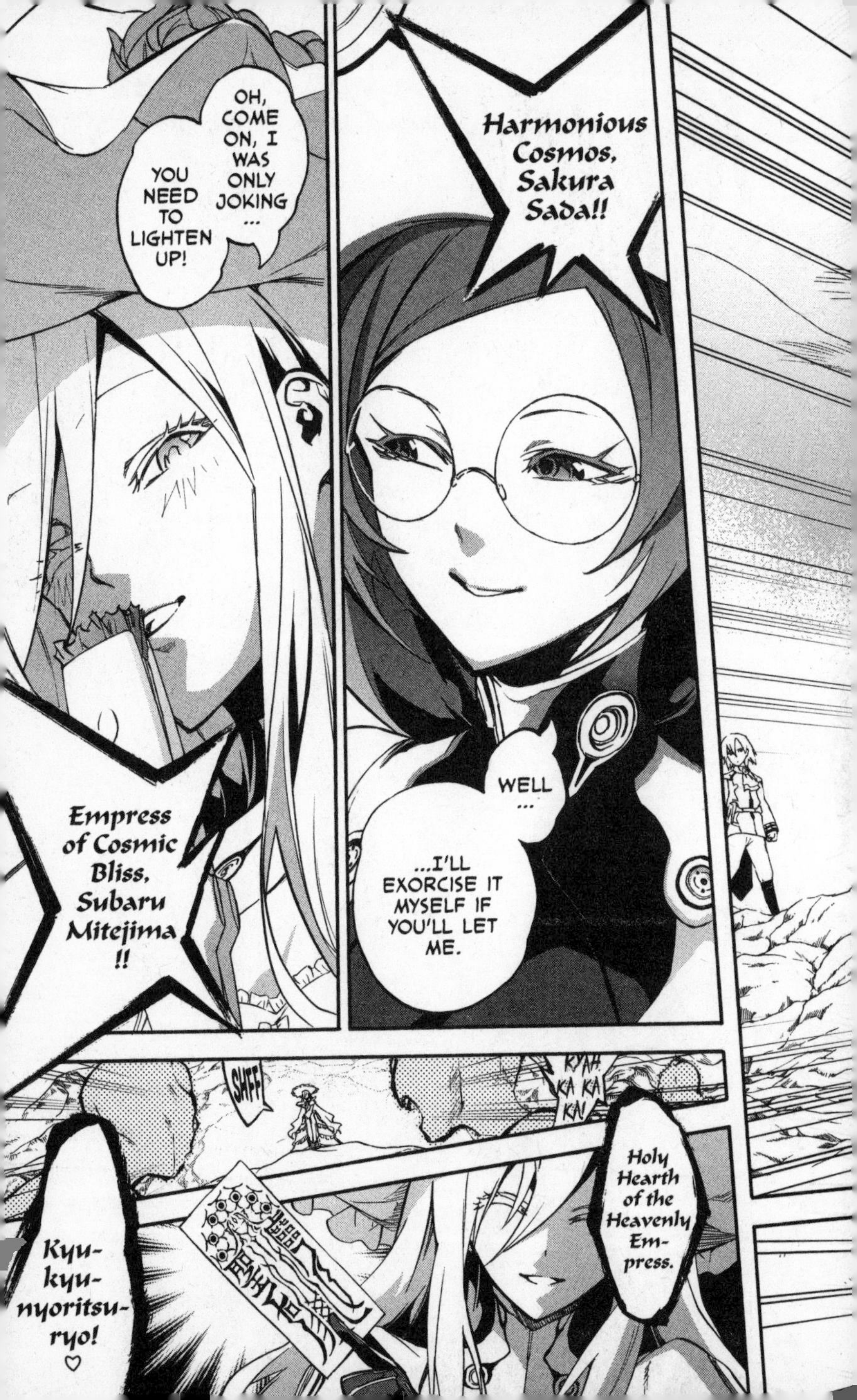
Harmonious Cosmos, Sakura Sada!!
WELL ...
...I'LL EXORCISE IT MYSELF IF YOU'LL LET ME.
OH, COME ON, I WAS ONLY JOKING ...
YOU NEED TO LIGHTEN UP!
Empress of Cosmic Bliss, Subaru Mitejima !!
KYAH KA KA KA!
SHFF
Holy Hearth of the Heavenly Em-press.
Kyu-kyu-nyoritsu-ryo! ♡

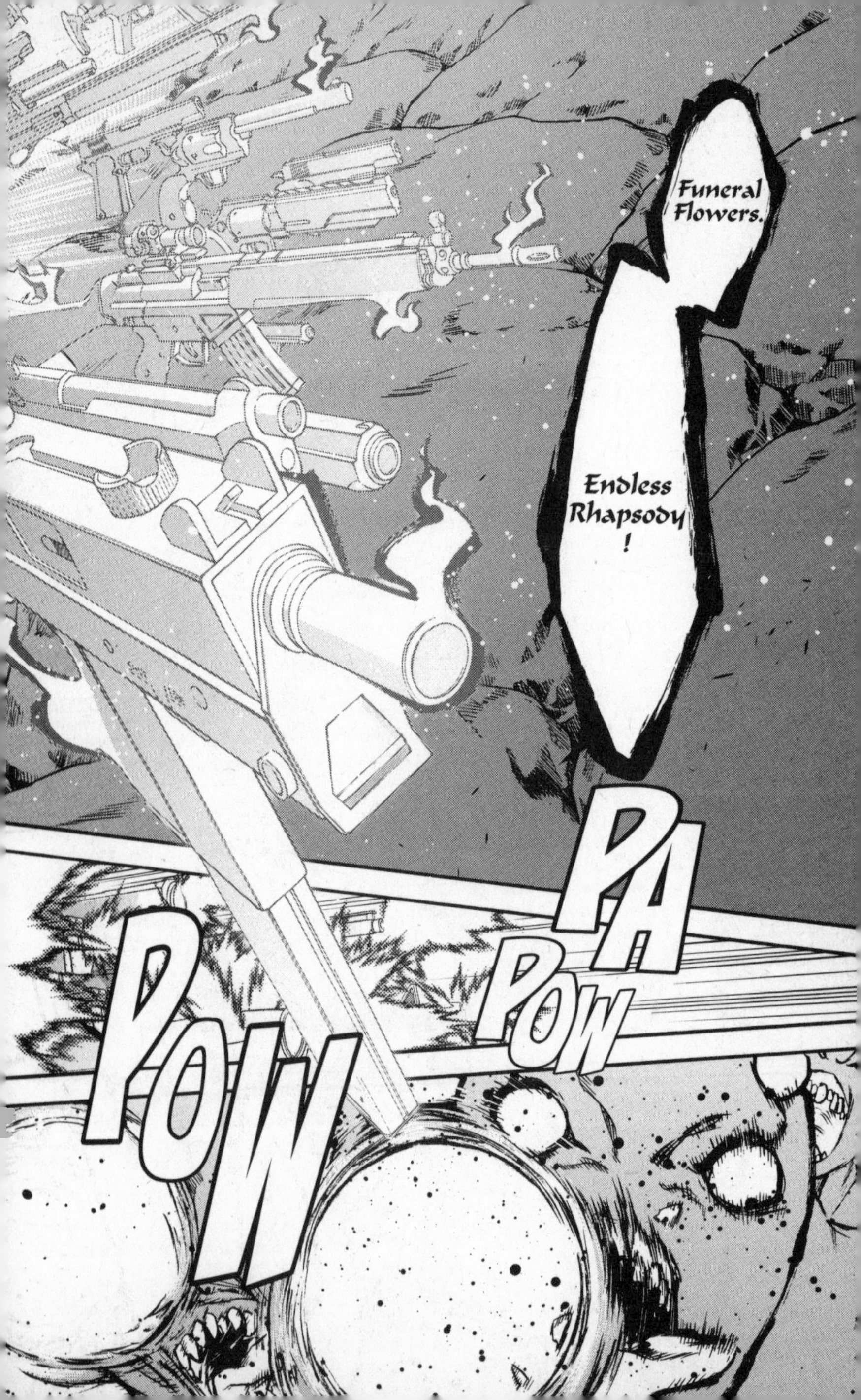
Funeral Flowers.
Endless Rhapsody!
PA POW
POW

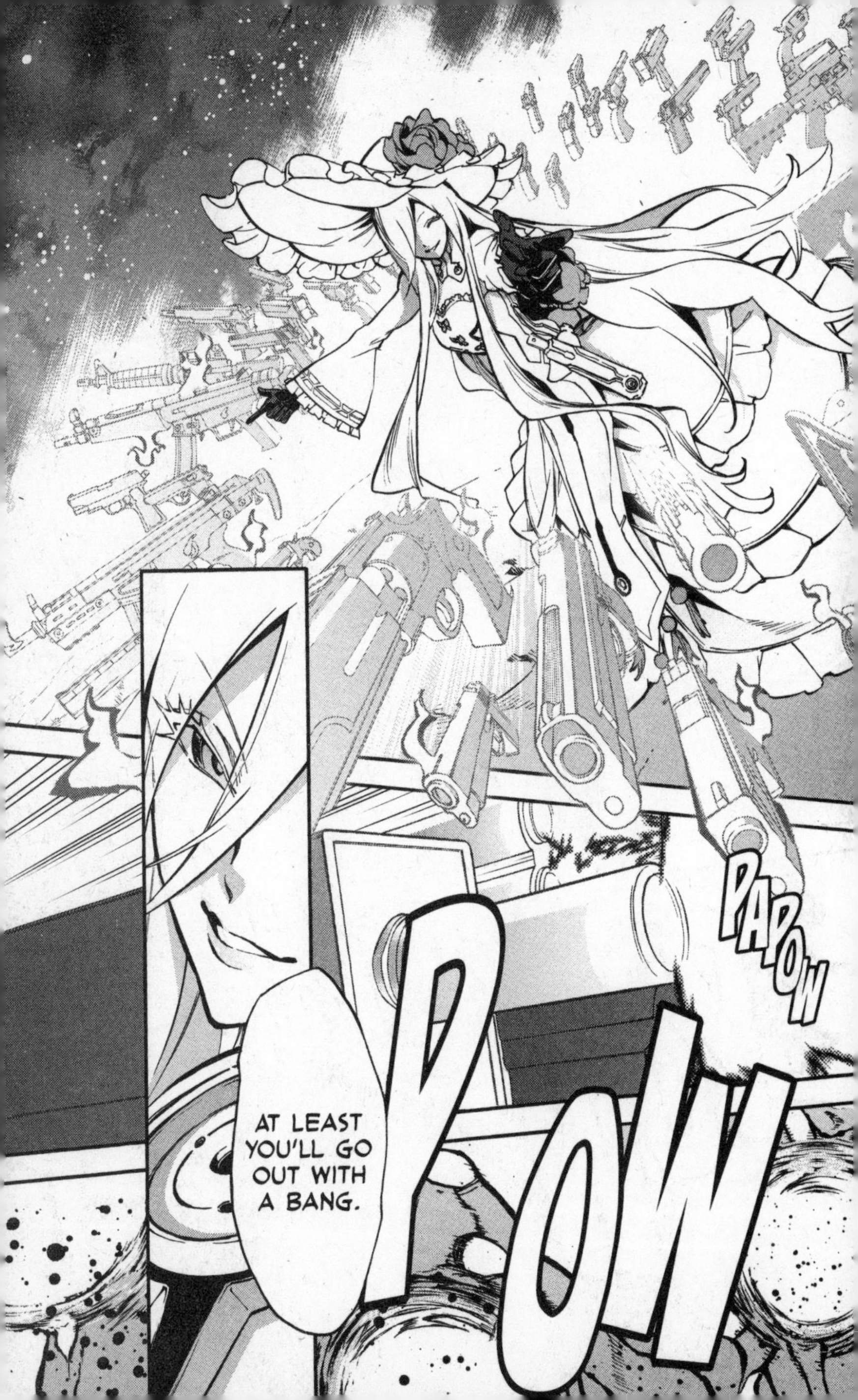
PADOW
AT LEAST YOU'LL GO OUT WITH A BANG.
POW

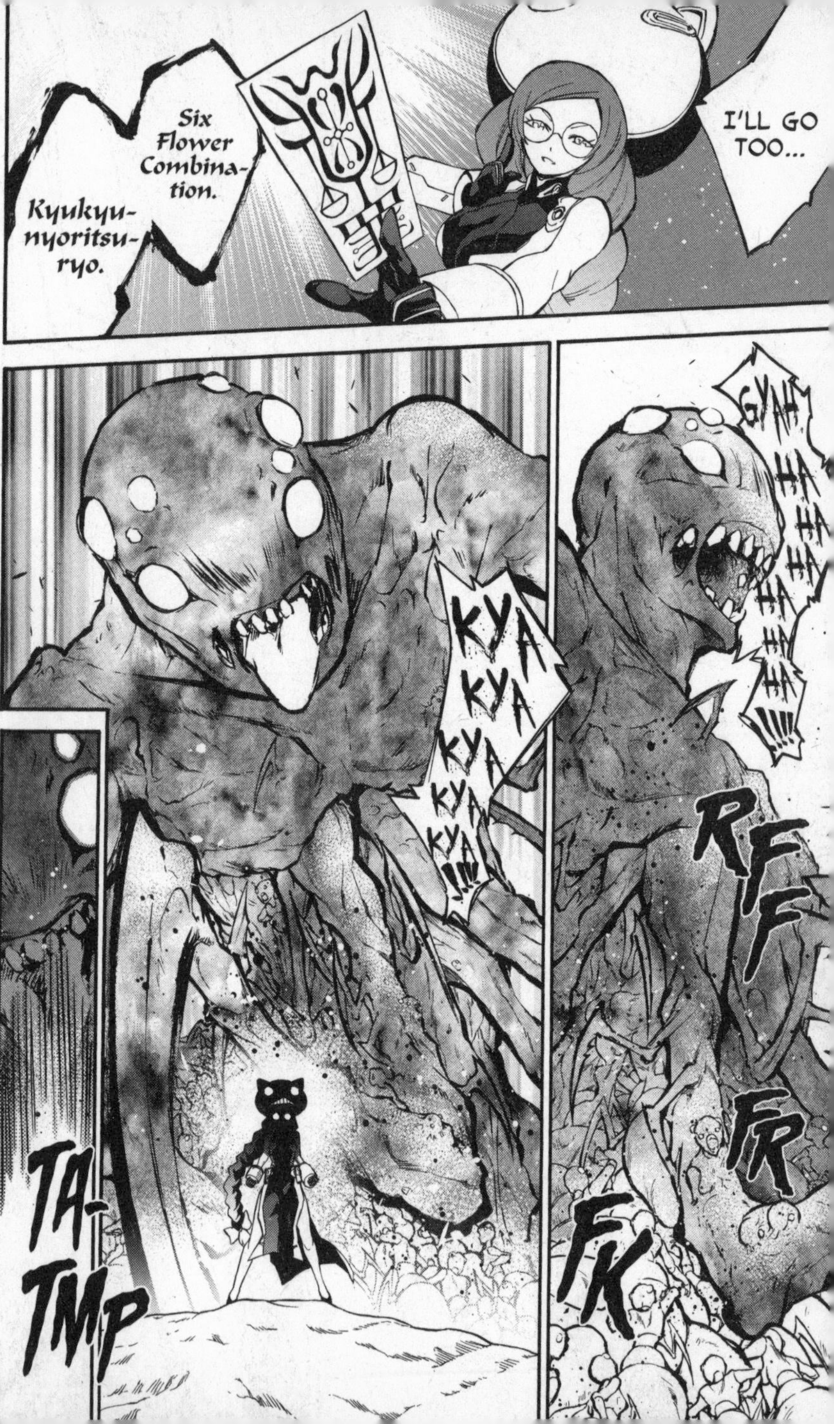
I'LL GO TOO...
Six Flower Combination.
Kyukyu-nyoritsu-ryo.
GYAH HA HA HA HA HA HA HA!!!!
RFF
FRFK
KYA KYA KYA KYA KYA!!!
TA-TMP

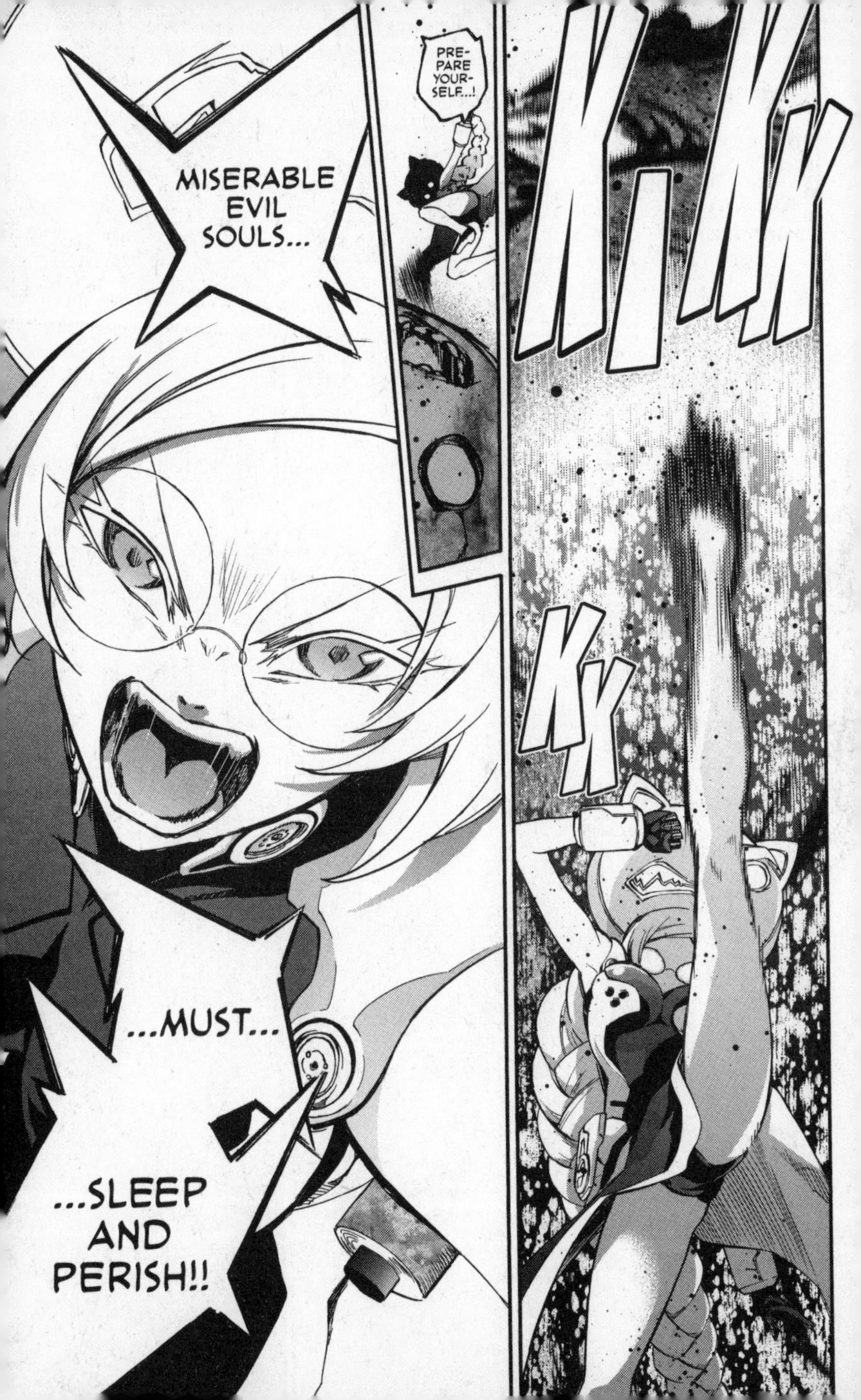
KINK
KK
PRE-PARE YOUR-SELF...!
MISERABLE EVIL SOULS...
...MUST...
...SLEEP AND PERISH!!

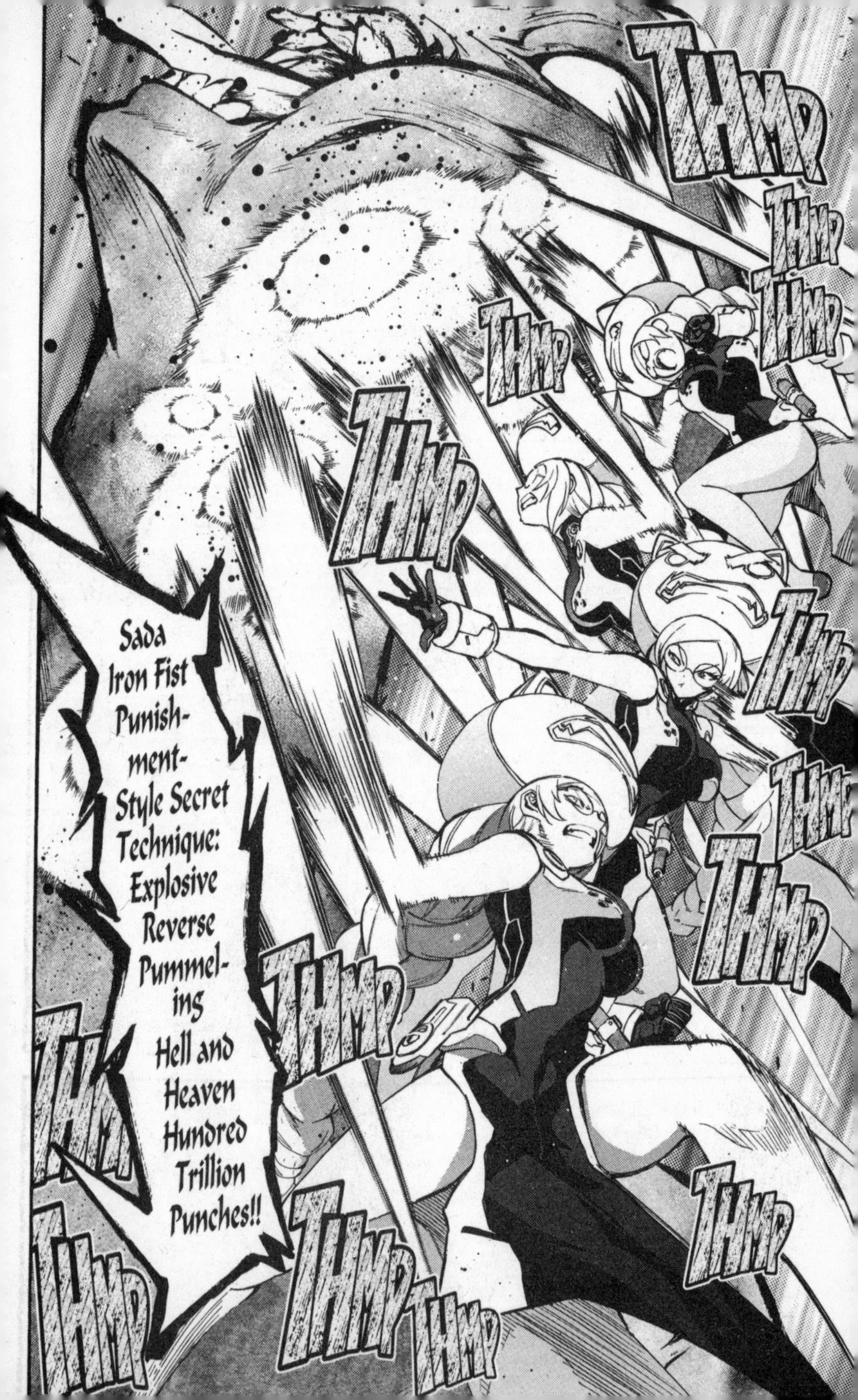
THMP
THMP
THMP
THMP
THMP
THMP
THMP
THMP
Sada Iron Fist Punish-ment-Style Secret Technique: Explosive Reverse Pummel-ing Hell and Heaven Hundred Trillion Punches!!
THMP
THMP
THMP
THMP
THMP
THMP

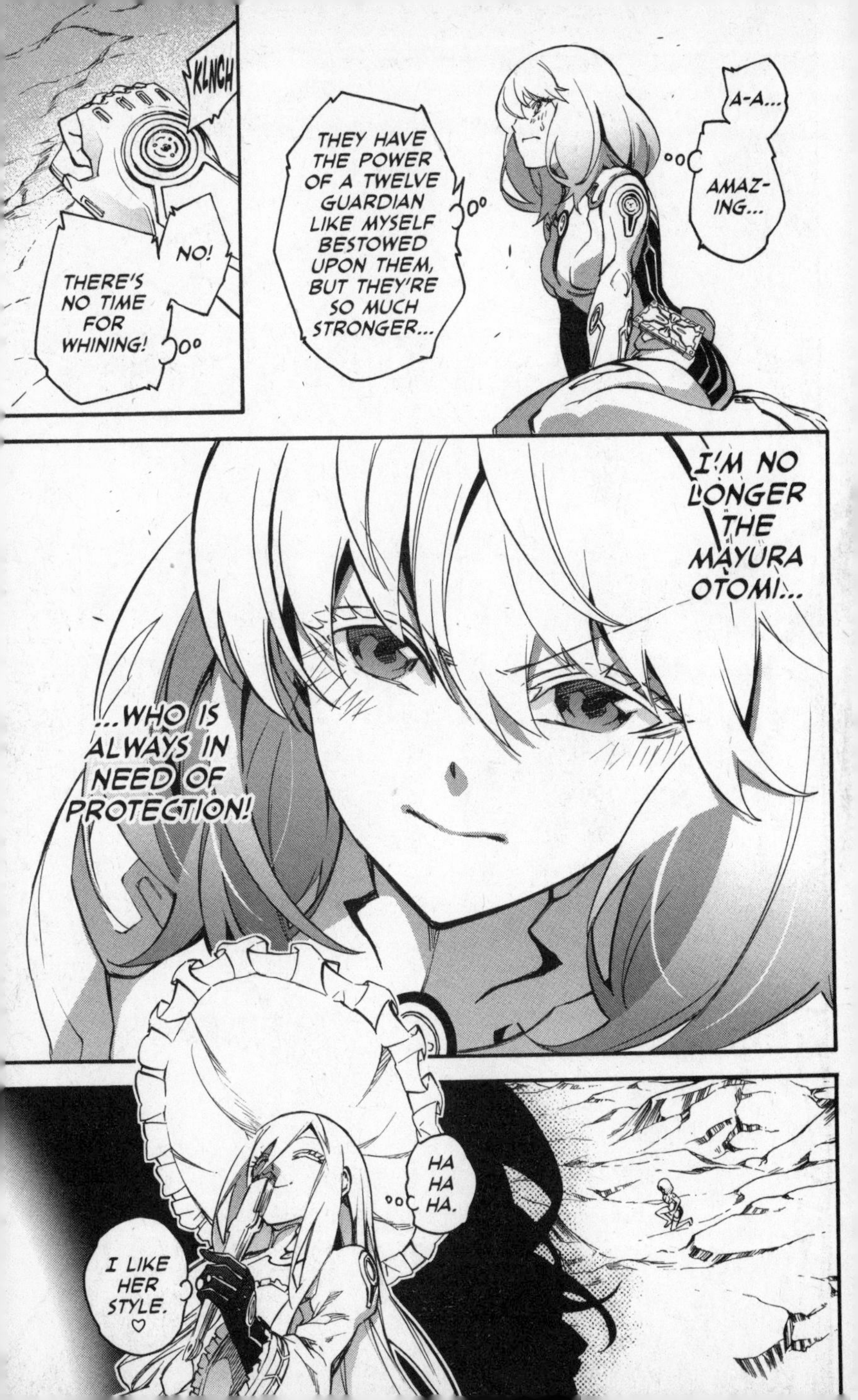
A-A...
AMAZ-ING...
THEY HAVE THE POWER OF A TWELVE GUARDIAN LIKE MYSELF BESTOWED UPON THEM, BUT THEY'RE SO MUCH STRONGER...
KLNCH
NO!
THERE'S NO TIME FOR WHINING!
I'M NO LONGER THE MAYURA OTOMI...
...WHO IS ALWAYS IN NEED OF PROTECTION!
HA HA HA.
I LIKE HER STYLE. ♡

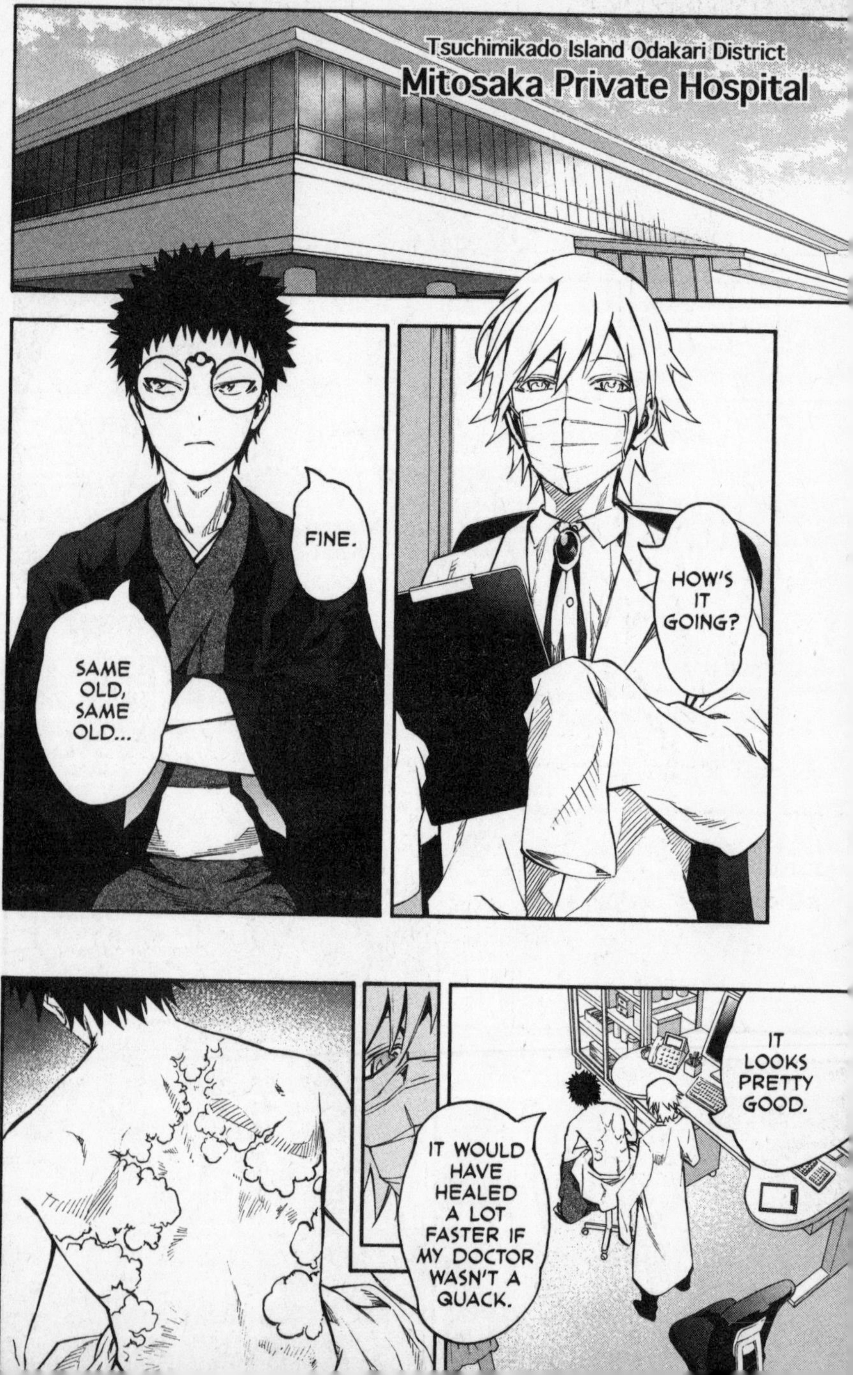
Tsuchimikado Island Odakari District
Mitosaka Private Hospital
HOW'S IT GOING?
FINE.
SAME OLD, SAME OLD...
IT LOOKS PRETTY GOOD.
IT WOULD HAVE HEALED A LOT FASTER IF MY DOCTOR WASN'T A QUACK.

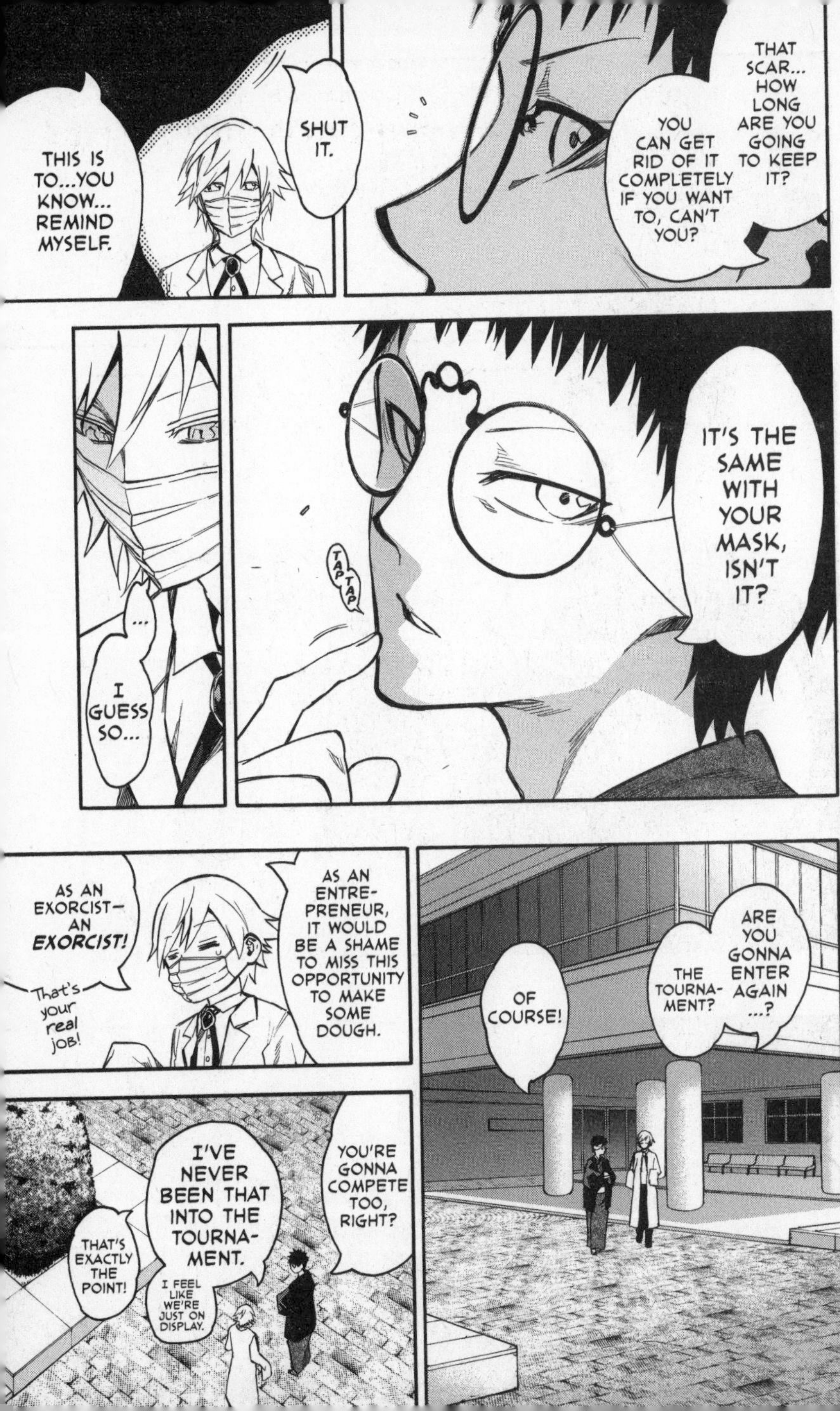
THAT SCAR... HOW LONG ARE YOU GOING TO KEEP IT?
YOU CAN GET RID OF IT COMPLETELY IF YOU WANT TO, CAN'T YOU?
SHUT IT.
THIS IS TO...YOU KNOW... REMIND MYSELF.
IT'S THE SAME WITH YOUR MASK, ISN'T IT?
TAP TAP
...
I GUESS SO...
ARE YOU GONNA ENTER AGAIN ...?
THE TOURNAMENT?
OF COURSE!
AS AN ENTREPRENEUR, IT WOULD BE A SHAME TO MISS THIS OPPORTUNITY TO MAKE SOME DOUGH.
AS AN EXORCIST— AN *EXORCIST!*
That's your real job!
YOU'RE GONNA COMPETE TOO, RIGHT?
I'VE NEVER BEEN THAT INTO THE TOURNAMENT.
THAT'S EXACTLY THE POINT!
I FEEL LIKE WE'RE JUST ON DISPLAY.

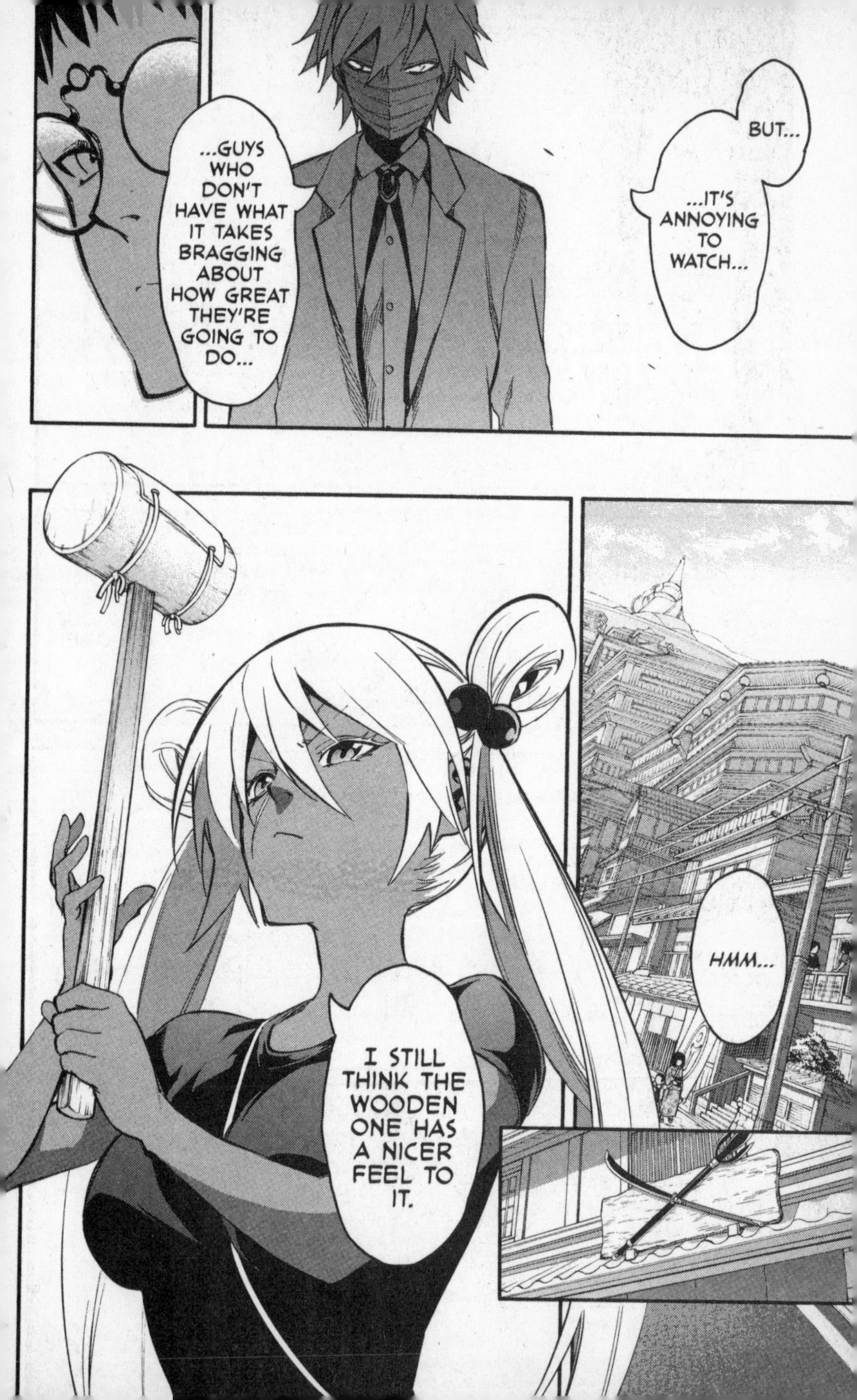
BUT... ...IT'S ANNOYING TO WATCH...
...GUYS WHO DON'T HAVE WHAT IT TAKES BRAGGING ABOUT HOW GREAT THEY'RE GOING TO DO...
HMM...
I STILL THINK THE WOODEN ONE HAS A NICER FEEL TO IT.

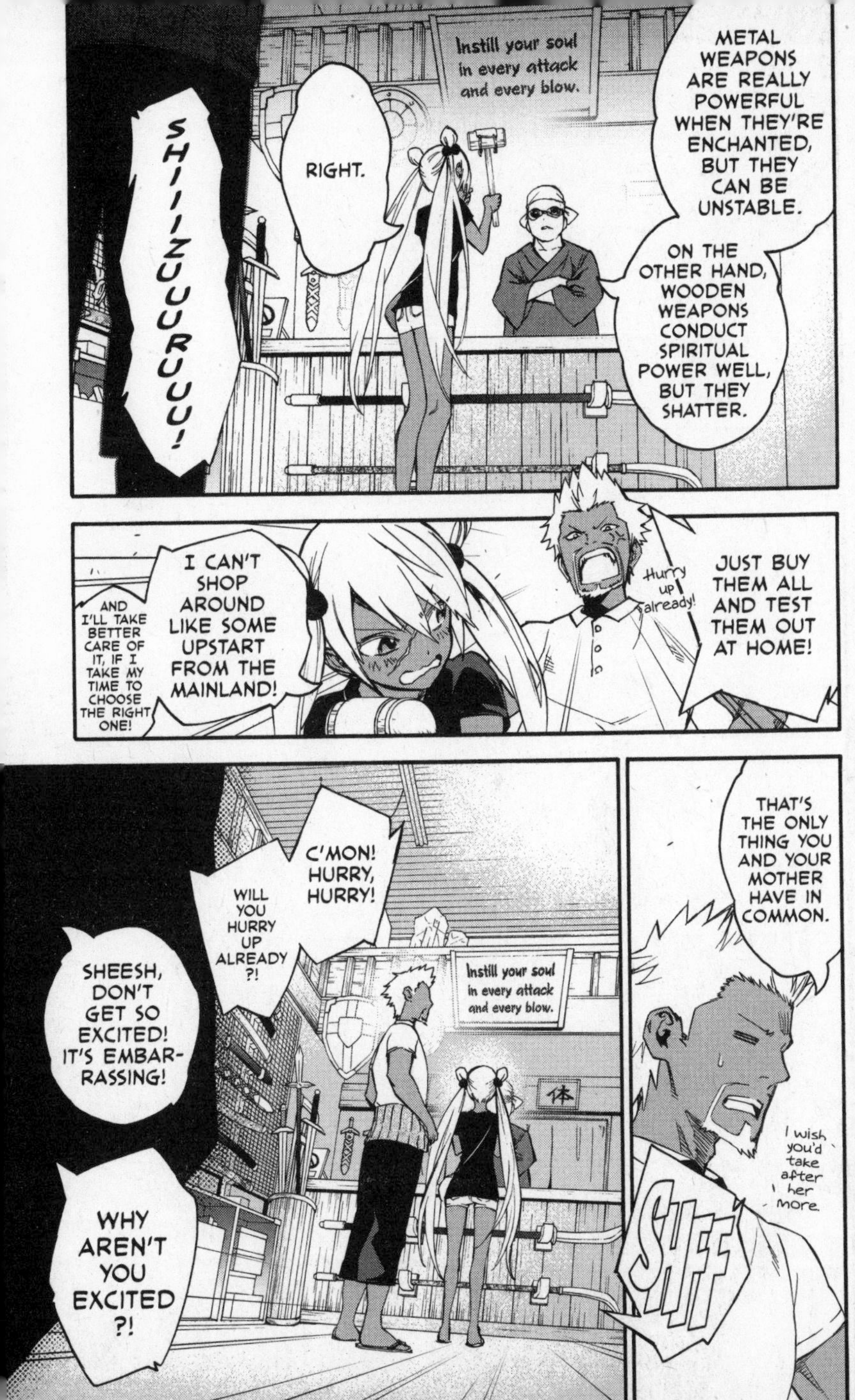
METAL WEAPONS ARE REALLY POWERFUL WHEN THEY'RE ENCHANTED, BUT THEY CAN BE UNSTABLE.
ON THE OTHER HAND, WOODEN WEAPONS CONDUCT SPIRITUAL POWER WELL, BUT THEY SHATTER.
Instill your soul in every attack and every blow.
RIGHT.
SHIIIIZUUURUUU!
JUST BUY THEM ALL AND TEST THEM OUT AT HOME!
Hurry up already!
I CAN'T SHOP AROUND LIKE SOME UPSTART FROM THE MAINLAND!
AND I'LL TAKE BETTER CARE OF IT, IF I TAKE MY TIME TO CHOOSE THE RIGHT ONE!
THAT'S THE ONLY THING YOU AND YOUR MOTHER HAVE IN COMMON.
I wish you'd take after her more.
SHFF
C'MON! HURRY, HURRY!
WILL YOU HURRY UP ALREADY?!
Instill your soul in every attack and every blow.
体
SHEESH, DON'T GET SO EXCITED! IT'S EMBARRASSING!
WHY AREN'T YOU EXCITED?!

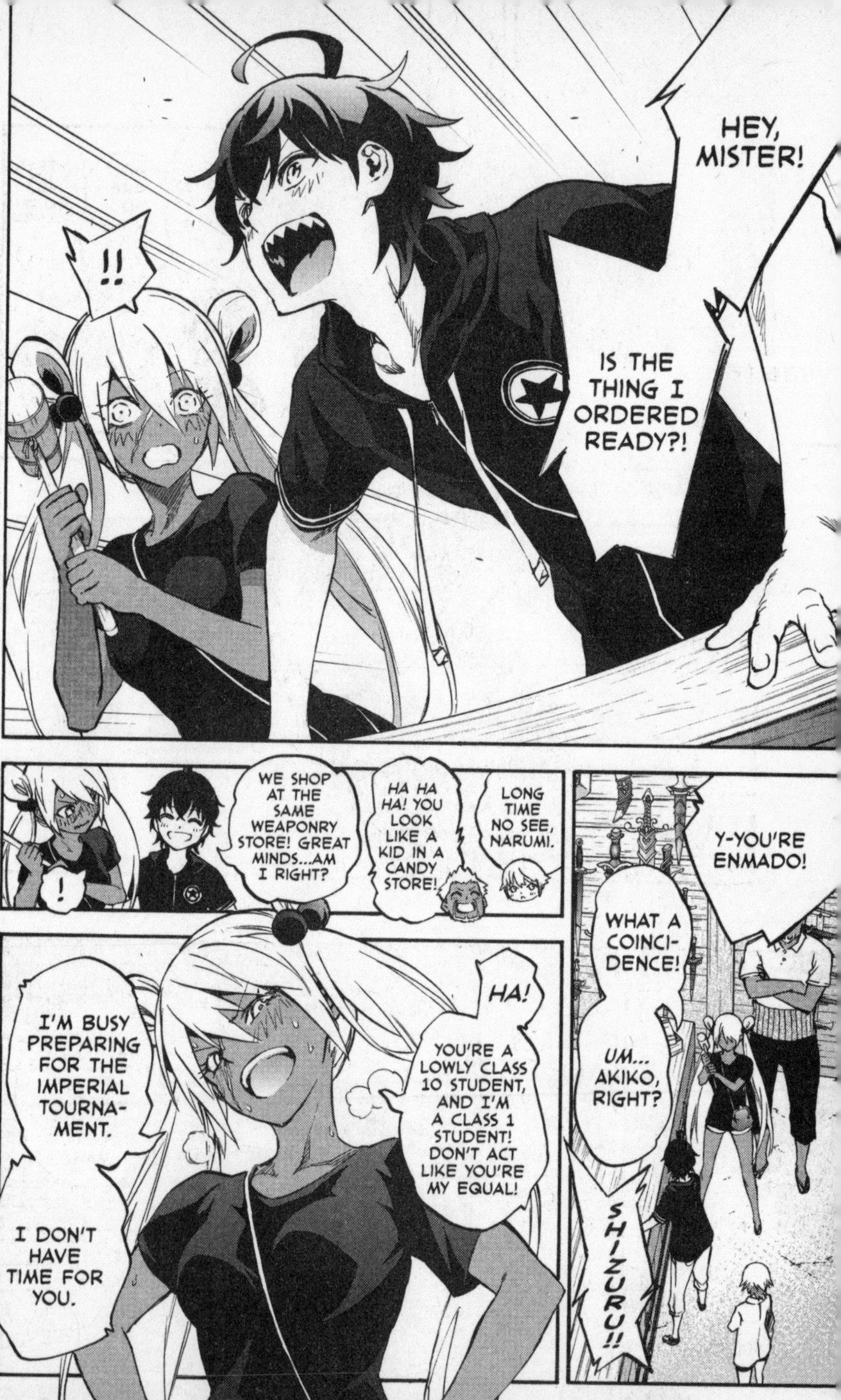
HEY, MISTER!
IS THE THING I ORDERED READY?!
!!
Y-YOU'RE ENMADO!
WHAT A COINCIDENCE!
UM... AKIKO, RIGHT?
SHIZURU!!
LONG TIME NO SEE, NARUMI.
HA HA HA! YOU LOOK LIKE A KID IN A CANDY STORE!
WE SHOP AT THE SAME WEAPONRY STORE! GREAT MINDS...AM I RIGHT?
!
HA!
YOU'RE A LOWLY CLASS 10 STUDENT, AND I'M A CLASS 1 STUDENT! DON'T ACT LIKE YOU'RE MY EQUAL!
I'M BUSY PREPARING FOR THE IMPERIAL TOURNAMENT.
I DON'T HAVE TIME FOR YOU.

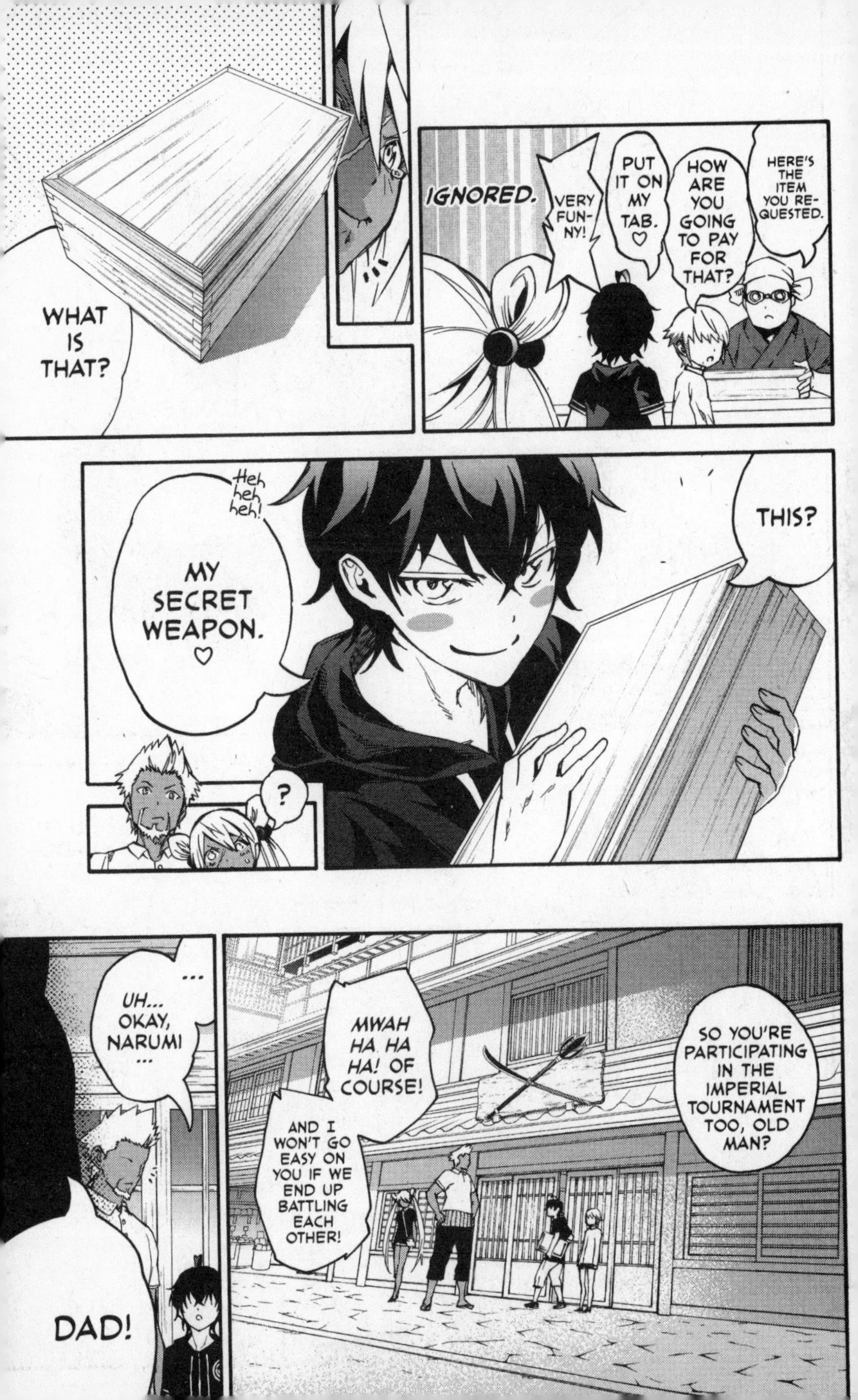

HERE'S THE ITEM YOU REQUESTED.
HOW ARE YOU GOING TO PAY FOR THAT?
PUT IT ON MY TAB. ♡
VERY FUNNY!
IGNORED.
WHAT IS THAT?
THIS?
Heh heh heh!
MY SECRET WEAPON. ♡
?
SO YOU'RE PARTICIPATING IN THE IMPERIAL TOURNAMENT TOO, OLD MAN?
MWAH HA HA HA! OF COURSE!
AND I WON'T GO EASY ON YOU IF WE END UP BATTLING EACH OTHER!
...
UH... OKAY, NARUMI...
DAD!

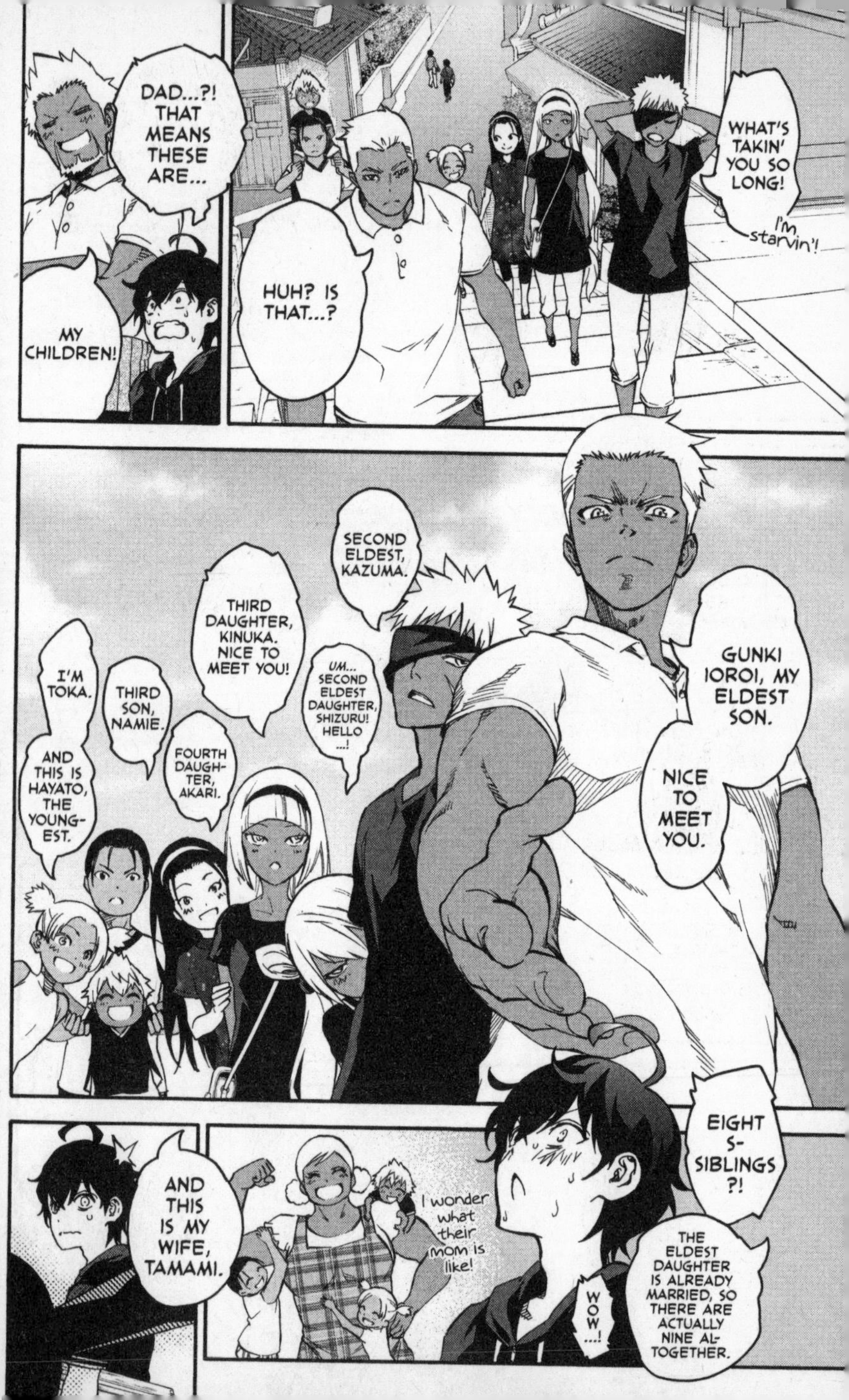
WHAT'S TAKIN' YOU SO LONG!
I'm starvin'!
HUH? IS THAT...?
DAD...?! THAT MEANS THESE ARE...
MY CHILDREN!
GUNKI IOROI, MY ELDEST SON.
NICE TO MEET YOU.
SECOND ELDEST, KAZUMA.
UM... SECOND ELDEST DAUGHTER, SHIZURU! HELLO ...!
THIRD DAUGHTER, KINUKA. NICE TO MEET YOU!
FOURTH DAUGH-TER, AKARI.
THIRD SON, NAMIE.
I'M TOKA.
AND THIS IS HAYATO, THE YOUNG-EST.
EIGHT S-SIBLINGS?!
THE ELDEST DAUGHTER IS ALREADY MARRIED, SO THERE ARE ACTUALLY NINE AL-TOGETHER.
WOW...!
I wonder what their mom is like!
AND THIS IS MY WIFE, TAMAMI.

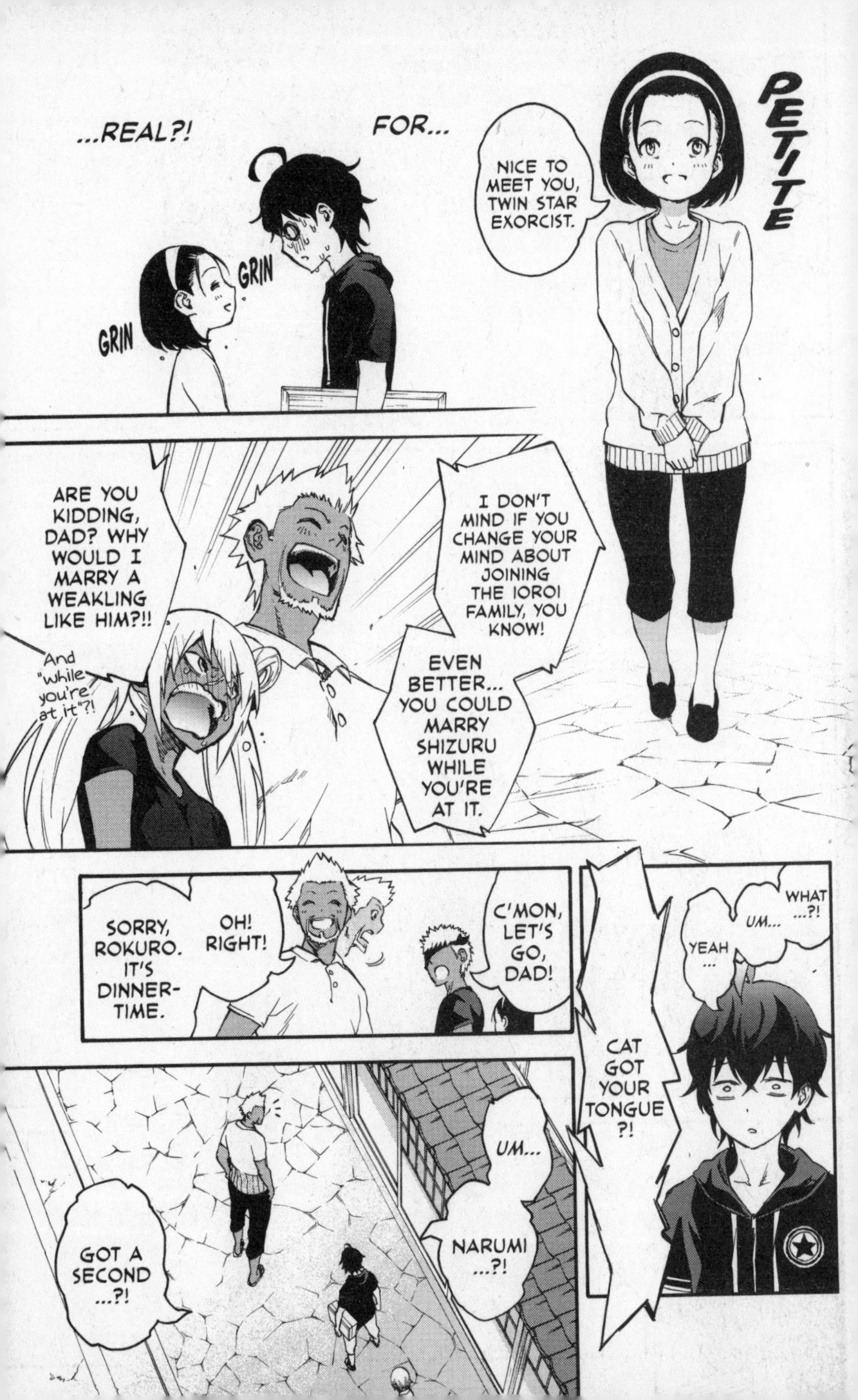
PETITE
NICE TO MEET YOU, TWIN STAR EXORCIST.
FOR...
...REAL?!
GRIN
GRIN
I DON'T MIND IF YOU CHANGE YOUR MIND ABOUT JOINING THE IOROI FAMILY, YOU KNOW!
EVEN BETTER... YOU COULD MARRY SHIZURU WHILE YOU'RE AT IT.
ARE YOU KIDDING, DAD? WHY WOULD I MARRY A WEAKLING LIKE HIM?!!
And "while you're at it"?!
WHAT ...?!
UM...
YEAH ...
CAT GOT YOUR TONGUE ?!
C'MON, LET'S GO, DAD!
OH! RIGHT!
SORRY, ROKURO. IT'S DINNER-TIME.
UM...
NARUMI ...?!
GOT A SECOND ...?!

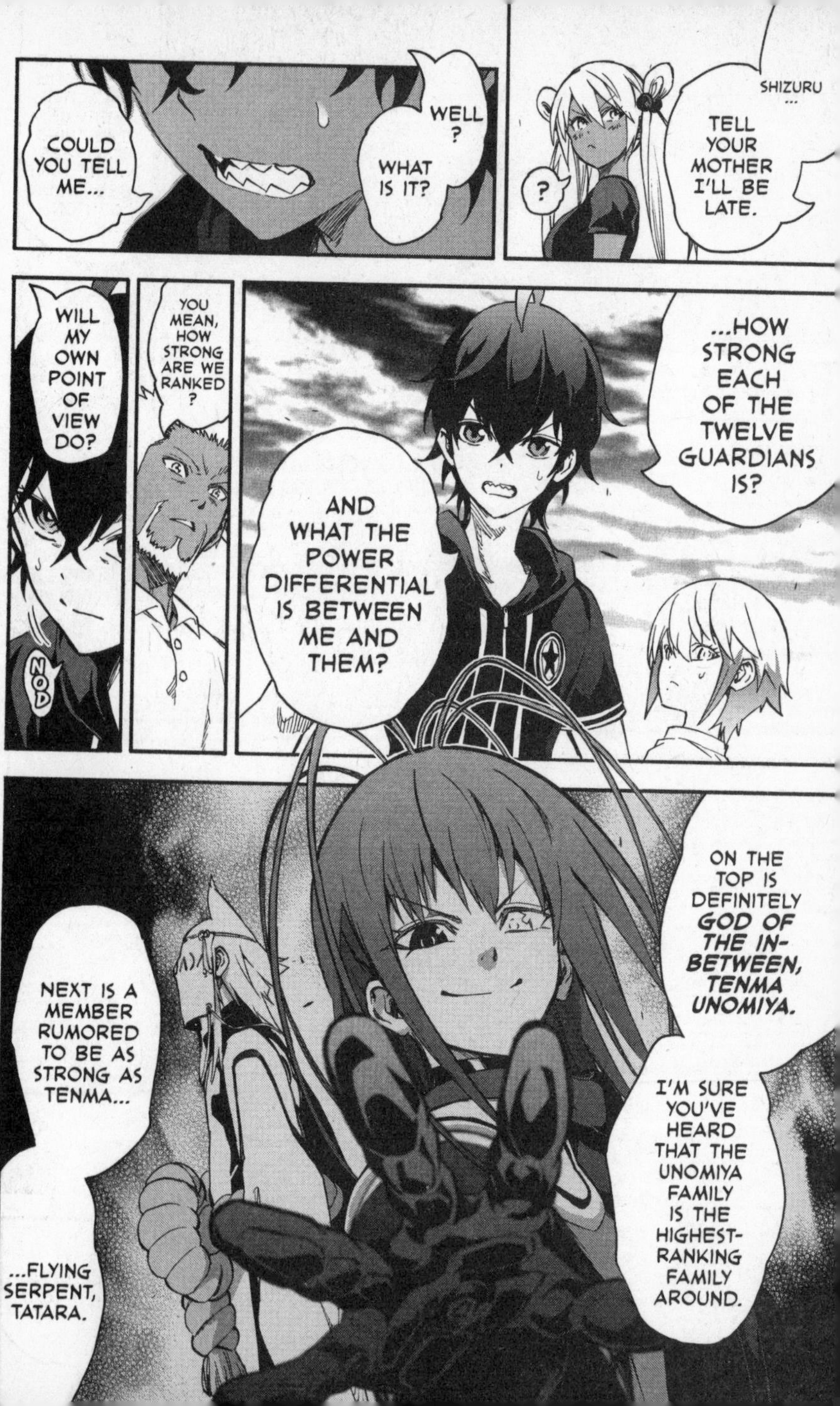
SHIZURU...
TELL YOUR MOTHER I'LL BE LATE.
?
WELL? WHAT IS IT?
COULD YOU TELL ME...
...HOW STRONG EACH OF THE TWELVE GUARDIANS IS?
AND WHAT THE POWER DIFFERENTIAL IS BETWEEN ME AND THEM?
YOU MEAN, HOW STRONG ARE WE RANKED?
WILL MY OWN POINT OF VIEW DO?
NOD
ON THE TOP IS DEFINITELY *GOD OF THE IN-BETWEEN, TENMA UNOMIYA.*
I'M SURE YOU'VE HEARD THAT THE UNOMIYA FAMILY IS THE HIGHEST-RANKING FAMILY AROUND.
NEXT IS A MEMBER RUMORED TO BE AS STRONG AS TENMA...
...FLYING SERPENT, TATARA.

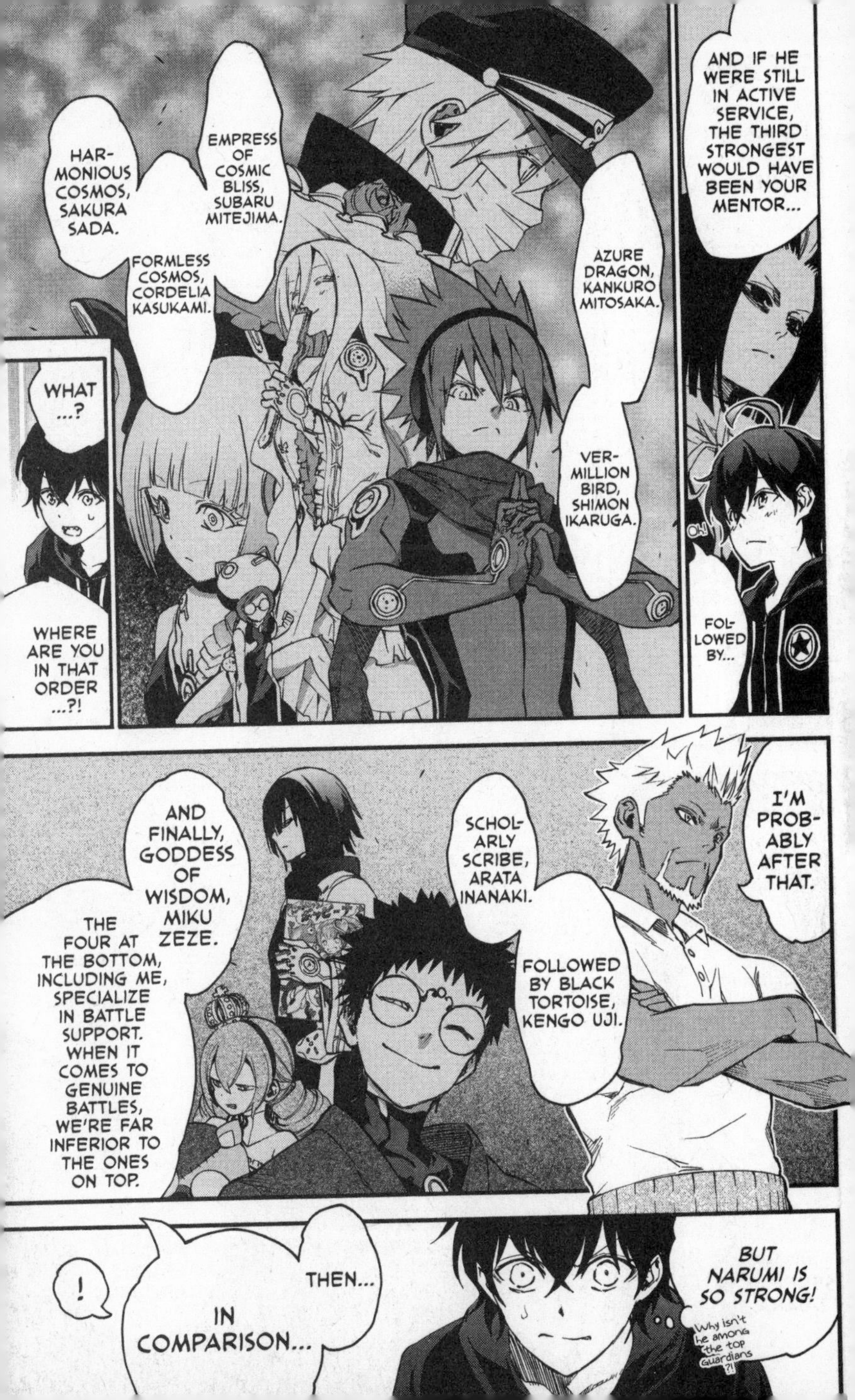
AND IF HE WERE STILL IN ACTIVE SERVICE, THE THIRD STRONGEST WOULD HAVE BEEN YOUR MENTOR...
OH!
FOLLOWED BY...
AZURE DRAGON, KANKURO MITOSAKA.
EMPRESS OF COSMIC BLISS, SUBARU MITEJIMA.
HARMONIOUS COSMOS, SAKURA SADA.
FORMLESS COSMOS, CORDELIA KASUKAMI.
VERMILLION BIRD, SHIMON IKARUGA.
WHAT ...?
WHERE ARE YOU IN THAT ORDER ...?!
I'M PROBABLY AFTER THAT.
SCHOLARLY SCRIBE, ARATA INANAKI.
FOLLOWED BY BLACK TORTOISE, KENGO UJI.
AND FINALLY, GODDESS OF WISDOM, MIKU ZEZE.
THE FOUR AT THE BOTTOM, INCLUDING ME, SPECIALIZE IN BATTLE SUPPORT. WHEN IT COMES TO GENUINE BATTLES, WE'RE FAR INFERIOR TO THE ONES ON TOP.
BUT NARUMI IS SO STRONG!
Why isn't he among the top Guardians ?!
THEN... IN COMPARISON...
!

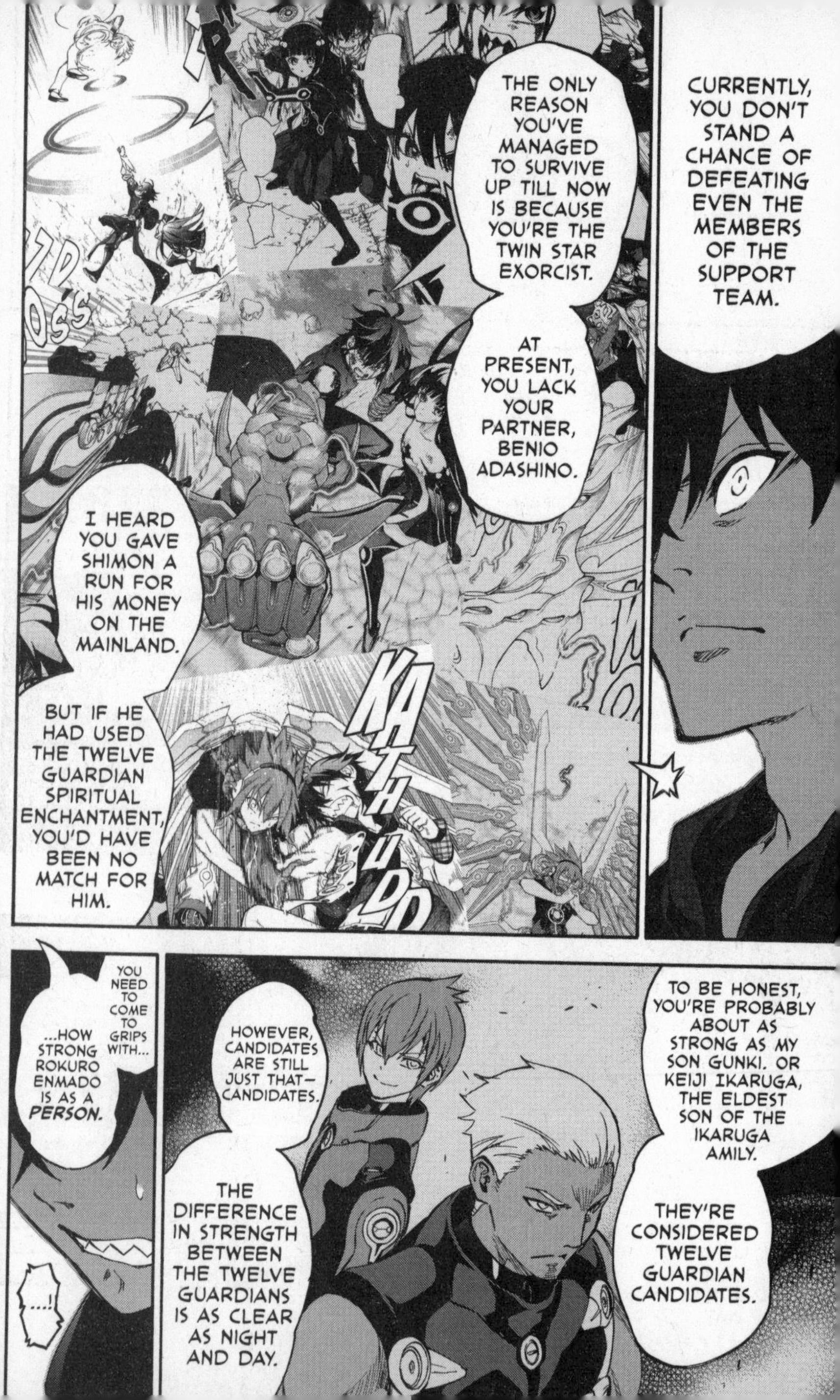
CURRENTLY, YOU DON'T STAND A CHANCE OF DEFEATING EVEN THE MEMBERS OF THE SUPPORT TEAM.
THE ONLY REASON YOU'VE MANAGED TO SURVIVE UP TILL NOW IS BECAUSE YOU'RE THE TWIN STAR EXORCIST.
AT PRESENT, YOU LACK YOUR PARTNER, BENIO ADASHINO.
I HEARD YOU GAVE SHIMON A RUN FOR HIS MONEY ON THE MAINLAND.
BUT IF HE HAD USED THE TWELVE GUARDIAN SPIRITUAL ENCHANTMENT, YOU'D HAVE BEEN NO MATCH FOR HIM.
TO BE HONEST, YOU'RE PROBABLY ABOUT AS STRONG AS MY SON GUNKI. OR KEIJI IKARUGA, THE ELDEST SON OF THE IKARUGA AMILY.
THEY'RE CONSIDERED TWELVE GUARDIAN CANDIDATES.
HOWEVER, CANDIDATES ARE STILL JUST THAT—CANDIDATES.
THE DIFFERENCE IN STRENGTH BETWEEN THE TWELVE GUARDIANS IS AS CLEAR AS NIGHT AND DAY.
YOU NEED TO COME TO GRIPS WITH...
...HOW STRONG ROKURO ENMADO IS AS A *PERSON.*
...!

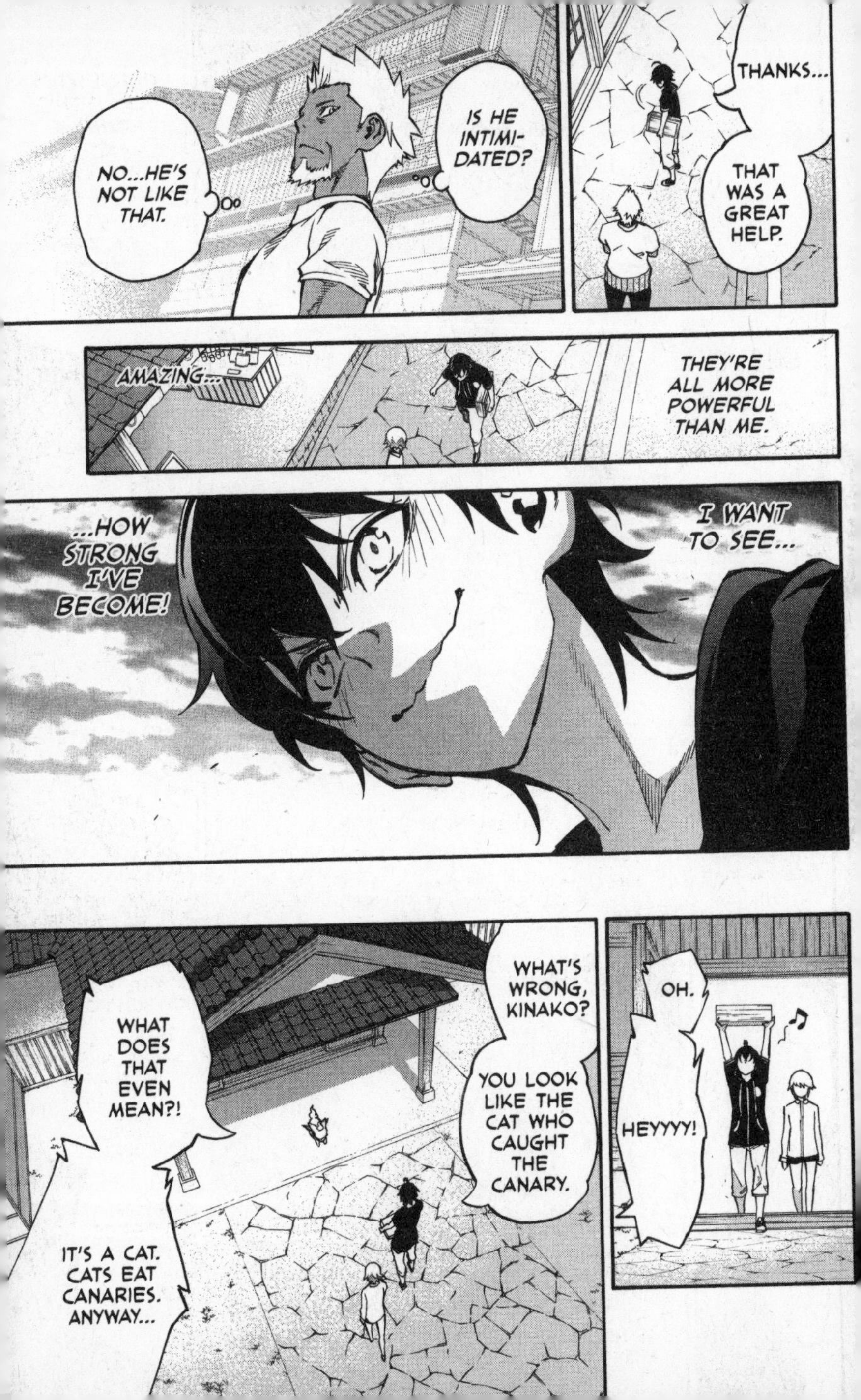
THANKS...
THAT WAS A GREAT HELP.
IS HE INTIMIDATED?
NO...HE'S NOT LIKE THAT.
THEY'RE ALL MORE POWERFUL THAN ME.
AMAZING...
I WANT TO SEE...
...HOW STRONG I'VE BECOME!
OH.
HEYYYY!
WHAT'S WRONG, KINAKO?
YOU LOOK LIKE THE CAT WHO CAUGHT THE CANARY.
WHAT DOES THAT EVEN MEAN?!
IT'S A CAT. CATS EAT CANARIES. ANYWAY...

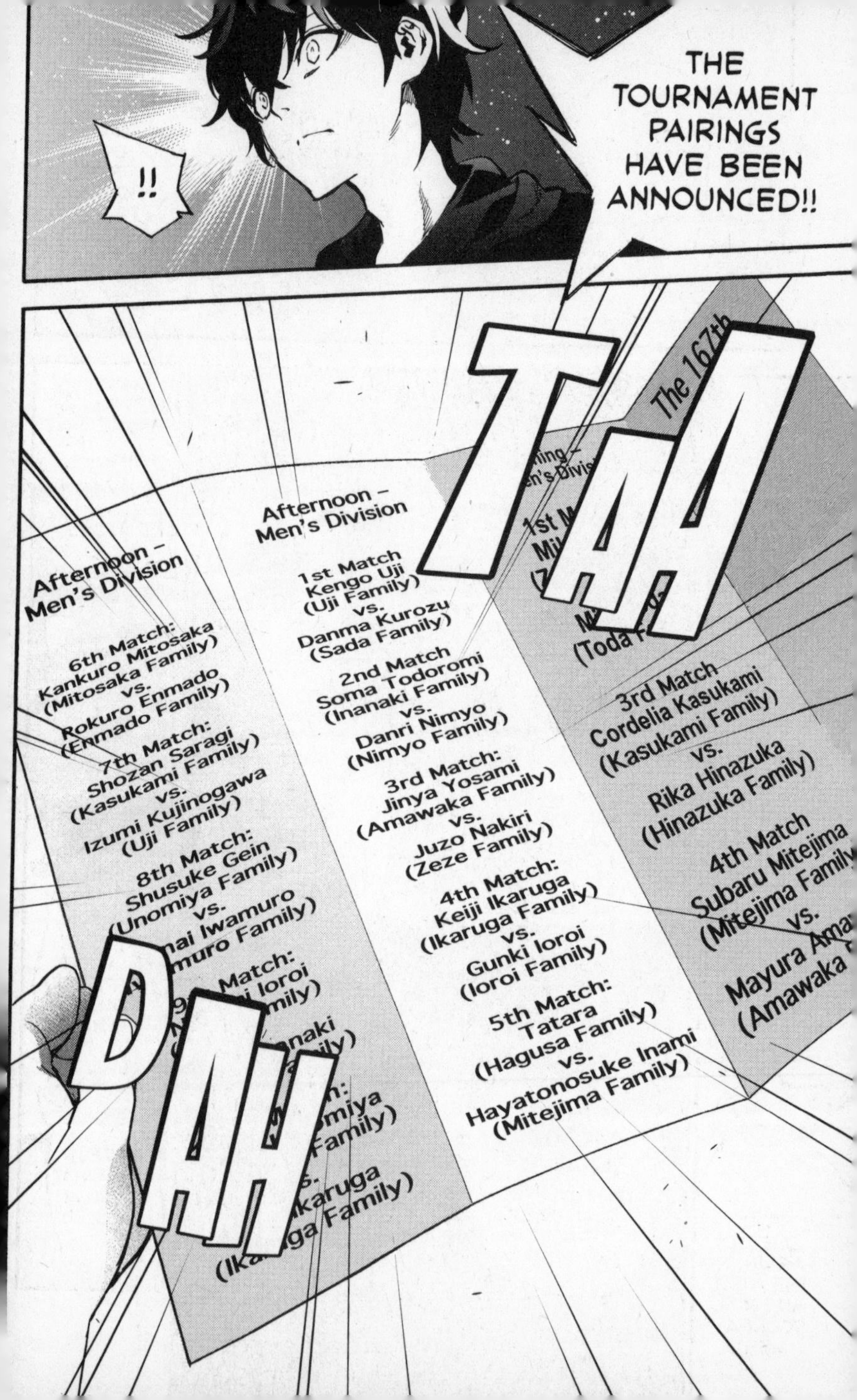
THE TOURNAMENT PAIRINGS HAVE BEEN ANNOUNCED!!
!!
TAA
The 167th
3rd Match
Cordelia Kasukami
(Kasukami Family)
vs.
Rika Hinazuka
(Hinazuka Family)
4th Match
Subaru Mitejima
vs.
Afternoon – Men's Division
1st Match
Kengo Uji
(Uji Family)
vs.
Danma Kurozu
(Sada Family)
2nd Match
Soma Todoromi
(Inanaki Family)
vs.
Danri Nimyo
(Nimyo Family)
3rd Match:
Jinya Yosami
(Amawaka Family)
vs.
Juzo Nakiri
(Zeze Family)
4th Match:
Keiji Ikaruga
(Ikaruga Family)
vs.
Gunki Ioroi
(Ioroi Family)
5th Match:
Tatara
(Hagusa Family)
vs.
Hayatonosuke Inami
(Mitejima Family)
Afternoon – Men's Division
6th Match:
Kankuro Mitosaka
(Mitosaka Family)
vs.
Rokuro Enmado
(Enmado Family)
7th Match:
Shozan Saragi
(Kasukami Family)
vs.
Izumi Kujinogawa
(Uji Family)
8th Match:
Shusuke Gein
(Unomiya Family)
vs.
DAH

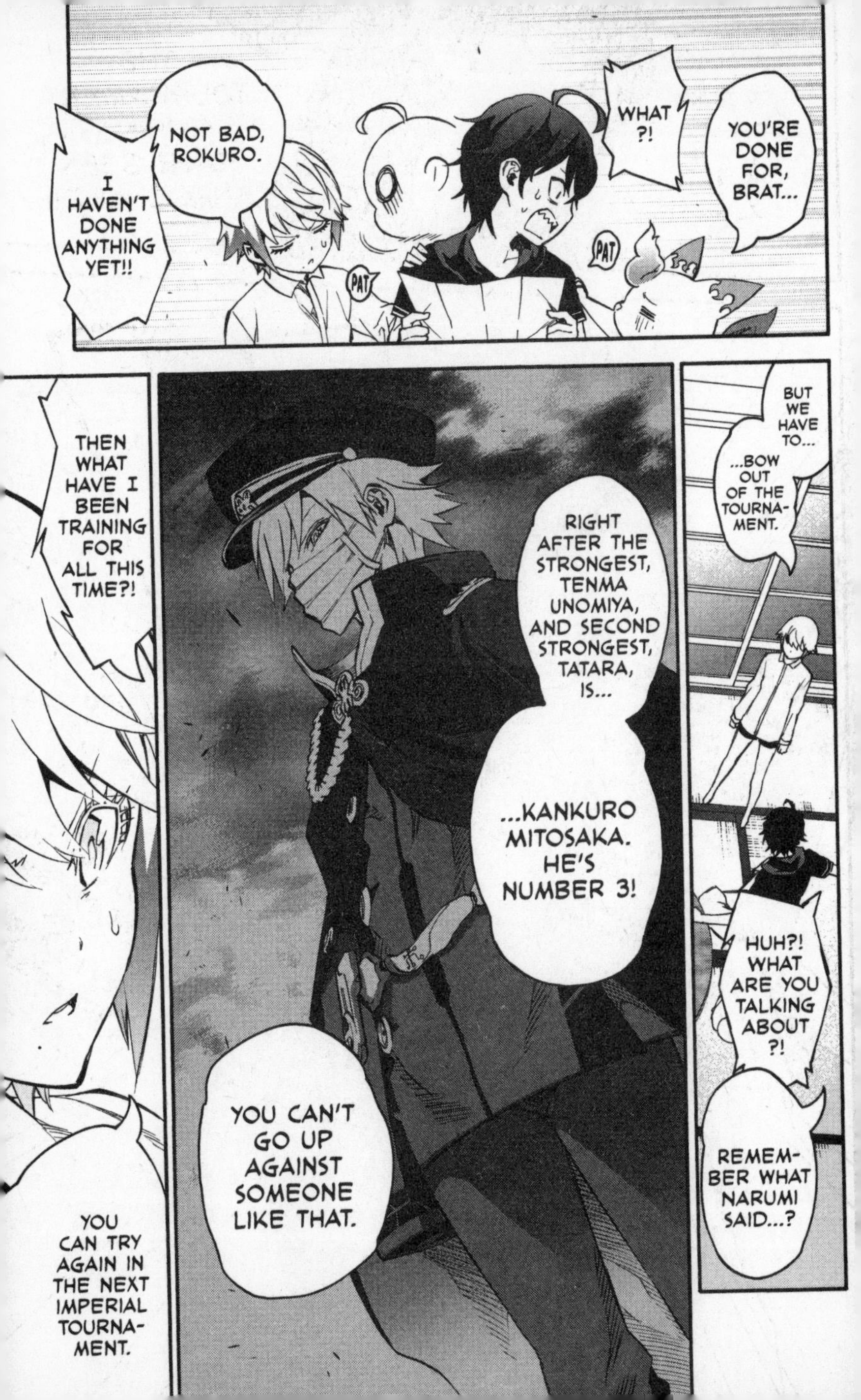

YOU'RE DONE FOR, BRAT...
WHAT?!
PAT
PAT
NOT BAD, ROKURO.
I HAVEN'T DONE ANYTHING YET!!
BUT WE HAVE TO...
...BOW OUT OF THE TOURNA-MENT.
HUH?! WHAT ARE YOU TALKING ABOUT?!
REMEM-BER WHAT NARUMI SAID...?
RIGHT AFTER THE STRONGEST, TENMA UNOMIYA, AND SECOND STRONGEST, TATARA, IS...
...KANKURO MITOSAKA. HE'S NUMBER 3!
YOU CAN'T GO UP AGAINST SOMEONE LIKE THAT.
THEN WHAT HAVE I BEEN TRAINING FOR ALL THIS TIME?!
YOU CAN TRY AGAIN IN THE NEXT IMPERIAL TOURNA-MENT.

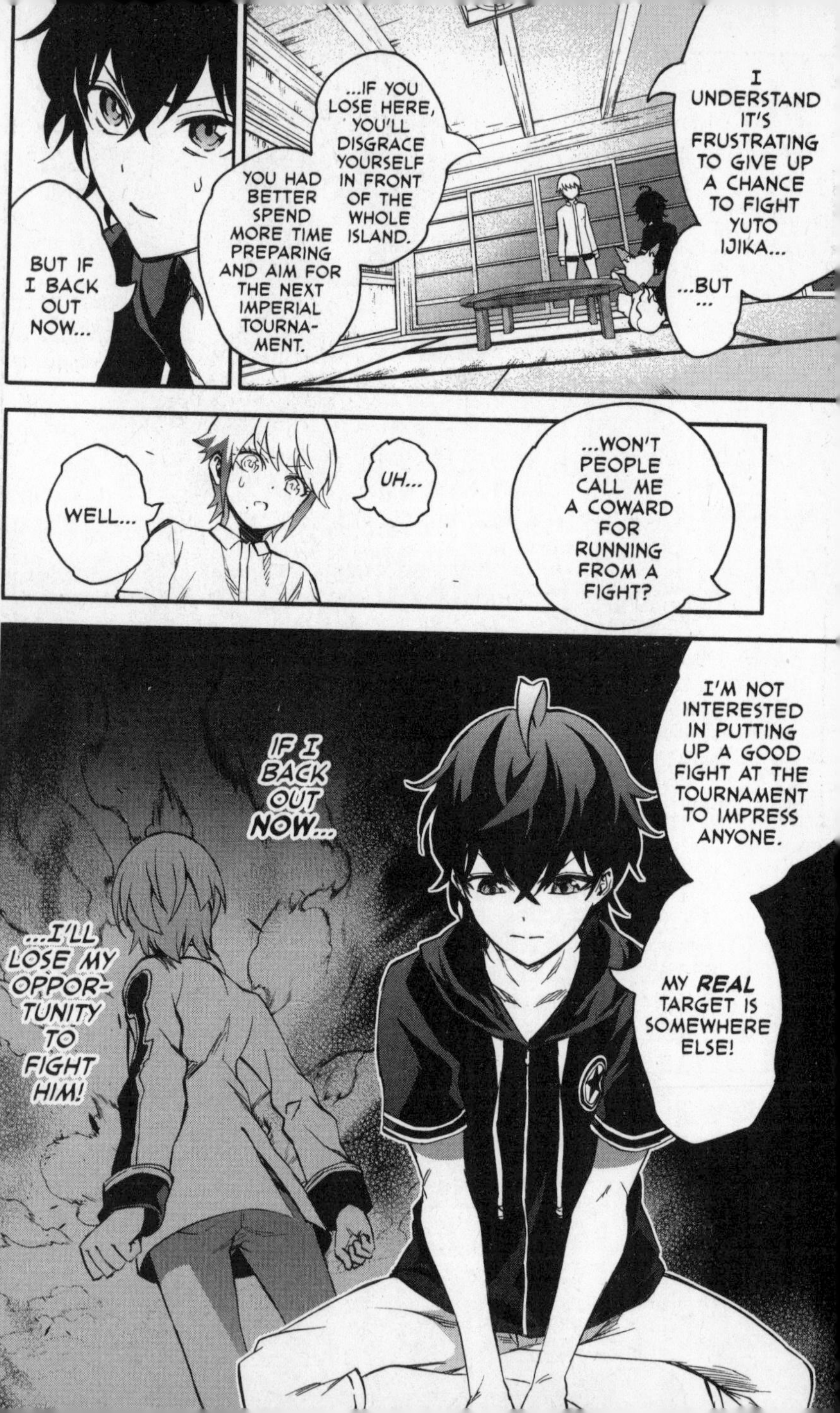
I UNDERSTAND IT'S FRUSTRATING TO GIVE UP A CHANCE TO FIGHT YUTO IJIKA...
...BUT ...
...IF YOU LOSE HERE, YOU'LL DISGRACE YOURSELF IN FRONT OF THE WHOLE ISLAND.
YOU HAD BETTER SPEND MORE TIME PREPARING AND AIM FOR THE NEXT IMPERIAL TOURNAMENT.
BUT IF I BACK OUT NOW...
...WON'T PEOPLE CALL ME A COWARD FOR RUNNING FROM A FIGHT?
UH...
WELL...
I'M NOT INTERESTED IN PUTTING UP A GOOD FIGHT AT THE TOURNAMENT TO IMPRESS ANYONE.
MY REAL TARGET IS SOMEWHERE ELSE!
IF I BACK OUT NOW...
...I'LL LOSE MY OPPORTUNITY TO FIGHT HIM!

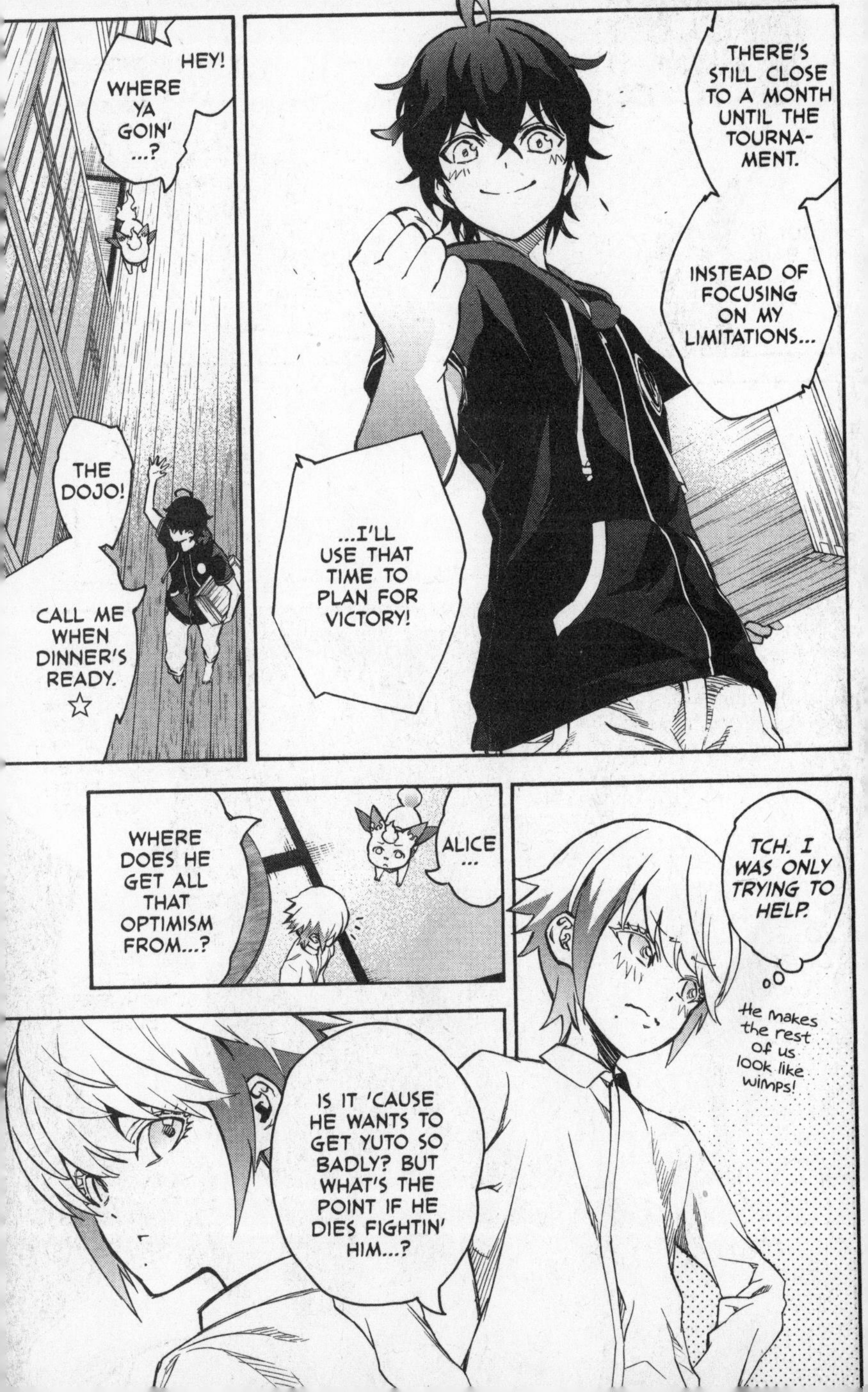
THERE'S STILL CLOSE TO A MONTH UNTIL THE TOURNA-MENT.
INSTEAD OF FOCUSING ON MY LIMITATIONS...
...I'LL USE THAT TIME TO PLAN FOR VICTORY!
HEY! WHERE YA GOIN' ...?
THE DOJO!
CALL ME WHEN DINNER'S READY. ☆
TCH. I WAS ONLY TRYING TO HELP.
He makes the rest of us look like wimps!
ALICE ...
WHERE DOES HE GET ALL THAT OPTIMISM FROM...?
IS IT 'CAUSE HE WANTS TO GET YUTO SO BADLY? BUT WHAT'S THE POINT IF HE DIES FIGHTIN' HIM...?

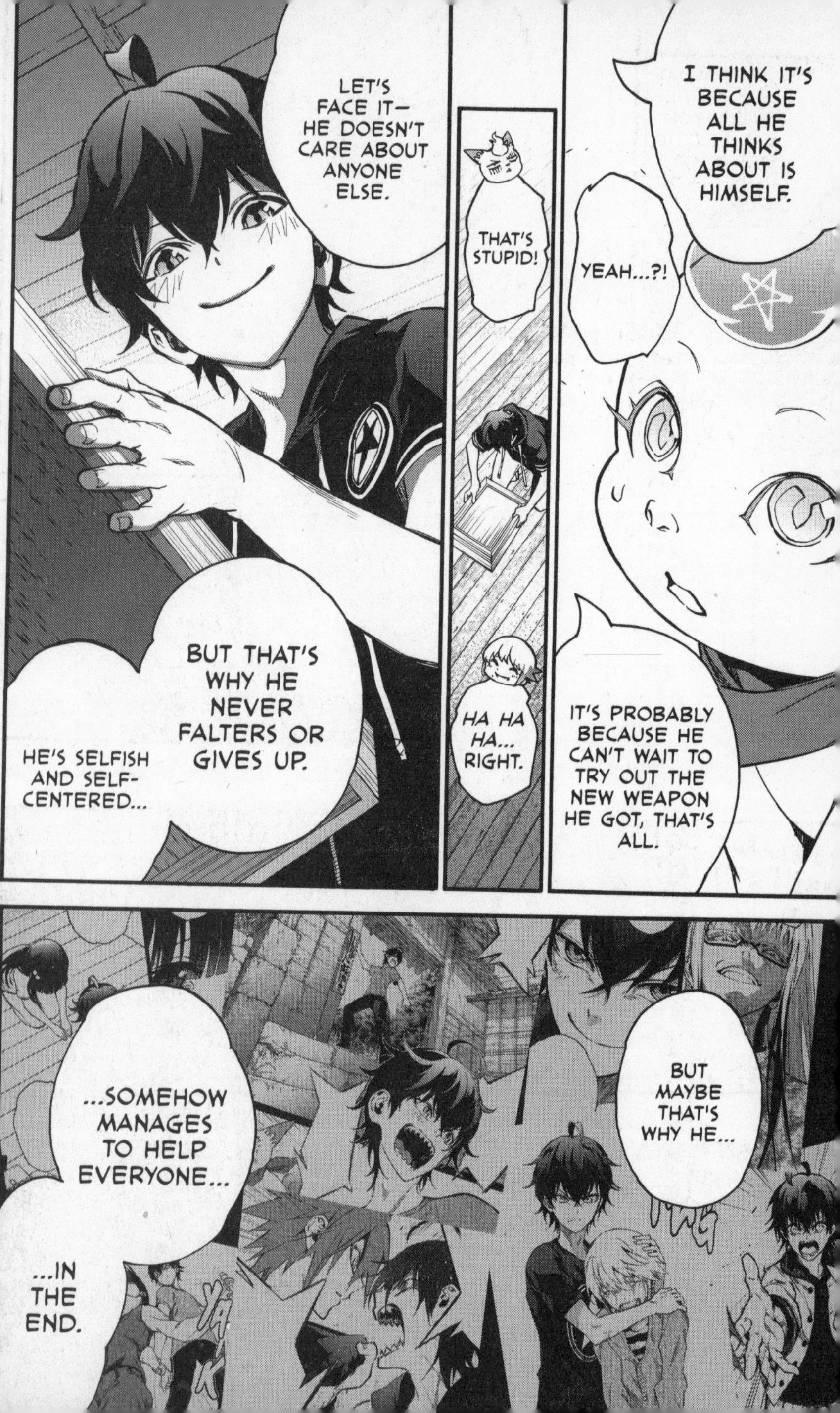
I THINK IT'S BECAUSE ALL HE THINKS ABOUT IS HIMSELF.
YEAH...?!
IT'S PROBABLY BECAUSE HE CAN'T WAIT TO TRY OUT THE NEW WEAPON HE GOT, THAT'S ALL.
THAT'S STUPID!
HA HA HA... RIGHT.
LET'S FACE IT— HE DOESN'T CARE ABOUT ANYONE ELSE.
HE'S SELFISH AND SELF-CENTERED...
BUT THAT'S WHY HE NEVER FALTERS OR GIVES UP.
BUT MAYBE THAT'S WHY HE...
...SOMEHOW MANAGES TO HELP EVERYONE...
...IN THE END.

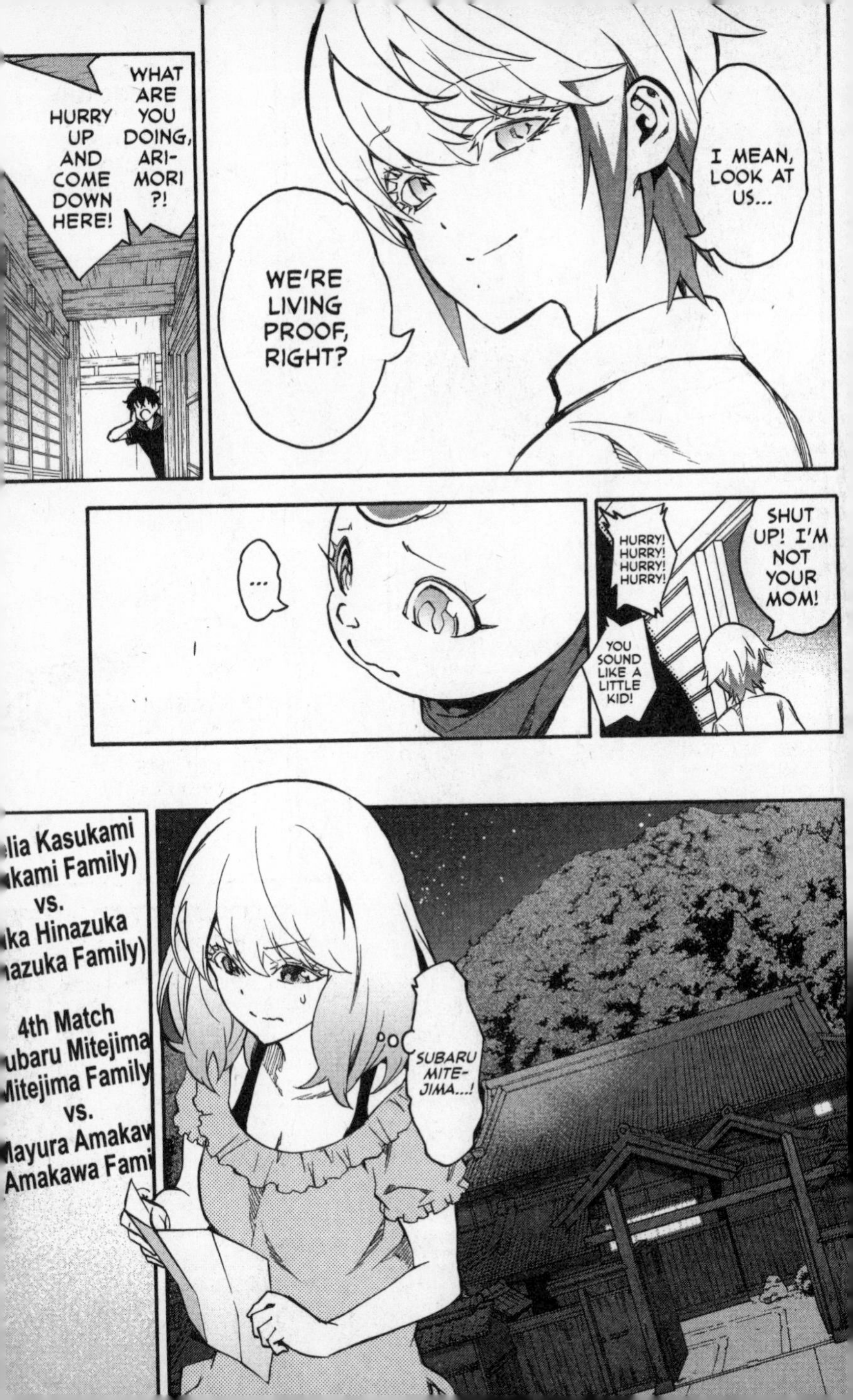
I MEAN, LOOK AT US...
WE'RE LIVING PROOF, RIGHT?
WHAT ARE YOU DOING, ARI-MORI?!
HURRY UP AND COME DOWN HERE!
SHUT UP! I'M NOT YOUR MOM!
HURRY! HURRY! HURRY! HURRY!
YOU SOUND LIKE A LITTLE KID!
...
elia Kasukami
ıkami Family)
vs.
ka Hinazuka
ıazuka Family)
4th Match
ubaru Mitejima
Mitejima Family
vs.
Mayura Amakaw
Amakawa Fami
SUBARU MITE-JIMA...!

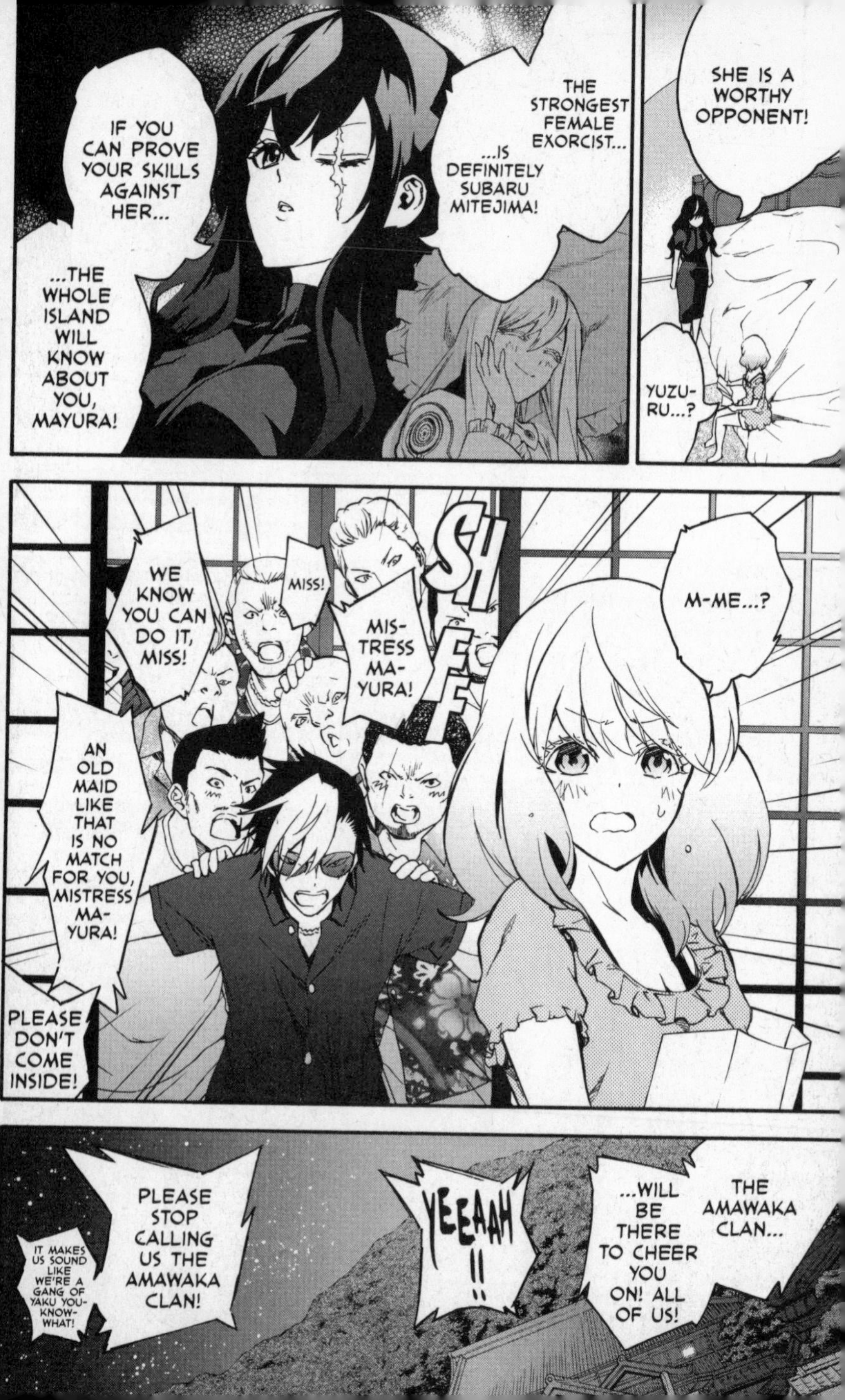
SHE IS A WORTHY OPPONENT!
YUZU-RU...?
THE STRONGEST FEMALE EXORCIST...
...IS DEFINITELY SUBARU MITEJIMA!
IF YOU CAN PROVE YOUR SKILLS AGAINST HER...
...THE WHOLE ISLAND WILL KNOW ABOUT YOU, MAYURA!
M-ME...?
SHFF
MISS!
MIS-TRESS MA-YURA!
WE KNOW YOU CAN DO IT, MISS!
AN OLD MAID LIKE THAT IS NO MATCH FOR YOU, MISTRESS MA-YURA!
PLEASE DON'T COME INSIDE!
THE AMAWAKA CLAN...
...WILL BE THERE TO CHEER YOU ON! ALL OF US!
YEEAAH!!
PLEASE STOP CALLING US THE AMAWAKA CLAN!
IT MAKES US SOUND LIKE WE'RE A GANG OF YAKU YOU-KNOW-WHAT!

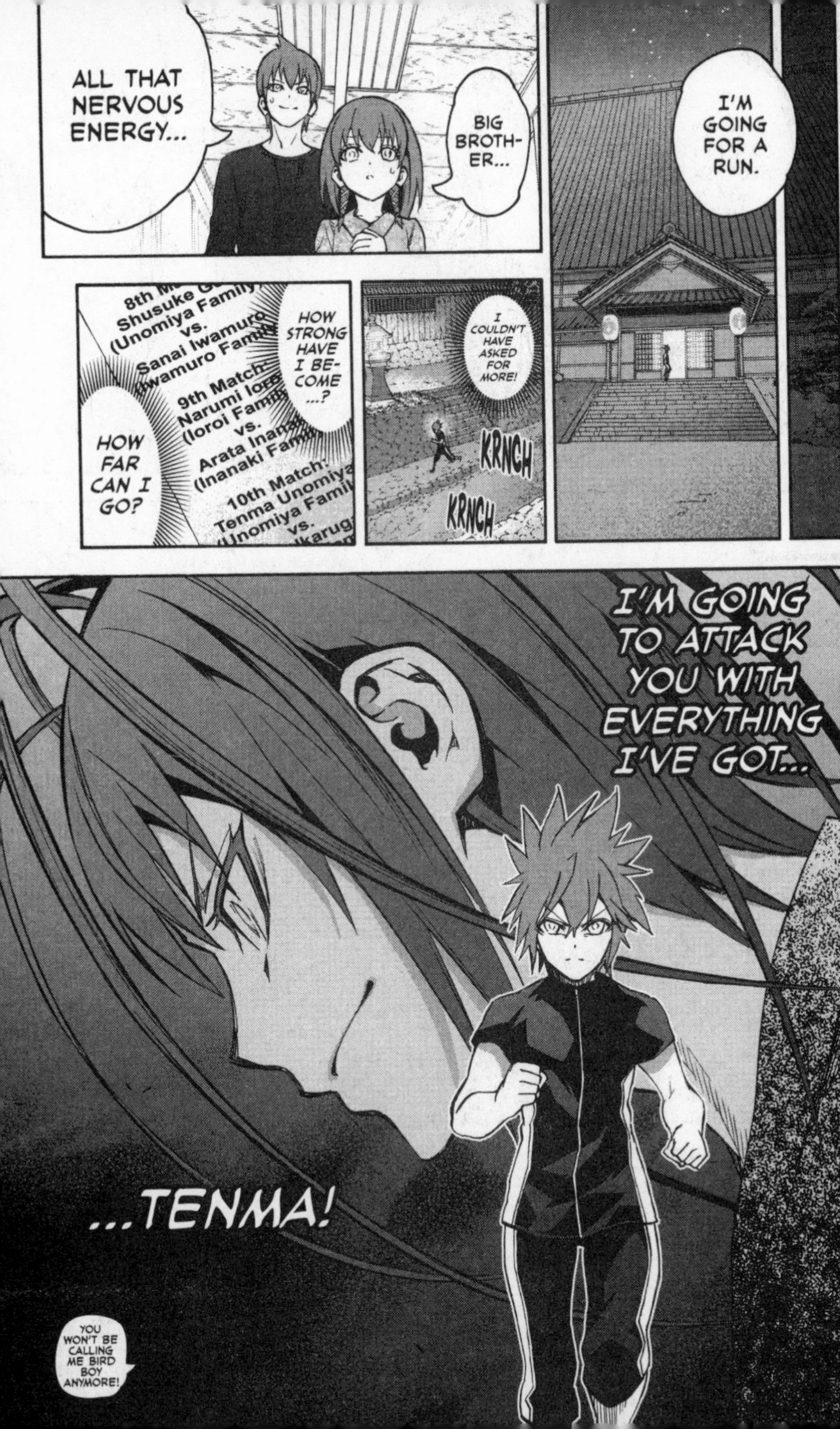
I'M GOING FOR A RUN.
BIG BROTH-ER...
ALL THAT NERVOUS ENERGY...
I COULDN'T HAVE ASKED FOR MORE!
KRNCH
KRNCH
HOW STRONG HAVE I BE-COME ...?
HOW FAR CAN I GO?
Shusuke
(Unomiya Family
vs.
Sanai Iwamuro
9th Match:
Narumi Ioroi
vs.
10th Match:
Tenma Unomiya
vs.
I'M GOING TO ATTACK YOU WITH EVERYTHING I'VE GOT...
...TENMA!
YOU WON'T BE CALLING ME BIRD BOY ANYMORE!

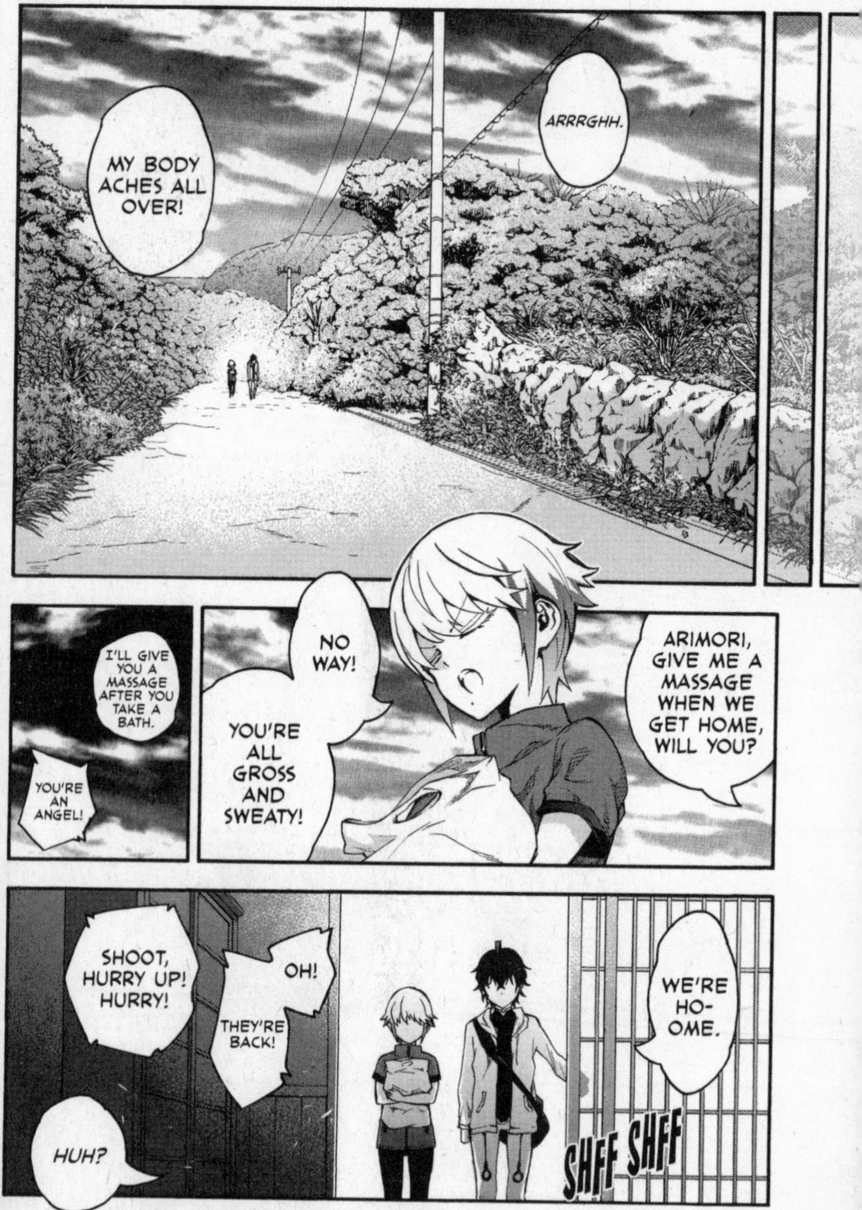
ARRRGHH.
MY BODY ACHES ALL OVER!
ARIMORI, GIVE ME A MASSAGE WHEN WE GET HOME, WILL YOU?
NO WAY!
YOU'RE ALL GROSS AND SWEATY!
I'LL GIVE YOU A MASSAGE AFTER YOU TAKE A BATH.
YOU'RE AN ANGEL!
WE'RE HO-OME.
SHFF SHFF
OH!
THEY'RE BACK!
SHOOT, HURRY UP! HURRY!
HUH?

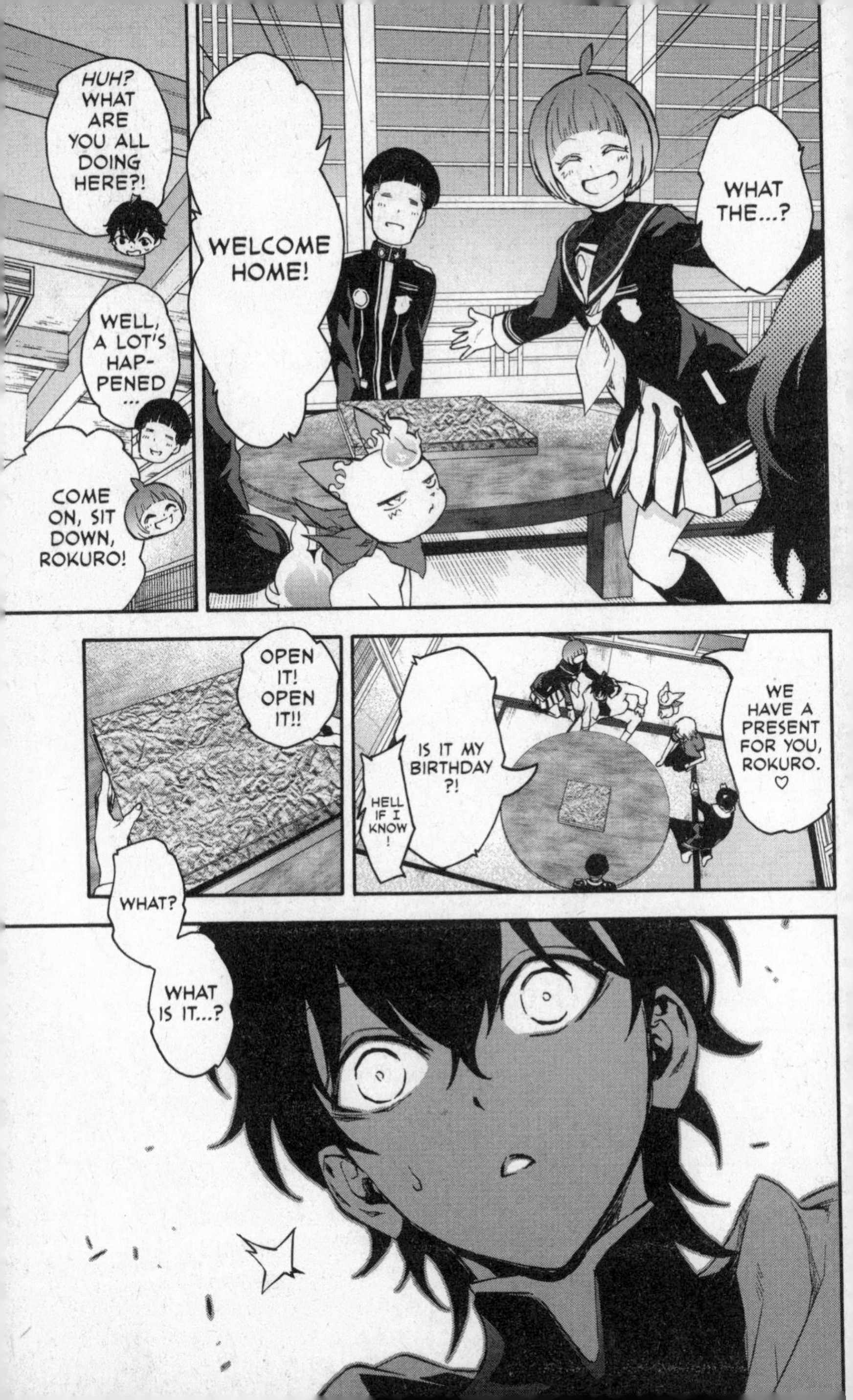
WHAT THE...?
WELCOME HOME!
HUH? WHAT ARE YOU ALL DOING HERE?!
WELL, A LOT'S HAP-PENED...
COME ON, SIT DOWN, ROKURO!
WE HAVE A PRESENT FOR YOU, ROKURO. ♡
IS IT MY BIRTHDAY?!
HELL IF I KNOW!
OPEN IT! OPEN IT!!
WHAT?
WHAT IS IT...?

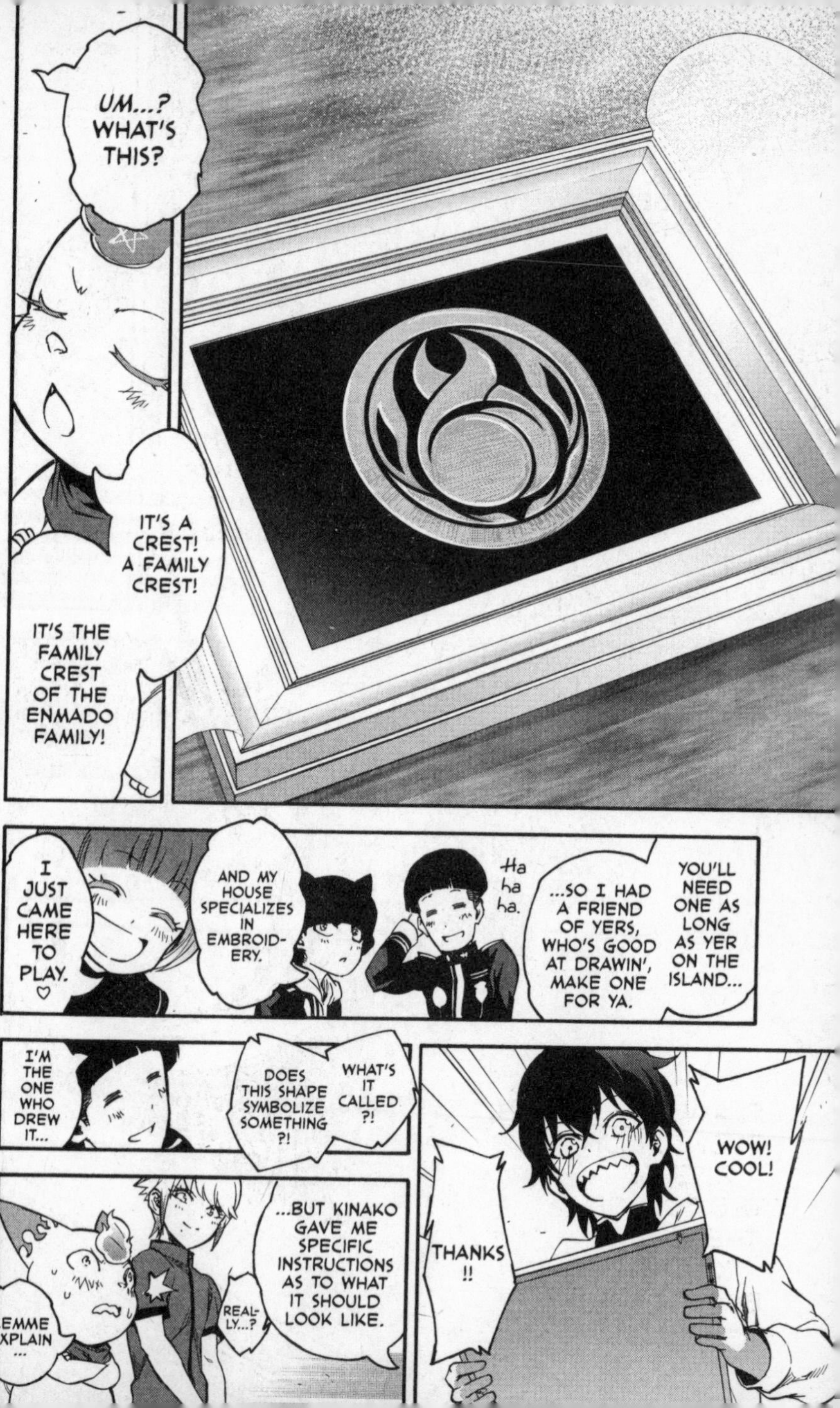
UM...? WHAT'S THIS?
IT'S A CREST! A FAMILY CREST!
IT'S THE FAMILY CREST OF THE ENMADO FAMILY!
YOU'LL NEED ONE AS LONG AS YER ON THE ISLAND...
...SO I HAD A FRIEND OF YERS, WHO'S GOOD AT DRAWIN', MAKE ONE FOR YA.
Ha ha ha.
AND MY HOUSE SPECIALIZES IN EMBROIDERY.
I JUST CAME HERE TO PLAY. ♡
WOW! COOL!
THANKS!!
WHAT'S IT CALLED?!
DOES THIS SHAPE SYMBOLIZE SOMETHING?!
I'M THE ONE WHO DREW IT...
...BUT KINAKO GAVE ME SPECIFIC INSTRUCTIONS AS TO WHAT IT SHOULD LOOK LIKE.
REALLY...?
LEMME EXPLAIN...

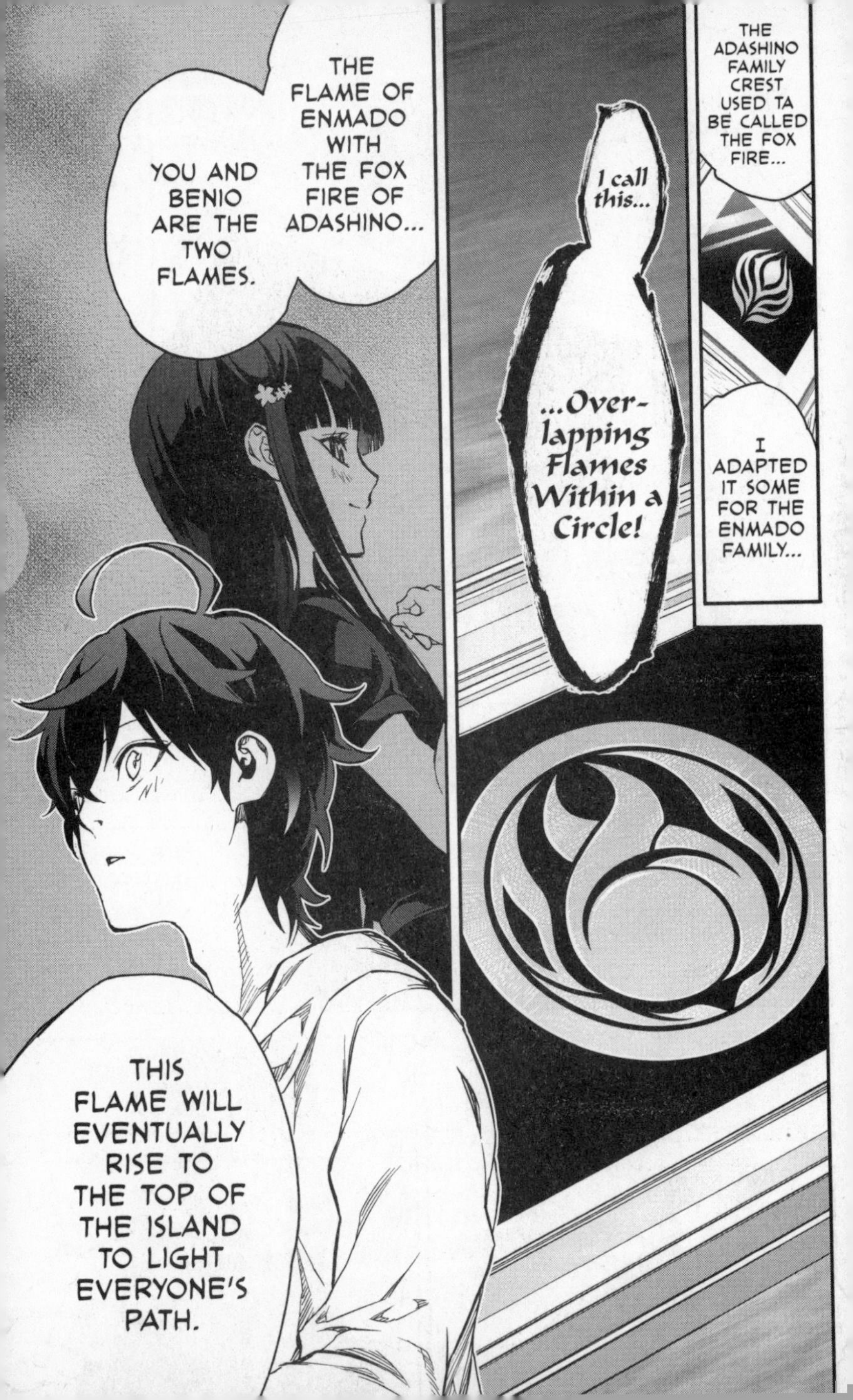
THE ADASHINO FAMILY CREST USED TA BE CALLED THE FOX FIRE...
I ADAPTED IT SOME FOR THE ENMADO FAMILY...
I call this...
...Over-lapping Flames Within a Circle!
THE FLAME OF ENMADO WITH THE FOX FIRE OF ADASHINO...
YOU AND BENIO ARE THE TWO FLAMES.
THIS FLAME WILL EVENTUALLY RISE TO THE TOP OF THE ISLAND TO LIGHT EVERYONE'S PATH.

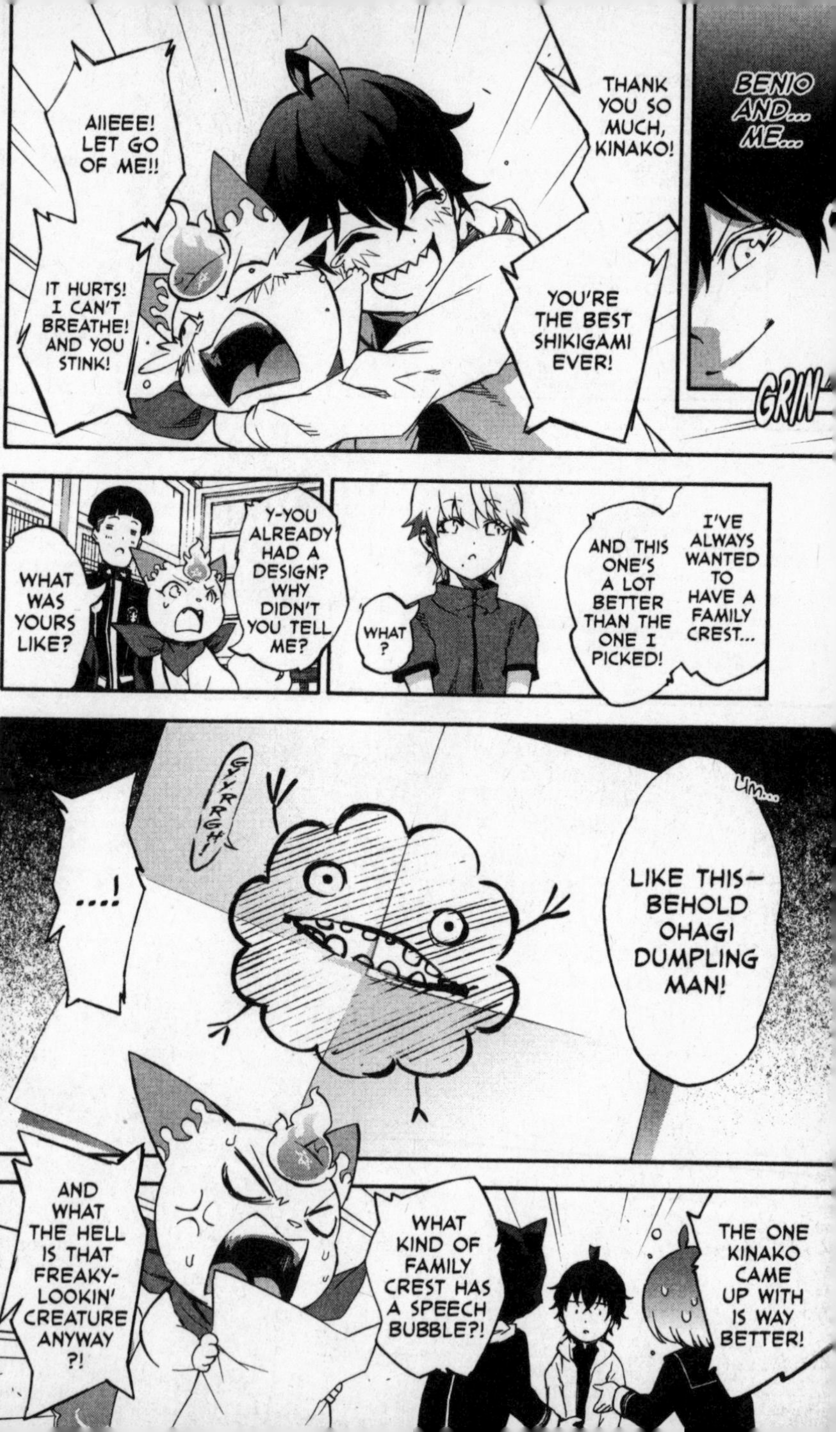
BENIO AND... ME...
GRIN
THANK YOU SO MUCH, KINAKO!
YOU'RE THE BEST SHIKIGAMI EVER!
AIIEEE! LET GO OF ME!!
IT HURTS! I CAN'T BREATHE! AND YOU STINK!
I'VE ALWAYS WANTED TO HAVE A FAMILY CREST...
AND THIS ONE'S A LOT BETTER THAN THE ONE I PICKED!
WHAT?
Y-YOU ALREADY HAD A DESIGN? WHY DIDN'T YOU TELL ME?
WHAT WAS YOURS LIKE?
UM...
LIKE THIS— BEHOLD OHAGI DUMPLING MAN!
GYYRRGH!
...!
THE ONE KINAKO CAME UP WITH IS WAY BETTER!
WHAT KIND OF FAMILY CREST HAS A SPEECH BUBBLE?!
AND WHAT THE HELL IS THAT FREAKY-LOOKIN' CREATURE ANYWAY?!

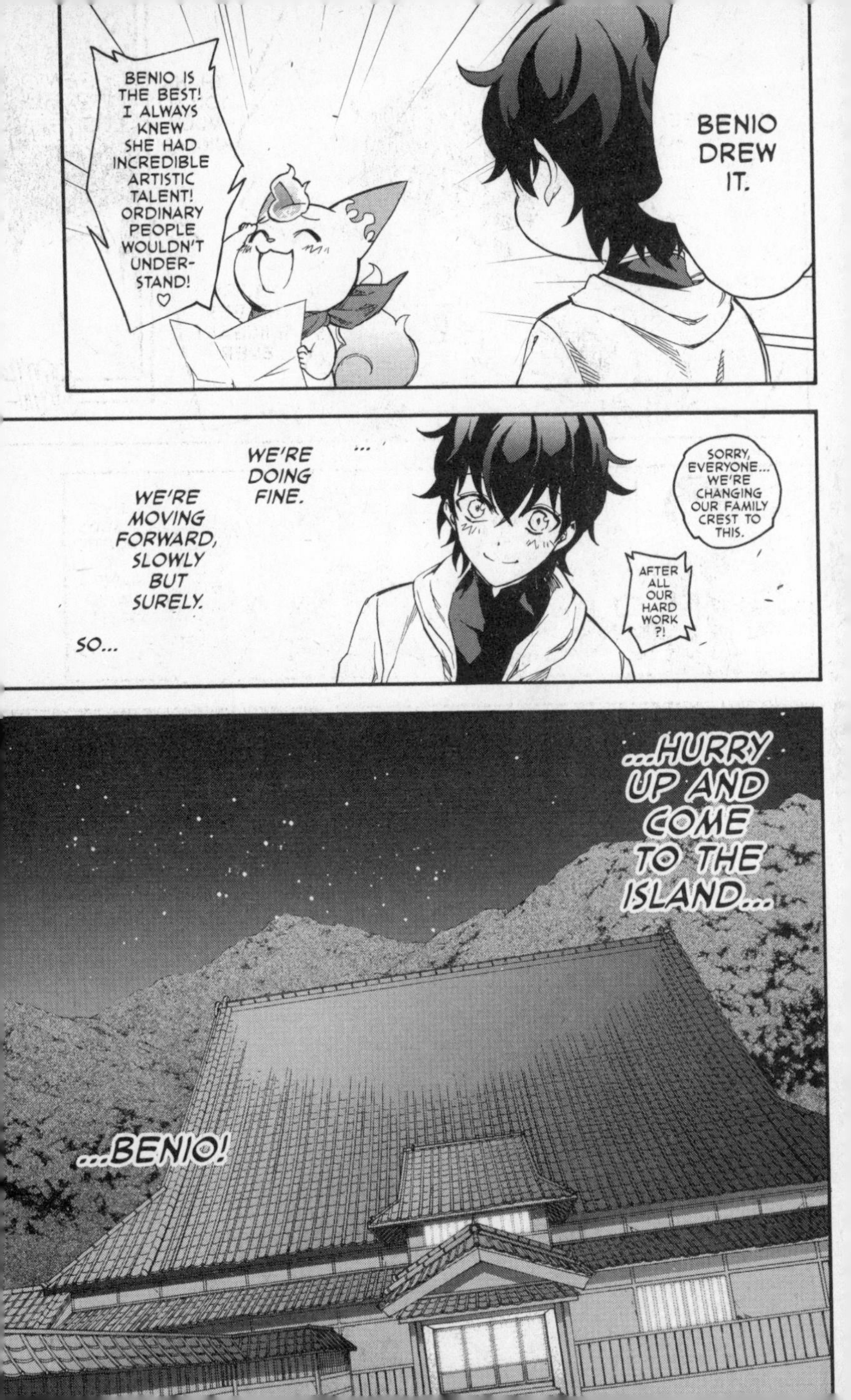
BENIO DREW IT.
BENIO IS THE BEST! I ALWAYS KNEW SHE HAD INCREDIBLE ARTISTIC TALENT! ORDINARY PEOPLE WOULDN'T UNDER-STAND! ♡
SORRY, EVERYONE... WE'RE CHANGING OUR FAMILY CREST TO THIS.
AFTER ALL OUR HARD WORK?!
...
WE'RE DOING FINE.
WE'RE MOVING FORWARD, SLOWLY BUT SURELY.
SO...
...HURRY UP AND COME TO THE ISLAND...
...BENIO!

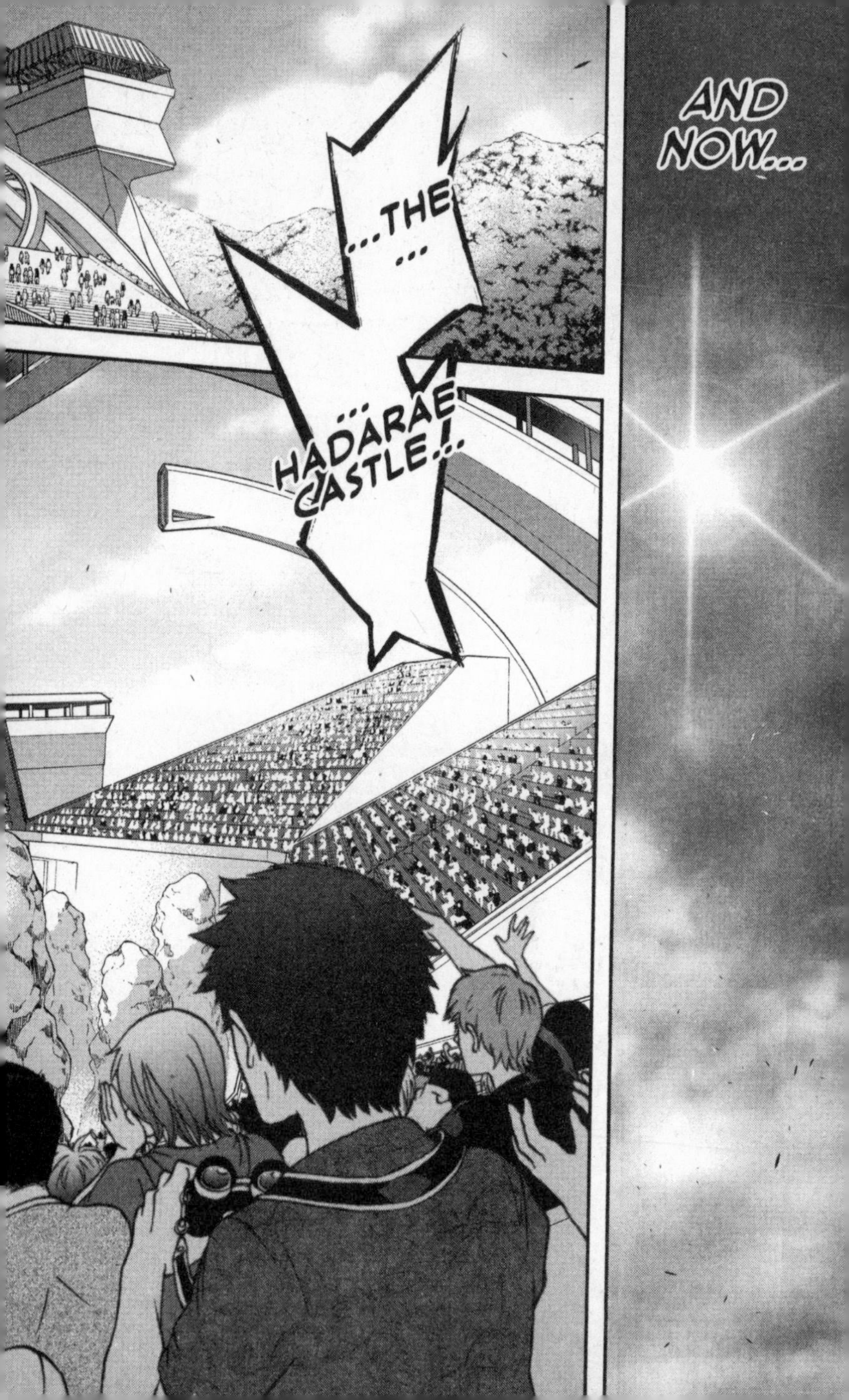
AND NOW...
...THE ...
...HADARAE CASTLE...!!

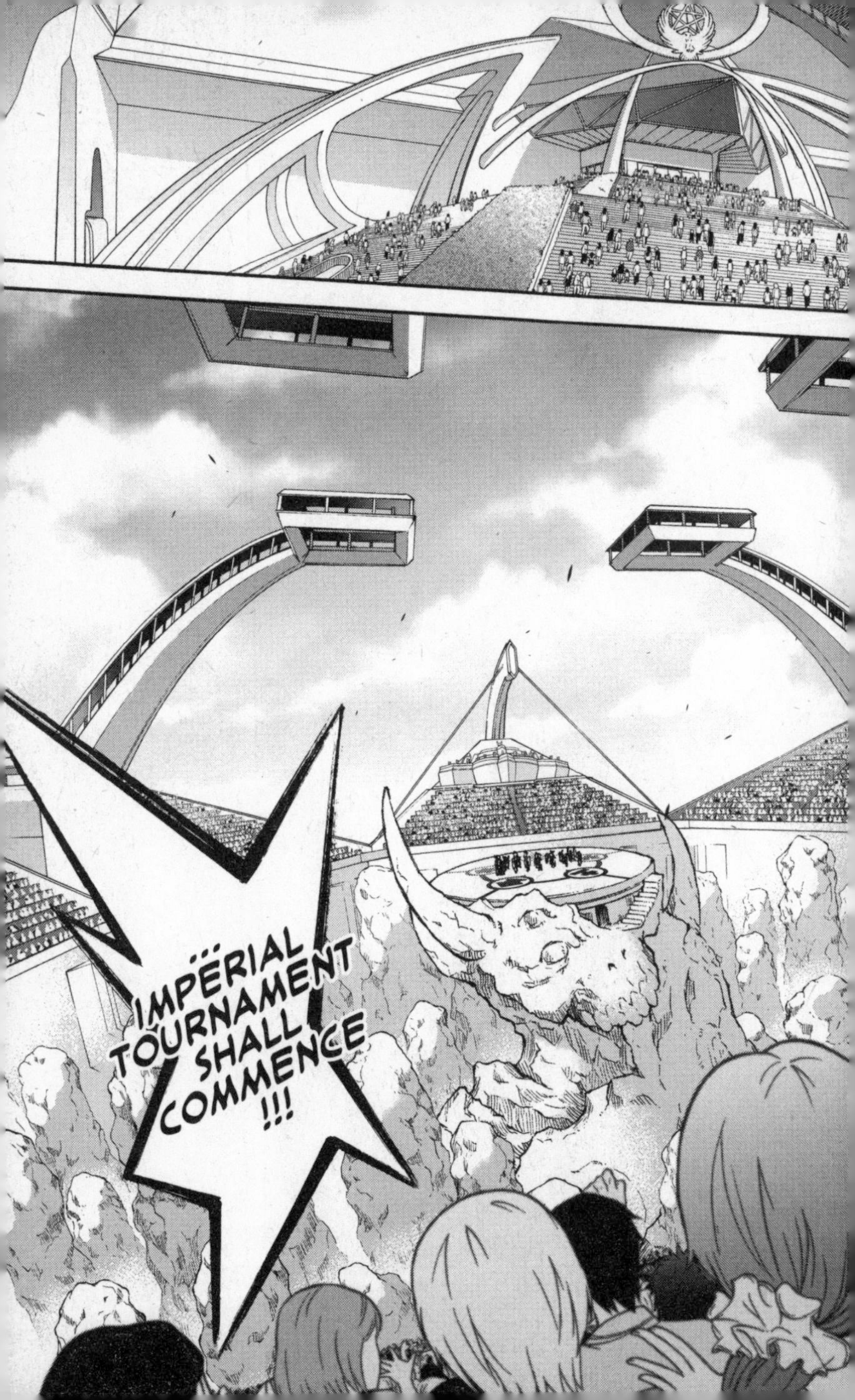
...IMPERIAL TOURNAMENT SHALL COMMENCE!!!

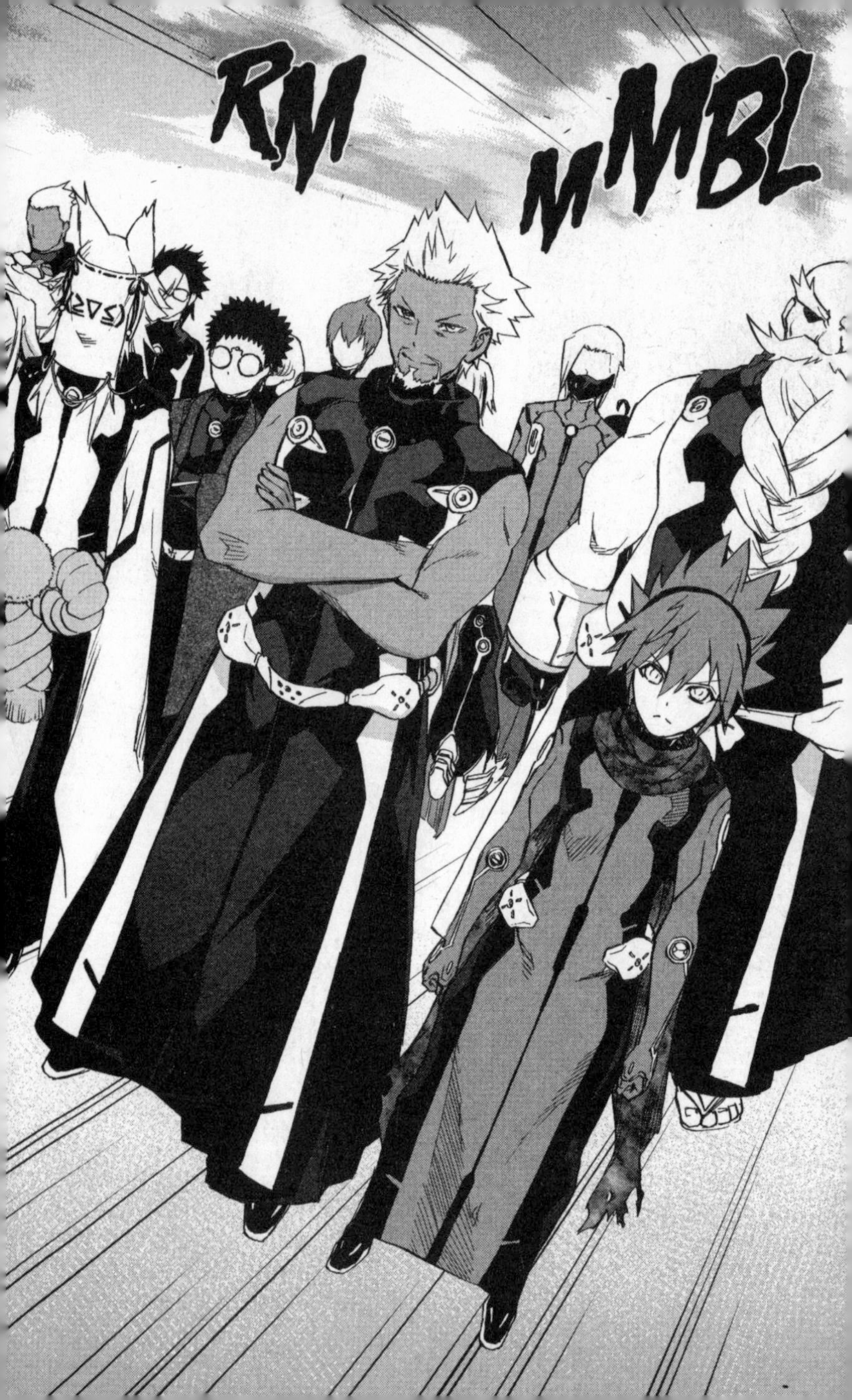
RM
MMBL

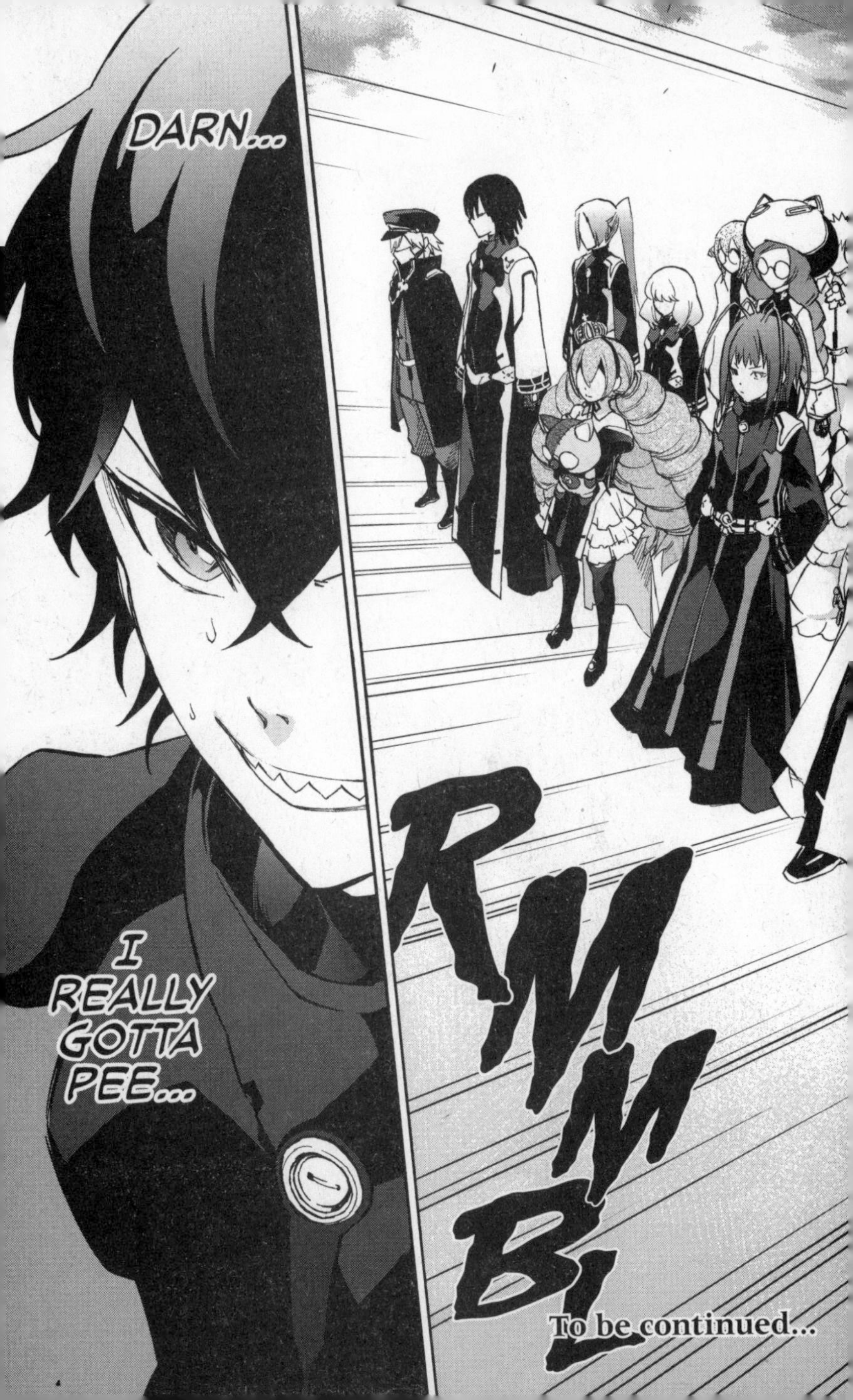
RMMB!
To be continued...
DARN...
I REALLY GOTTA PEE...

# Bonus: Twin Stars' Excursion

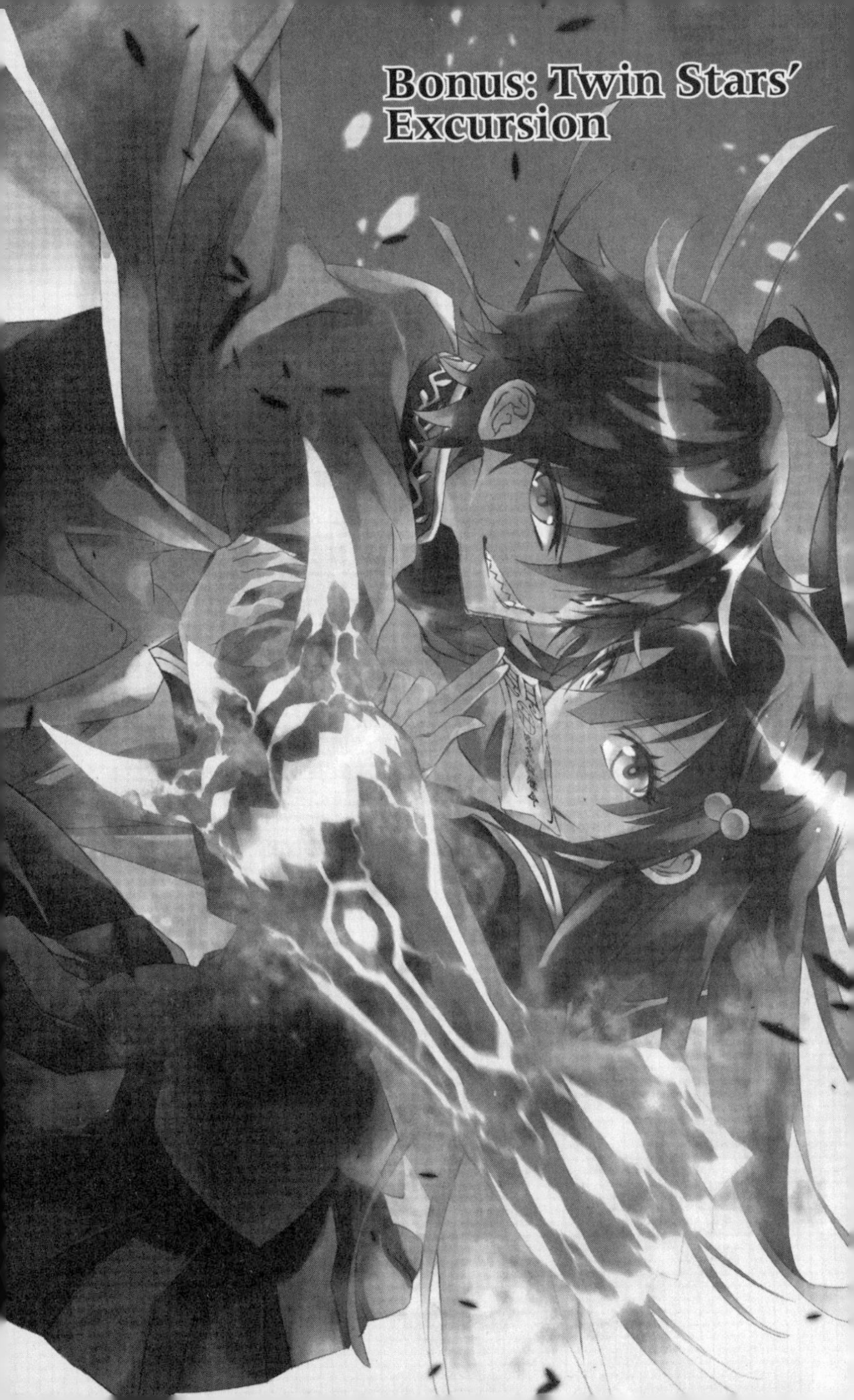

Twin Star Exorcists

ONMYOJI

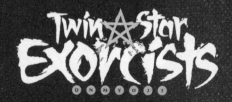

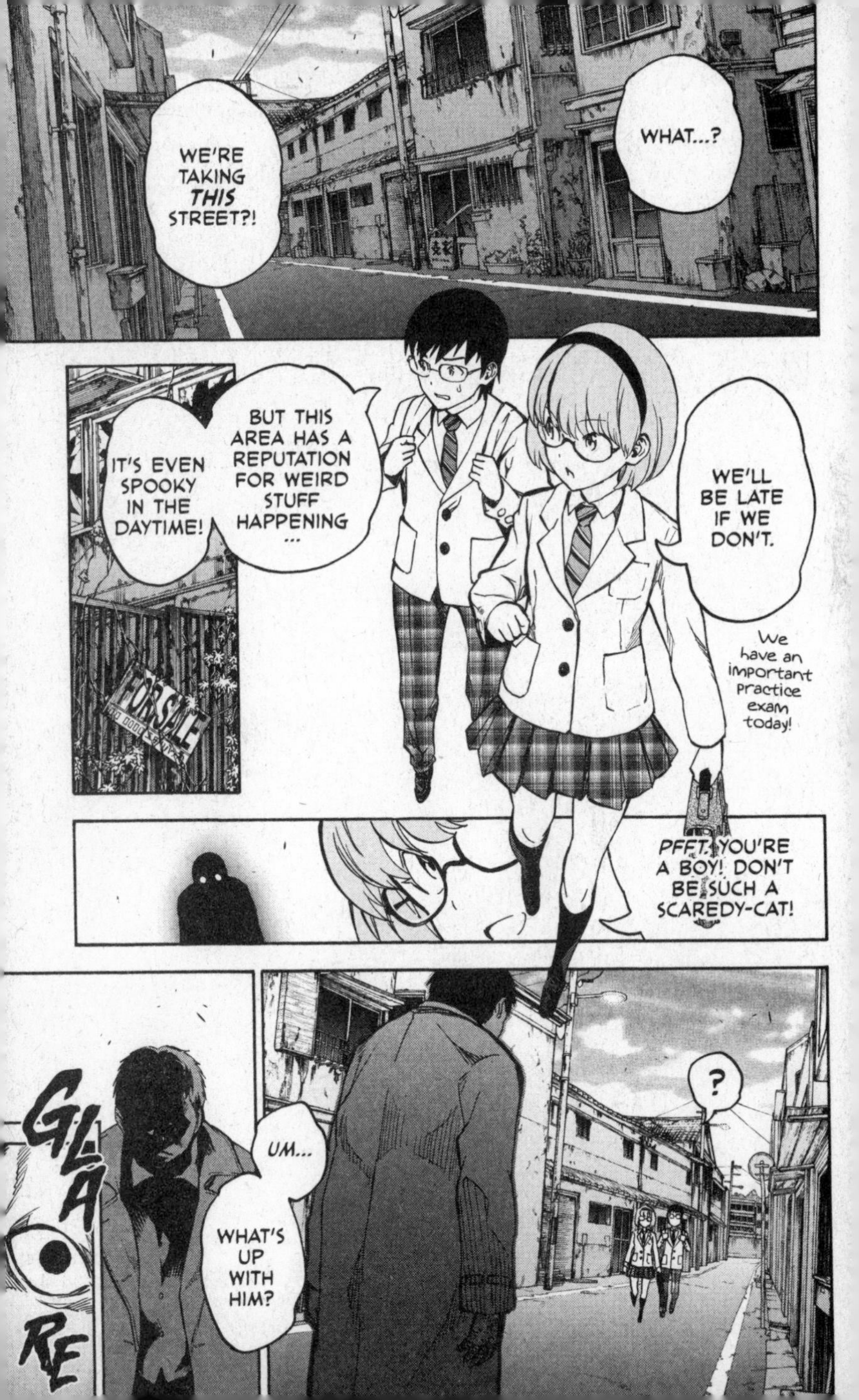
WHAT...?
WE'RE TAKING *THIS* STREET?!
WE'LL BE LATE IF WE DON'T.
We have an important practice exam today!
BUT THIS AREA HAS A REPUTATION FOR WEIRD STUFF HAPPENING...
IT'S EVEN SPOOKY IN THE DAYTIME!
FOR SALE
*PFFT.* YOU'RE A BOY! DON'T BE SUCH A SCAREDY-CAT!
?
UM...
WHAT'S UP WITH HIM?
GLARE

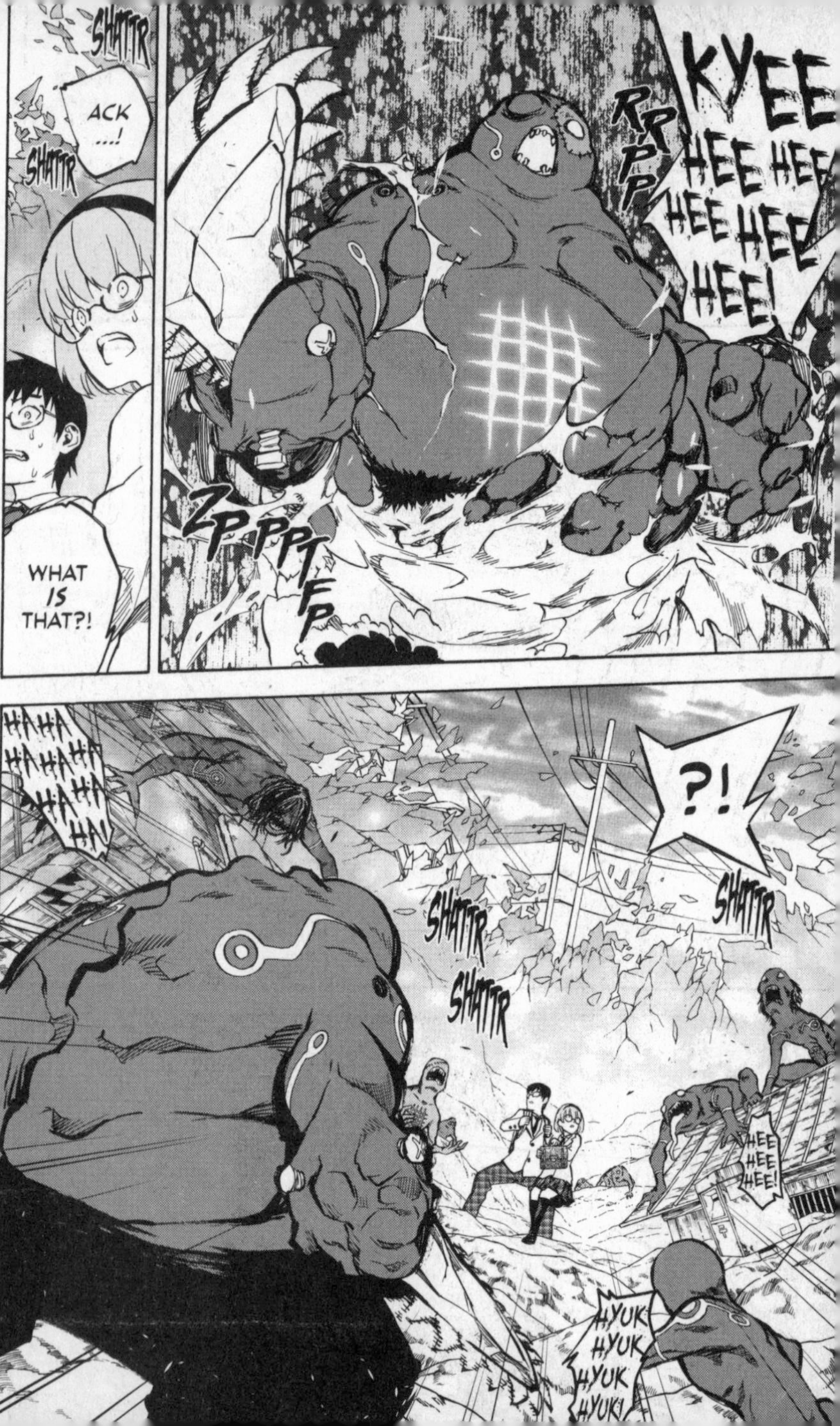
KYEE HEE HEE HEE HEE HEE!
RRPP
ZPPPTFP
SHATTR
ACK ....!
SHATTR
WHAT IS THAT?!
?!
SHATTR
HAHA HAHAHA HAHA HA!
SHATTR
SHATTR
HEE HEE HEE!
HYUK HYUK HYUK HYUK!

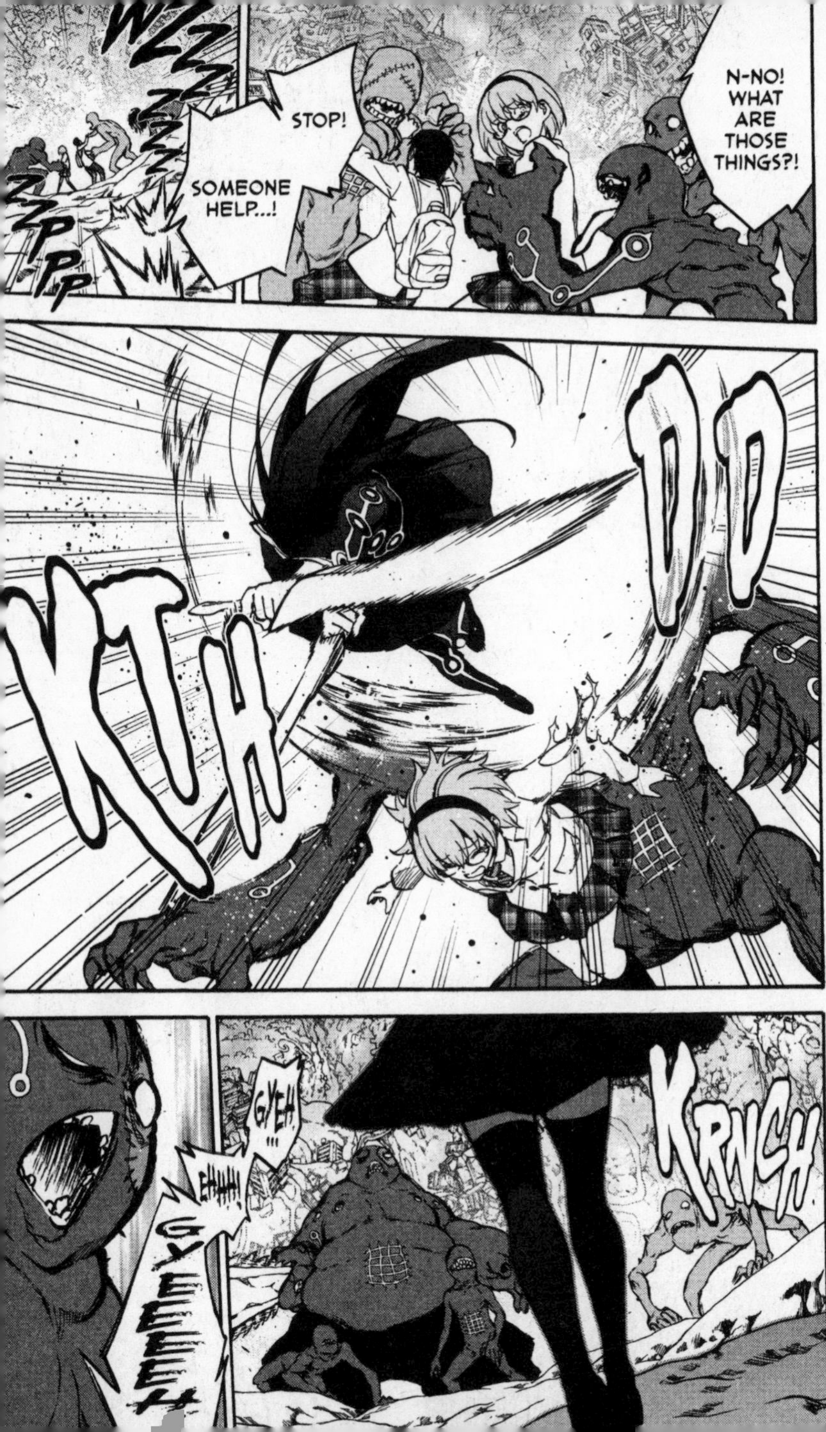
N-NO! WHAT ARE THOSE THINGS?!
STOP!
SOMEONE HELP...!
KRNCH
GYEH!!!
EHHHH!
GYEEEEEEEH!

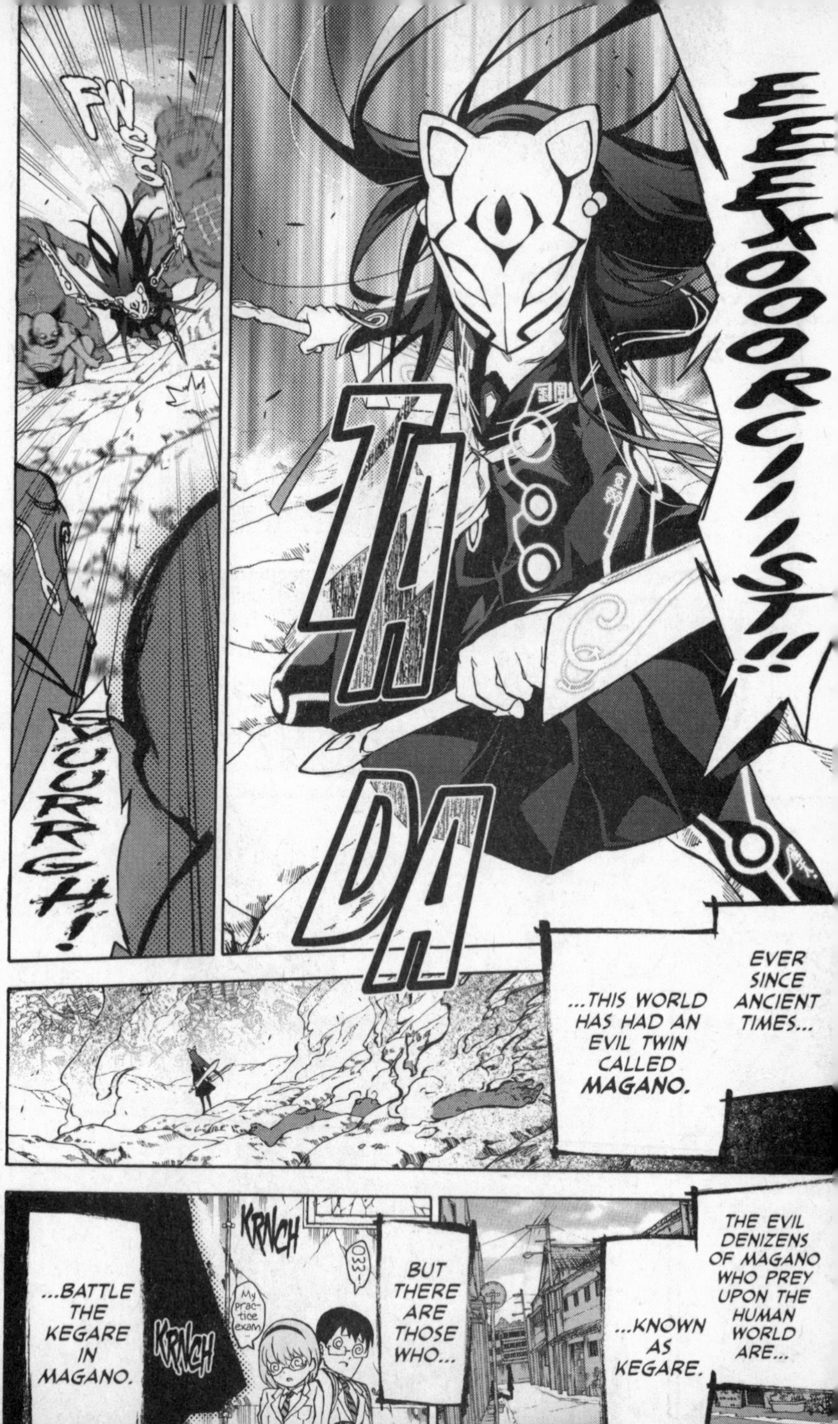
EEEXOOORCIIIST!!
TA
DA
FNSS
GYURRGH!
EVER SINCE ANCIENT TIMES...
...THIS WORLD HAS HAD AN EVIL TWIN CALLED MAGANO.
THE EVIL DENIZENS OF MAGANO WHO PREY UPON THE HUMAN WORLD ARE...
...KNOWN AS KEGARE.
BUT THERE ARE THOSE WHO...
OWW!
KRNCH
My practice exam...
KRNCH
...BATTLE THE KEGARE IN MAGANO.

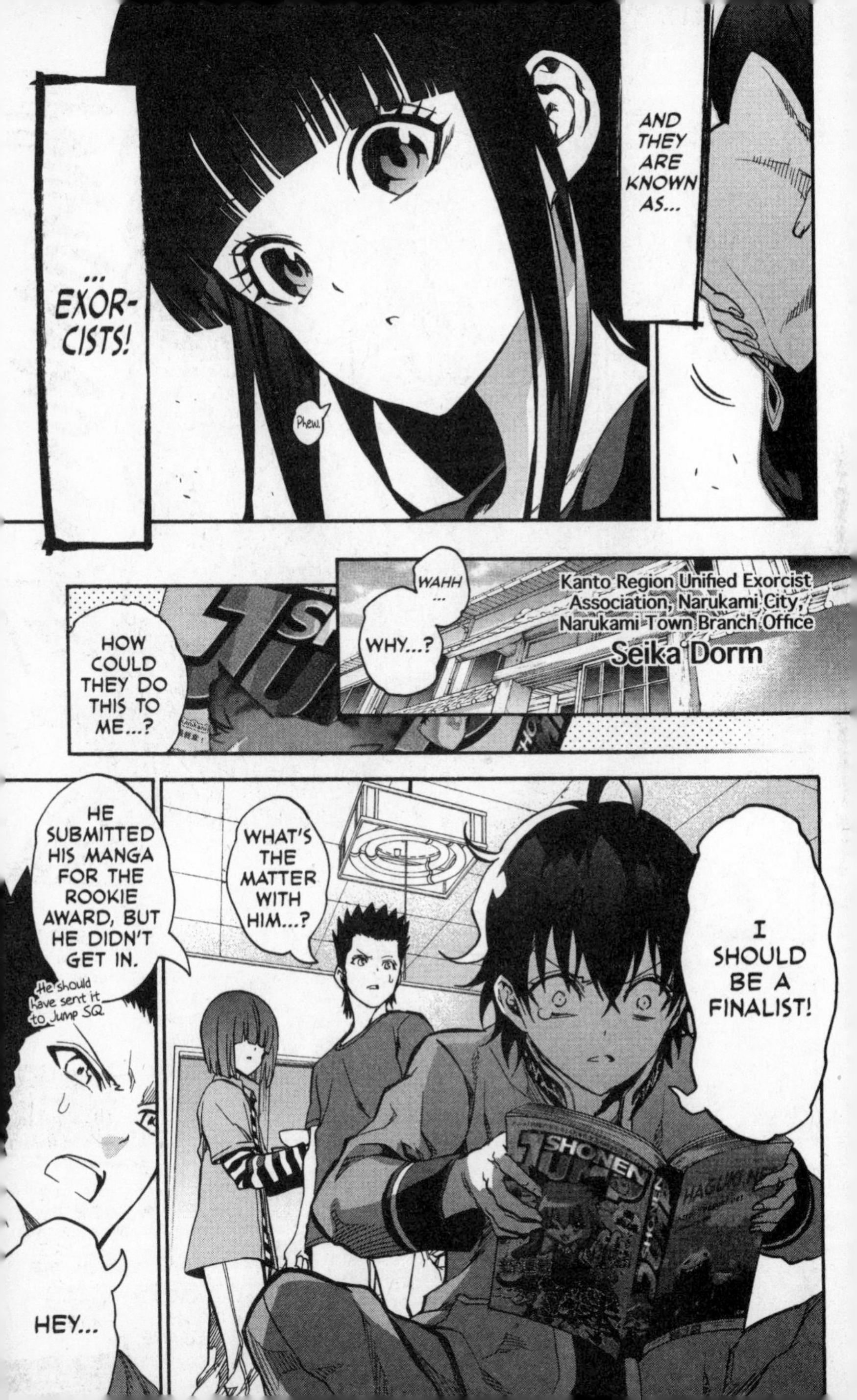
AND THEY ARE KNOWN AS...
...EXÖRCISTS!
Phew.
Kanto Region Unified Exorcist Association, Narukami City, Narukami Town Branch Office
Seika Dorm
WAHH...
WHY...?
HOW COULD THEY DO THIS TO ME...?
I SHOULD BE A FINALIST!
WHAT'S THE MATTER WITH HIM...?
HE SUBMITTED HIS MANGA FOR THE ROOKIE AWARD, BUT HE DIDN'T GET IN.
He should have sent it to Jump SQ.
HEY...
SHONEN JUMP

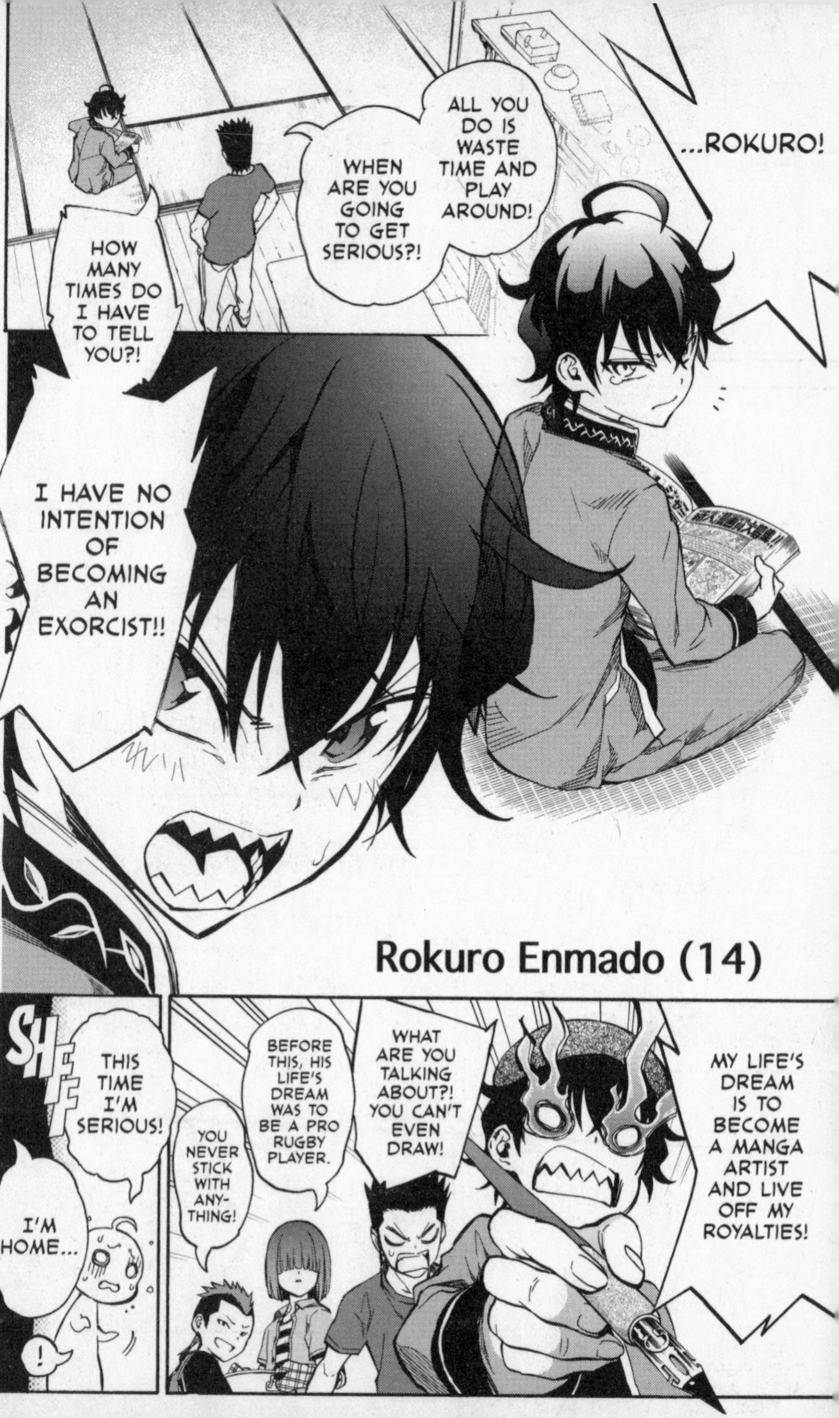
...ROKURO!
ALL YOU DO IS WASTE TIME AND PLAY AROUND!
WHEN ARE YOU GOING TO GET SERIOUS?!
HOW MANY TIMES DO I HAVE TO TELL YOU?!
I HAVE NO INTENTION OF BECOMING AN EXORCIST!!
Rokuro Enmado (14)
MY LIFE'S DREAM IS TO BECOME A MANGA ARTIST AND LIVE OFF MY ROYALTIES!
WHAT ARE YOU TALKING ABOUT?! YOU CAN'T EVEN DRAW!
BEFORE THIS, HIS LIFE'S DREAM WAS TO BE A PRO RUGBY PLAYER.
YOU NEVER STICK WITH ANY-THING!
SHFF
THIS TIME I'M SERIOUS!
I'M HOME...
!

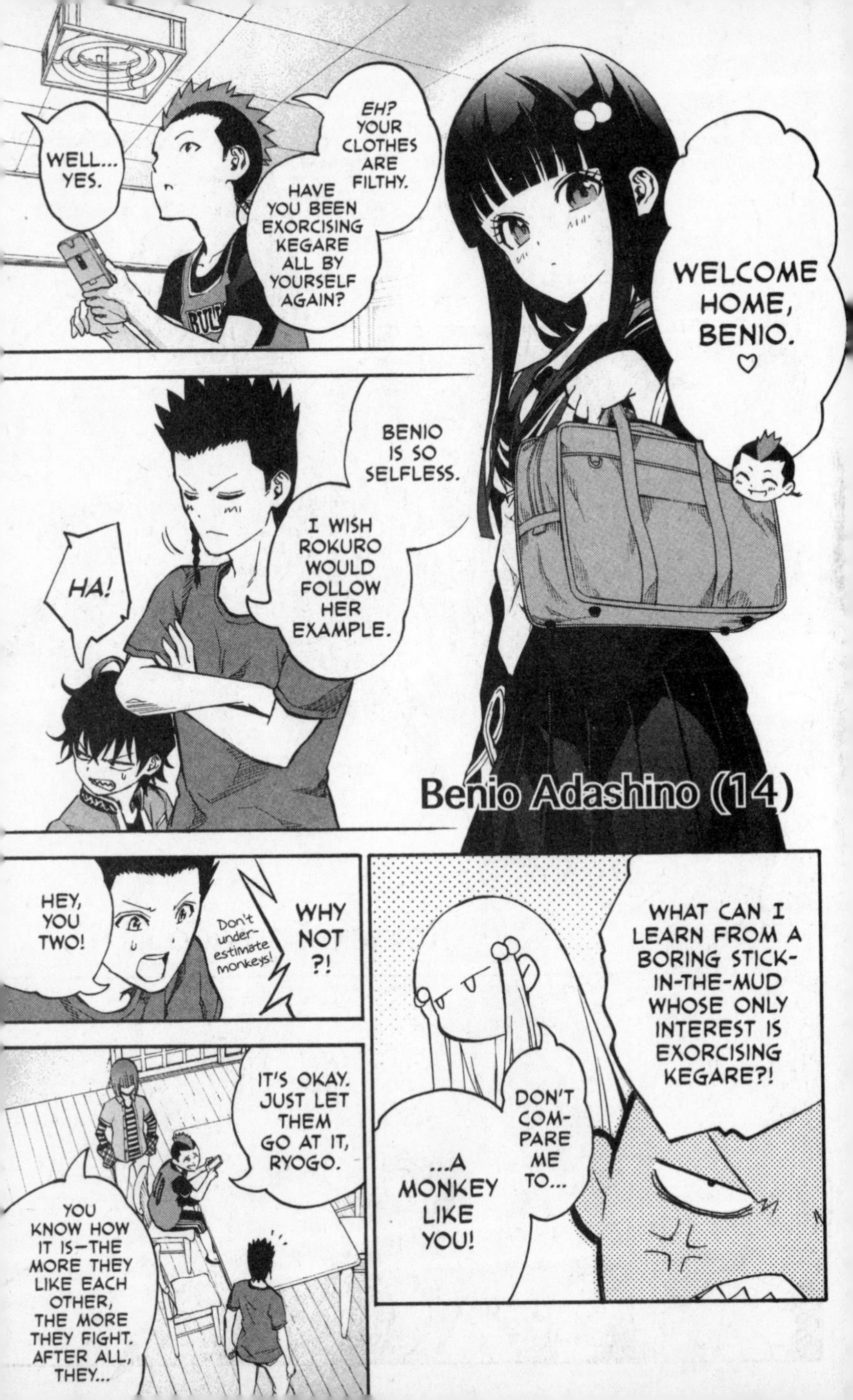
WELCOME HOME, BENIO. ♡
Benio Adashino (14)
EH? YOUR CLOTHES ARE FILTHY. HAVE YOU BEEN EXORCISING KEGARE ALL BY YOURSELF AGAIN?
WELL... YES.
BENIO IS SO SELFLESS.
I WISH ROKURO WOULD FOLLOW HER EXAMPLE.
HA!
WHAT CAN I LEARN FROM A BORING STICK-IN-THE-MUD WHOSE ONLY INTEREST IS EXORCISING KEGARE?!
DON'T COM-PARE ME TO...
...A MONKEY LIKE YOU!
WHY NOT ?!
Don't under-estimate monkeys!
HEY, YOU TWO!
IT'S OKAY. JUST LET THEM GO AT IT, RYOGO.
YOU KNOW HOW IT IS—THE MORE THEY LIKE EACH OTHER, THE MORE THEY FIGHT. AFTER ALL, THEY...

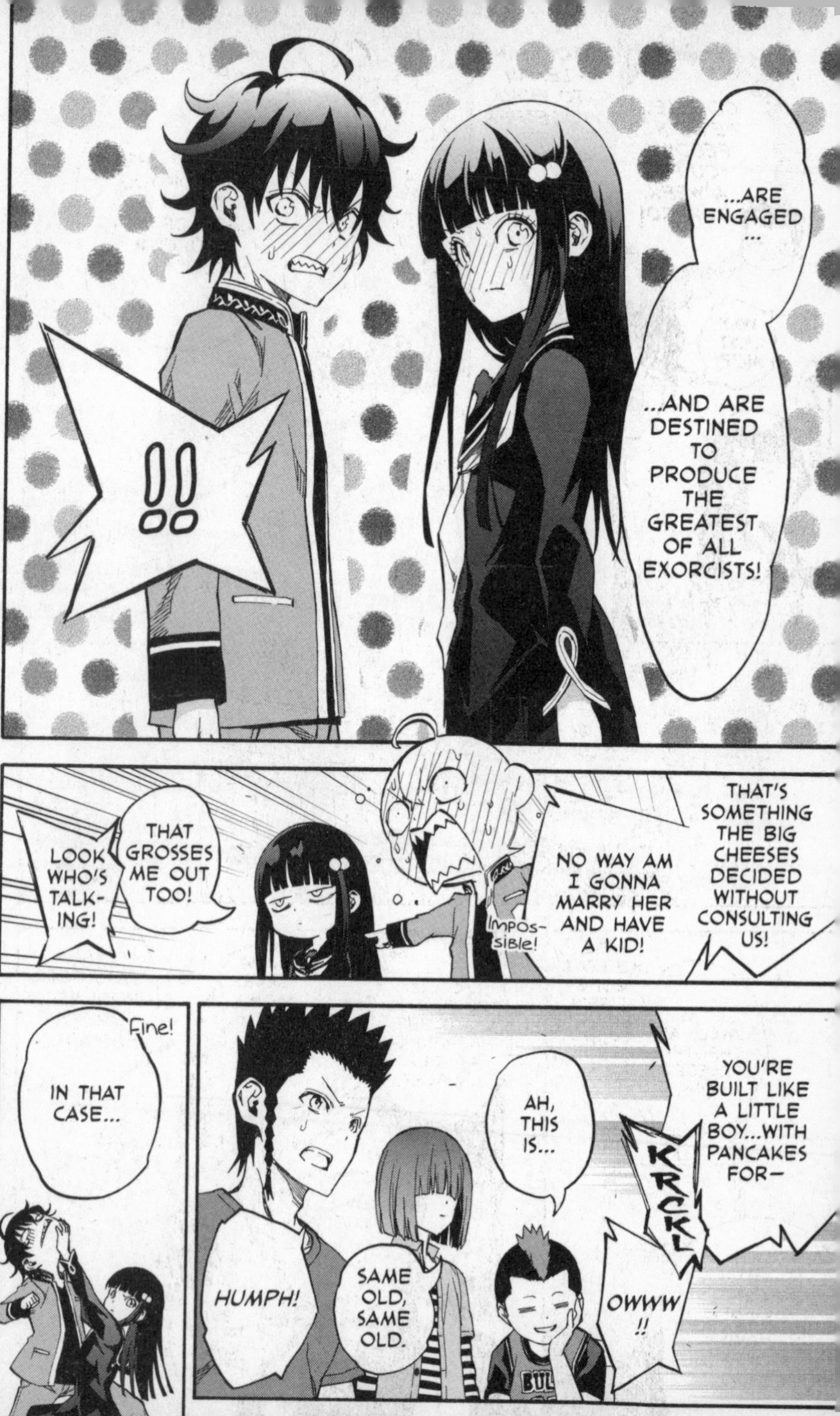
...ARE ENGAGED ...
...AND ARE DESTINED TO PRODUCE THE GREATEST OF ALL EXORCISTS!
!!
THAT'S SOMETHING THE BIG CHEESES DECIDED WITHOUT CONSULTING US!
NO WAY AM I GONNA MARRY HER AND HAVE A KID!
Impos-sible!
THAT GROSSES ME OUT TOO!
LOOK WHO'S TALK-ING!
YOU'RE BUILT LIKE A LITTLE BOY...WITH PANCAKES FOR—
KRCKL
OWWW !!
AH, THIS IS...
HUMPH!
SAME OLD, SAME OLD.
Fine!
IN THAT CASE...

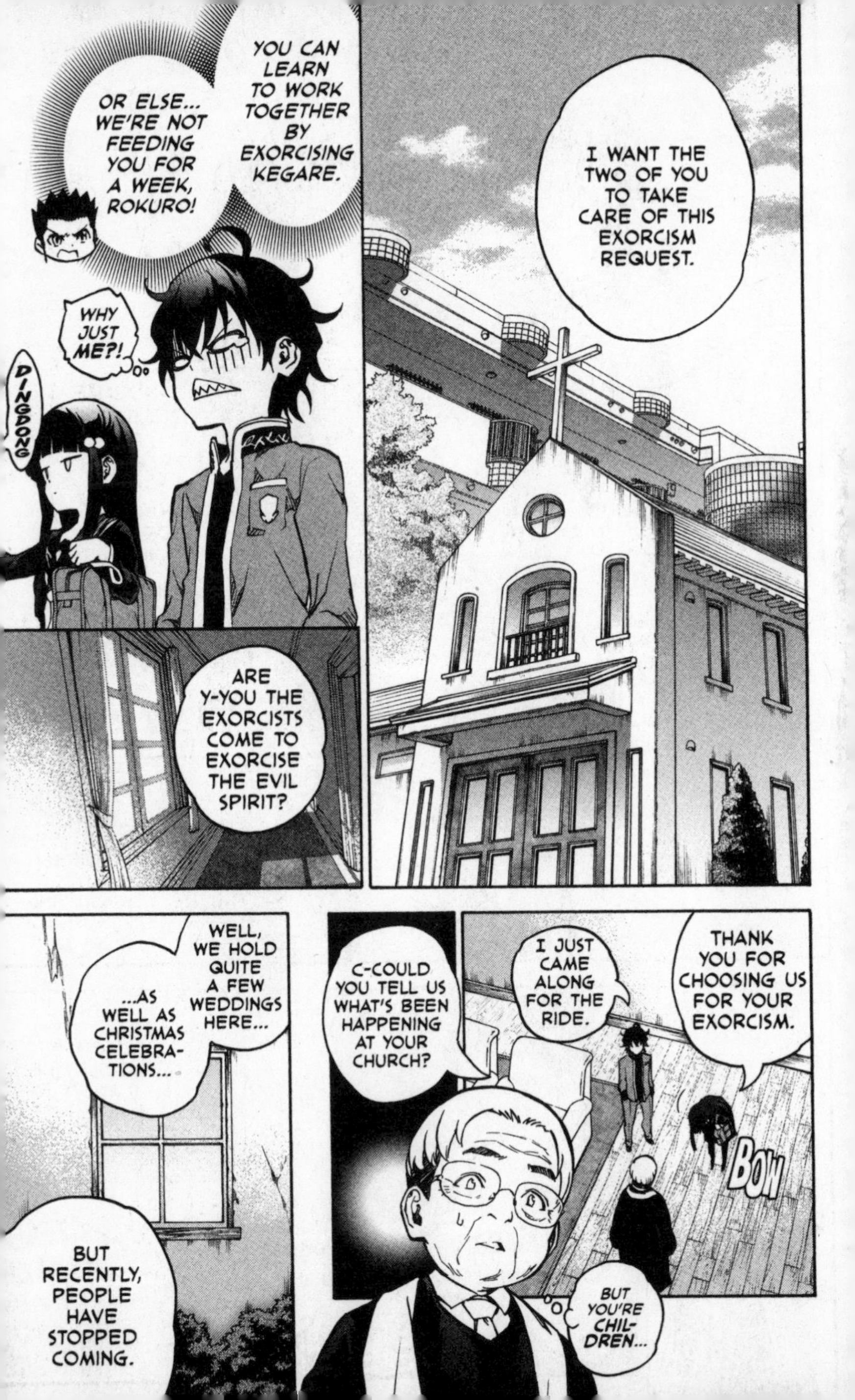
I WANT THE TWO OF YOU TO TAKE CARE OF THIS EXORCISM REQUEST.
YOU CAN LEARN TO WORK TOGETHER BY EXORCISING KEGARE.
OR ELSE... WE'RE NOT FEEDING YOU FOR A WEEK, ROKURO!
WHY JUST ME?!
DINGDONG
ARE Y-YOU THE EXORCISTS COME TO EXORCISE THE EVIL SPIRIT?
THANK YOU FOR CHOOSING US FOR YOUR EXORCISM.
I JUST CAME ALONG FOR THE RIDE.
BOW
BUT YOU'RE CHIL-DREN...
C-COULD YOU TELL US WHAT'S BEEN HAPPENING AT YOUR CHURCH?
WELL, WE HOLD QUITE A FEW WEDDINGS HERE...
...AS WELL AS CHRISTMAS CELEBRA-TIONS...
BUT RECENTLY, PEOPLE HAVE STOPPED COMING.

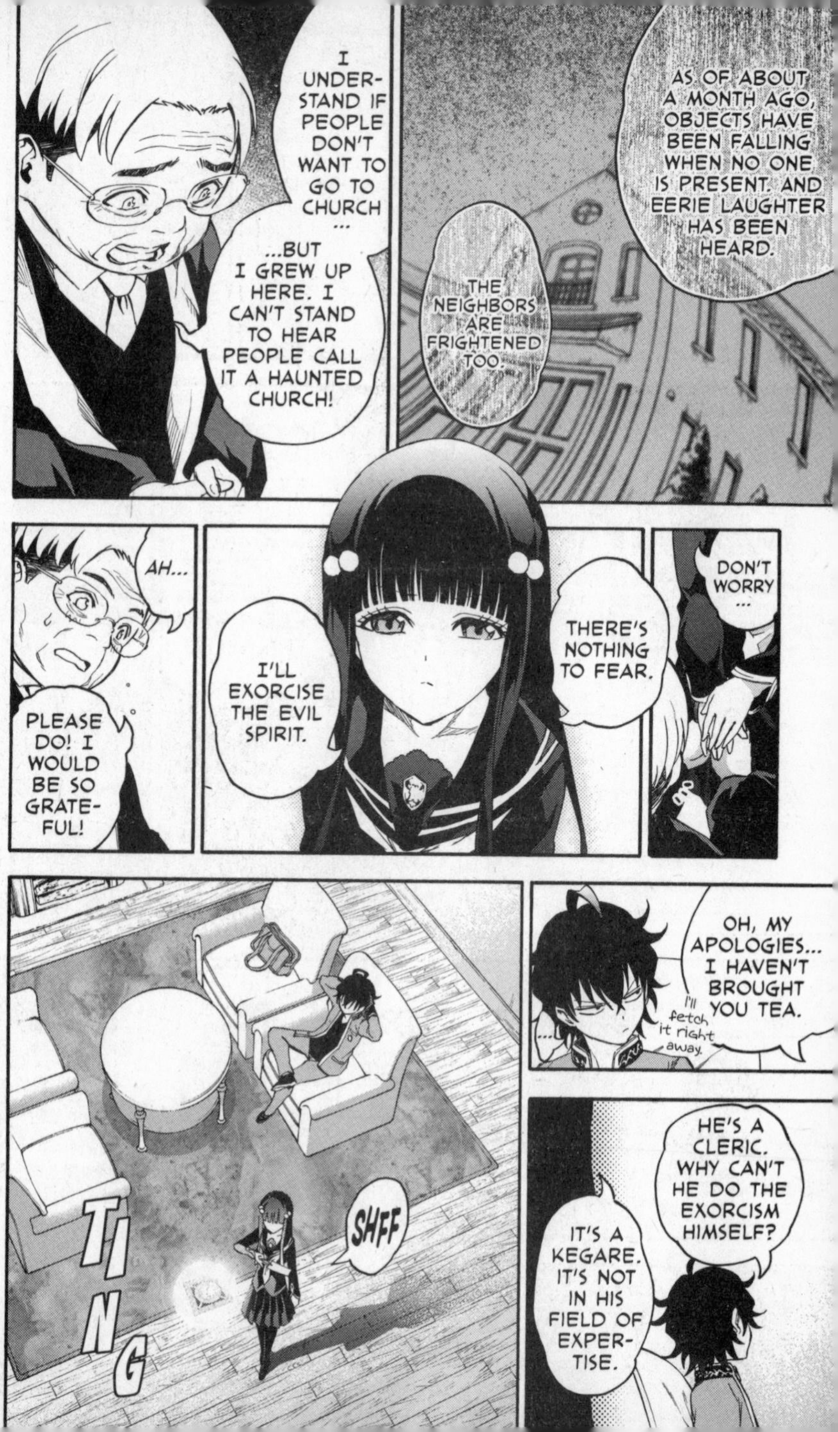
AS OF ABOUT A MONTH AGO, OBJECTS HAVE BEEN FALLING WHEN NO ONE IS PRESENT. AND EERIE LAUGHTER HAS BEEN HEARD.
THE NEIGHBORS ARE FRIGHTENED TOO.
I UNDER-STAND IF PEOPLE DON'T WANT TO GO TO CHURCH...
...BUT I GREW UP HERE. I CAN'T STAND TO HEAR PEOPLE CALL IT A HAUNTED CHURCH!
DON'T WORRY...
THERE'S NOTHING TO FEAR.
I'LL EXORCISE THE EVIL SPIRIT.
AH...
PLEASE DO! I WOULD BE SO GRATE-FUL!
OH, MY APOLOGIES... I HAVEN'T BROUGHT YOU TEA.
I'll fetch it right away.
...
HE'S A CLERIC. WHY CAN'T HE DO THE EXORCISM HIMSELF?
IT'S A KEGARE. IT'S NOT IN HIS FIELD OF EXPER-TISE.
SHFF
TING

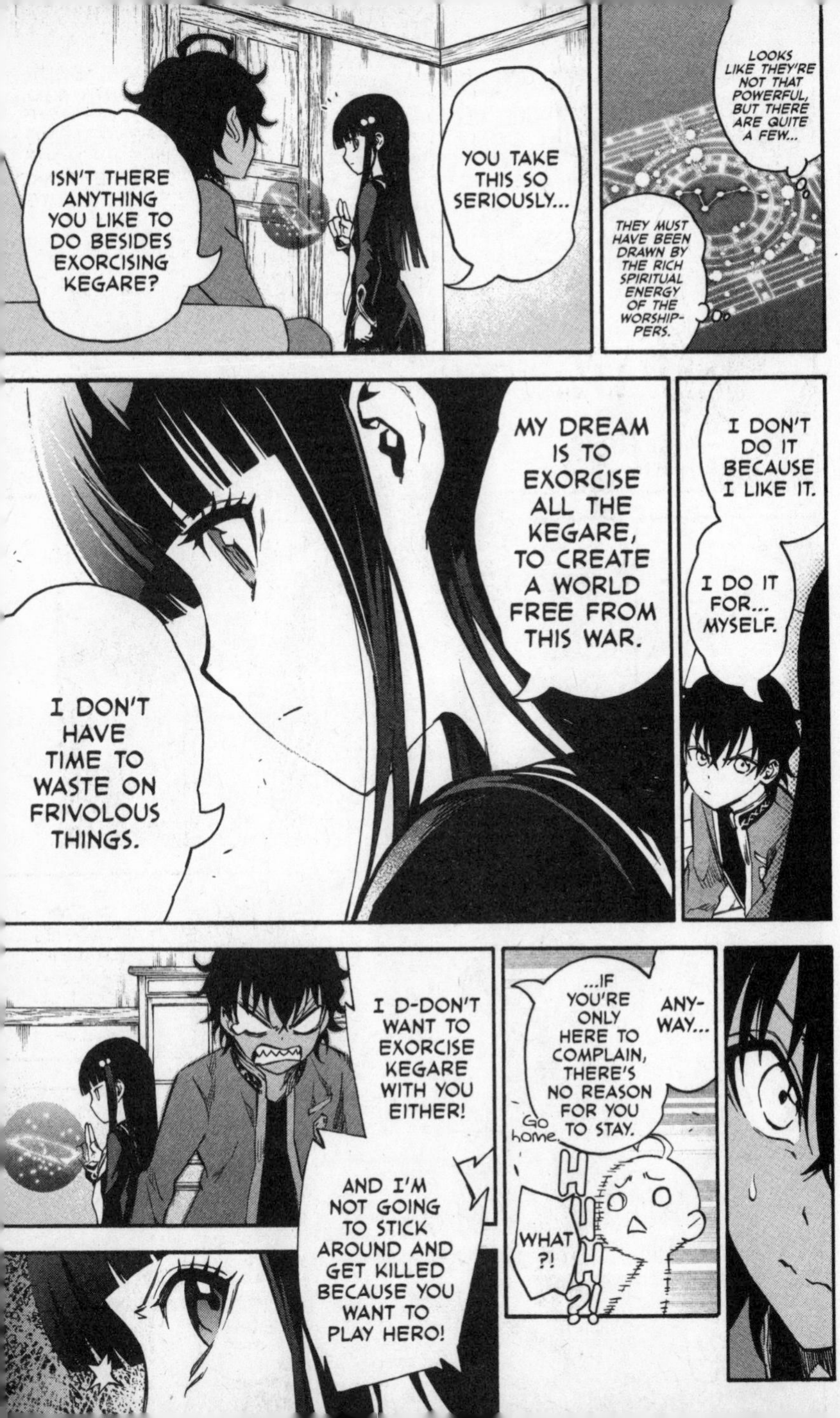
LOOKS LIKE THEY'RE NOT THAT POWERFUL, BUT THERE ARE QUITE A FEW...
THEY MUST HAVE BEEN DRAWN BY THE RICH SPIRITUAL ENERGY OF THE WORSHIP-PERS.
YOU TAKE THIS SO SERIOUSLY...
ISN'T THERE ANYTHING YOU LIKE TO DO BESIDES EXORCISING KEGARE?
I DON'T DO IT BECAUSE I LIKE IT.
I DO IT FOR... MYSELF.
MY DREAM IS TO EXORCISE ALL THE KEGARE, TO CREATE A WORLD FREE FROM THIS WAR.
I DON'T HAVE TIME TO WASTE ON FRIVOLOUS THINGS.
ANY-WAY...
...IF YOU'RE ONLY HERE TO COMPLAIN, THERE'S NO REASON FOR YOU TO STAY.
Go home.
WHAT ?!
I D-DON'T WANT TO EXORCISE KEGARE WITH YOU EITHER!
AND I'M NOT GOING TO STICK AROUND AND GET KILLED BECAUSE YOU WANT TO PLAY HERO!

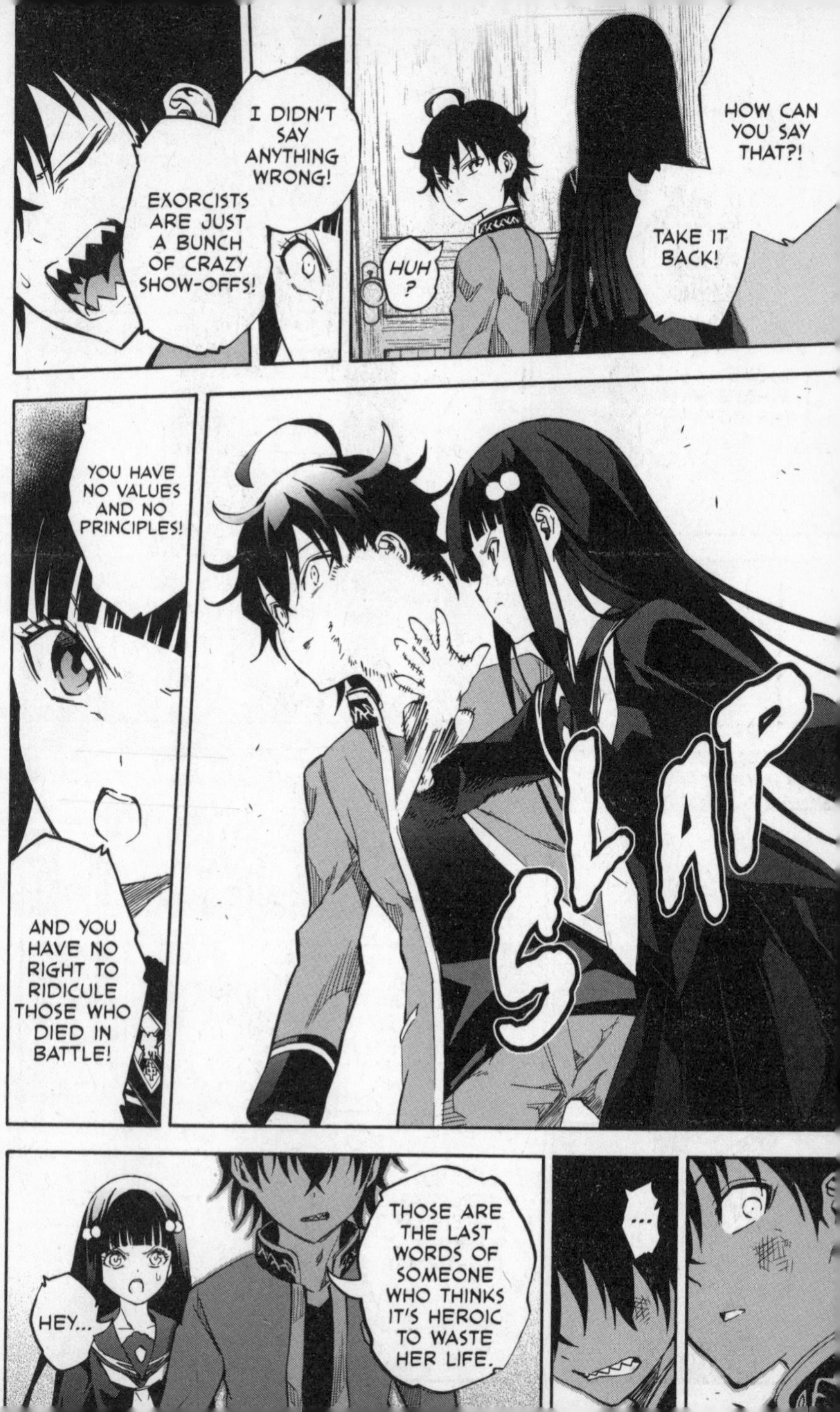
HOW CAN YOU SAY THAT?!
TAKE IT BACK!
HUH?
I DIDN'T SAY ANYTHING WRONG!
EXORCISTS ARE JUST A BUNCH OF CRAZY SHOW-OFFS!
SLAP
YOU HAVE NO VALUES AND NO PRINCIPLES!
AND YOU HAVE NO RIGHT TO RIDICULE THOSE WHO DIED IN BATTLE!
...
THOSE ARE THE LAST WORDS OF SOMEONE WHO THINKS IT'S HEROIC TO WASTE HER LIFE.
HEY...

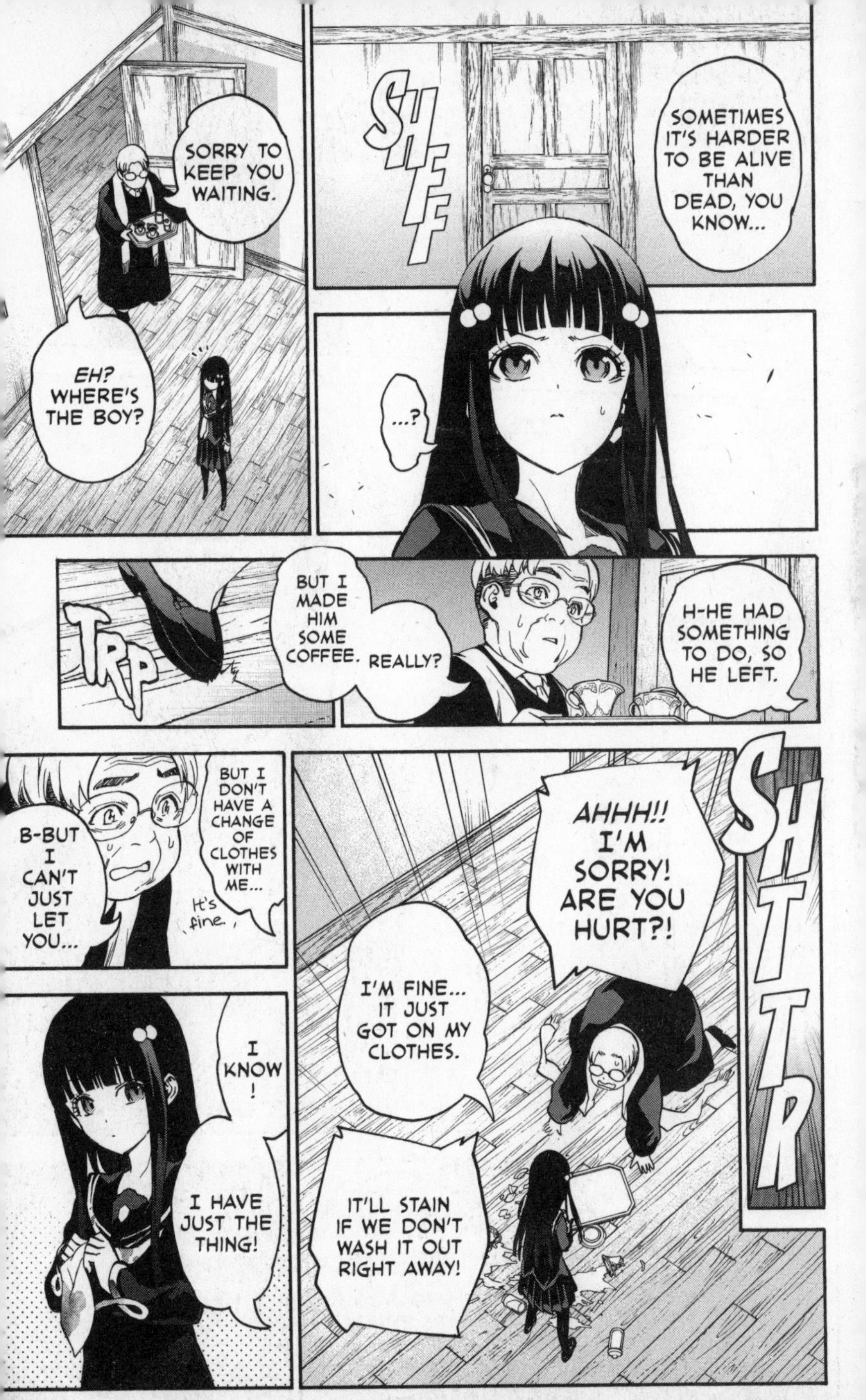
SHFF
SOMETIMES IT'S HARDER TO BE ALIVE THAN DEAD, YOU KNOW...
...?
SORRY TO KEEP YOU WAITING.
EH? WHERE'S THE BOY?
H-HE HAD SOMETHING TO DO, SO HE LEFT.
REALLY?
BUT I MADE HIM SOME COFFEE.
TRP
SHTTR
AHHH!! I'M SORRY! ARE YOU HURT?!
I'M FINE... IT JUST GOT ON MY CLOTHES.
IT'LL STAIN IF WE DON'T WASH IT OUT RIGHT AWAY!
BUT I DON'T HAVE A CHANGE OF CLOTHES WITH ME...
It's fine.
B-BUT I CAN'T JUST LET YOU...
I KNOW!
I HAVE JUST THE THING!

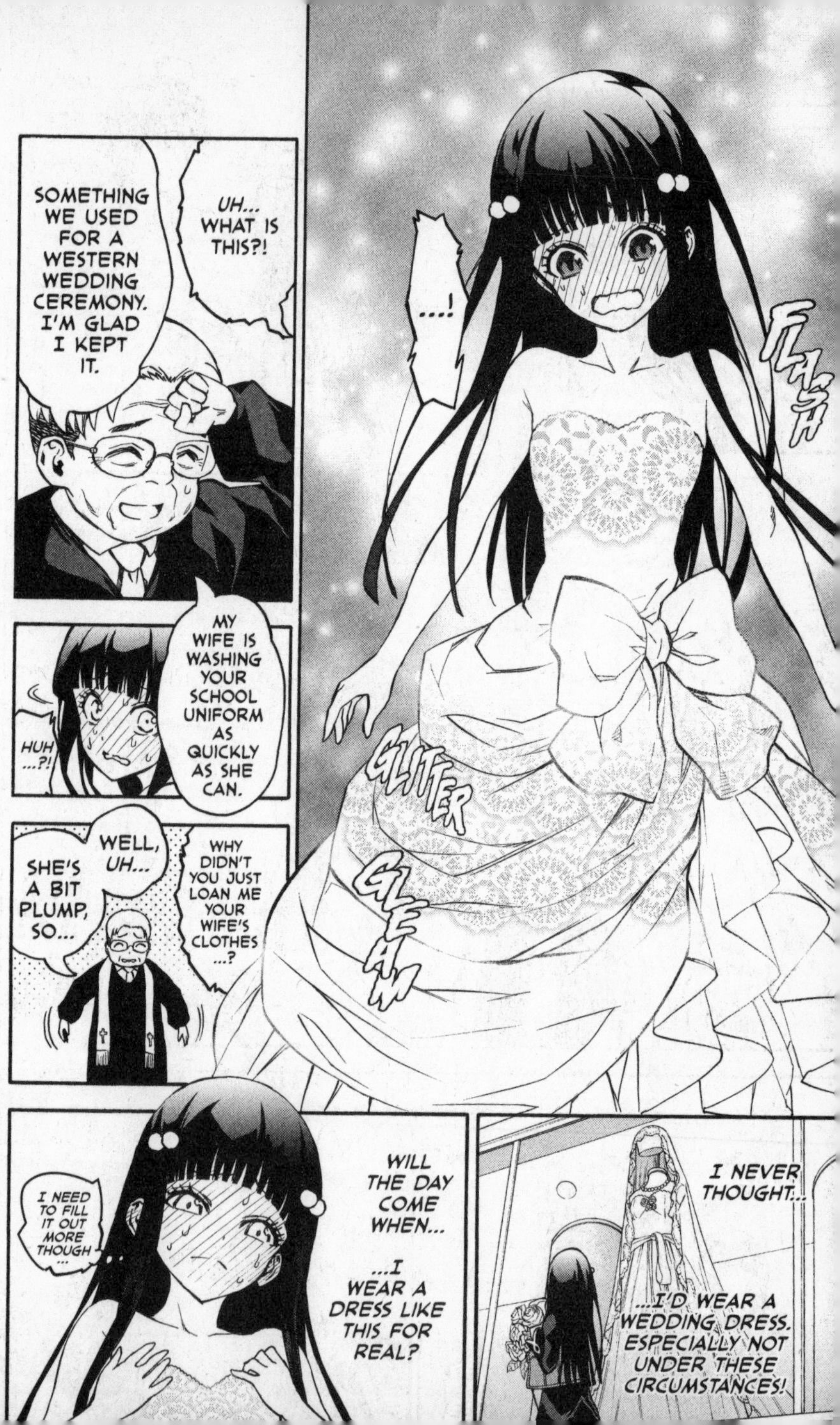
...!
FLASH
GLITTER
GLEAM
UH... WHAT IS THIS?!
SOMETHING WE USED FOR A WESTERN WEDDING CEREMONY. I'M GLAD I KEPT IT.
MY WIFE IS WASHING YOUR SCHOOL UNIFORM AS QUICKLY AS SHE CAN.
HUH ...?!
WHY DIDN'T YOU JUST LOAN ME YOUR WIFE'S CLOTHES ...?
WELL, UH...
SHE'S A BIT PLUMP, SO...
I NEVER THOUGHT...
...I'D WEAR A WEDDING DRESS. ESPECIALLY NOT UNDER THESE CIRCUMSTANCES!
WILL THE DAY COME WHEN...
...I WEAR A DRESS LIKE THIS FOR REAL?
I NEED TO FILL IT OUT MORE THOUGH...

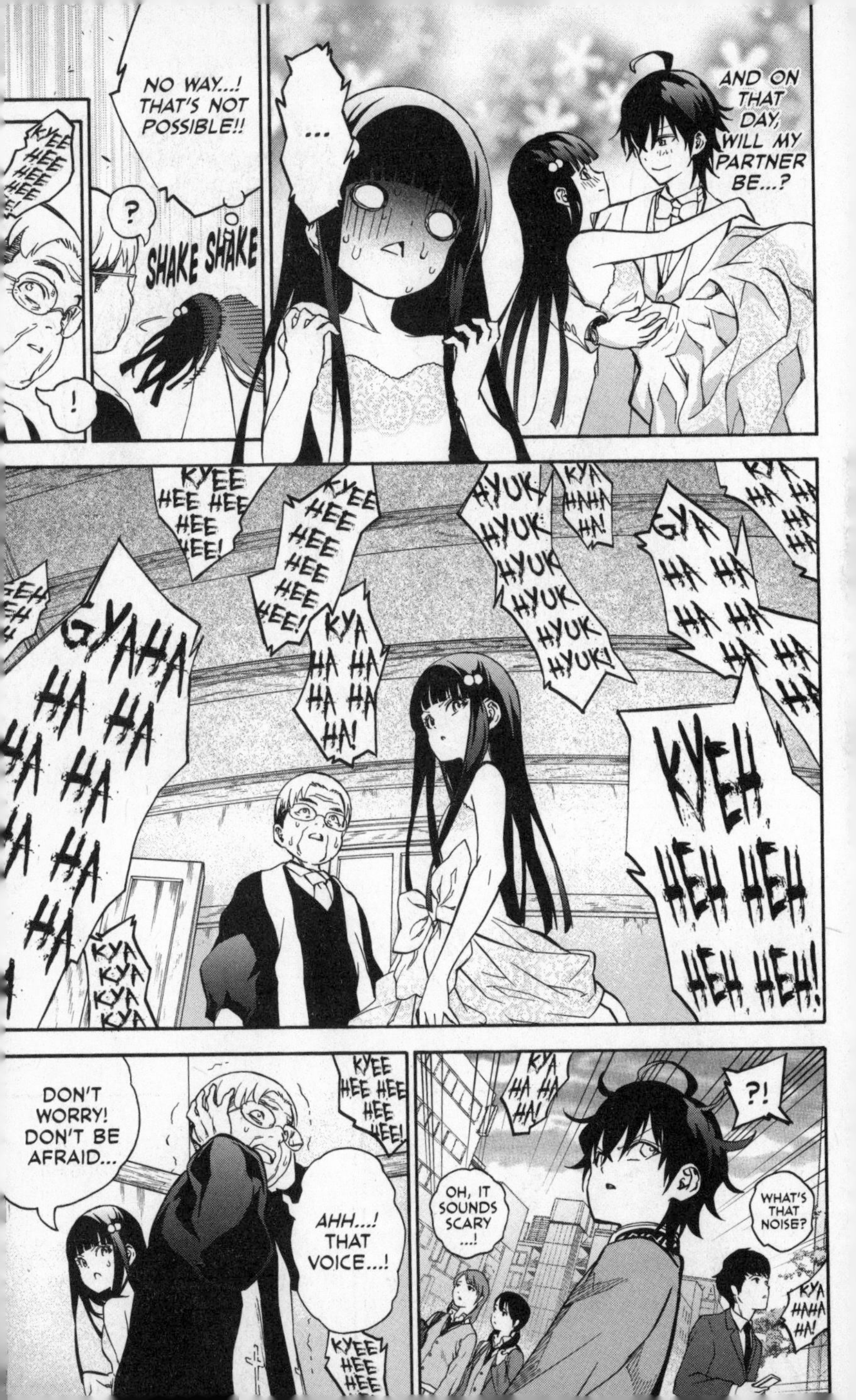
AND ON THAT DAY, WILL MY PARTNER BE...?
...
SHAKE SHAKE
NO WAY...! THAT'S NOT POSSIBLE!!
?
KYEE HEE HEE HEE HEE!
!
GYA HA HA HA HA HA HA HA
KYA HAHA HA!
HYUK HYUK HYUK HYUK HYUK HYUK!
KYEE HEE HEE HEE HEE HEE HEE!
KYEE HEE HEE HEE HEE!
KYEH HEH HEH HEH HEH!
KYA HA HA HA HA HA HA!
GYAHA HA HA HA HA HA HA HA HA HA HA
KYA KYA KYA KYA
?!
KYA HA HA HA!
WHAT'S THAT NOISE?
OH, IT SOUNDS SCARY...!
KYA HAHA HA!
KYEE HEE HEE HEE HEE!
AHH...! THAT VOICE...!
DON'T WORRY! DON'T BE AFRAID...
KYEE HEE HEE

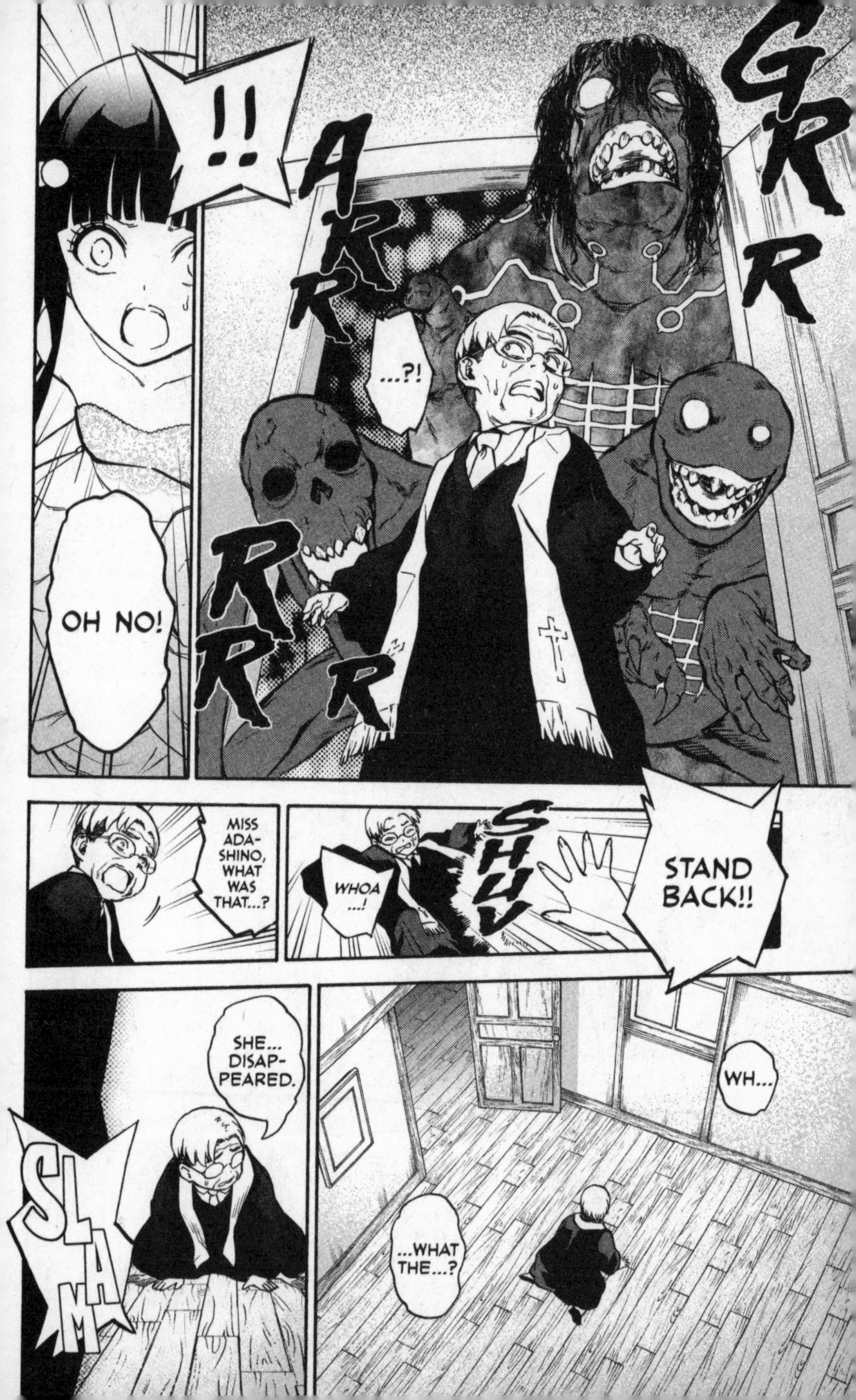
GRR
ARR
...?!
RRRRR
!!
OH NO!
STAND BACK!!
SHUV
WHOA ...!
MISS ADA-SHINO, WHAT WAS THAT...?
WH...
...WHAT THE...?
SHE... DISAP-PEARED.
SLAM

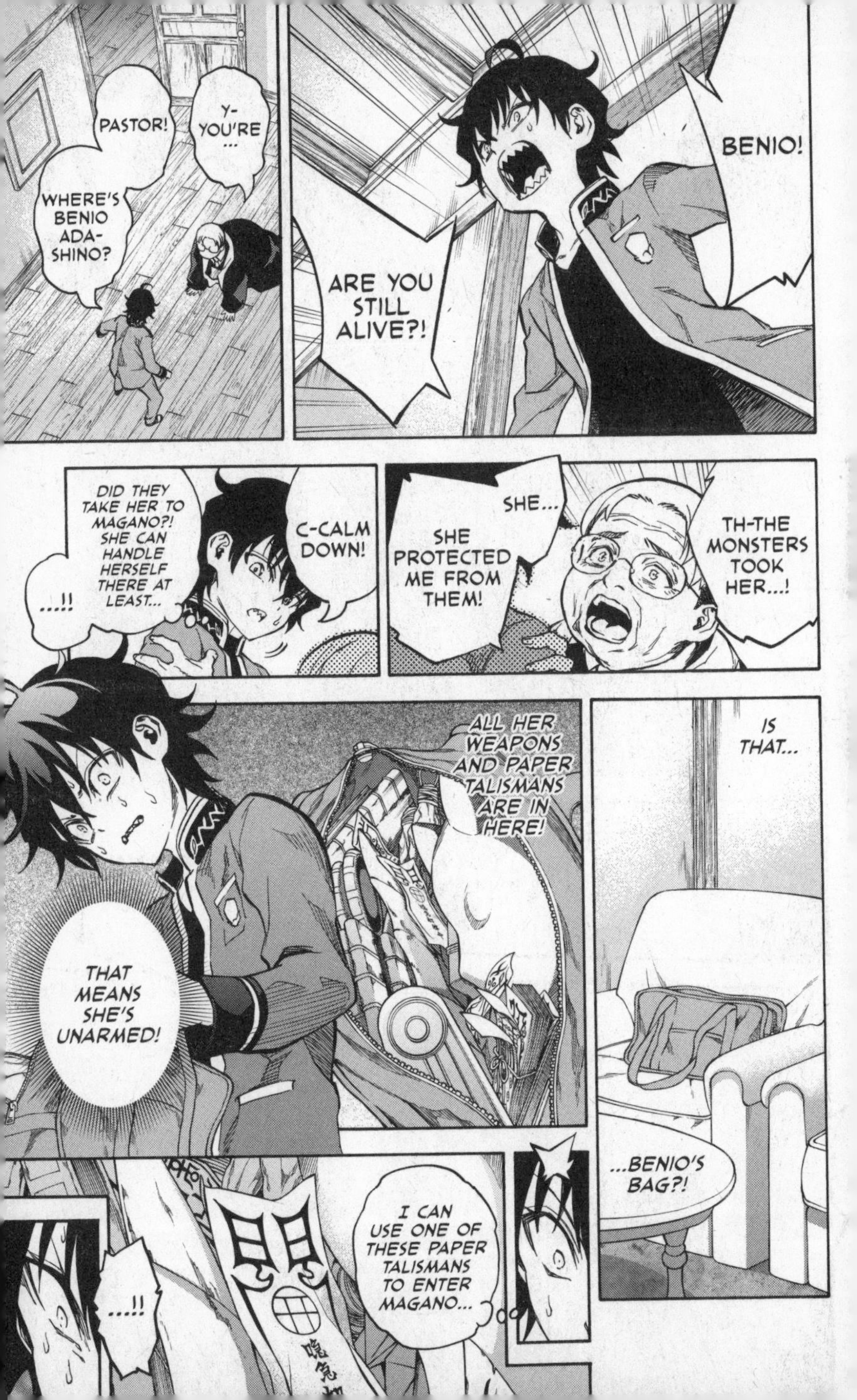
BENIO!
ARE YOU STILL ALIVE?!
Y- YOU'RE ...
PASTOR!
WHERE'S BENIO ADA- SHINO?
TH-THE MONSTERS TOOK HER...!
SHE...
SHE PROTECTED ME FROM THEM!
C-CALM DOWN!
DID THEY TAKE HER TO MAGANO?! SHE CAN HANDLE HERSELF THERE AT LEAST...
...!!
IS THAT...
...BENIO'S BAG?!
ALL HER WEAPONS AND PAPER TALISMANS ARE IN HERE!
THAT MEANS SHE'S UNARMED!
I CAN USE ONE OF THESE PAPER TALISMANS TO ENTER MAGANO...
...!!

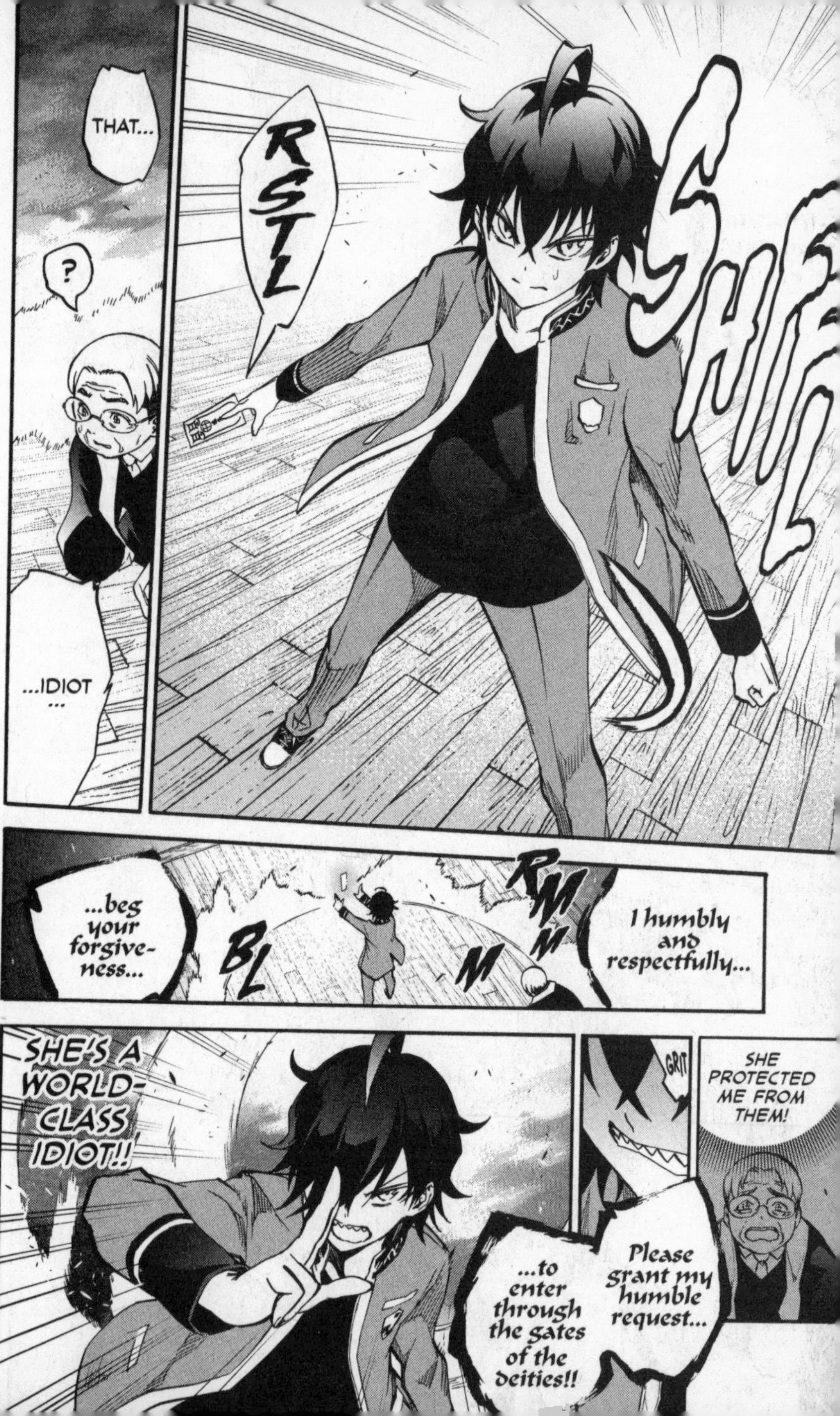

SHF
RSTL
THAT...
?
...IDIOT...
I humbly and respectfully...
RMMM
BL
...beg your forgive-ness...
SHE PROTECTED ME FROM THEM!
Please grant my humble request...
...to enter through the gates of the deities!!
GRIT
SHE'S A WORLD-CLASS IDIOT!!

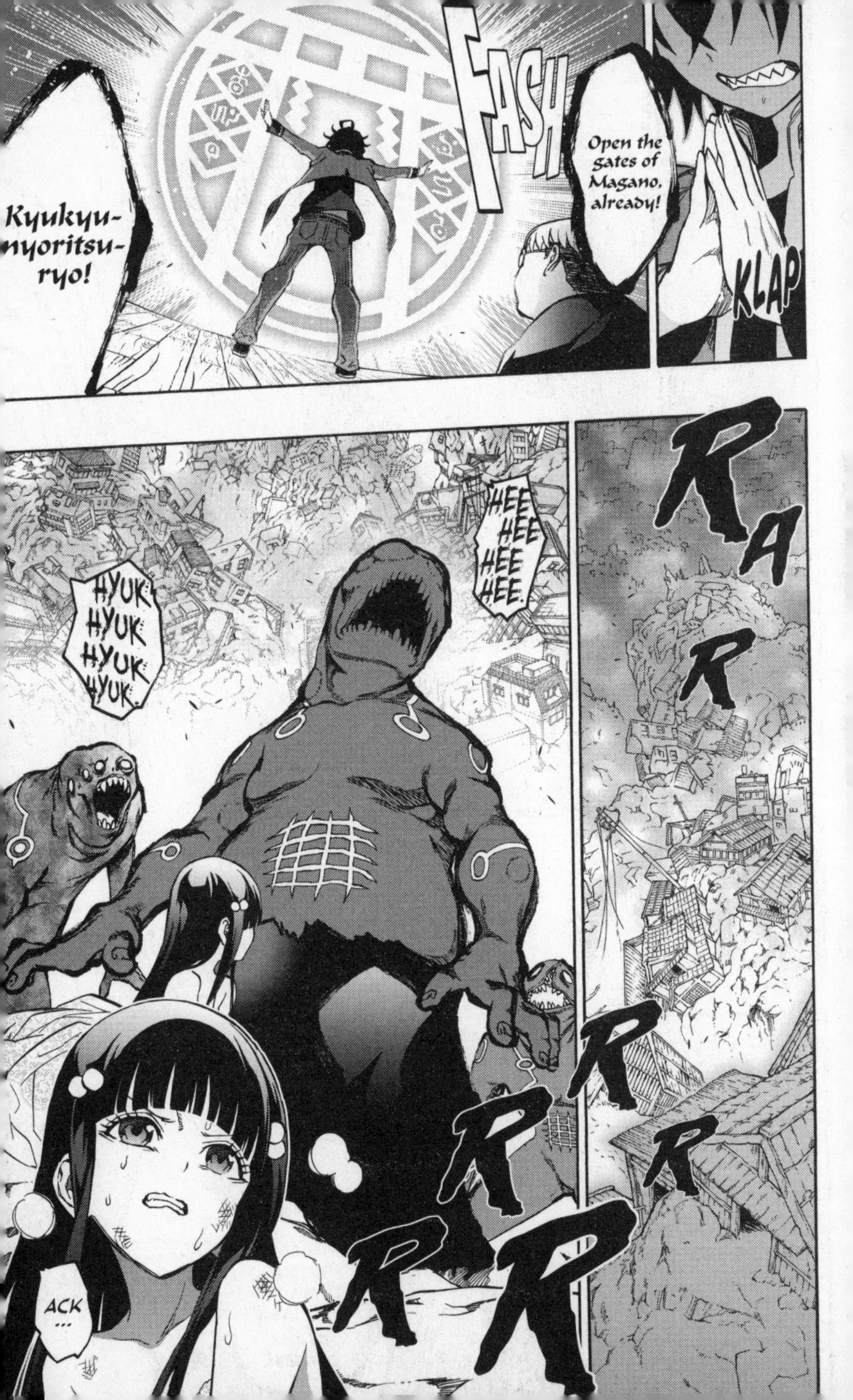
Open the gates of Magano, already!
KLAP
FASH
Kyukyu-nyoritsu-ryo!
RAR
HEE HEE HEE HEE.
HYUK HYUK HYUK HYUK.
RRRRR
ACK...

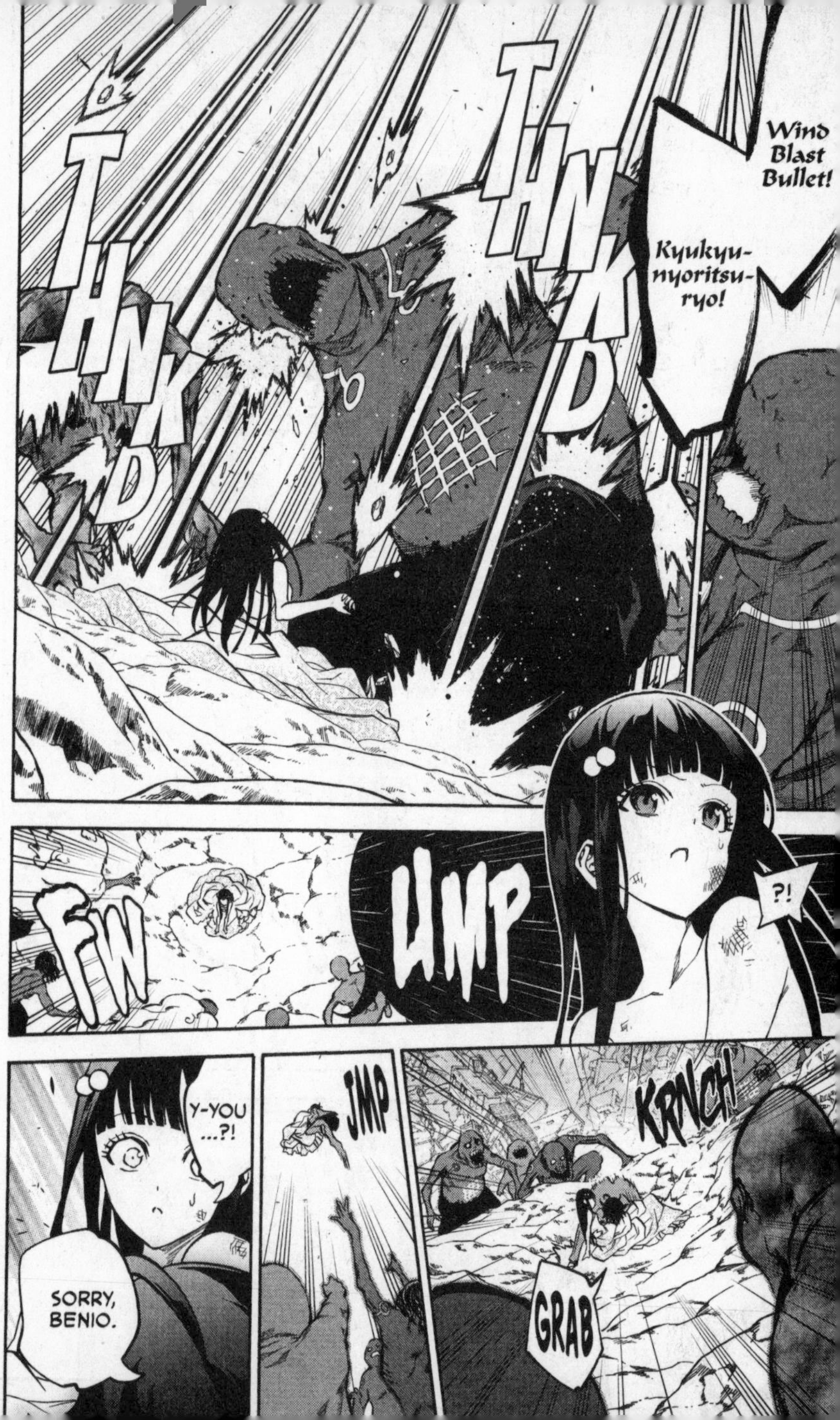
Wind Blast Bullet!
Kyukyu-nyoritsu-ryo!
THNK D
THNK D
?!
UMP
FWN
KRNCH
GRAB
JMP
Y-YOU ...?!
SORRY, BENIO.

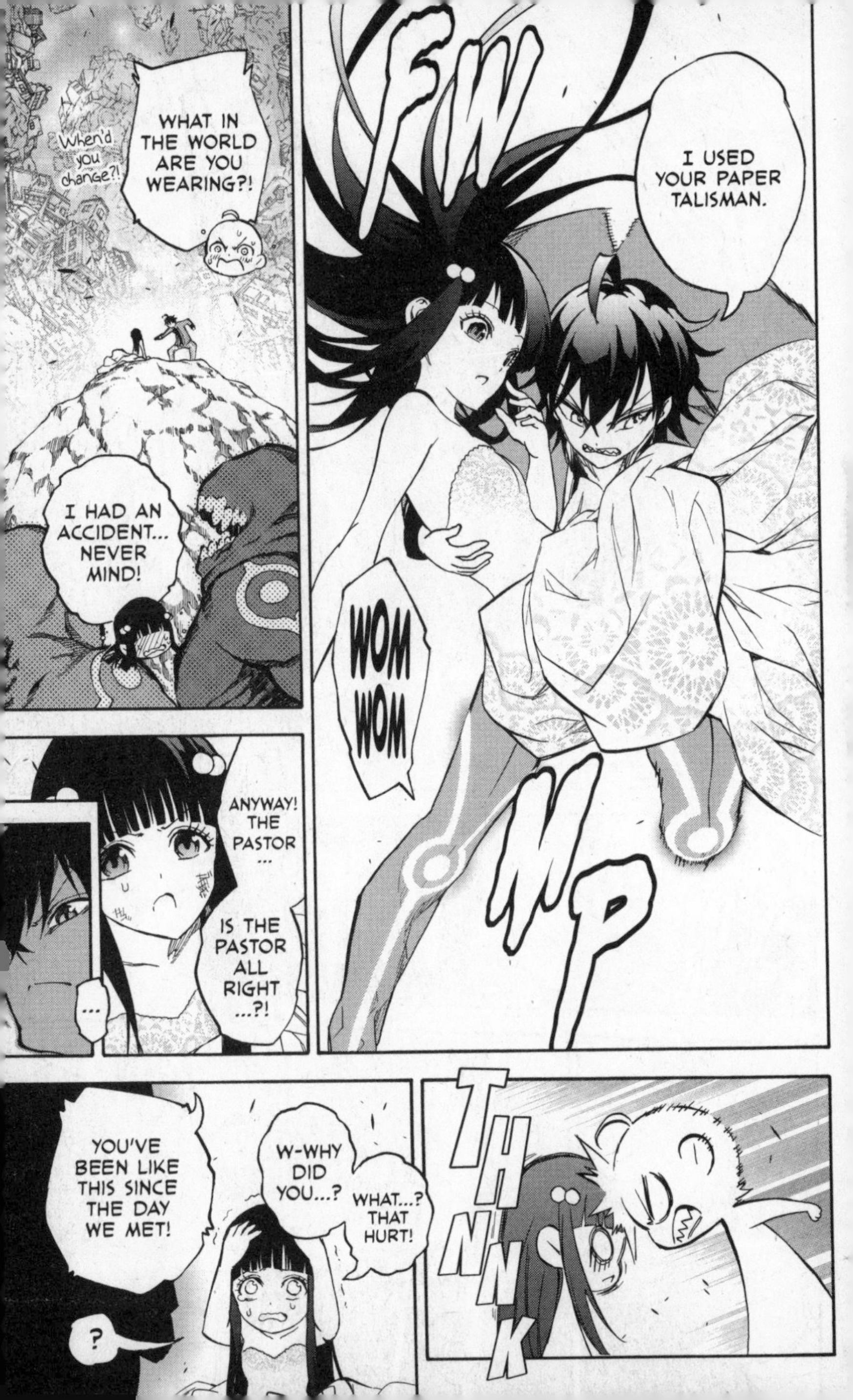
I USED YOUR PAPER TALISMAN.
FWI
WOM WOM
MP
WHAT IN THE WORLD ARE YOU WEARING?!
When'd you change?!
I HAD AN ACCIDENT... NEVER MIND!
ANYWAY! THE PASTOR...
IS THE PASTOR ALL RIGHT...?!
...
THHNNK
WHAT...? THAT HURT!
W-WHY DID YOU...?
YOU'VE BEEN LIKE THIS SINCE THE DAY WE MET!
?

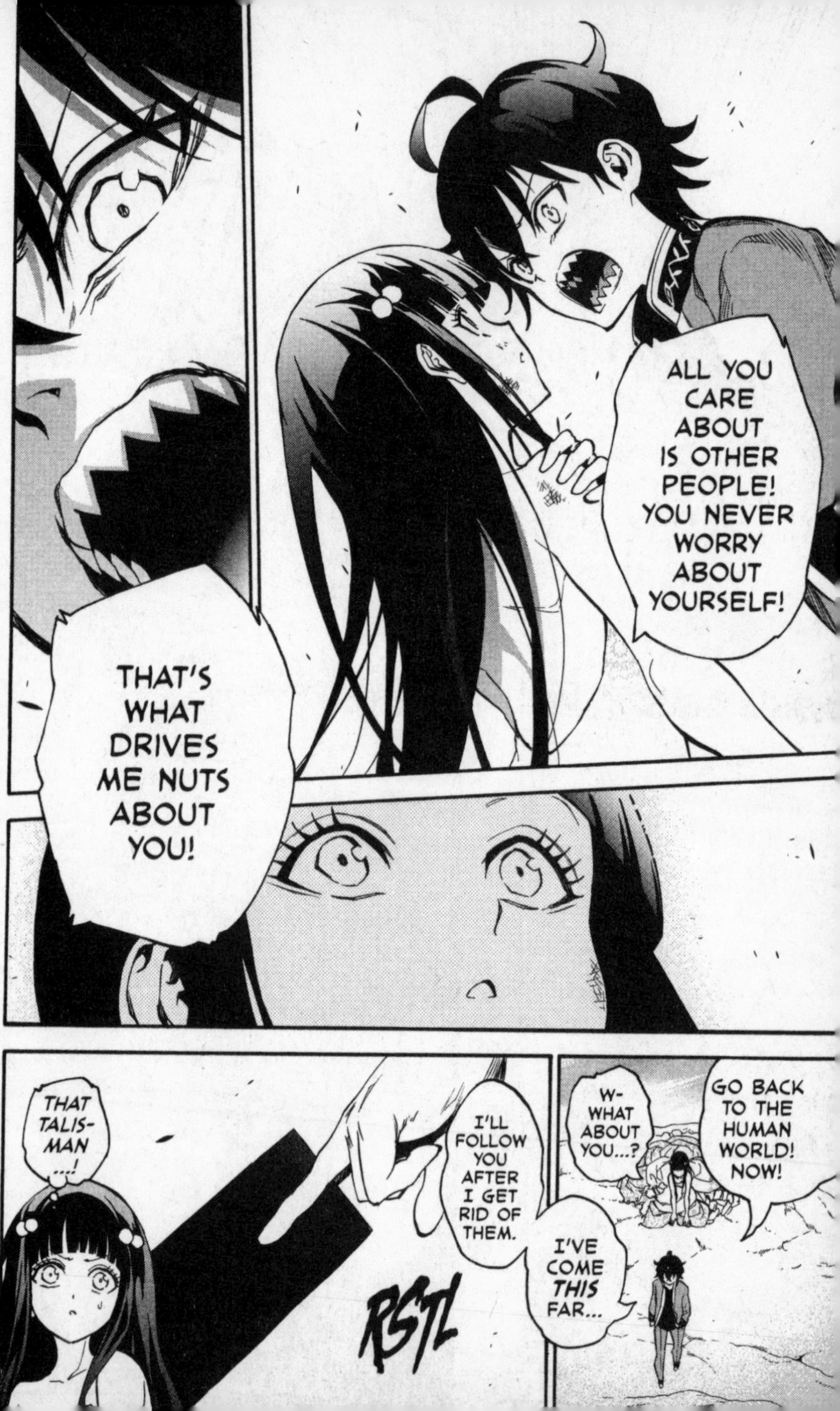
ALL YOU CARE ABOUT IS OTHER PEOPLE! YOU NEVER WORRY ABOUT YOURSELF!
THAT'S WHAT DRIVES ME NUTS ABOUT YOU!
GO BACK TO THE HUMAN WORLD! NOW!
W-WHAT ABOUT YOU...?
I'VE COME *THIS* FAR...
I'LL FOLLOW YOU AFTER I GET RID OF THEM.
RSTL
*THAT TALISMAN...!*

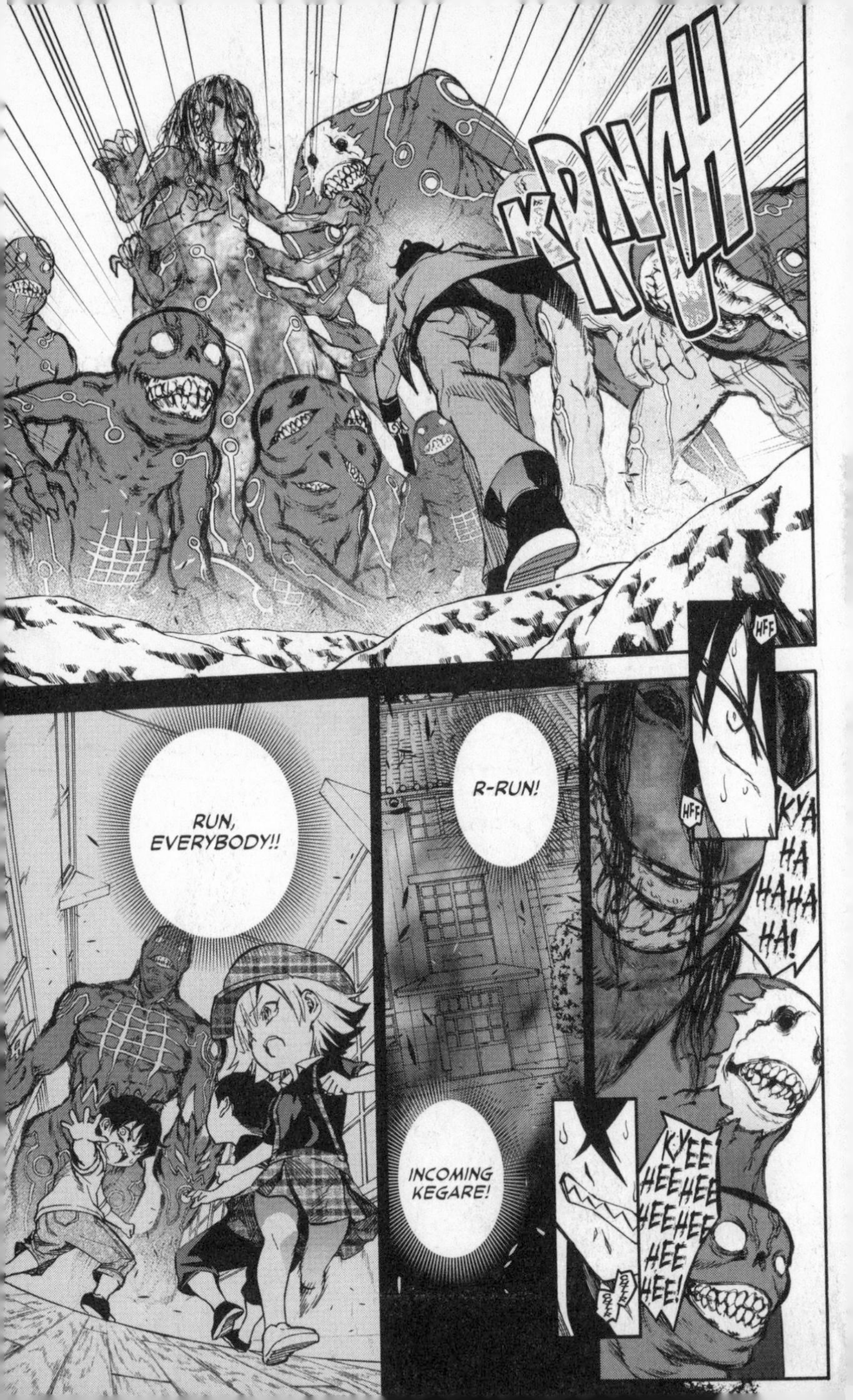
KRNCH
HFF
HFF
KYA HA HA HAHA HA!
KYEE HEE HEE HEE HEE HEE HEE HEE!
R-RUN!
INCOMING KEGARE!
RUN, EVERYBODY!!

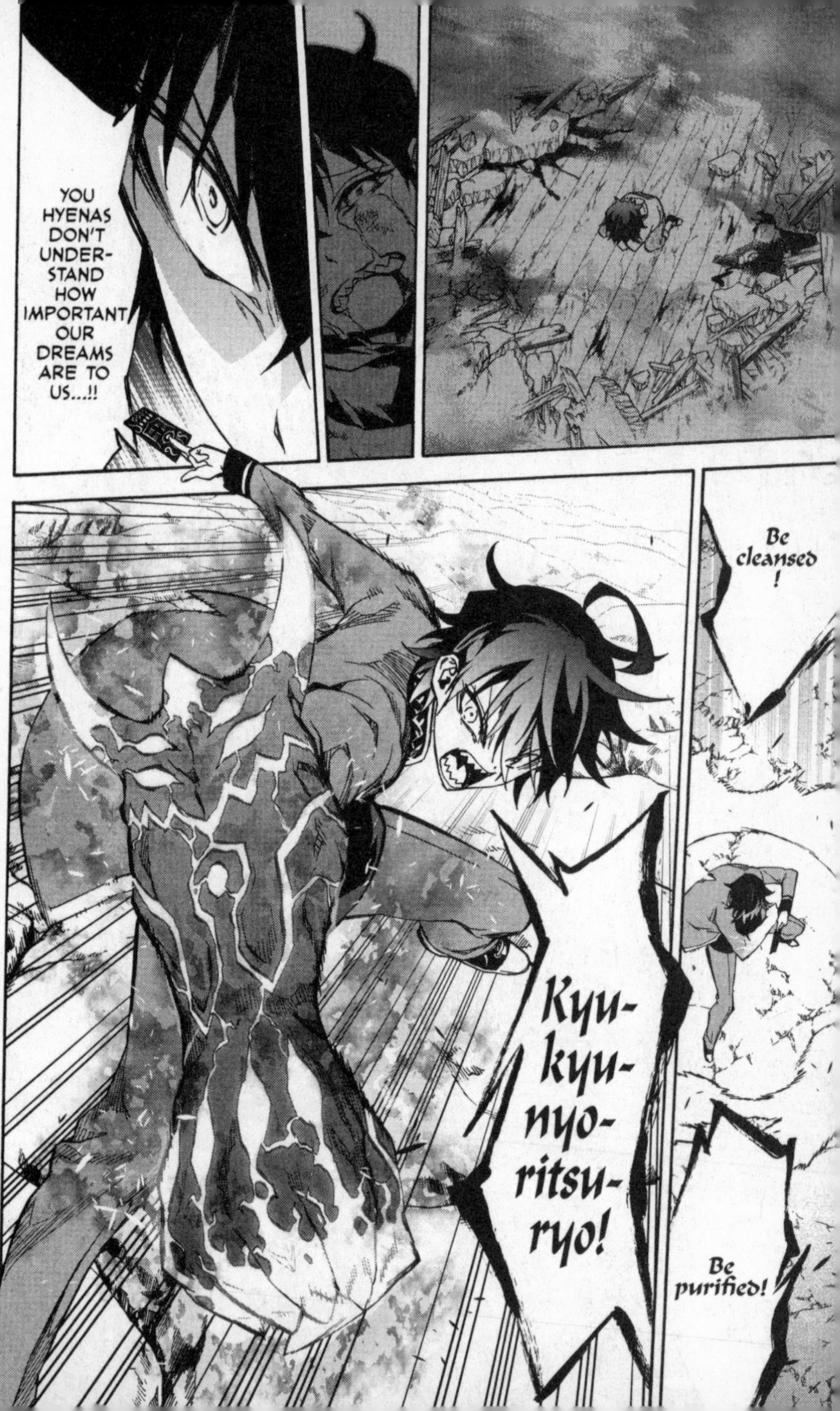
YOU HYENAS DON'T UNDER-STAND HOW IMPORTANT OUR DREAMS ARE TO US...!!
Be cleansed!
Be purified!
Kyu-kyu-nyo-ritsu-ryo!

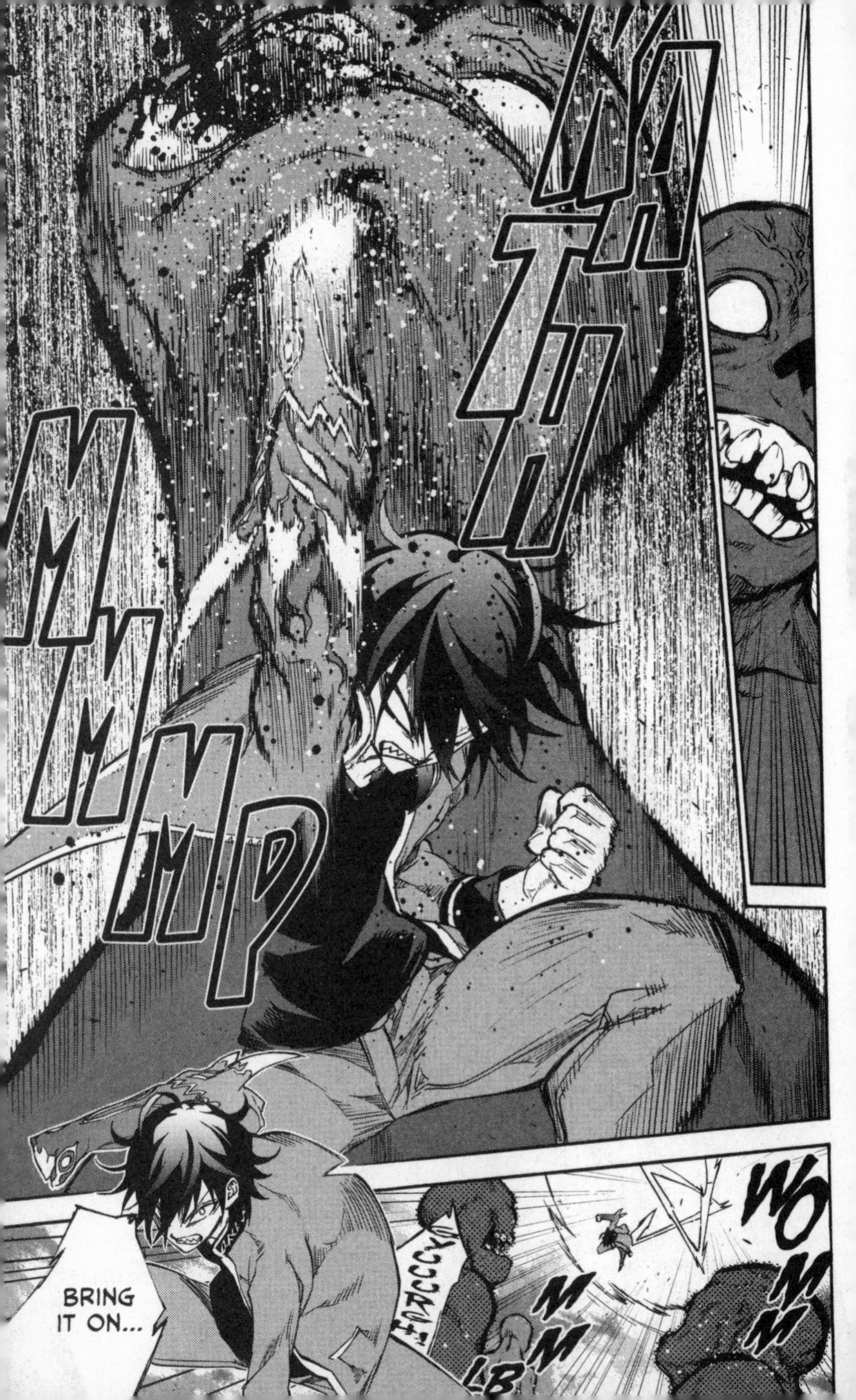
BRING IT ON...

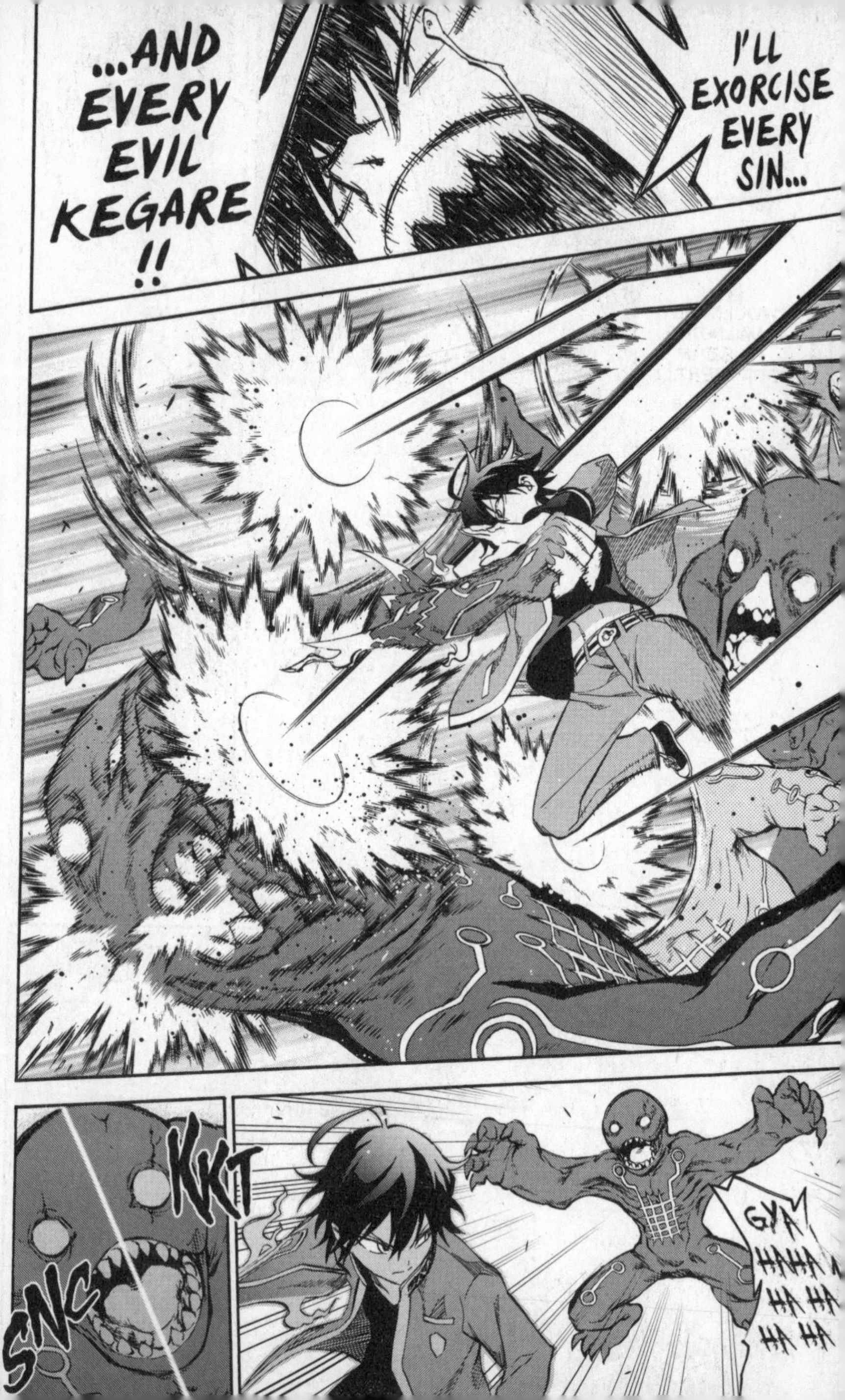
I'LL EXORCISE EVERY SIN...
...AND EVERY EVIL KEGARE!!
GYA HAHA HA HA HA HA
KKT
SNC

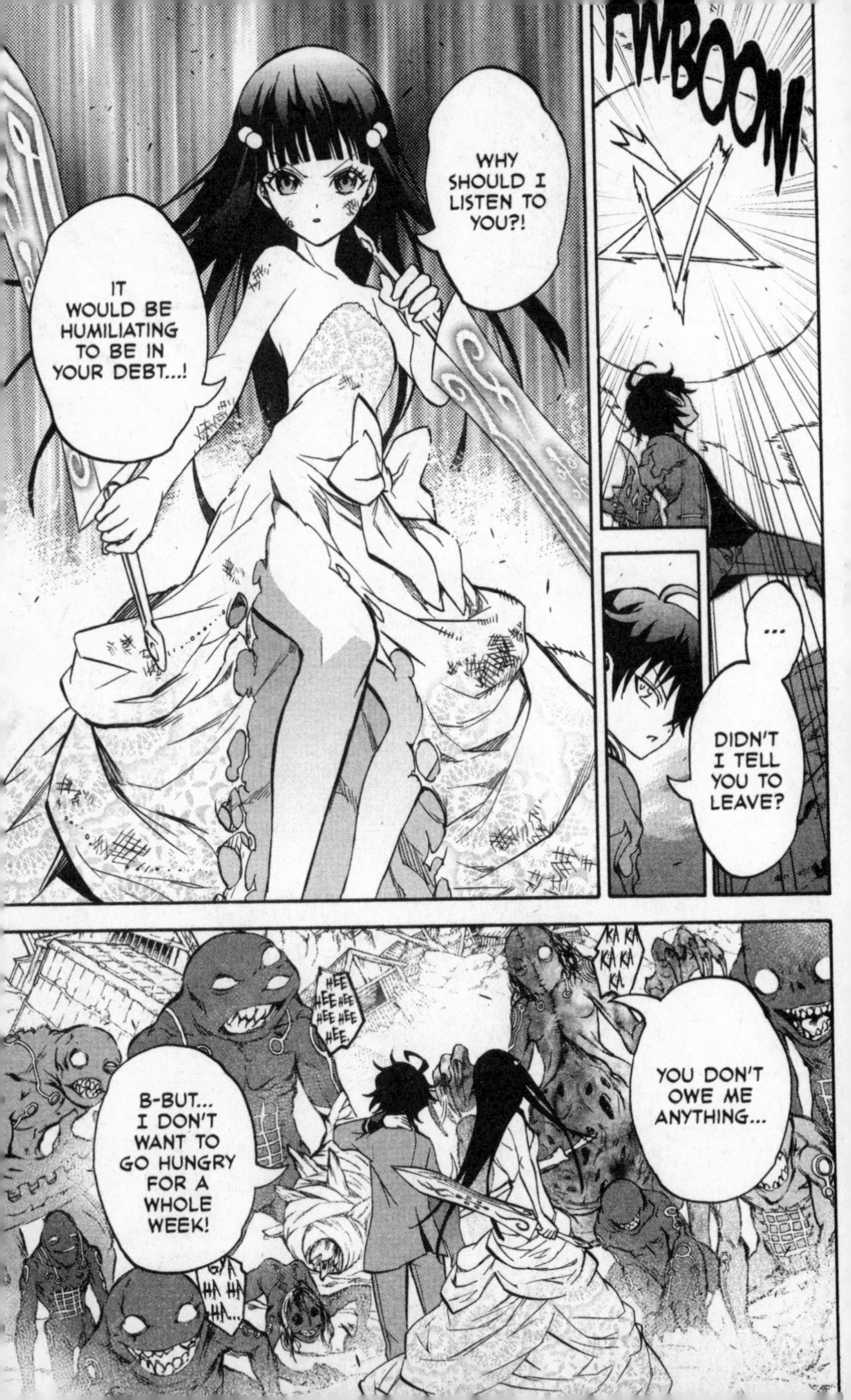
FWBOOM
...
DIDN'T I TELL YOU TO LEAVE?
WHY SHOULD I LISTEN TO YOU?!
IT WOULD BE HUMILIATING TO BE IN YOUR DEBT...!
KA KA KA KA KA
YOU DON'T OWE ME ANYTHING...
HEE HEE HEE HEE HEE HEE
B-BUT... I DON'T WANT TO GO HUNGRY FOR A WHOLE WEEK!
GYA HA HA HA...

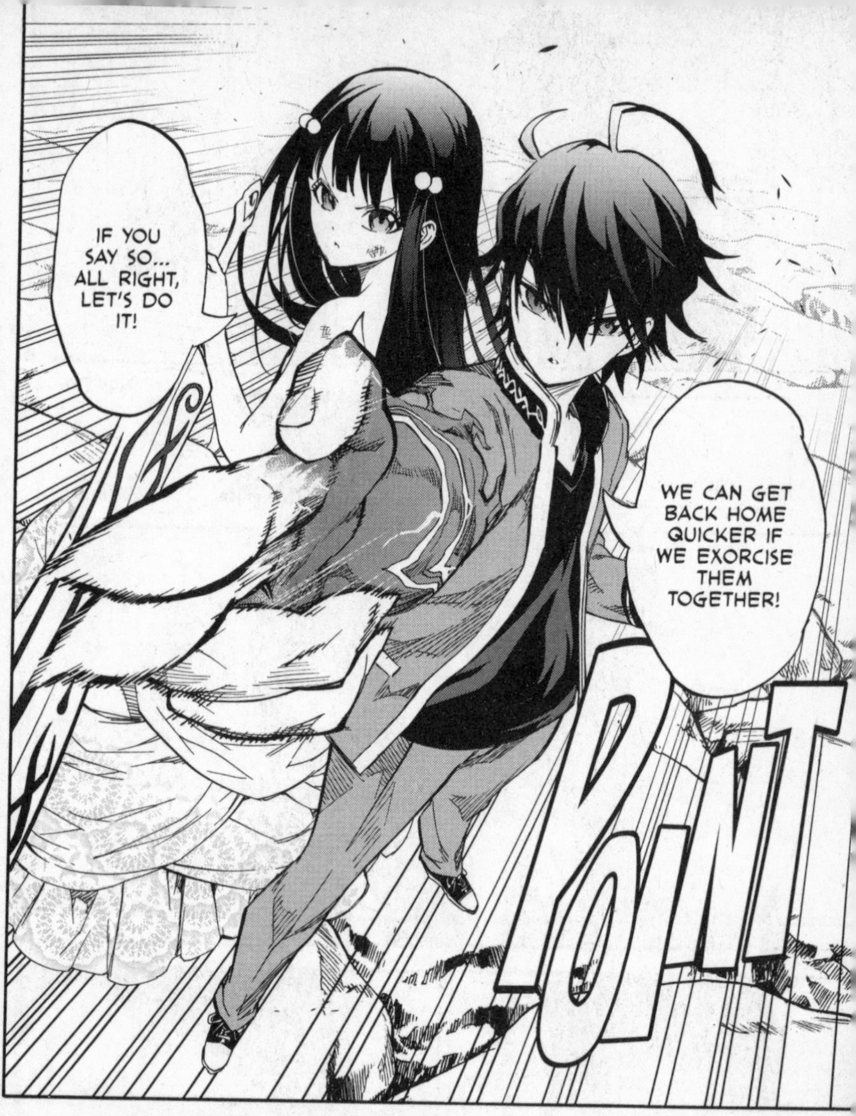
WE CAN GET BACK HOME QUICKER IF WE EXORCISE THEM TOGETHER!
IF YOU SAY SO... ALL RIGHT, LET'S DO IT!
DOINT

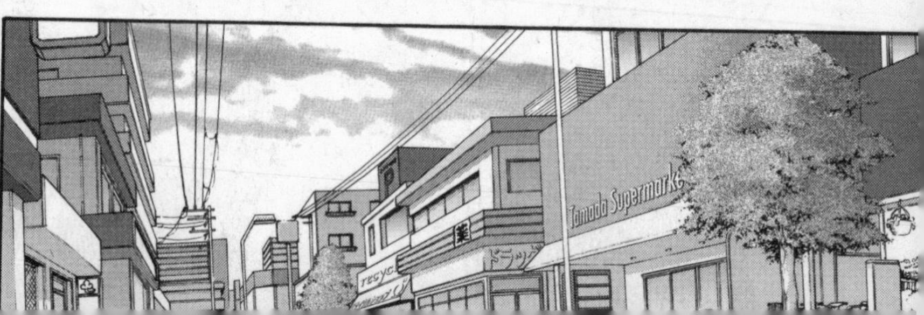
Tamada Supermarke

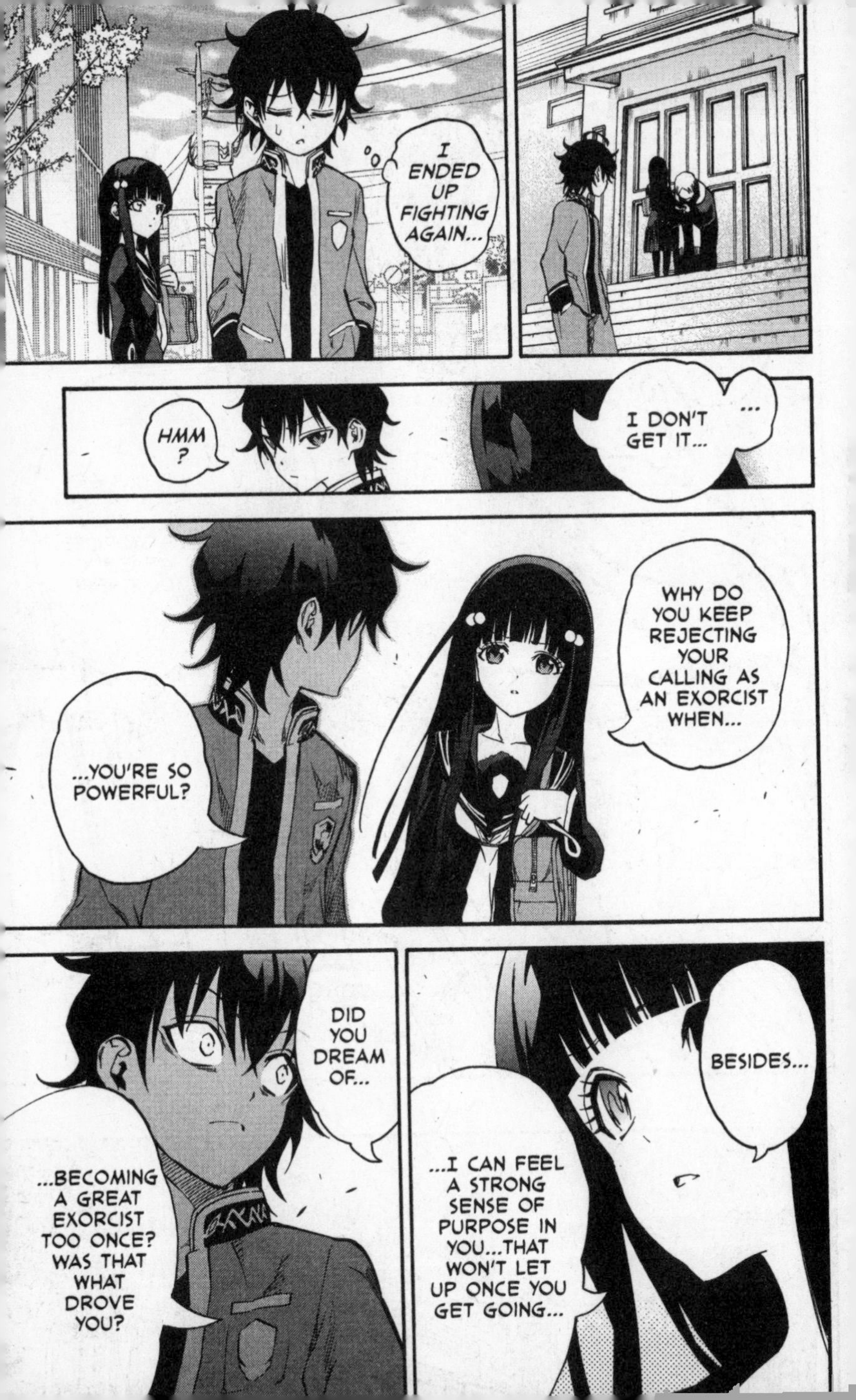
I ENDED UP FIGHTING AGAIN...
...
I DON'T GET IT...
HMM?
WHY DO YOU KEEP REJECTING YOUR CALLING AS AN EXORCIST WHEN...
...YOU'RE SO POWERFUL?
BESIDES...
...I CAN FEEL A STRONG SENSE OF PURPOSE IN YOU...THAT WON'T LET UP ONCE YOU GET GOING...
DID YOU DREAM OF...
...BECOMING A GREAT EXORCIST TOO ONCE? WAS THAT WHAT DROVE YOU?

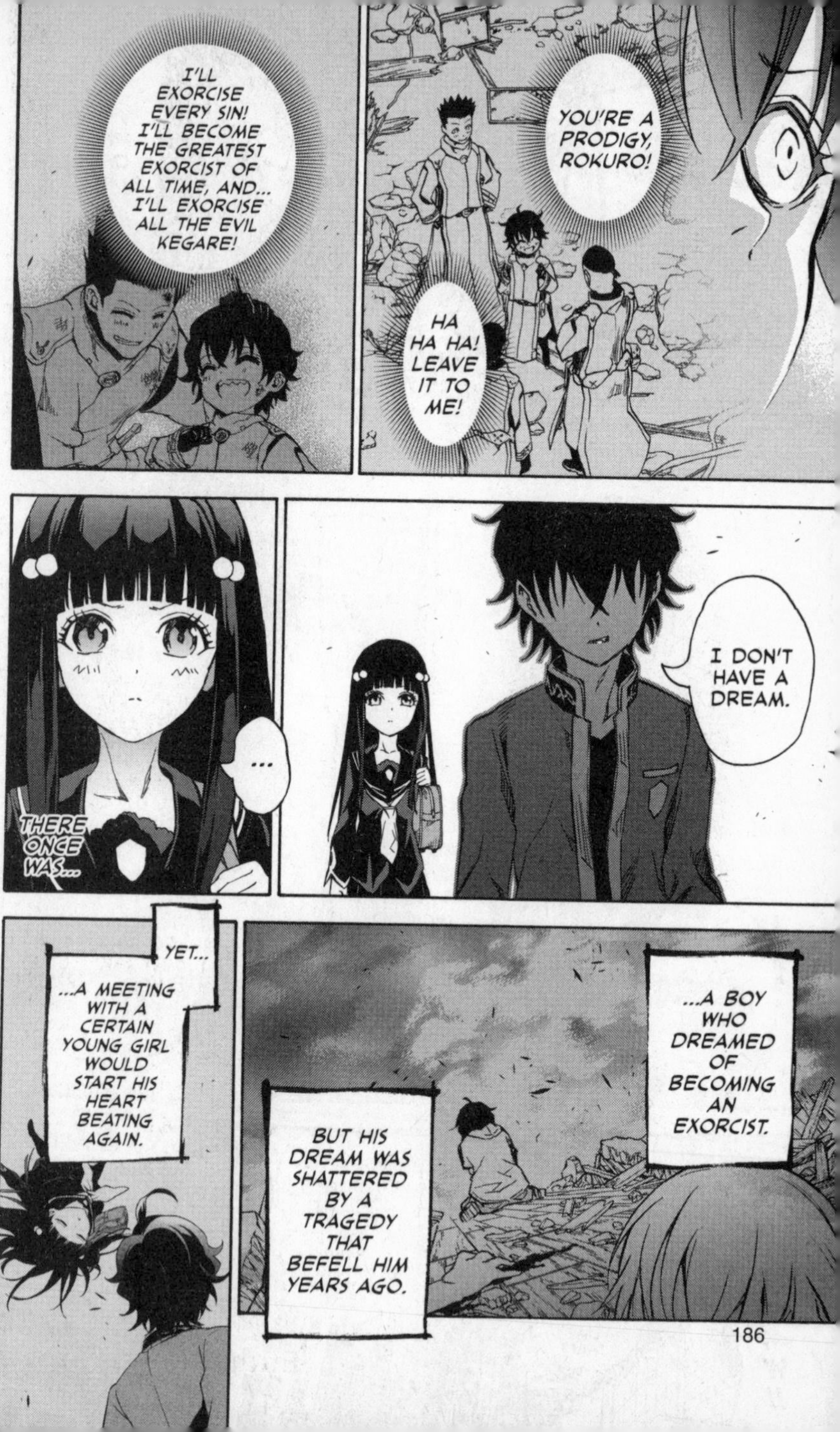
YOU'RE A PRODIGY, ROKURO!
HA HA HA! LEAVE IT TO ME!
I'LL EXORCISE EVERY SIN! I'LL BECOME THE GREATEST EXORCIST OF ALL TIME, AND... I'LL EXORCISE ALL THE EVIL KEGARE!
I DON'T HAVE A DREAM.
...
THERE ONCE WAS...
...A BOY WHO DREAMED OF BECOMING AN EXORCIST.
BUT HIS DREAM WAS SHATTERED BY A TRAGEDY THAT BEFELL HIM YEARS AGO.
YET...
...A MEETING WITH A CERTAIN YOUNG GIRL WOULD START HIS HEART BEATING AGAIN.

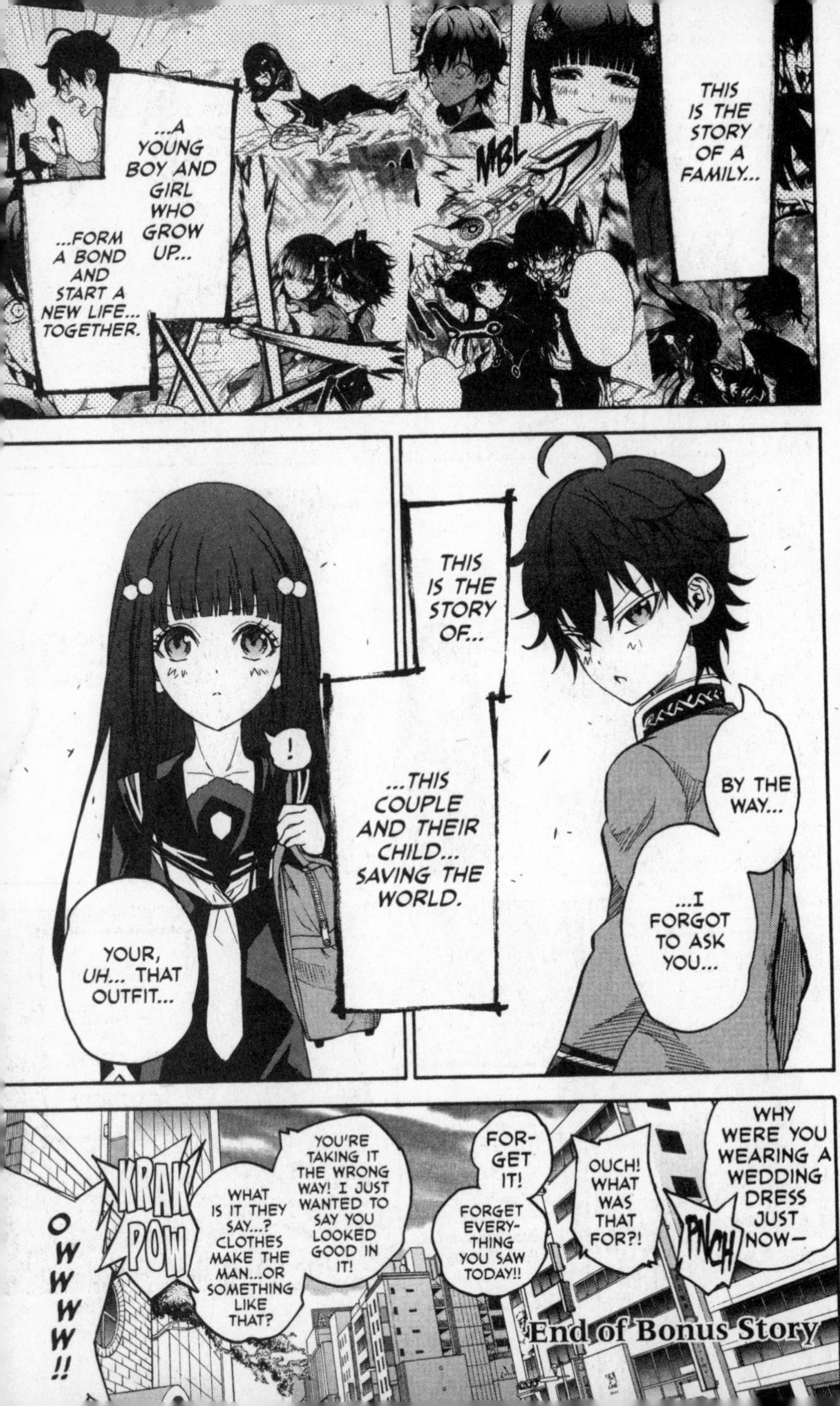
THIS IS THE STORY OF A FAMILY...
MBL
...A YOUNG BOY AND GIRL WHO GROW UP...
...FORM A BOND AND START A NEW LIFE... TOGETHER.
THIS IS THE STORY OF...
...THIS COUPLE AND THEIR CHILD... SAVING THE WORLD.
BY THE WAY...
...I FORGOT TO ASK YOU...
!
YOUR, UH... THAT OUTFIT...
WHY WERE YOU WEARING A WEDDING DRESS JUST NOW—
PNCH
OUCH! WHAT WAS THAT FOR?!
FOR-GET IT!
FORGET EVERY-THING YOU SAW TODAY!!
YOU'RE TAKING IT THE WRONG WAY! I JUST WANTED TO SAY YOU LOOKED GOOD IN IT!
WHAT IS IT THEY SAY...? CLOTHES MAKE THE MAN...OR SOMETHING LIKE THAT?
KRAK POW
OWWWWW!!
End of Bonus Story

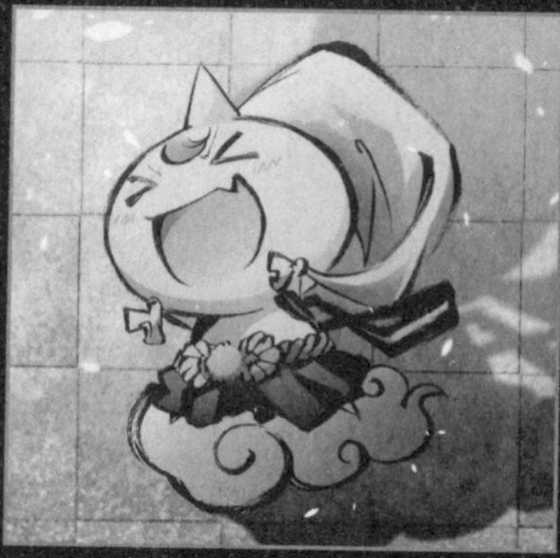

I had the honor of appearing on the Super Stage, the biggest stage of Jump Festa 2016, with the voice actors of the *Twin Star Exorcists* anime.

The place was packed, and I had really bad stage fright about speaking in front of such a big audience. But it turned out to be the most memorable experience of my life!

I'm working on my manga now with an eye to repeating that peak experience.

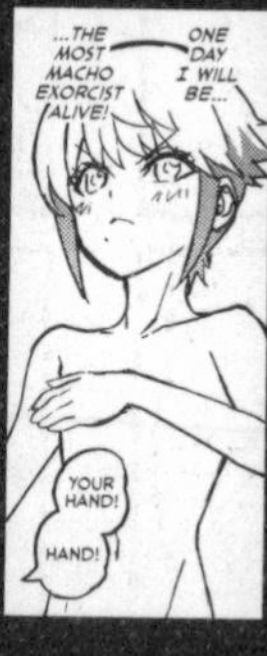
ONE DAY I WILL BE...
...THE MOST MACHO EXORCIST ALIVE!
YOUR HAND!
HAND!

**YOSHIAKI SUKENO** was born July 23, 1981, in Wakayama, Japan. He graduated from Kyoto Seika University, where he studied manga. In 2006, he won the Tezuka Award for Best Newcomer Shonen Manga Artist. In 2008, he began his previous work, the supernatural comedy *Binbougami ga!*, which was adapted into the anime *Good Luck Girl!* in 2012.

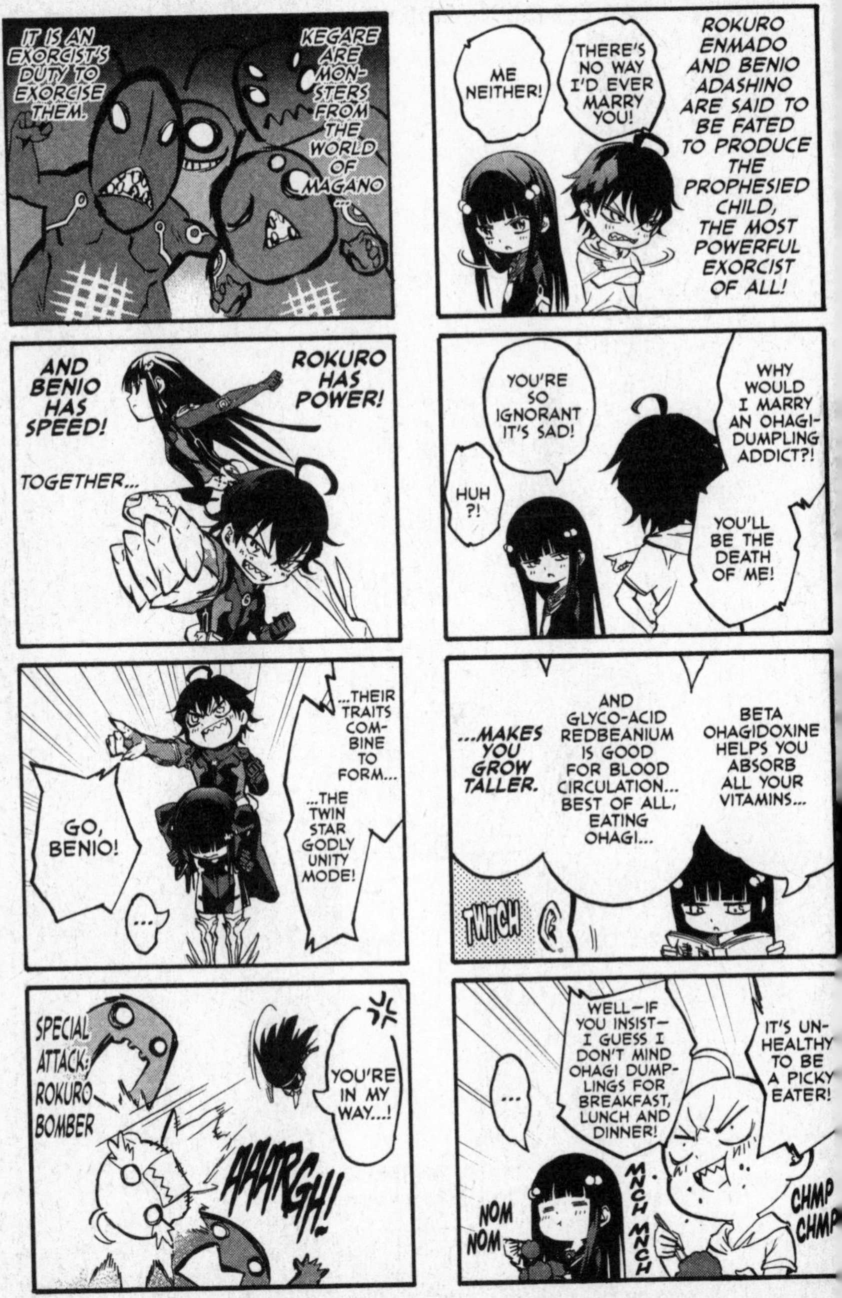
ROKURO ENMADO AND BENIO ADASHINO ARE SAID TO BE FATED TO PRODUCE THE PROPHESIED CHILD, THE MOST POWERFUL EXORCIST OF ALL!
THERE'S NO WAY I'D EVER MARRY YOU!
ME NEITHER!
WHY WOULD I MARRY AN OHAGI-DUMPLING ADDICT?!
YOU'LL BE THE DEATH OF ME!
YOU'RE SO IGNORANT IT'S SAD!
HUH?!
BETA OHAGIDOXINE HELPS YOU ABSORB ALL YOUR VITAMINS...
AND GLYCO-ACID REDBEANIUM IS GOOD FOR BLOOD CIRCULATION... BEST OF ALL, EATING OHAGI...
...MAKES YOU GROW TALLER.
TWITCH
IT'S UNHEALTHY TO BE A PICKY EATER!
WELL—IF YOU INSIST—I GUESS I DON'T MIND OHAGI DUMPLINGS FOR BREAKFAST, LUNCH AND DINNER!
...
CHMP CHMP
MNCH MNCH
NOM NOM
KEGARE ARE MONSTERS FROM THE WORLD OF MAGANO...
IT IS AN EXORCIST'S DUTY TO EXORCISE THEM.
ROKURO HAS POWER!
AND BENIO HAS SPEED!
TOGETHER...
...THEIR TRAITS COMBINE TO FORM...
...THE TWIN STAR GODLY UNITY MODE!
GO, BENIO!
...
YOU'RE IN MY WAY...!
SPECIAL ATTACK: ROKURO BOMBER
AAARGH!

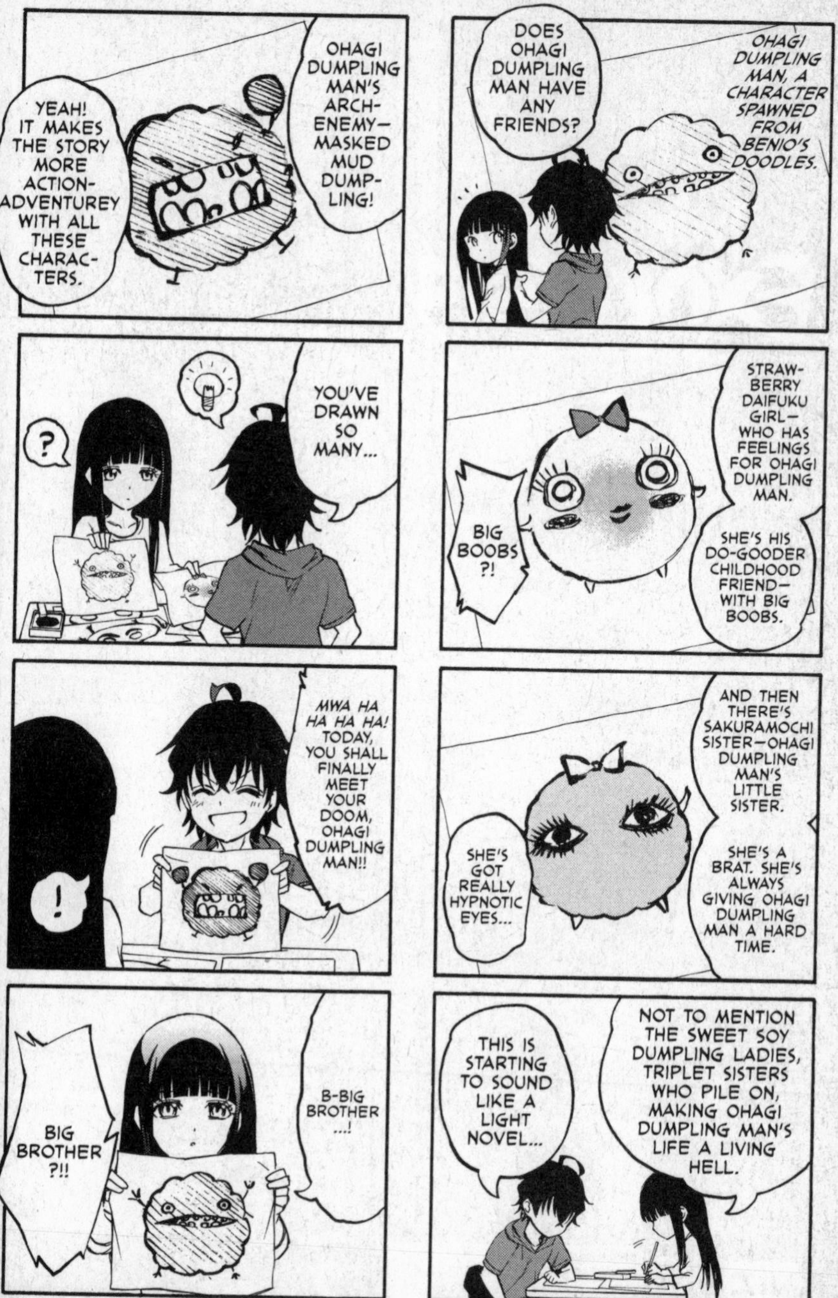
OHAGI DUMPLING MAN, A CHARACTER SPAWNED FROM BENIO'S DOODLES.
DOES OHAGI DUMPLING MAN HAVE ANY FRIENDS?
STRAWBERRY DAIFUKU GIRL—WHO HAS FEELINGS FOR OHAGI DUMPLING MAN.
SHE'S HIS DO-GOODER CHILDHOOD FRIEND—WITH BIG BOOBS.
BIG BOOBS?!
AND THEN THERE'S SAKURAMOCHI SISTER—OHAGI DUMPLING MAN'S LITTLE SISTER.
SHE'S A BRAT. SHE'S ALWAYS GIVING OHAGI DUMPLING MAN A HARD TIME.
SHE'S GOT REALLY HYPNOTIC EYES...
NOT TO MENTION THE SWEET SOY DUMPLING LADIES, TRIPLET SISTERS WHO PILE ON, MAKING OHAGI DUMPLING MAN'S LIFE A LIVING HELL.
THIS IS STARTING TO SOUND LIKE A LIGHT NOVEL...
OHAGI DUMPLING MAN'S ARCH-ENEMY—MASKED MUD DUMPLING!
YEAH! IT MAKES THE STORY MORE ACTION-ADVENTUREY WITH ALL THESE CHARACTERS.
YOU'VE DRAWN SO MANY...
?
MWA HA HA HA HA! TODAY, YOU SHALL FINALLY MEET YOUR DOOM, OHAGI DUMPLING MAN!!
!
B-BIG BROTHER...!
BIG BROTHER?!!

─SHONEN JUMP Manga Edition─

STORY & ART **Yoshiaki Sukeno**

TRANSLATION **Tetsuichiro Miyaki**
ENGLISH ADAPTATION **Bryant Turnage**
TOUCH-UP ART & LETTERING **Stephen Dutro**
DESIGN **Shawn Carrico**
EDITOR **Annette Roman**

SOUSEI NO ONMYOJI © 2013 by Yoshiaki Sukeno
All rights reserved.
First published in Japan in 2013 by SHUEISHA Inc., Tokyo.
English translation rights arranged by SHUEISHA Inc.

The stories, characters and incidents mentioned in this
publication are entirely fictional.

Printed in Canada

Published by VIZ Media, LLC
P.O. Box 77010
San Francisco, CA 94107

10 9 8 7 6 5 4 3 2 1
First printing, January 2018

www.shonenjump.com

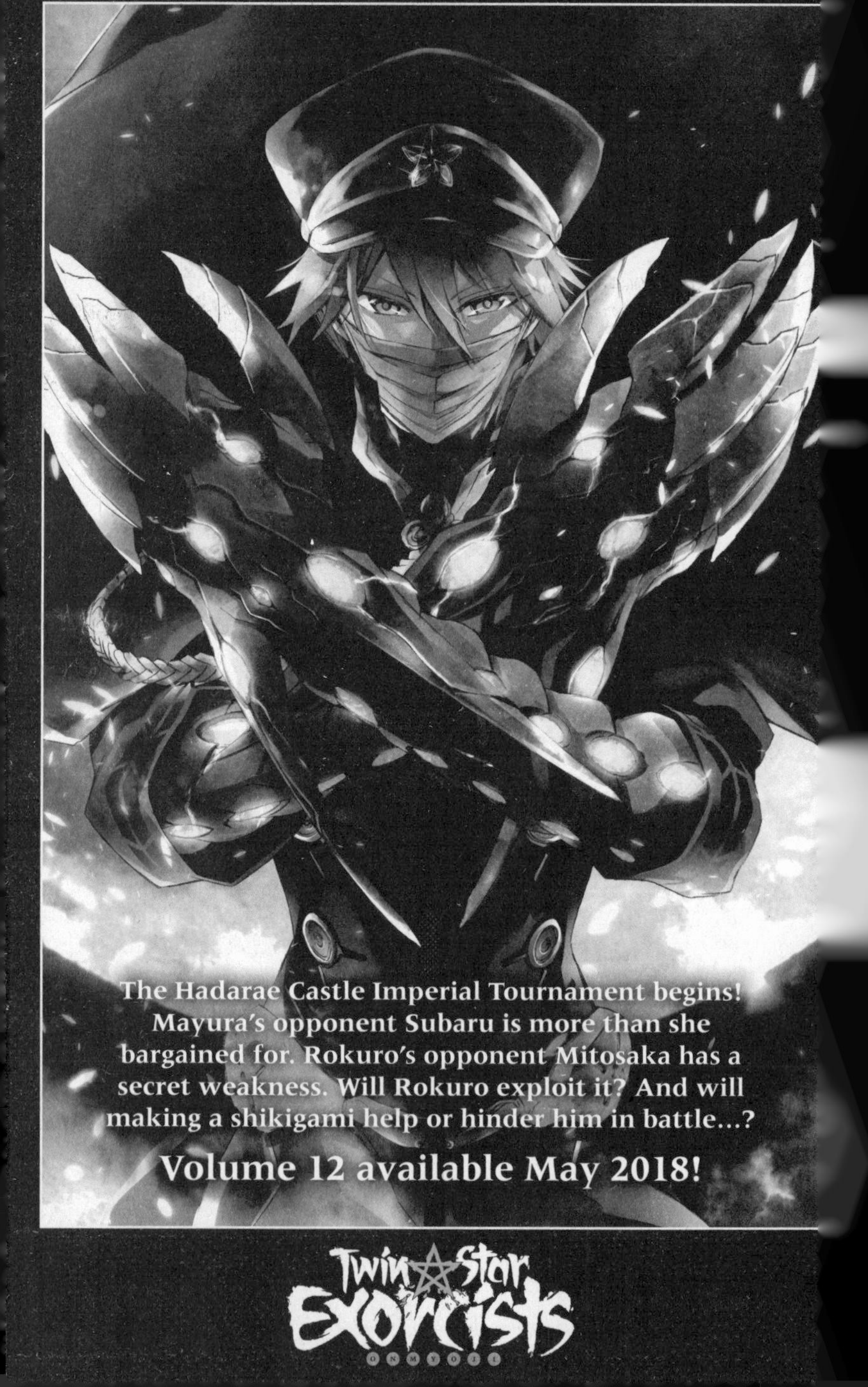
The Hadarae Castle Imperial Tournament begins! Mayura's opponent Subaru is more than she bargained for. Rokuro's opponent Mitosaka has a secret weakness. Will Rokuro exploit it? And will making a shikigami help or hinder him in battle...?
Volume 12 available May 2018!

Twin Star Exorcists
ONMYOJI